God's Assassins
State Terrorism in Argentina in the 1970s

Between 1976 and 1983 an estimated 30,000 Argentines "disappeared" under the military junta. Most were imprisoned and tortured before being murdered by the military. In the two years preceding 1976, another 2,000 were assassinated by paramilitary death squads loosely organized by the Argentine government of Isabel Perón.

God's Assassins tells the story of state terrorism in Argentina through interviews with participants on all sides of this issue. These include military officers, "Third World priests," Catholic Church officers who supported military objectives and methods, former members of guerrilla movements, survivors of prison camps, journalists, trade unionists, and others who experienced state terrorism in Argentina. Patricia Marchak combines excerpts from these interviews with documents and media reports from the time and her own insightful study of Argentina's history to provide an analysis of the process as well as the causes of state terrorism.

The graphic and moving interviews in *God's Assassins* show the complexity of these causes and indicate that there is no simple explanation of the period. Was the head of a major guerrilla movement a double agent? Did the intelligence service actually believe it was engaged in the third world war? Why did the Catholic Church turn on its own priests? Through her interviews, Marchak reveals much that will never appear in official documents.

PATRICIA MARCHAK is a professor in the Department of Anthropology and Sociology at the University of British Columbia.
WILLIAM MARCHAK is retired after thirty years in the newsprint export sales business to newspaper publishers throughout Latin America, including Argentina.

God's Assassins

State Terrorism in Argentina in the 1970s

PATRICIA MARCHAK

In collaboration with
WILLIAM MARCHAK

McGill-Queen's University Press
Montreal & Kingston · London · Ithaca

ISBN 0-7735-2013-9

Legal deposit fourth quarter 1999
Bibliothèque nationale du Québec

Printed in Canada on acid-free paper

McGill-Queen's University Press acknowledges the
financial support of the Government of Canada through
the Book Publishing Industry Development Program for
its activities. We also acknowledge the support of the
Canada Council for the Arts for our publishing program.

Canadian Cataloguing in Publication Data

Marchak, M. Patricia, 1936–
    God's assassins : state terrorism in Argentina
    in the 1970s
    Includes bibliographical references and index.
    ISBN 0-7735-2013-9
    1. Political violence – Argentina – History – 20th century.
    2. Disappeared persons – Argentina – History –
    20th century. 3. Terrorism – Argentina – History –
    20th century. 4. Argentina – Politics and government –
    1955–1983. I. Marchak, William. II. Title.
    F2849.2.M36 1999   982.06'4   C99-900997-4

Typeset in Sabon 10/12 with Akzidenz Grotesk display
by Caractéra inc., Quebec City

CONTENTS

TABLES

ACKNOWLEDGMENTS

The Social Sciences and Humanities Research Council of Canada granted research funds for this project, and the University of British Columbia allowed me to take research leave time. I am most grateful to both organizations.

The first contact that William and I had on this project was with Maud and Robert Cox. Robert, a former editor of the *Buenos Aires Herald*, was obliged to escape from Argentina in 1979 after repeated threats to his family. The Coxes encouraged us to proceed, and we thank them for lengthy discussions that helped us on our way.

Many Argentine citizens aided us with this project. The human rights groups were extremely helpful, and we thank all the truly remarkable people whom we met under their auspices. Jorge Vibes and Silvia Delfino, whom we met through the Canadian Studies Program in Buenos Aires, were extremely supportive of the research and became dear friends. Dr Emilio Mignone, María Alicia Gutierrez, Marta Maffei, Pampa Mercado, Dr Juan Carlos Marín, Dr Carlos Acuña, Dr Alfredo Bravo, Dr Adolfo Dorfman, Professor María Virginia Babot de Bacigaluppi, Dr Rut Diamint, Maximo Gainza, and many others helped us locate individuals, gave us copies of important material, and were most concerned that we should be able to pursue this line of research. These individuals represent very diverse positions in the ideological and social spectrum in Argentina today, but all were more concerned that the project be thorough and fair than that it represent their personal beliefs.

We are greatly indebted to the numerous individuals who presented us with copies of relevant publications, including those which they themselves had authored. The Canadian Embassy in Buenos Aires was most helpful, and we especially want to thank Beatriz Ventura, who suggested contacts in that great city.

We will not forget the kindness of the staff and volunteers at the Centro de Estudios Legales y Sociales, in particular Martín Abregu, Caroline Nieto, and Cristina Caiati, who found us a desk in the crowded quarters of CELS and helped us comb through years of newspaper clippings in their library. We also thank Andrew Graham-Yooll, editor of the *Buenos Aires Herald*, and the staff there who permitted us to photocopy many pages from their newspaper archives.

Gustavo, Wanda, and Pedro Wahren were wonderful friends during our stay in Buenos Aires, and we trust that our friendship will continue long past the publication of this book. Jorge and Bunty Fasceto were most kind and generous, and we thank them especially for their help during a spell of illness. These friends shared with us their own thoughts on these events, though they must not be held responsible for anything we have written here.

There are many others who made our stay interesting and helped us with our research; we cannot name them all, but we do think of them with gratitude. Most particularly, we thank all who granted us the opportunity to interview them. They shared their thoughts with us, and it is their thoughts that we have recorded here.

There were no permanent assistants on the project, but many were employed in the transcribing and translating tasks, both in Vancouver and in Buenos Aires. In particular, we want to thank Dolly del Pozzo, Alejandra Médellin, Marina Niks, Gabriel and Shirly Patrich, Raul Pechiera, Gloria Schwartz, Shireen Shiraz, and Dominique Yupangco for their patience and skill in working with the tapes.

Sensitive and intelligent editing is characteristic of Carlotta Lemieux, and her hand in this project is much appreciated. We also thank Eileen Oertwig, who looked after the financial statements and correspondence in Vancouver while we were in the field, and herself and Brian Milligan who cared for our house and dog in our absence. Finally we thank many dear friends in Vancouver who patiently tolerated our obsession with Argentina as we puzzled our way through this project.

Map of Argentina

PART ONE

Introduction

CHAPTER 1

Introduction

An estimated 30,000 people disappeared in Argentina between 24 March 1976 and 30 October 1983. Many others were imprisoned illegally, and thousands went into exile. Abducted people were taken to one of the hundreds of concentration camps throughout the country, where they were tortured and ultimately murdered by armed men employed by the military forces of the Argentine state. The state was controlled by a military junta, who called the reign of terror *el Proceso*, the Process for National Reorganization. Possibly no officers were aware that Franz Kafka's classic novel about bureaucratic authoritarianism, *The Trial*, is called *El Proceso* in Spanish.

Prior to the military coup, there was a period of political anarchy and economic decline, which the military forces who were active in clandestine roles called "the dirty war." Under the (third) elected government of Juan Domingo Perón, from September 1973 until his death at the beginning of July 1974, and then under the government of his third wife, María Estela, better known by her stage name, Isabel, up to two thousand people were murdered by paramilitary groups known as the Triple A, organized by a ministry of the government.[1] In addition, at least two hundred people (some estimates are much higher) were killed in open battle between guerrilla fighters and the army.

Under both the elected governments and the junta, the stated objective of state agencies engaged in killing people was to destroy subversives, communists, atheists, and dissidents who, in their view, constituted a serious threat to the well-being of "Western civilization and Christianity." Guerrilla organizations had become established in the late 1960s, and armed guerrillas were committing robberies, kidnappings, and assassinations. Both foreign and domestic businesspeople were potential targets of guerrilla violence. Army barracks were attacked and arms were stolen from them; other arms were procured outside the country with ransom money obtained by kidnapping executives. There was, in short, a genuine threat of subversion.

However, the killings by the paramilitary Triple A under the aegis of the government and, later, the killings by the military government went far beyond guerrilla members. Apparently innocent young people, union members, academics, artists, journalists, lawyers, priests, social workers, psychiatrists, and psychoanalysts were killed or imprisoned in the first phase, and were among the "disappeared" within days of the military coup that ushered in the second phase. The criteria for selection were not known. No one could be sure what constituted a crime or whether one was guilty. People who were not members of any of the suspected subversive groups were also at risk. Their names might have been noted in the address book of someone already picked up; they might have been an involuntary witness to a kidnapping; or they might be picked up accidentally. Some people were kidnapped because their possessions were coveted by secret police; some because an influential individual did not like them. Some were picked up for absolutely no known reason. Fear thus permeated the society, and it became greater as disappearances became endemic and neither police nor religious authorities acknowledged that they were occurring. This was state terrorism.

Guerrilla kidnappings and bombings, together with paramilitary kidnappings and bombings, were the immediate antecedents to the state terrorism. Before the guerrillas and Triple A were established, however, there was a longer period of violence. Rebellion against the repeated military coups and military governments was widely expressed by the young. Resistance to military attempts to control union activities was manifested by labour. The powerful Catholic Church was beset by a small group called the Third World Priests' Movement, which put service to the poor ahead of sermons on sin and salvation. The military's attempt to destroy the unique political ideology of Argentina, Peronism, merely resulted in its glorification by vast masses within the population. Police forces were frequently violent, and repression was commonplace, though before 1973 there was not yet systematic state terrorism.

Violence in this society went back a long way. In the history of Argentina, military force had been the frequent recourse of the rich against the poor. After the rise of state-centred unions under Juan Perón in the late 1940s, violence was also exerted by unions against dissident locals or members. The Roman Catholic Church, while not actively violent, was rigidly authoritarian. In general, the society operated in an authoritarian fashion, and it failed to develop – or, when developed, it failed to sustain – the rule of law or civil respect for the legal resolution of conflict. Pluralism, that is, tolerance for diverse political and social ideas, did not emerge, and consequently political institutions were subjected to violence far more than to debate. A volatile mixture of competing interest groups struggled within a society that had already dismantled if not fully destroyed its judicial system, its free press, the possibility of independent academic inquiry in its universities, its political parties, and independent or disengaged police action. All activities were therefore political in the rawest sense and were concerned with the competing power demands of various sectors of the population. Thus, even before Juan Perón's return from exile in Spain in 1973, and then his death, and before Isabel Perón's disastrous attempts to control subversion by force, Argentina was a deeply divided, troubled country. In view of this history, one might ask: Was state terrorism inevitable?

This book is partly a response to that question. However, the methodology is indirect. The objective here is not so much to address the historical question as to listen carefully to a large number of Argentine citizens who experienced the terrorism. These interviewees tell us their own stories, whether as witnesses or as participants in the events of the 1970s. Some tell us about the anxiety of the pre-coup years and their support for military intervention; others, of their anger and resistance to military rule. Some tell us why they became revolutionaries, what it meant to be a guerrilla, and how they survived the 1970s. Some tell us why they were "Third World priests" and how they survived within their own church as well as in the state. Still others, conservative churchmen, tell us why they agreed with the military government; and military men tell us why, from their perspective, the terrorism was necessary and justifiable. These interviews do not provide "proof" in support of a hypothesis about why state terrorism occurred, but they do provide a rich understanding of the conditions in which it emerged and of people's experiences under its spell. People acted in response to what they perceived and believed, and it is these perceptions and beliefs that we encounter here.

The interviewees also disclose information and offer their own interpretations of events. From these, together with the historical record, we are able to construct an explanation of why and how state terrorism occurred in Argentina from about 1974 (two years before the coup) through to the end of 1983, when the military forces handed over state power to a democratic government. Our objective is to explore the nature of state terrorism and its impact on a population and, in the process, to identify the structural origins and proximate causes of the events.

There is an international literature on state terrorism, particularly with reference to Nazi Germany and Stalin's Russia. Writers have also considered possible explanations for the authoritarianism and repression in Latin American countries. We refer to these works where they are helpful in our search for explanations of the Argentine case, but this is not a book about theory; it is book about experience. Our primary source is the autobiographical accounts of our interviewees. The historical record supplements these accounts.

WHAT IS STATE TERRORISM?

We adopt a definition of state terrorism that was originally advanced by theorist Hannah Arendt in her classic analysis of the Nazi regime in Germany.[2] This definition distinguishes terrorism as not merely force or even violence imposed by the agencies of the state. All states, ancient as well as modern, have sometimes imposed their authority by force or by the threat of force. Under ideal conditions, force may be used sparsely; moral authority and the rule of law may suffice to maintain peace and order in a society. In Argentina before the dirty war and the military coup of 1976, the frequent resort to force indicated the lack of moral authority and the breakdown of legal constraints. But even such violence as occurred then was short of terrorism. Terrorism is an instrument designed to frighten a larger population. In contrast to the violence that typically precedes it, it is not designed merely to kill political opponents; it is intended to terrify people.[3] There is no adequate explanation for the choice of victims; fear is engendered by unpredictability. Although some potential victims recognize themselves as the probable targets (in the case of Argentina, these were members of armed guerrilla organizations), many others who are not identified targets are caught. There are no rules. There is no certainty about what constitutes a trespass. It seems that anyone could be in the wrong, anyone could be a victim.

But there is always a caveat to generalizations. Terrorism is intended to terrify the population, yet it is possible for a state to initiate a terrorist campaign only if a substantial part of the population supports it. The explanation of this seeming paradox is that state terrorism is a process, not a single event. The process begins when a majority of the population is eager to see the end of violence and shares some ideas about which groups are responsible. A repressive regime appears as the way to end it, to bring order to the society, and to rid the society of the troublemakers. Exhausted by years of public atrocities, the population is prepared to believe a government that promises peace. Of those who are imprisoned or disappear, there is a widespread belief that "they must have done something."

In the early stages of state terrorism, there is very little uncensored information about what is happening, and there does seem to be a cessation of open violence. Guerrilla activity seems to decline; bodies stop appearing on the streets. The mass media say nothing at all about disappearances and torture, though they provide pictures and stories about the capture of subversives and the discovery of arms caches in guerrillas' houses. Propaganda informs the population that the troublemakers are under control and that the government is successfully eliminating a serious threat to the well-being of the nation. Gradually, all sources of alternative information and opposition are eliminated.

Over time, the repression widens to include more people. Guerrilla activity and political subversion are redefined so that ever more people are potentially affected. While terrorism begins with action against opponents – or persons whom government officials believe to be opponents – it moves beyond these narrow confines when a fully developed intelligence service is established. The longevity of the service depends on its ability to widen the net indefinitely. Eventually, it turns on its own functionaries, those who know too much and who can testify about what happened.

WHAT IS THE OBJECTIVE OF STATE TERRORISM?

The stated objective of a terrorist campaign is to eliminate some subpopulation that is defined as an enemy or as being composed of inferior beings who are somehow "impure" and unacceptable. The explicit argument put forward by the state is that such people cannot be controlled except by the most ruthless weeding out and that terrorism, with its kidnapping and torture, is a necessary means of identifying and eradicating the enemy. Terrorism is thus not open warfare.

But we need to dig further to explain this behaviour. Why would a government want to eliminate some of its own citizens? The apparent answer is that the government, with the tacit consent of a fair part of the population, proposes to reconstitute the society according to its version of "pure," "good," and "perfect." The government is engaged in social engineering, or ethnic cleansing. Since the impure people are not all easily identified, terrorism becomes the method of social engineering. The definition of "pure" is clearly ideological.

In the Argentine case, there are three ideologies to examine: that of the conservative church and military, that of the bureaucratic unions, and that of guerrilla fighters and dissident unions. Each had a strong, uncompromising version of perfection in its projected society, and each was prepared to struggle for the opportunity to impose its version on the whole society.

IS SOCIAL ENGINEERING
RELATED TO ECONOMIC
RESTRUCTURING?

As the reader will recognize in the interviews that constitute the larger part of this book, many of the interviewees believed that terrorism in Argentina (and also in Chile) was a consequence of an economic restructuring plan that had its origins outside the country. In their opinion, monetarism or neoliberalism was the guiding ideology, and the military undertook the task of imposing this market ideology on the economy of the country.[4] To do this, the military had to kill off all actual and potential opponents, and to destroy the strong union movement.

There is no doubt that the military government was engaged in restructuring the economy at the same time as it was involved in kidnapping and killing workers, students, and others who might have mounted an offensive campaign. But the question is whether state terrorism was undertaken in order to restructure the economy and, if so, at whose behest. We suggest that one can best understand the economic restructuring as part of the more general social engineering which the military undertook; further, that while external military forces played an influential role in the anticommunist crusade, the economic plans were not introduced on behalf of international capital or even under the aegis of a cohesive capitalist class within the country – though it does seen reasonable to assume that the economic planners expected that a liberalized economy would attract both foreign and new domestic investment.

Our own interpretation is that the attempts to develop the economy over the previous four decades had resulted in an extremely uneven state-centred society. By the late 1960s, stagnation and capital outflow were endemic.[5] Both the military governments and the quasi-elected governments from the mid-1950s onward had run into economic difficulties. All governments were engaged in a struggle with the Peronist, state-centred unions, but the military forces were not aligned with and certainly not controlled by a capitalist class or fraction of a class; they had a high degree of autonomy, due to various historical circumstances.

Whoever took over government at that stage would have had to undertake a restructuring to reignite the economy; the issue was who would control the state and how the restructuring would take place. the various contenders were the union leaders, organized students and their supporters, the conservative church, and the military – all components of the middle class. Of primary importance is the fact that a wide range of institutional sectors that we might expect to find in developed industrial societies – including strong political parties, independent judiciary and media, and organizations independent of the state – were not part of the established social fabric. Although financial, industrial, agribusiness, and small-business sectors did exist, there does not seem to be much evidence that their leading members acted in concert, had the same long-term or even short-term interests, or actively participated in politics. Thus, it was the ideological leaders of unions, universities, church, and military who shared the stage and who struggled amongst themselves for control of it. To some degree, this remains true today; as the interviews suggest, a subdued struggle continues for control of the interpretation of what occurred at that time.

PLANNING STATE TERRORISM

State terrorism is not a random occurrence, not even when, in its later stages, its targets are randomly selected. To impose a state terrorist regime, the potential terrorists have to be very well organized. Clandestine camps have to be established. Torture methods have to be taught. The technology for torture has to be available. Transportation, communication, and other institutional conditions have to be arranged. Indoctrination has to be well advanced to ensure loyalty and obedience. In short, coordination and advance planning are required, and these things take time and a high degree of organizational expertise. State terrorism in Argentina was certainly planned long in advance by the leaders of the three military forces. Clandestine concentration camps were established throughout the country before the coup, and the instruments of torture were installed. Army and police personnel were taught how to use the instruments, how to inflict terror. An intelligence unit was established with wide-ranging powers.

This degree of advance organization involves an extensive bureaucratic decision-making and implementation capacity. Yet bureaucratic organizations are normally the antithesis of arbitrary operations; there is a hierarchy of authority, there are rules, records, and well-defined procedures.[6] Thus, the question that theorists grapple with is: How does a modern bureaucracy lend itself to decisions to eliminate sectors of the population? The answer given by some theorists is that the goal of organizations is not necessarily moral or rational from various perspectives, but the means are rational in the sense that they constitute the best-known way of attaining the explicitly defined goal. Others argue that bureaucracy, indeed the entire technical and organizational format of "modernity," is essential to and in a sense produces the conditions for terrorism.[7]

If the goal is to eliminate Jews, gypsies, cripples, and homosexuals, as it was in Nazi Germany, or rightists as in Stalin's USSR, or leftists as in Argentina and Chile of the 1970s, then terrorism, torture, and murder may constitute rational means. Obviously, such a decision would have to be supported by the many functionaries who are expected to carry out brutal orders; success would otherwise be impossible. Yet there is a limit to the capacity of any regime to force recruits to torture and murder their compatriots (or indeed noncompatriots, even during a war). The limits of force are exceeded when there is faith, missionary zeal, and loyalty to the leaders and co-workers who are part of the terrorist regime.

Another approach, for those who view "modernity" as the underlying condition, is to argue that bureaucracies, together with modern science and technology, separate the human agent from the victim in such a way as to destroy all sense of personal responsibility for one's actions. We do not take this alternative approach in this book; there does not seem to be a sufficient body of evidence, either in the history or in the interviews, to indicate that the context of state terrorism in Argentina was modernity as understood in this way. The process of modernization and the growth of bureaucracies, on the other hand, could be important conditions, and we will examine the process and development of bureaucratic organization in the chapters on history.

METHODOLOGY

The historical record, which is set out in part 2, is essential reading for an understanding of the origins and causes of state terrorism. The sources for this interpretation include, in addition to the historical and journalistic literature, a wide range of contemporary materials and informants. We sought out information on the history from many university and independent researchers who have studied and published works on political and economic issues. We examined newspaper archives, including especially the extensive library of clippings maintained at the Centro de Estudios Legales y Sociales (CELS) and the *Buenos Aires Herald*. We also sought out representatives of human rights and other organizations to hear their versions of history. However, this is not primarily a history book; our objective in this first section is to provide a reasonable and concise depiction of the historical context before proceeding to the interviews.

Autobiographical accounts do not provide proof about what happened in the past. Imperfect memories, selective memories, and repressed knowledge, as well as the influence of current interests on how the past is reconstructed, all affect the accounts. These interviews are subjective renditions by people who have been through a traumatic period in their lives and are trying to explain it to themselves as well as to the strangers from Canada. The interviews should not be read as "truth" but as a revelation of the fears, beliefs, ideologies, loyalties, and betrayals of the period, and of the historical record as interpreted by those who participated in it, whether as the repressed or the repressers.

Most of our interviewees were asked to tell us their personal stories. Our questions were of the nature "Where were you when ...?" "What happened ...?" and "What did you do?" They also gave us their interpretation of the historical context or the immediate conditions of the 1976 coup. They had theories about the causes: Peronism, militarism, and an authoritarian church were among these; so was an international conspiracy to test neoliberal economic policies and the strategic defence policy initiated by the United States. Their views on the causes are important, and we have included many of them.

Because of the positions which a few of the interviewees then occupied, the autobiographical material about them had to be omitted from this report in order to protect their identity. For others, whose present situation likewise required us to be extremely discreet, aliases have been provided, and their depictions of what happened and why have been included in a much-edited form. But the editing has never involved additions or invention; only deletions to protect a person's identity. This is especially the case for individuals in the church and the military forces, and occasionally for former guerrilla fighters.

The interviewees did not all describe their own experiences. Some of them, either because of the positions they occupied then or now, or because they did not wish to provide a personal account, talked about the historical context or about particular circumstances of the repression. As well, there were many interviews with persons who led human rights organizations, with women who participated in the marches of the Mothers of the Plaza de Mayo, or with members of the grandmothers' group that has documented the kidnapping of newborn babies (the Abuelas). There were interviews with academics who had specialized knowledge of specific events or organizations, and with politicians in government or opposition parties. Many of these interviews were obtained for information or background and are not reported here. However, where individuals had a version of certain events that went beyond general knowledge (for example, the relationship between Montonero leaders and the army, which is described in the final interviews of this book), those discussions are reported in some detail.

We anticipated that when we put together a large number of these autobiographical and interpretive accounts, even taking for granted that memories would be defective or carefully chosen to fit current interests, we would have a richer understanding of the complexities of a society under state terrorism than we could have achieved by relying solely on documents or official accounts. This is an unusual methodology for the study of a historical event, but we believe it has been successful. Unlike documentary studies combined with interviews that are designed only to obtain or verify "facts," this method has allowed us to recognize different perspectives and, through them, to understand a troubled society in a way that no alternative methodologies would have permitted.

These retrospective, highly subjective accounts give us insight into the culture of the 1970s (and, indirectly, into the culture of the 1990s when the interviews took place). Although a theory of state terrorism could be developed without these accounts, it would lack the fibre and vibrancy that make the events of the 1970s understandable. These qualities, which the interviews exude, illuminate the nature, more than the chronological history, of state terrorism.

Selection of Interviewees

The interviewees were a diverse selection of people that included guerrillas, "Third World priests," conservative members of the hierarchy of the Catholic Church, military officers, military rebels, and bereaved family members. Also included were nonrevolutionary students, business people, actors and artists, housekeepers and others who had lost no loved ones, experienced no personal threats, and carried on with their lives almost as if the repression around them was not occurring.

Although we tried to interview a wide range of individuals, we most actively sought out those who had been members of targeted groups in 1974–79, during the pre-coup and immediate post-coup terrorism. These were, first of all, individuals who were between the ages of sixteen and thirty in 1975, since their peers were an estimated 81 per cent of the victims. In all, we interviewed 118 individuals. Of these, eighty-two (69 per cent) were in this age group, and thirty (25 per cent) were in the critical group aged between twenty and twenty-four. Five were fifteen years old or younger at the time and were interviewed because of the effects they experienced as young children. The remainder were older and were interviewed either because of their particular roles in the events of the 1970s or to ensure that we heard the views of persons who were not directly involved even though they were very much present.

The second criterion was occupational role. Unionized workers, students, teachers and professors, and professionals in the human sciences or journalism were targeted during the repression. Not surprisingly given the age group of most of those interviewed, thirty-five of them (29 per cent) were students in 1975. Fourteen were teachers or professors, and thirteen were unionized workers in industry or business (about 11 per cent each). Business people and lawyers, medical professionals, including psychiatric and psychoanalytic workers, and people in occupations related to the humanities and arts (including journalism and architecture) were represented by nine, six, and ten interviewees, respectively. Readers should be alerted to the difference between North American and Argentine occupational labels and training requirements. After high school, Argentines generally go directly into professional training in such fields as law and medicine, and may become practitioners in as few as four or five years. Law is frequently a choice for a career in business. Psychologists, psychiatrists, and psy-choanalysts all work together in a medical setting, and the training and roles for these professionals are much less distinct than in North America; also, psychoanalysis is popular and well regarded in 1990s Argentina. Secondary-school teachers and professors are less clearly demarcated, and sometimes the same individuals teach at both levels. One may designate oneself a professional in social science or some other field at the conclusion of an undergraduate degree program.

Our interviewees included members of two groups that had particular roles during the repression: priests, ministers, and church administrators (nine in the sample); and members of the armed forces (six in the sample). The current papal nuncio (whose predecessor had recently received negative media attention in Rome for his role in Argentina of the 1970s) refused our request for an interview.

The victims of the repression are estimated to have been 70 per cent male. In the 1970s there were only men in the church and the military (and in the church this is still true), but there were many women in guerrilla movements, and there were women (in varying proportions) in targeted occupations. Our sample included seventy-five men (63 per cent) and forty-three women, so it somewhat overrepresented women relative to the estimated proportion of victims and their numbers (or lack thereof) in targeted occupations.

We were aware that throughout the early 1970s and during the early phases of the repression, there were numerous violent actions against Jewish businesses. In 1976 the army claimed that these were the work of unauthorized paramilitary forces. The attacks declined in frequency after international attention was focused on them. There can be little doubt that anti-Semitism has had a long run in Argentina, whether it originated with the Spanish conquest and the ideology of Christendom at that time, or whether it arose in a more recent period of history that includes the corporatism of Juan Perón's government and the fascism of many sectors of the army. But the history is not all of a piece. On the one hand, there is clear evidence of anti-Semitism in the bombing of a synagogue in the 1980s and in the acceptance of known Nazis as immigrants following the Second World War. On the other hand, Buenos Aires has the second-largest Jewish community outside Israel (New York is first), and in the years immediately preceding the Second World War, Argentina received 50,000 Jewish refugees from Europe. By comparison, Canada (with only a slightly smaller population and with a similar economic capacity) took only 5,000.

In view of the history, we asked leaders of the Jewish community whether Jews had been targeted during the repression. Although we heard that there were many anti-Semites in the armed forces and that certain army officers had been especially vicious in their treatment of Jewish prisoners, the leaders we consulted told us that they did not think Jews had been targeted. In addition to these general consultations, we included among our interviewees a number of persons who identified themselves as Jews, and we asked them whether they thought Jews had been especially singled out during the repression. The answer was "probably not," with the additional response that if Jews were caught and identified as Jews, they were probably subjected to particularly harsh treatment. Martin Andersen, however, a journalist of solid reputation, argues that the proportion of Jews who disappeared exceeded their proportion of the population, and he unhesitatingly attributes this to anti-Semitism.[8] As it happened, we had no difficulty contacting Jews as well as Catholics. Indeed, several went out of their way to ensure that we met survivors who had been young and involved in leftist organizations during the 1970s. So Jews are well represented in the final sample.

Protestants, Muslims, and people of other religions were more difficult to find because they form a very small proportion of the population and were even fewer in number then. However, there was no reason for us to suspect that any of these religious groups were targeted. The same can be said of the various immigrant groups – British, Lebanese, Turkish, Russian, Polish, German, and others – that are a minority among a population that is largely of Italian or Spanish descent. Indeed, we found no evidence of any kind, no hint, no grumble, that ethnicity as such was a factor in the repression. (As an aside, it should be noted that contrary to some "explanations" of the terrorism in Argentina, neither the total number of persons of German descent nor the influence of German immigrants immediately after the Second World War was of sufficient significance to explain much of anything. This is said to offset the notion that what occurred was the work of neo-Nazis.)

Native peoples and mestizo populations are certainly oppressed in Argentina as elsewhere in Latin America; but no one has suggested, and there is no evidence to suggest, that native peoples as such were among the disappeared. This should not be surprising, because on this occasion the targets were in the middle class and the organized working class, not in the populations living in poverty or on the margins of society.

A defect of our selection method is, of course, that we cannot say that it is representative of the general population in a statistically reliable form, and in fact we offer no statistics based on the sample. What we do offer are interviews that display a range of experiences and opinions and provide the reader with a sense of what happened, its impact at the time, and the memory of it today. The interviews that are reproduced here, either in whole or in part, are similar to the other interviews we conducted. While each individual is of course unique, the experiences and views of those published here are typical of the interviewees as a whole, though the selection may have been somewhat arbitrary. But since we are not trying to prove something and there is no hypothesis to be rigorously tested, this procedure is offered as a means of understanding a social situation rather than of measuring it.

Why Argentina?

We chose Argentina, rather than the many other societies that have undergone similar repressions, because it is not now in a situation where fear of reprisal is a dominant and pervasive experience for citizens, yet the fear is not so ancient that it has been forgotten. We were able to speak with people who had lived through these events and retained a strong memory of them, and who were not afraid to talk about the past.

PREPARATION AND PRESENTATION OF PUBLISHED INTERVIEWS

The interviews were conducted in 1996 and 1997 – that is, twenty years after the military coup of March 1976 and about thirteen years after the conclusion of the military dictatorship. They were conducted by the author and her collaborator during two periods totalling six months, and they took place in Buenos Aires, Tucumán, Córdoba, Rosario, and Mar del Plata. They were taped, except when an interviewee requested otherwise. Notes were also taken to supplement the tapes. Then the taped interviews were transcribed (usually twice by separate typists), translated (also done twice in many cases), and edited, with scrupulous attention to maintaining close correspondence with the spirit of the original in the English version presented here.

The edited interviews are presented here under a heading that begins with the word "Voice" and gives a name (the actual name or an alias of the interviewee). These are presented without intervention by the author except where essential historical information, translation of acronyms, and the like is required; this information is inserted in square brackets, where possible, but in the endnotes if more space is required. For reasons of space, the interviewer's questions have been omitted when the interviewee was narrating a personal history and the questions were simply for clarification or to encourage the speaker to continue. However, the questions are included (in italics) where the reader would need to know a particular question in order to appreciate why the response took the form it did, or where the question included information, a challenge, or a sudden change of topic.

Of necessity, the author severely cut the interviews, omitting extraneous and redundant material. This was done with as much care as possible in order to preserve the content, the contextual information, and, where possible, the style of speaking in the original.

NOTES ON LANGUAGE

Where interviewees used Spanish words for which there is no equivalent English phrase, or Spanish titles and names, the original has been given and the closest equivalent is provided in square brackets or in an endnote. Similarly, when the English equivalent has been used in the translation but the reader might wish to know the Spanish name, the Spanish word or title has been added in square brackets or in a note.

The word "disappeared" has become a noun and an intransitive and transitive verb in Latin-American Spanish as a consequence of the terrorist regimes in Argentina and neighbouring societies. Thus, one speaks of "the disappeared" and says, "The army disappeared him" as well as "She disappeared." Because the word is so pervasive in all the literature and interviews, we have adopted these usages even though the English language (reflecting a very different experience) is less flexible with that verb. The noun in Spanish is *los desaparecidos* and we have sometimes left it like that in the text of the edited interviews rather than translating it, because it is a word that belongs to Latin America as no other word does.

The term *compañero* has no English equivalent. It is inadequately rendered as "companion," "friend," "co-worker," or "colleague," because it implies a stronger bond between equals than any of those terms does. The closest term might be "mate" as used in Australia. We have chosen to let *compañero* stay in the English text.

When referring to abductions by the military, our respondents frequently used the terms "taken" and "fallen." We have generally translated these as "kidnapped." Individuals who participated in the Montoneros or in other groups opposed to the various governments frequently stated that "he/she/I was a militant." For persons who were not members of armed organizations or engaged in violent actions, we have translated the word "militant" as "activist"; but where violence was indicated, we have kept the literal translation, "militant."

In English we talk about "the army" or "the navy," but we normally use an adjective together with the word "forces" (for example, "armed forces") to describe any combination of the services. In Latin-American Spanish the term "the military" is the equivalent of our "armed forces," and because "military" is used as a noun throughout the literature and interviews, we have adopted it in the English translations. Also, there is the word *militar* in reference to a member of the armed forces. English has the word "soldier," but the word *militar* embraces any member of the armed forces, from a foot soldier to a general. We use the term in the Spanish sense. The plural "militaries" refers both to military forces and to military personnel.

Che Guevara had a profound influence on a generation of young people throughout Latin America, and their version of what he stood for and said is known as Guevarism. We retain the term in this book.

There are certain titles, names of organizations, or names of events for which an English equivalent might be devised but where the colour of the original would fade in translation. For example, young Argentines in 1970 often belonged to the Juventud Peronista. Literally, this is the Peronist Youth, or Young Peronists' Association. The translation might be interpreted as akin to the Young Liberals or Young Conservatives in a country such as Canada, but in fact the Juventud was very different – a powerful association that trained thousands of young Argentines for revolutionary activity under a military dictatorship. In organization and style it was fascist; in ideology, it was a curious mixture of Peronism, Guevarism, and socialism. We have used both Juventud and Young Peronists, but readers should recognize that the latter cannot be equated with similar political associations in other countries.

There is no translation for the Montoneros (the senior and more militant arm of the Juventud). The name has historical meaning, referring to frontier cowboys (*gauchos*) who, according to legend, defended Argentina in its infancy. The guerrilla organization that adopted the name captured its romantic and nationalist connotation.

Another set of words that we decided to leave unedited are the colourful terms for events and social movements so typical of Latin-American Spanish. *Peronismo* and *justicialismo* (both referring to the Peronist movement) and *Cordobazo* (a general strike that occurred in the city of Córdoba in 1969) are among these.

CONFIDENTIALITY AND A PARADOX

For the record, we ran into a curious paradox. In accordance with the ethical requirements of the Social Sciences and Humanities Research Council of Canada, which provided the funding for this project, and the University of British Columbia, where the author is employed, we have carefully ensured confidentiality of all research documents that could identify individuals. The paradox is that our concern for confidentiality was not shared by all the informants. Many of them preferred to be identified. They did not want to disappear again. So although we have given false names and altered some identifying features of many informants, in other cases we have named persons and organizations that are on the public stage, academics and film makers whose analyses are in the public realm, and others who made it clear that they preferred to tell their story under their own name. In order that those who wanted to speak without identification are assured of confidentiality, there is no identification system in the text. Real names are given in full for persons who requested identification, but not all apparently full names are real. Aliases have no external meaning: they were chosen because they are popular names in Argentina.

ORGANIZATION OF THE BOOK

Throughout the text, the narrative history of Argentina and interviews are interspersed. As a continuation of the introductory section, chapter 2 consists of interviews that convey the experiences of ordinary people trying to cope with a violent society. These interviews provide a sense of the range of experiences and reflections amongst our interviewees. The range includes both fear of the military regime and support for it, with many perspectives between the two extremes. The events to which these interviewees refer will be discussed in later chapters.

Part 2 is concerned with the history up to the early 1970s. A very short chapter 3 covers selected features, as background material, of the historical period up to 1945. Chapter 4 focuses on the Peronist decade and the subsequent military and quasi-military governments up to 1973. Chapter 5 concentrates on the growth of unions and their interaction with military governments during the post-Peronist period. It also contains three interviews with people who resided in the industrial city of Córdoba in the turbulent 1960s and 1970s. The final chapter of this section provides a fairly detailed description of some of the guerrilla groups that formed during the 1960s and early 1970s, together with an account of the return of Juan Perón. (Further details of the guerrilla groups can be found in the appendix.)

Part 3 includes many interviews that provide insights on the escalating violence after 1970. The interviews are interspersed with information from newspapers of the time and interpretation. The section opens with a discussion of the dirty war that began under Juan Péron and continued under Isabel's government. Interviews describe the impact of this on a major Argentine writer, several young students, and a guerrilla fighter. Chapter 8 includes interviews with people who were imprisoned during the dirty war. These people provide insights on union organization and infighting, as well as giving first-hand accounts of their painful experiences in jail.

Still within part 3, chapter 9 is a study of *el Proceso* following the 1976 coup. Chapter 10 consists of several fascinating interviews with people who were members of the guerrilla movements. The pervasive sentiment in these interviews is regret, and it is a very complex emotion because their current understandings of what they did is so often disjunctive with what they believed at the time. Chapter 11 is a study of survivors in the impoverished rural town of Tucumán, where one of the revolutionary armies was decimated. Finally, in chapter 12, we listen to a publisher and an editor describe their reactions to both the military regime and the guerrillas. This chapter also examines international reaction to events in Argentina.

Part 4 concentrates on the two major institutional sectors of this society: the Roman Catholic Church and the military. Here there are contradictory views within the church on its proper role and how it behaved during the repression. The military voices are equally at odds with one another: there are defenders, denouncers, and sceptics in their ranks too. These interviews reveal many of the extreme tensions and conflicts that emerged during the dictatorship and that still bedevil these organizations.

The conclusion returns to the discussion with which we began the book. What were the origins and causes of state terrorism? What have we learned from the interviews about the social context and the process, and about the experiences of the interviewees who lived through these events?

We urge readers to tackle this text in its chronological order, because the interviews are incremental in their revelations about experiences, interpretations of events, and even in the knowledge of what occurred. The suspicions of some of the people interviewed are either confirmed or negated by what others actually know; the tragedies of some are shown to be heightened by the meaninglessness of their suffering. What was deadly serious for some was seen as absurd or was disbelieved by others.

The interviews, much more than the historical narrative – compelling as it is – tell us how very complex is the tapestry of state terrorism. Seemingly, nothing is as it first appears, and nothing can be reduced to simple causes. The reader will find in these pages a number of sub-themes that run through the history. One of these is about a leader of the Montoneros who, in the opinion of some of our interviewees and of several writers, was a double agent. Another sub-theme concerns the infighting between the unions and its effect on the ability of the union movement to prevent the terror. A third theme is about the dilemma of the Catholic Church as it moves toward the millennium, urged by the pope to face its past honestly but still unable to admit its share of responsibility for what happened in that tragic time. There is one question which no existing theory has tackled: Why did the torturers save the newborn babies of imprisoned (and subsequently murdered) mothers, and why did military families and their friends adopt these children as their own? No other example of state terrorism includes this seemingly bizarre behaviour. If our argument about the importance of ideology is correct, the answer must be that the military saw the newborns as innocents in need of appropriate socialization. Unlike the nazis, they did not label the mothers as genetically unfit; merely as ideological enemies.

When we reach the conclusion of this study, we are less inclined than when we started to view this conflict as a military behemoth pitted against an innocent population – not, we hasten to add, because the military was justified in its attack on the population. No, the military's terrorist war was monstrous. But the military itself was a creation of the society on which it preyed.

CHAPTER 2

Coping with State Terrorism

This chapter consists of excerpts from interviews with people who experienced the terrorism in Argentina. These people were not guerrilla fighters, not church officials, not police or army officers. They were just ordinary folk trying to cope with a difficult situation. Their voices tell of fear, confusion, cynicism, anger, and also of sadness, indifference, and even smugness. The military coup was a disaster or a blessing; the military forces were idiots or saints; social life was totally disrupted or it went on without interruption. These are ordinary voices in a time of social upheaval: voices that give us diverse interpretations of what happened and why it happened. They represent a fair cross-section of the range of perspectives that we heard during our interviews with citizens who were not on the front lines.

VOICE: WALTER

When I left Argentina in 1977, during the military period, I really hated to live here. I was very afraid to live here. I was nineteen and I thought that there must be another place where people can be logical and not all stupid, because here people were dying. I was living afraid, everybody was living afraid, and I thought, this is not logical, this country's reality. There must be another reality.

How can I tell you? I felt afraid all the time. Afraid of being young. For example, we had to agree with the haircut, with the short haircut all the time, and not to have a beard, for example, and not to wear green things, not to wear green clothes because they were the symbol of the guerrillas. It was forbidden to have a green coat. If you were young and different, that was dangerous. You always had to have your identity documents when you went out. If you forgot, you would hurry home again because this was dangerous. I was not in a political party, but I felt nervous all the time.

It was very dangerous to be young at that time in Argentina. You were not supposed to speak about your thoughts. The law ensured that you would stay silent. Classes were carried on, and we learned, but it was like trying to be in another world. We were trying not to speak about another subject, only studies, because we were afraid of being heard by policemen or military people.

VOICE: SEBASTIAN

I was still in primary school, ten years old, in 1970. My father, a professor, was a left-wing activist in a small socialist party. They were socialists but thought that the left in Argentina had to review the relationship with Perón and Peronism. In 1971 I was allowed to attend meetings of this party, and I began to read about the history of my country. The next year, all over the city, there were signs saying "Perón will return."

I entered a public secondary school. Political commitment in secondary schools was strong. At the student centre, the Peronist Youth were the dominant group. There were a lot of Montoneros – thirteen- and fourteen-year old Montoneros – and a little group of activists. I was not a Montonero, but my relationship with Peronist Youth was good. I became increasingly involved in politics. In 1974 the government intervened[1] in my secondary school. Political activity was absolutely prohibited, so I stopped being involved. Had I continued, my life would have been in danger.

My family life was not quiet because my father had to leave the University of Buenos Aires for the second time. He had been ousted from the university in 1966 when General Onganía staged a military coup. He had returned to the university in 1973 when Héctor Cámpora, followed by Juan Perón, became president. But in 1975 the government intervened at the University of Buenos Aires, and my father again had to leave it. He continued to teach at the University in Bahía Blanca, so our family went there when I was fifteen years old.

Bahía Blanca is a city very near a military base. There are strong right-wing and fascist groups in that city. In Argentina in the 1970s, we did not have conservatives and liberals. It was socialists and fascists. There was no middle ground. One day, I think it was around February or March 1975, there were some armed men at the Hotel Austral where we were staying. These armed men went through the streets with guns. They said that people who were teaching at universities were Marxists and that they had to be killed. It was the first time I witnessed real violence.

My father tried to calm us, but he sent my mother, sister, and me to another town, where he visited on weekends. Later, in 1976, a lot of teachers of the university were detained by armed troops. Some of them were just detained, but most disappeared. At that time we did not know the system of disappearance. We knew that some of them had been detained, but we did not know what had happened to them. We thought they would reappear in time.

My father left the university at Bahía Blanca by the middle or end of 1975. We went to live for several months at my grandmother's house in Buenos Aires. My father was worried when some friends of his who were neither Montoneros nor leftists were detained. One of his friends was jailed for one month and was told to leave the country. Though my father was afraid of what could happen to him, he never thought he could die. He thought that he might be in jail for a week or a month, but nothing worse. A friend of my father's, whom he had met in university and who worked in the Israeli Embassy, told him of a way to escape from Argentina. He told my father that if he wanted, we could be in Israel within forty-eight hours. He said to my father, "Tell me when you want to get out of the country and we will put you and your family on a plane and you will be in Israel within forty-eight hours." Then my father met us and asked the whole family what we wanted to do. He said, "I didn't do anything. I want to stay because I am not guilty of anything." So we decided to stay. Of course, we were not aware of the consequences of this decision. He did not know at that time that people had died. He knew that Montoneros were kidnapped and killed. But he thought, "Well, I'm not a Montonero, so nothing bad will happen to me." That seemed rational at the time.

When my father thought there was nothing more to worry about and that the danger had passed, we went back to our home in Buenos Aires. But there was an atmosphere of horror there. Day after day, we heard sirens. We would see armed men, often not in uniform, and also uniformed police or the military surrounding a house. Also sometimes there were fires and this all happened near our house. When that happened, my father would tell us to go to the basement. Six months after the coup, the police came to our house.

The police came, without uniforms, and they asked the concierge to knock on our door. When my mother went to the door to ask who it was, the person who answered said it was the concierge. My mother asked, "What do you want?" It was eleven in the evening. The person said, "I have to deliver something." When my mother opened the door, there were two men with guns and another by the stairs. All of them faced my parents and sister as though they were waiting to shoot them. Then they pushed the concierge away.

They began to search the house. After ten minutes or so, they realized that there were no guns and said that they were policemen and that they were working under the orders of the army. They began to speak against the military, claiming that they were forced to do terrible things to families. Then they told us they had to take and burn the books because the real danger was books. My father had previously put away all his "dangerous" books in the basement, including Marx's works, Lenin's, and such. So when these policemen looked for the books they didn't find those. But they took the books by Jean Paul Sartre and Aldo Ferrer, the leftist economist. They took a book by Pablo Neruda, the Chilean poet. Then they took my father away. They didn't steal anything else. After that we found out that often when they went to houses they stole or broke things. Sometimes they took women as well. So perhaps we were fortunate.

They arrested my father and told us that they would take him to a judge in Bahía Blanca. The next day my mother went to Bahía Blanca. When she arrived, the judge told her that he did not know anything about my father and had heard nothing. The judge said he did not recognize the name. Much depended on who captured you. If they were crazy, they would kill you. Well, my father was lucky, and they did a *simulacro*, they simulated killing him. The judge in Bahía Blanca knew that my father had been kidnapped, but he did not tell my mother because he thought that my father, on the way from his house to Bahía Blanca, might have been killed. So he did not want to be involved in the situation. For a month we had no knowledge of my father's whereabouts.

We went to the police, and finally a lawyer who was our friend obtained a writ of habeas corpus and we learned where he was. My mother went to that jail with food and clothes for him. They told her that my father would receive them, but he never did. When my mother came back the next day, she was told that he was not there any more. So again we did not know where he was. After fifteen days we received his first letter from jail. He was in jail for one and a half years before we were allowed to visit him. He was accused of – well, there was a law, I'm not sure exactly what it was – but it was for something like ideological crimes.

We visited him first in Bahía Blanca and then in La Plata until September 1978. I will always remember that the first time we saw my father, he told us what a Russian novelist had once said: "There are some moments in the life of countries where the best place to be is jail." As time went by, I thought he was right, and for two reasons. I think that, in a way, he and I were proud of the fact that he was in jail; but also he was lucky that he did not disappear.

When we were looking for my father, we met mothers of people who had disappeared. It was then that we realized what was happening. It was difficult to be really aware of that because my mother, sister, and I had only a few friends. Former friends did not want to know us when we tried to get their help. When we phoned friends, they would say things like, they were busy and for us to not phone them for a while. We were alone ...

Some of my father's friends were released, and then, finally, he was released in November 1978. We knew of people who, when they were freed, were shot. They waited for people. I don't know if it was the army, the police, or other armed groups. They waited for them to come out of jail and then they killed them. So when we knew that my father was getting out of jail, we waited at the jail entrance for the whole day. I don't know what we could have done. I remember that day, after he was released, coming from the jail to the bus station and travelling by bus to Buenos Aires; that was a very happy day. From then on we had no problems. By the time political parties began to appear again, we knew about the disappearances, but the worse part of our story was over.

Looking back, I think there was no explanation for anything. When Peronism was ousted in the coup of 1955, the military repression afterwards made Peronism look much better than it had really been. People who wanted to fight against the regime, the military, and against everything they considered to be wrong with the country started to call themselves Peronists. Then people who remained anti-Peronists, especially the owners of the fields in the pampas and some of the richer people, began to think that what was happening was very dangerous. So they had to give a lot of power to the army in order to stop this strange political movement. It was something like an explosive culture, a very strange and powerful movement composed of people with conflicting opinions, and a powerful army out of control, and terrorists fighting them. The violence increased. The army thought that most terrorists were idealists; they were people from university. So they thought that politically they had to kill not only the people with the guns but people with the books, because they thought that the people with the books taught the people with the guns. Then it all became monstrous. There were no limits. Everyone could be suspected of being a terrorist. Every military shift wanted to prove themselves, to catch dissidents and ideological enemies. Well, that's how it was then.

VOICE: MARTÍN

Before the coup, I was employed in a government department. My position had a certain degree of responsibility. I didn't make important decisions, but the matters I had to deal with were quite important, and the industrial sectors I worked with were big and powerful. They had strong lobbies, and I learned how they influenced economic policies. Ministers of commerce and industry, and the secretariats that depended on them were almost all chosen by influential people in these industries. In that way there was a link with the officials designated by them.

A great part of the efforts of the secretariats of industry consisted of trying to obtain exceptions to the law for the private sector. The senior levels in the ministry supported the requests of the lobbies, but at my middle level it was my duty to identify where the proposals were against the law.

Then, in the two years before the military coup, I was required to sit on a commission dealing with the [named] industry. There were strong pressures from certain deputies in Congress to get this job done according to the law. I was obliged to investigate a particular firm ... Well, I knew that this firm could not have obtained its many advantages without the involvement of the officials of the Ministry of Industry. In 1976 three of us prepared and signed a long report, noting all these irregularities and including the names of Argentines who were supposed to have been accomplices and executors.

Shortly afterward, I obtained a grant to take postgraduate studies in Italy. The coup here occurred a month after I arrived in Italy. A month later, I received a telegram from the ministry, signalling that I was being fired. I finished my course in five months, returned to Argentina, and asked the new authorities of the ministry to explain why I had been dismissed. They did not tell me this clearly, but I was able to find out that the accusations against me were based on two things: first, it was a personal vendetta of the officials who were affected by the matter I have told you about; the second, which was very dangerous, was that I belonged to a leftist revolutionary party. They alleged that my trip to Europe had included attendance at a meeting of the Fourth International in Paris.

It was nonsense, there was no truth in it. I had no knowledge then, nor have I to this day, that there was a meeting of the Fourth International. Anyway, I came from an ultra-right-wing family. Nevertheless, shortly after I returned to Argentina, I could sense the tactic and the practice of state terrorism. I had never participated in any political movements or in any unacceptable politics, not even in a political party, nor in any revolutionary movements; not of the left or right. It is beyond imagining.

My leaving had apparently coincided with the opening meeting of the Fourth International. But the real problem was that our group of four or five people who worked together were accused of being leftists by our bosses, who wanted to get rid of us. I had never participated in political movements. I had strong personal and rational reasons for this. The first is that I did not see in the left or right an effective program. They both recited dogmas. Also, I tended to see the political leaders and the leaders of the leftist movements as upstarts. From both sides, left and right. Further than that, there were family reasons: my father had been a political exile, which he regretted all his life. He came from France. He was a refugee from the Second World War because he had belonged to the Vichy regime. And because of his experience, I was able to understand that I was someone who did not have a special aptitude for politics. My father's experience made quite an impression on me. He never told me – I suppose I knew – that the big mistake he had committed was his very small participation during the German occupation of France.

When I was in Italy I did not understand what was going on in Argentina, but a few days after returning I recognized that this military coup was unlike its predecessors. It had institutionalized terrorism. It didn't leave anyone sure of anything where personal security was concerned. The newspapers published a great deal about the military occupation of the University of Bahía Blanca. As I read, my eyes were opened because it became evident to me that it was a witch-hunt. It was exactly like events in the Middle Ages. That day, I had to go to the house of my mother-in-law. I felt panicky because I had books in the library there in my in-laws' house, an important library of economics textbooks, of history and philosophy. I had to burn a cubic metre books.

I knew that the army was conducting operations in the neighbourhoods and that they came into people's houses. They were particularly interested in the ideological orientation and the politics of members of each family. In fact, a few days later, a patrol spent the whole day searching through the block where my in-laws lived in Buenos Aires. They operated principally in the outskirts of the city because they were looking for union leaders or leftist intellectuals. In reality, as we learned much later, the technique of the armed forces – the army, navy, marines, police – was to take a hundred in order to catch one.

I was able to speak with one of the disappeared who returned; we used the phrase "born-again." It was rare that someone who had disappeared was freed. This boy was released from jail after he had been hooded for many days and tortured. They demanded that he give them names of leftist activists, but he absolutely didn't know of anyone. Something happened that caused the military to realize that this was an error. The prisoners were always hooded, without being able to take off the hood. They took him to a distant suburb in a car, and they told him that this was the day that he would be born again; starting that day, he had a new birthday. And in effect, he was saved. He was saved from a certain death.

The same thing happened with an old boss of mine who had been a government minister in a provincial Peronist government, in the leftist sector. He was kidnapped, tortured, interrogated, and later he promised to give names if they permitted him to leave and to make one telephone call. Once he left, he took refuge in the offices of the United Nations and he managed to leave the country.

Now I must tell you a very odd story. It is something that has occurred to me only once in my life. A premonition. I dreamed that I and my old boss, this person who took refuge at the United Nations, were walking in the street and he was behind me. He told me he had to hide because they were following him and were on the point of kidnapping him. In the dream I was able to give him the address where we could meet so that I could protect him. It had been years since I had seen this man. I felt very altered when I awoke.

The following day I encountered him on the street. This was in 1976, shortly after I returned from Italy. In amazement, I told him of the dream from the previous night, and he told me that in fact he had to report once a week to the police, because he was already being watched. Some two months later, they kidnapped him. So it was not a surprise for me what had happened because of that very strong nightmare I had. And furthermore, I found out immediately about the kidnapping from mutual friends. I found out that he was able to find refuge in the United Nations through mutual friends. This episode that I have just told you about, I am not sure how to describe it. A psychologist friend said it was the pressure of the time.

There are many people who were kidnapped or who had to leave the country. I myself had neither leftist tendencies nor right-wing; yet, like many people, we lived in a state of tension because we knew that for every one person that could be a terrorist, ninety-nine were going to be kidnapped who had nothing to do with it. And I am not alone in saying this now. This was admitted by one of the higher military people in the Supreme Court in 1985. What I wanted to say to you, in any event, is that in many ways, apart from the state terrorism, in no way was I able to agree with the new political economy that they were implementing at this time under the minister Martínez de Hoz.

It was the beginning, the seed, the germ that gave birth to the neo-liberal policy of today's government. This policy ignored the profound and grave problems of Argentina in the economic and social sense ... Argentina in the 1970s had already come to a point of no return; this was my view. But the solution, in my eyes, was not neoliberal economic policy, and in this I was influenced by the French tradition, where a strong state sector cohabits with a private sector that had to open up to external competition. This explains, in part, my rejection of the discourse of the intellectuals from the left and the right, when they proposed either an absolute corporate state or a totally socialist state. I thought they lacked a correct vision of these things. The only thing they did – in my eyes – was to recite the catechism as though it were the little red book of Mao or the Friedman manifesto.

In this way, direct participation was practically impossible in those political movements. It was not because I was a visionary. I understand that nature is dialectic, but of the Hegelian mode. Society evolves with internal contradictions that people discover in one way or another. But it is not the market god that resolves the contradictions, nor is it socialism that is going to resolve them. There is no historical example of a country that has reached a certain level of economic development based simply on the market or simply on socialism.

Once I almost ran into a problem. Some magazines arrived for me from France. When I went to claim a package, I had to spend the entire afternoon with a censor officer who, page by page, analysed the content of the French magazines. They were strongly critical of the military in Latin America. I don't know if he understood, but I am sure he could recognize some French words. I imagine that even today there is an interesting record about me in the Information Services of the SIDE.[2] And there is a paradox here. My father also has a record, from the opposite side.

VOICE: ANATOL HERMÁN

The military was just another government apart from the torture, and there was no resistance here. I didn't see people that frightened. People were comfortable. People were shopping and travelling and everything was fine. In the early 1970s people were happy, too. Public opinion was in favour of the rebels in a romantic, frivolous way. No one took seriously that these people were genuinely violent. To understand Argentine society, you have to realize that there is no law, no sense of right or wrong. People get upset by an extreme problem, but short of that they have no legal system for dealing with everyday problems. People demonstrate against applications of the law.

I was not into democracy then, but I joined some of the rebel groups. When I was at university I tried various ones. I was a Bob Dylan fan. I may be lukewarm on the Catholic Church, but I do care about the poor. I don't like being bossed around. The revolutionaries were violent and authoritarian. They had an inclination toward revolution. They believed that the workers were being fooled by propaganda. They thought that if the propaganda was removed, workers would join the revolution. By 1974 I was out of it. They were crazy ...

The military, however, were always inept. The ERP [the People's Revolutionary Army] had only 2,000 people. The military, provincial police, federal police, gendarmerie, and other police and military groups numbered at least 200,000. They built up the machinery for everything – extortion, all kinds of business. So by 1982 they were inept at everything. At the command level they didn't have the training to combine forces for a real operation. The three forces were totally uncoordinated in the Malvinas[3]. There was no single military command. I think they were crazy. The whole Perón–López Rega[4] period was crazy too. No reality check. Public opinion just swings around throughout the 1960s and the 1970s.

VOICE: ELENA

I was lucky. I moved to Venezuela in 1966, when I was twenty-three. I worked there for eight years, so when all my friends signed up with the guerrillas, I was not caught up with them. When I returned shortly before the coup, I was able to get a good job. Everybody here was frightened. The priests were frightened because some of their brothers had been assassinated, so the church offered no support for people. People were demoralized. The middle class and workers supported the military. People I worked with had to keep a low profile. Actually, I think it was more dangerous to stay here than we realized at the time. There was nothing I could do, just get on with my own life.

VOICE: GUILLERMO

I finished high school in La Plata in 1974. La Plata is the capital of the province of Buenos Aires, with maybe half a million people. It was a traditional middle-class bureaucratic city. It had a prestigious and traditional university, and much of the life of the city was organized around the university. Student life was important. Students came from different parts of Argentina and from other Latin American countries. It was safer, supposedly, smaller than Buenos Aires, the place to send your kids to study. And, of course, for all these reasons it was a highly explosive political environment in the late 1960s and early 1970s. In per capita terms, it was apparently the city with the most *desapareci-dos*. It was one of the cities in which the repression was more, let us say, efficient. The size of the city, the type of life, everybody knew everybody; and the houses were easily accessible for capturing people.

Like most students, I was studying in a national college, a traditional school affiliated with the university,[5] the place where everybody in the middle class wanted to go, and it was highly political. Every political organization in the country had its organization in the school at the time, the right and the left. So I got involved in politics when I was in my fourth year. I joined student organizations, groups for reading and discussing Marx, more oriented towards the left. I never was a Peronist, nor am I now. I was part of a small political party at the end of my second year, a splinter group from the communist party, a group with Maoist inclinations, but I did not stay with it for long.

Then, amazingly, after some very complex orientation and explanation, this communist Maoist party ended up providing support for Isabel Perón. Can you imagine it – a Maoist communist party in Argentina supporting Isabel Perón! It had something to do with nationalism: the explanation was that in the view of that generation, democracy was an American invention and we did not trust America. So why not support this woman? It was part of supporting the national movement of women – well, maybe it was more complex, I'm sure it was, but I can't recall now what it was.

I started university during the Peronist years. I decided not to continue with politics. From the end of my high school to the end of the first two years of university, we had three or four presidents: the last military president of the previous dictatorship, General Alejandro Lanusse, the one who organized the return of Juan Domingo Perón, the short tricky government of Héctor Cámpora, then Perón, then Isabel Perón, and I finished my university with the military in power again. Five presidents altogether. One could imagine what university life had been like in Istanbul during the invasion of the Turks. I finished university surrounded by military forces. Those were difficult years.

My private life was very important in terms of my survival. I concluded that political action was over for me, so no more life on the streets, no more meetings with a couple of friends to discuss literature and politics. Actually, most of my friends in one way or another got into the Peronist organizations, most to the Juventud, the youngest branch of the Montoneros. Maybe I had no interest in violence or – well, maybe this was also important so I will mention it. You see, from my infancy I had lived in working-class neighbourhoods. I was sure that none of the trade unionists that I knew when I was an adolescent would ever back a socialist revolution. Frankly, to me it was a fantasy of the middle-class students that there would be a revolution and that they could use violence as a means of changing society. To me, the Juventud and Montoneros were conservative organizations. And in that particular idea, I have never changed my view.

Some of my friends were murdered. Two members of my high school class were kidnapped. One of them was living with me after escaping from the police. He lost his documentation, which was then an essential part of one's body. We were obsessed with not losing our documentation. We had hours and hours of discussion when I tried to persuade him to quit the Montoneros. He stayed with them and he was murdered. In my view, the Montoneros were a bunch of – well, the idea that Mario Firmenich [Montonero leader] was some kind of socialist was impossible to swallow. I never met him personally, but I learned from ex-members of the Montoneros. It was some kind of fascism for the middle-class young. This was amazing because in those families, in La Plata, Peronism never won an election and the population was anti-Peronist in the 1950s. So the second generation were going against the tradition of their families in a place where family was important. I was not a saint in the eyes of the military, either. I got the impression, particularly in the study of philosophy, that the military regarded it as similar to communism. I was sure they knew all the students very well.

For people of my age, kidnappings by the Montoneros, like the kidnapping and murder of the director of the major newspaper,[6] had no impact. They were concerned with the social structure. For people who were eighteen to about twenty-three years old coming from middle-class professional families, clearly the majority were in favour of the Montoneros. And you can find in the list of the *desaparecidos* most of these kids who got into the Peronist organizations. For that generation and the previous one, there was not a single liberal value in terms of politics; it was a matter of revolution, of national values, so it was expediency that counted. There were infinite ways to explain the use of violence. Violence is capitalism; violence is inequality, poverty. So making a decision to use violence against any particular person was acceptable.

In the time I was growing up, it was so different from how it is today. Even rock and roll – sure, I was interested in politics, but I liked rock and roll – yet it was not easy to talk about such things as rock and roll if you were in a group that was seriously interested in politics. It was a kind of deviation. Revolution was the topic. It was to be conducted by the working class. Music – well, we never went to a dance or a disco – it was a petty-bourgeois deviation. It was not allowed. We had serious relations with the world, it was a commitment. Many of us married before we were twenty years old; we considered it a commitment, part of the project, the historical mission. Politics then swallowed up almost everything. It was difficult not to be part. I went to a reunion with my fellows at the high school last year. I met one after twenty-something years. He had not been part of any of these developments, and he told me that he hadn't understood most of what was happening. He felt detached from all the groups. He said that in those years he had had a terrible life, being mistreated by the majority because he was interested in dancing and had a "soft" approach to life, which today is what most young people enjoy ...

The brutality organized by the military was made in Argentina. I don't believe in this theory of international involvement. Any theory of outside involvement has to deal with this: our society created that government, and to me it is very important to make this clear, particularly for my fellow Argentines.

VOICE: JOSÉ LUIS FASCE

I was already forty years old and practising law in Mar del Plata[7] in 1970. There was a struggle between the military government and guerrillas, who were animated by external forces, especially by Perón. The revolutionaries killed General Aramburu, an important man in Argentine history. The Montonero movement was initiated by brilliant students from select schools in Buenos Aires, and they had the protection and support of the third world priests. Simultaneously, there began to appear subversive and guerrilla movements with a clearly leftist tendency, more left than the Montoneros at the beginning. The ERP [People's Revolutionary Army] was influenced from Cuba, and its leaders were trained there in guerrilla tactics.

I remember that in our town at that time there was a young member of the ERP who was trying to leave the organization. In a bar he explained to me how he had gone to Cuba, without leaving any trace, without being identified by the Argentine government. There he had been trained in military action. He wanted to leave the organization, but when he tried to get out he disappeared, because the subversive organizations did not let people leave.

In Mar del Plata, there were also people who belonged to revolutionary groups but who had a normal life. They were on reserve for the fight in specific moments. This was public and notorious knowledge; we knew of the existence of these groups, already formed or in formation. We could not identify specific individuals. Many of them were not identified. There were groups on the left and on the right. The groups on the right were supported by the military. On one occasion, a student was killed in a leftist students' meeting when a group of about ten right-wingers entered and started shooting. These right-wing groups in Buenos Aires were called the Triple A, and they were supported by the government. Anyway, as a response, a leader of the right-wingers, a young lawyer, was having coffee in a bar next to the courts, and the people of the left arrived suddenly and killed him. That night approximately six were killed. This was before the coup. The killers were on the left; young students, armed.

I was outside all of this, outside the left and the right. So all the time I was looking from outside. But all of this gives you an idea of the uncertainty and anguish of the people. Everybody was waiting for the misgovernment of Isabel to end. And I am going to give you an example. The union leaders at that time had so much influence in the government, 1975, that they got labour laws which are still in place today and which the unions consider so favourable for them that all they now want is simply to keep them.

At that time, did you think that the guerrilla movements were allied with the unions?

No. And I am going to tell you why. The unions were embedded in the government in such a way that they provided 33 per cent of the candidates for the legislature. The CGT [General Confederation of Labour] was still Peronist. I want to point out that in these subversive organizations, some of the members were working totally within the organization, clandestinely, and fighting. The majority, however, were living apparently normal lives. They were doctors, lawyers, veterinarians, and common people. And they were at the service of the organization when it required them.

I have read a lot about Cuba recently, and I have visited there several times since 1990. I know that the Cuban government was selling arms to the guerrilla movements. Even in the 1970s I believed that the Argentine movements received instruction or arms from Cuba. The Guevarist theory of focus was incorrect in the Cuban case because, actually, Sierra Maestra[8] received support from sympathizers outside, especially from North America, which sent money and arms.

Let's go back to the military coup in Argentina. Were you glad when it occurred?

Yes. I was happy because finally an epoch of misgovernment had ended. I expected inflation to stop, and I hoped there would be a balanced government in which the unions would have an important part but would not have control over the country. And finally I expected what is happening right now, that Argentina's economy would grow. Also, it was necessary for the government to combat the guerrillas. Back in 1970, the military created a special tribunal to consider subversive crimes. The subversives were defended by lawyers with many guarantees. The first thing done by Cámpora's government in 1973, when he took power, was to set them free. Those subversives said that they were only opposed to the military and that they wanted a democratic government. One of the members of the tribunal was murdered in the street. At least Isabel ordered the annihilation of the subversives.

To understand what happened, you have to recognize that this was a genuine war, dirty, but still a war. There was a subversive group with its military code, with its clandestine hospitals, with its clandestine secret services, with its clandestine espionage, even with its public relations. We need to differentiate between those who were really armed fighters and those who were sympathizers and collaborators. For each combatant there was a wide logistic support of money, medicine, propaganda, etcetera. I calculate that there were 10,000 actual combatants. That's what I thought then, and I still think so.

There were places in Argentina that were considered liberated subversive zones. In the north, in the province of Tucumán, one had to pay a revolutionary toll. The subversive movement occupied towns and openly attacked legal regiments ... In this attack I calculate there were about five hundred subversives. The combatants, following the focus theory of Guevara, had carefully chosen a place in the jungle – rugged, with mountains. But there were also many other combatants who were urban guerrillas. They robbed banks, they kidnapped people, and killed people who did not support them. And they killed union leaders, such as José Rucci and Augusto Vandor.

It is very difficult to say whether the military government could have used any other means than the ones it did use. This was a war, dirty as all wars are, in which the parties had to adopt similar methods to achieve success. It was the same thing the subversives were doing, torturing, murdering. I believe there were not as many people who were disappeared and tortured as the subversives say. I believe there were far fewer than 10,000 persons. There were persons who wanted to work, to study, to raise their children. Out of 30 million people, 10,000 persons is less than the 0.03 per cent. In that number, 10,000 persons, I am including those who died and those who were tortured but not killed. Many of them collaborated with the repressers, denouncing their companions. And now they even appear as heroes.

Did you think at that time that it was necessary to kill so many people?

I repeat that the 10,000 persons included both the dead and the tortured. I believe the dead could have numbered about 3,000, of which more than half died in open combat with the legal forces, police forces and gendarmeries.

After the military period, the CONADEP *commission was set up to study* el Proceso. *Do you accept its findings?*

Yes, I think so. But simultaneously with the CONADEP, the minister of interior under President Alfonsín formally promised to establish a national commission to identify and investigate the disappearances, tortures, and deaths which had been committed by the subversives. This was formally promised by the Ministry of Interior, but it was never carried out.

I am not clear about your answer. You said you accepted the evidence in CONADEP, *as reported in its publication,* Nunca Más?

Yes.

But that documents nearly 9,000 people who disappeared, were tortured, and were killed. And many of the cases that are reported there are of people who were not subversives.

We need to get back to what I indicated earlier, that there were many subversives who continued their normal life and were the logistical support of the combatants ...

What about the children?

Yes. We need to refer to the ideas of the subversives. Mario Firmenich, the highest chief of the Montoneros, stated that when one went into clandestine life, the whole family went into clandestinity so that the children would grow up in a completely revolutionary environment. There is precise documentation of Firmenich stating this.

Actually, I meant the babies who were born in prison. The ones who were taken from their mothers by the military or others.

I must repeat for you so that I am totally clear, this was a war, a big war. Children brought up by strangers occur in any war. Some of the children of the subversives are now grown up and have received education, food, and, above all, love from the people who had them in their charge. In some cases it has been proved that they do not want to go back to their real family, even when they know that they are adopted. I understand the pain of the grandparents who do not have their children with them, but it is also true that life continues, sometimes despite us.

Let me change topics. In a number of universities and public libraries, there were many books burned because the books were regarded as subversive by the military. Do you think that was necessary?

I do not have any proof of that. Furthermore, I know that the military governments had commercial relations with the Soviet Union, and here in Argentina the relations with the Soviet Union were never broken. I personally have, and had at that time, books – and I read them – that were on the left or on the right, and I never was bothered.

Now, we have actually talked with people who burned books and who watched books being burned, and the books were not about Marxism; they were books that are usually found in university libraries in Humanities. For example, Sigmund Freud or Jean Piaget or mathematical set theory. Do you believe that?

I do not think that happened. I have a friend who is a psychiatrist whom we can ask. I do not have any problem in contacting him, but this is the first I have heard about that happening with Freud, Piaget, or advanced mathematics.

I have one more question about the military period. Again, according to Nunca Más *and other historical accounts of the period, the military and police engaged in robberies. Do you think that occurred?*

That is possible. I admit that. I think it was true. I think it happened. At that time, on both sides there were circumstances where human beings were both at their most beautiful and most vile. The heroism – sometimes giving one's own life. And the vile – the human miseries like violations and robbery, as happens in any war.

Back to something you mentioned earlier: you estimated that there were 10,000 guerrillas who were armed, and you estimated that 10,000 were killed or tortured. With respect to those who were killed or tortured, you pointed out that they were less 0.03 per cent of the population. But then the question arises, if the subversives were also merely 0.03 per cent of the population, why was it necessary to bring so much force to destroy them?

It is very simple. Part of the guerrilla forces were known, part hidden. For example, Firmenich established that when they undertook military action, they had to use the uniform with symbols of their rank. This was when the operation was open. In other cases, when the operation was clandestine, they did not use uniforms or ranks. Sometimes, according to the instructions from Cuba, they used the uniforms of the legal forces, purposely to take advantage of the confusion which they provoked in the armed forces.

This strategy continued to be used, even in the attack on La Tablada in 1989, during the government of President Alfonsín, in which the remainder of the ERP was involved.[9] The ERP chief, Gorriarán Merlo, attacked La Tablada wearing a military uniform.[10] He escaped to Mexico after the attack. Then he gave an interview to two journalists, and the videotape was openly transmitted on Argentine television. In that video, Gorriarán described how the operation had been conducted. After that, the Argentine judicial authority contacted Interpol to find him and his wife, who had also been involved in the La Tablada attack. Mexico extradited him and he was tried in Argentina, with all the legal guarantees.

Your question was why was it necessary for such a powerful army to fight against such a small guerrilla force. It was because guerrilla war is different from the type of war for which the army is usually trained. Normally, army men wear their uniforms. But in this kind of warfare, they did not wear uniform because they had to avoid being recognized. Keep in mind that many of the military were not combatants against the guerrillas. Many continued with their normal jobs. I think that only between 10 and 20 per cent of the army were engaged in the actual battle against the guerrillas. Some army men were mentally and physically trained for a very different war, very dirty and not clear. Many of the officers received special instruction in other countries. I think it was provided by the United States in Panama, and many Latin American officers were trained there.

I personally did not have any contact with or any benefit from the military; or public jobs, profits ... nothing. In 1976 the military government of the province offered me a position as a judge. But I declined because I prefer to be a lawyer. I never had relations with the military or any benefits from them. But I believe that there was a cultural and economic revolution occurring here. What happened during the 1960s and the 1970s was a war in which the winners have been put in the seat of the accused. It is the first time that an upside-down Nuremberg has occurred.

Were laws abrogated during el Proceso?

No. Some laws were suspended. Publication of subversive propaganda was forbidden. But all the people worked, played, without problems. In other countries, people thought that in Argentina we had trenches, that there were people fighting in the street. It was not true.

Some people have said they were unable to get the habeas corpus process attended to, that many judges refused to touch it. Is that true?

That is true.

So was that a legal right which was not available for many people? How did you as a lawyer feel about it?

Many lawyers have problems with habeas corpus. But in my line of work, I did not have to deal with it.

PART TWO

Historical Origins

CHAPTER 3

A Violent History

Violence in the name of imposing order in Argentina had been a long-standing policy of governments. Elites of the country had often initiated – or had readity accepted – repressive forms of social control over workers and dissidents. The church hierarchy likewise could be expected to consent to, if not actively collaborate in, the suppression of dissidents. Argentina had become, over its history, an undemocratic, intolerant, rigidly polarized society. One might have predicted that it was on a collision course. Yet there were many surprises in the way the case unfolded.

There are two distinct periods of the history before the 1970s. The first is a colonial and immediate postcolonial history, which is of continuing interest because it established the original institutions and culture of the country. The second begins about 1930 when the military forces first took over the reins of government. In this chapter, we will very briefly consider the outstanding events, economic development, and immigration patterns of the early period. Then we will examine the military period before Juan Perón's mid-century governments.

COLONIAL HISTORY
AND THE OLIGARCHY

The Spanish conquest of Latin America left a legacy in Argentina as elsewhere. Genocide against native people was brutal and widespread, and much of the country in its first couple of centuries consisted of strongmen (*caudillos*), who controlled territories or vital ports, and the poor who were obliged to live under their control.

However, the country's economic and social development from about the 1850s to the 1920s is actually not very different from the process in other European settler colonies, such as Australia and Canada, with the important exception of the landholding pattern. Canada, the United States, and Australia all made room for numerous family farms so that there were many small property holders and small commodity producers in the total population. The oligarchy in Argentina, by contrast, monopolized the land. A few powerful families occupied huge estates in the exceptionally fertile lands (*pampas*) that spread in a large semicircle inland from Buenos Aires and in the sugar-growing and other plantation-crop areas to the north.

On the sugar-cane estates in the province of Tucumán, the oligarchy created labour conditions that were pre-capitalist in nature – serfdom would not be too strong a term – and the condition persisted into the twentieth century. However, across the fertile agricultural lands of the south, the crops were cereals, sheep for the wool trade, and beef cattle, and these did not require large pools of repressed labour. Thus, for much of the rich rural area there was a strong oligarchy on huge estates (*estancias*) but very few peasant farmers (*campasinos*). The kind of labour used on the sugar plantations was unnecessary here. The labour force that was retained on these estates consisted of cowboys (*gauchos*), and while they may have had a servile beginning, they fairly soon became a rural proletariat earning wages. In most (but not all) of the country, they were capable of moving on to the cities, where they obtained wage work. Unions were being formed in the cities by the 1850s, and were well organized before the turn of the century. Labour conditions were often cruel, always unpleasant, but in this respect Argentina was similar to many other countries in the late nineteenth century.

The oligarchy split into two groups fairly early in Argentine settler history. One group remained locked in traditional landowning patterns in the mode of a rural aristocracy whose wealth derived from the produce of the land. A larger group, became engaged in mercantile business, finance, and eventually in secondary industry, in the same way as those with land and capital in other settler colonies. The sheep, wheat, and cattle businesses required an infrastructure of roads, railways, ports, banks, and backward linkages in manufacturing. Although British capital quickly became dominant in the railways and banks (just as it did in Canada), established Argentine landowners participated fully in the development of industries in Buenos Aires and other coastal cities. The commodity export trade, primarily with Britain, was the major source of income; but secondary industries, especially those linked to the export trade, grew at rates similar to or better than those of other former colonies.

ECONOMIC GROWTH
TO THE 1930S

Before the turn of the century, the Argentine per capita income was equal to that of Germany and higher than that of most other western and northern European countries.[1] Argentina had one of the fastest-growing economies in the world between 1800 and 1913.[2] Between 1900 and 1914, the gross domestic product (GDP) grew by 6.3 per cent per annum; and in 1914 Argentina's per capita GDP was almost equal to that of Switzerland, higher than that of Sweden and France, twice that of Italy, and five times that of Japan.[3] It was in the same league as Canada, with a slightly lower per capita income but with very similar natural resources, combined with a low population density.[4]

Foreign direct investment by Britain, and to a lesser extent by other European countries, was greatest in railways, utilities, transit services, telephone, telegraph, shipping, and packinghouses throughout the early development and right up to the onset of the First World War. This investment was essential for building the infrastructure that allowed Argentine capitalists to sell their agricultural products on world markets. European investment declined after the war, but direct private investment by United States companies gradually increased.[5]

Economic growth slowed after 1914, as it did elsewhere, but it was still at a high level in the postwar years. In 1929 Argentina was ranked eighteenth of the world's nations in per capita product, and even during the Depression and the Second World War it sustained considerable, if less spectacular, growth rates.[6] Its economic decline began later, toward the end of the 1940s. During the early period and until the early 1930s, then, Argentina was unlike other nations of Latin America. Although the terms of trade with Britain were in British interests and continued so with the 1933 Roca-Runciman Treaty, it would be inappropriate to apply to Argentina, during these formative years, a theory of underdevelopment which might be suitable for other South American countries. Certainly, the terms of trade were uneven, but progressive underdevelopment was not the outcome in Argentina in the pre-1930 period. Consequently a theory of underdevelopment by way of explaining state terrorism would dissolve fairly quickly.

IMMIGRATION

There are some writers who suggest that the difference between Argentina and other European settler colonies lies primarily in the source of immigrants. There are two arguments: one, that the settlers were not literate and were unskilled for industry; the other, that they possessed a "Latin temperament" that was not conducive to the development of democratic institutions.

It is factually correct that the largest group of immigrants during the nineteenth century came from Italy, and the next largest from Spain, and that the majority were impoverished peasants. In the 1890s some 86 per cent came from the poorest regions of southern and central Europe, though there were also skilled workers from northern Europe who provided the initial population of tradespeople. By the last decade of the nineteenth century, there were about four million settlers in Argentina. But it is questionable whether the above facts lead to a conclusion that these immigrants were unsuitable for development of either industry or democracy. Industry did develop, and it developed at a pace just as rapid as in Canada and Australia, where the immigrants were primarily northern and western Europeans with higher literacy levels and more industrial skills.

Furthermore, constitutional government prevailed in the country for nearly seventy years prior to 1930, Latin temperament notwithstanding. Uruguay and Chile, both with Latin immigrant populations, sustained democracies for most of the century preceding the breakdown of the 1970s. Thus, while the landholding and immigration patterns of the nineteenth century are components of Argentine history that should be recognized, there is no compelling evidence that they alone or even in combination with other conditions were major influences on the events of the 1970s.

On the other hand, the flood of new immigrants – the sheer number of them – in the early years of the twentieth century and after the First World War, combined with very rapid modernization of industry, created social and economic problems that were not susceptible to immediate solutions. In the short period from 1900 to 1914, some 3.5 million people immigrated, half of whom became permanent citizens.[7] (The other half were seasonal workers who returned to southern Europe after the harvesting season.) Immigrants were frequently blamed for tensions that were rooted simply in the inability of society to absorb them at the rate of induction.

Electoral reforms in 1912 introduced the secret ballot, universal male suffrage, and a few other essential ingredients of a more mature democracy, but at least one-third of the population was not naturalized and could not vote. More than two-thirds of urban entrepreneurs and businesspeople retained their original citizenship and did not participate in Argentine political life in the first decades of the new century.[8] This lack of participation in political life may have been a more significant problem for the society than the source or nature of the immigrants.

CLASS DIVISIONS:
EARLY TWENTIETH CENTURY

The divergence of Argentina from the pattern found in Canada and Australia became evident in 1919 and 1921–22. Until then, trade union evolution, the emergence of socialist and anarchist movements, the growth of Buenos Aires as the major port city, and other developments in the late nineteenth and early twentieth centuries had been similar to those elsewhere.[9] But now a couple of bloody mass murders of workers signalled a difference in the way economic elites and governments dealt with dissidence and rebellion. These other societies to which we are comparing Argentina because of the general similarities in resources, settlement, and early development have certainly also had some bloody class conflicts in their history, but these two events in Argentina are on a larger scale than occurred elsewhere.

The first took place in the second week of January 1919, known as the "tragic week" (semana trágica). A mass uprising in Buenos Aires was met by the army and during the affray and its aftermath more than a hundred workers were killed and many more wounded by the army and by right-wing death squads hired by employers. (The young lieutenant in charge of the troops who machine-gunned the workers was Juan Domingo Perón.)[10]

In the Patagonian Rebellion of 1921–22, soldiers killed 1,500 workers who had rebelled against British and Argentine sheep ranchers, bringing to a halt most economic activity in the province of Santa Cruz. Miserable living and working conditions, combined with lack of alternatives when there were massive layoffs, had sparked the unrest. The workers had already surrendered, after being promised amnesty, when they were massacred. Their bodies were interred in mass graves.[11] On this occasion, the commanding officer, Colonel Héctor B. Varela, was assassinated in revenge. This act of revenge was costly. The armed forces have referred to it ever since as proof of the need to quell subversion. The uprising itself was important in persuading the propertied classes and employers that the working class could no longer be controlled in traditional ways. As a result, increasingly repressive action was taken against workers. These measures were accompanied by ideological justifications that continued into the period under examination in this study.

DEMOCRACY:
EARLY TWENTIETH CENTURY

Throughout the long period of oligarchic rule, the ruling groups supported immigration, public education, separation of church and state, and free markets. Until 1912, when electoral reforms introduced the secret ballot and universal male suffrage, democracy offered no challenge to the elite's continued control, and, without challenge, they maintained a fairly liberal state in a restricted democracy.

There is surely some irony in this, because these reforms, accepted as a means of containing growing labour unrest, led to a political situation which the oligarchy was unwilling to accept, even though the reforms were consistent with changes occurring in industrial societies elsewhere. The changes allowed for the growth of alternative political parties and for their electoral success. Thus was formed the Radical Party, or UCR (Unión Cívica Radical), which won the election of 1916. Under Hipólito Yrigoyen the Radicals were moderates, inclined toward more liberal policies than previous governments. Conservatives viewed them as more left-wing than they were. In the "tragic week," the failure of the government to quell the strikers was immediately interpreted as evidence of its weakness, at best, and possibly of its connivance.

Events external to Argentina also influenced the upper-class interpretation of the Buenos Aires uprising. The Russian Revolution, the Spartacist threat in Germany, and militant strikes in Chile fuelled fears of even greater violence and loss of life or property. Members of the upper class blamed the local rebellion on the Soviet Union and targeted Jewish immigrants from Russia and eastern Europe as subversive elements. Jewish neighbourhoods were invaded by armed civilians and police, Jewish property was vandalized, and individuals were imprisoned simply because they had immigrated from Russia.

Emergence of Right-Wing Movements

Following the democratic reforms and the electoral success of non-oligarchic parties, Argentina began to spawn some extremely right-wing, nationalist, and fundamentalist Catholic movements. In 1919 an ultra-rightist nationalist movement was formed, the Argentine Patriotic League (Liga Patriótica Argentina). This group advocated stricter control of schoolteachers, more teaching of Argentine history, defence against immigrants with "alien" ideas, and protection of the society in an unchanging form. It attracted support from some parts of the military and also both from the elite and from unaffiliated urban workers as it became ever more militantly opposed to unions. The Liga organized itself through neighbourhood brigades and by November 1919 claimed it had 833 brigades throughout Argentina with about 20,000 activists.[12] It represented a threat to Yrigoyen's government, the more so since its members included Radicals, and it had the

Table 1
Elected Governments, 1910–1930

Date	How Power Obtained	President
1910–14	Election	Roque Sáenz Peña
1915–16	Election	Victorino de la Plaza
1916–22	Election	Hipólito Yrigoyen
1922–28	Election	Marcelo T. de Alvear
1928–30	Election	Hipólito Yrigoyen

effect of developing a more anti-union stance within the government party. In the early 1920s, members of the Liga actively engaged in anti-union activities, broke strikes, and recruited mercenaries and criminals to provoke bloody confrontations.

In the period between 1920 and 1928, 69 per cent of the Liga's executive groups were of upper-class origin; about half of the male leaders owned land or were members of landowning families; 31 per cent had been elected or appointed to office before 1916; and 19 per cent of the central authorities for whom occupational information was available were military officers. At the same time, members of the neighbourhood (or otherwise organized) brigades included more non-unionized workers, professionals, business owners, and business or government employees. The Liga included a number of upper-class young people at the universities, who formed groups within the Catholic Church and became known as the Social Catholic Movement. Opposed to unions, the Social Catholics collected money to alleviate working-class problems and thus, so the theory went, to create social peace. These students provided funding in the 1920s for a study group with values of the Catholic Middle Ages. They and other intellectuals became enamoured of the counterrevolutionary thought of the French writer Charles Maurras.[13]

Another ultra-right group, the Nationalists (Nacionalistas), formed in 1920, were likewise enamoured of Maurras and other antiliberal, antidemocratic, antisecular European writers. Added to these was Leopoldo Lugones, an Argentine poet, whose eloquent defence of authoritarianism had already become popular with Liga members. On average, the Nationalists were younger than Liga members, and fewer were in the military. Sandra McGee Deutsch, in her detailed study of the pre-1930 organizations, found the Nationalists to be much more radical in their opposition to unions. They desired a Mussolini-style corporatist system, they opposed "foreigners," especially Jews, and supported armed force in defence of their ideology.[14]

Table 2
Dictatorships and Governments, 1930–1946

Date	How Power Obtained	President
1930–32	Military coup	General José F. Uriburu
1932–38	Restricted elections	General Agustín P. Justo
1938–42	Rigged elections	Roberto M. Ortiz
1942–43	Ortiz resigned	Ramón S. Castillo
1943	Military coup	Arturo Rawson
1943–44	Military coup	General Pedro Ramírez
1944–46	Military designation	General Edelmiro Farrell

The right-wing groups opposed President Yrigoyen, his successor Marcelo T. de Alvear, and, following de Alvear's term, Yrigoyen yet again. By 1928, the opposition was focusing on democracy itself. In expressions that sound remarkably familiar to the ear of a North American in the late 1990s, they complained that democracy was an unworkable system of government, that the poor were harmed by unions and should have the right to remain free of them, and that Yrigoyen's continued power constituted the "dictatorship of the masses" or "oppression by the majority." Among Yrigoyen's sins were his opening of university faculties to greater middle-class participation and broadening the range of liberal professions represented in the curriculum. But Yrigoyen was elderly, and he was faced with a hostile Senate by the time the Great Depression hit Argentina. Congress was unable to solve the political or economic crisis, and the Liga gained wide support in its efforts to oust the government with the help of the military. Thus, in September 1930, Yrigoyen was overthrown in a military coup.

MILITARY GOVERNMENTS: 1930–45

The military forces of the country had undergone a process of professionalization over several decades, and by 1930 had become large and powerful organizations, the most powerful being the army. However, the forces were continually fractured by differing political commitments. Like the society in general, they were divided into moderate liberals and Catholic nationalists when it came to concocting remedies for the country's ills. Neither of these factions was enthusiastic about democracy, though the liberals at this stage were content with a restricted form of it. Catholic nationals wanted a more authoritarian approach. (Their respective positions changed after the Peronist years.)

Until 1943, these two major factions continued to compete with one another for political power.

In 1930 the Supreme Court ruled that the armed forces could legally oust an elected government. The rationale was that they alone would be in a position to protect life, liberty, and property if the established order broke down. To obtain legitimation for coups already performed, all the military had to do was provide the courts with reasons for its intervention, an outline of its intentions, and a promise to obey the constitution and uphold existing legislation.

That year, following the military coup, a Catholic nationalist, General José F. Uriburu, legally installed a fascist-type corporatist regime modelled on Mussolini's Italy. His government imposed a state of siege, dissolved trade unions, deported unnaturalized union leaders, arrested other leaders suspected of being anarchists and communists, also arrested members of the legal Socialist Party and the Radical Party, and fired or exiled many other politicians. Argentina was by now in the grips of the Great Depression, though the effects were not as staggering as in North America. Political instability was joined to the economic problems, and the blame for the economic problems was attached to Argentina's dependence on external markets for its raw materials. Uriburu's objectives included a reorganization of the state along corporatist lines. But he was not supported by the head of the army, and the state of siege was lifted in 1931. Shortly afterward, a palace coup brought about Uriburu's resignation, and elections were scheduled. The two governments that followed – under Augustín P. Justo and Roberto M. Ortiz – came into being through fraudulent elections. Although the economy improved under authoritarian rule, especially that of Ortiz and his successor, Ramón S. Castillo (who were installed as president in 1938 and 1942, respectively), these governments had very little credibility with the population

O'Donnell's Theory of Modernization

These military bureaucracies attempted to impose economic policies that substituted import-related industry in place of export orientation. This policy direction has been identified by Guillermo O'Donnell as typical of the modernizing process in the developing countries of Latin America.[15] O'Donnell argued that modernization involved a reduced reliance on commodities exports, attempts to create import-substitution industries, growth in domestic consumption, and eventually the exhaustion of "the easy" horizontal phase of import substitution. During the initial, generally successful period, a major consequence of the policies was the expansion of the state itself. O'Donnell suggested that the tensions created by rapid economic change in these countries led to increased repression by the government bureaucracy – which was often a military bureaucracy – rather than to development of political democracy.

O'Donnell contended that this process occurred in the Latin American societies that modernized most rapidly and extensively. These societies were Argentina and Brazil, because they had a fair level of affluence, a middle class, an organized working class, and a large domestic market. Consequently, the possibility of developing horizontal industrial growth through import substitution was greater than in smaller and less affluent regions. His view of the subsequent stages, after the "easy" range of import-substitution industries had been established, is less sanguine. We will encounter it in the next chapter when we discuss how the economy began its decline in the latter years of Juan Perón's second government.

Uneven Development

The economic strategy adopted by the military improved the manufacturing sector and gradually displaced the agrarian hold on the economy. But although the economy improved during the 1930s, the real wages of workers declined. Over the course of that decade, their number, but not their fortunes, increased. By 1940 there were nearly one million people in the labour force, and in manufacturing there were twice as many in 1944 as there had been in 1930. Women had gradually become one-third of the labour force (though they did not gain the vote until it was granted under the first Peronist government). Labour unrest increased and strikes became more frequent, even though at this stage only 20 per cent of industrial workers were unionized. The unionized sector managed, despite internal political divisions, to create a central organization, the General Confederation of Labour, or CGT (Confederación General del Trabajo) in 1930.

Then, in 1941–42, a popular front of radicals, socialists, and communists was formed to contest the power held by the united front of conservatives and the military. Although far from coherent as a movement, the left was beginning to take shape as a political entity in an industrial country. Meanwhile, in the external theatre, the Spanish Civil War had followed the electoral success of the Popular Front in the Spanish elections of 1936. This development, combined with the threat of working-class uprisings and political change, had created unrest in Argentina's military circles. Furthermore, by 1942 it was beginning to appear that the Allied powers might win the Second World War – a cause of consternation in the armed forces, where many members supported the Axis powers.

Putting all these developments together, the armed forces concluded that unless they took pre-emptive action, communists and socialists – whom they regarded as subversives – would gain power in Argentina. An army lodge known as the Working Group for Unification, or GOU (Grupo Obra de Unificación) had become a major anticommunist organization. Dominated by Colonel Juan Domingo Perón, its objective was to prepare Argentine officers to combat communists, and in its written articles of foundation it anticipated the "menace of a communist revolution of a Popular Front type."

Coups within Coups: Early 1940s

In 1943 there were two coups, the first on 4 June against President Castillo, led by General Arturo Rawson (a liberal), and the second, two days later, by a group of Catholic nationalist military personnel, who installed a relatively moderate Catholic nationalist general, Pedro Ramírez, as president. Historian Donald Hodges says of this coup within a coup: "The GOU became the vehicle by which a small group of middle-ranking officers wormed their way into key government positions and took over the reins of the army through their control of the decisive Ministry of War. It was a conspiratorial organization dominated by Catholic nationalists."[16] He also argues that this was a turning point when the informal alliance between the armed forces and the agro-export oligarchy was severed. It was certainly a turning point for Juan Perón, who was a leader of the GOU and made full use of his opportunity to gain access to key government positions.

The government under Ramírez engaged in a general crackdown on labour and anyone it defined as subversive. The editor of the communist newspaper *La Hora* was executed by firing squad. Leaders of the meat workers' union were arrested and their local closed. José Peter, general secretary of the meat workers' union, was imprisoned without trial for almost one and a half years. A labour federation that involved political activists in the socialist and communist parties was forcibly dissolved. Congress was dissolved as well, and all elected provincial authorities were removed from office. Political parties were banned, and freedom of the press was suspended.

In his position as secretary of labour and welfare, and later also as minister of war, Perón was very much involved in these decisions. However, he was also instrumental in persuading his government colleagues and the military to change their tactics – to engage less in direct repression and more in concessions to the working class. He was able to see that the growing number of urban workers in Argentina's industrializing cities would have political clout if they became more organized. By assiduously forging linkages with them and speaking on their behalf, he created a personal support base with the CGT as the central unit. His policies were successful in keeping the military in power, even though it lost the support of the oligarchy as labour gained ascendancy.

State-led Industrialization under the Military

By the mid-1940s, the Argentine army was emerging as an independent force with its own interests. It had created its own aircraft industry in 1927 and had since established industries for the production of munitions, chemicals, electrical equipment, and pig iron. In 1943 these industries were put under the management of a company called the General Agency for Military Industry. Thus was the army developing independent economic momentum.

As well, the army was showing an independence of spirit vis-à-vis the oligarchy. A national plan was created by which the state would determine all prices, wages, credit, and allocations of raw materials. Then the landowners were ordered to reduce and freeze rents, and the government nationalized all private grain elevators, which effectively ended the grain merchants' oligopoly. There were takeovers of private national and international businesses in 1943 and 1944, and in order to manage all these state-owned properties the government's employment rose from just under 200,000 to over 312,000 between 1940 and 1945. The military's portion of the total government budget rose from 27.8 per cent to 50.7 per cent between 1942 and 1946. All this created a growing deficit, which was financed by borrowing abroad and by increasing the money supply.[17]

In the beginning, sectors of the business community that could produce goods for the domestic market were pleased with the policies that stimulated private consumption and encouraged import-substitution industrialization. Between 1939 and 1945, local manufacturers dramatically increased their share of the domestic market. Small entrepreneurs prospered under military rule, and both the expanding middle class and the working class were, on balance, beneficiaries of the import-substitution policies.[18]

However, the industrial and financial elite, the former oligarchy, was less agreeable. While the military was developing its independent momentum, the oligarchy itself was changing. No longer was it a landed aristocracy, even if its members typically owned estates or had been born into landowning families. The agro-export industries had led to linkages with foreign capital, and the dominant class that emerged in this changing economy was a financial elite linked to foreign monopolies.(During this same period, the Canadian financial elite moved in the same direction. In both cases, the linkages were increasingly with U.S.–based monopolies, though British and European companies also participated.)

The military, and subsequently the Perón government, were thus moving in an opposite direction from the elite. The elite's interests lay in a more open economy, while the military favoured an increasingly closed one, with high levels of state control (though it should be noted that some members of the Argentine elite also favored import-substitution policies at that time).[19] Donald Hodges, considering the growing economic and political independence of the army, commented: "The army constituted a rival oligarchy based on selection and merit rather than inherited wealth, which also set them apart. It was the traditional defender of Argentine independence, which sooner or later brought it into collision with the oligarchy's dependence on foreign capital. Thus their coincidence of interests on political issues testified at best to a common front against the two mass-based civilian parties."[20]

Pressure from the United States

Under pressure from the United States, the Argentine government was obliged to break diplomatic ties with the Axis powers. The armed forces expressed indignation, and on this note Perón and others forced the resignation of Ramírez in February 1944. Perón became the new minister of war and vice-president. The United States regarded the changes as hostile to its interests and put pressure on the Argentine government to declare war on the Axis and to repress Nazi fascists. Although the government complied, the United States, represented in Argentina by its new ambassador, Spruille Braden, became a subversive agent against the military government and in favour of democratic reforms. It gave tacit support to the demonstrations of university students and socialists against the military regime. The regime responded to the unrest by reimposing the state of seige that had been established in December 1941 but had been lifted in May 1944. A liberal faction within the army then staged a coup, arrested Perón, and forced his resignation in October 1945. But their success was short-lived.

Workers in the CGT called a general strike for 18 October 1945, and the evening before, thousands of them converged on the Plaza de Mayo demanding Perón's release. The leaders of the coup were forced to abdicate under pressure not only from workers but also from Catholic nationalists and reformers in the army. The most the coup leaders could do was insist that elections be called in 1946.

Although most of the army were not enthusiastic about Perón, they preferred him to a popular front of socialists and communists, even when these groups were allied with conservatives and radicals in the Unión Democrática (UD). They realized that the military could continue to have influence by supporting Perón, even though this meant giving concessions to labour. Perón thus became the armed forces' candidate.

CHAPTER 4

Peronism and Militarism

Perón became president in 1946 with a comfortable 52.4 per cent of the vote. Peronist candidates won landslide victories in both houses of Congress and in provincial legislatures and governorships. Throughout his period as president, Perón maintained the strong support of organized labour, but he never had absolute support in the military or the church, and when he introduced new initiatives for labour in his second term, the military, backed by the church, led the revolt.

PERONIST POLICIES

In his first term as president, Perón created a centralized government, and in economic policy he concentrated on redistribution of income.[1] He staffed public bureaucracies with loyal followers and ostracized others. He soon had a secret service numbering 30,000. They wore brown suits and gabardine raincoats, following the Gestapo model, and they silenced opposition. A thousand-strong storm-trooper military force, the National Liberating Alliance, also was created. Perón nationalized the railroads, and he took over foreign-owned companies in many sectors, including ports and telephones. Although these purchases – plus their expanded employment costs – were expensive, nationalization was popular.

Dismantling of the Judicial System

Of crucial importance for our study is the fact that Perón dismantled the judicial system and severely reduced the capacity of opposition politicians to function independently of his government. Within weeks of his inauguration, Peronists initiated impeachment proceedings against four of the five Supreme Court justices, along with similar proceedings against provincial courts. By the end of 1949 more than seventy federal judges had been replaced with Peronist appointees. The civil service also was purged. A contempt law increased the penalties for anyone who defamed the authorities, and it denied the right of the defence to present evidence. This law was applied, in particular, to members of non-Peronist groups in Congress, who could be deprived of their seats for speaking disrespectfully of Peronists. Members of Congress were expelled and even imprisoned for "bad behaviour." As well, a number of laws were enacted to ensure that opposition parties could not hold mass meetings or have regular access to the mass media.

Intimidation of the Press and
Opposition Political Parties

The new constitution, effective as of May 1949, permitted the president to serve consecutive terms. Soon afterward, newspapers were raided, and the purchase of newsprint was nationalized. Radio stations and all newspapers except *La Nación* were controlled by Peronists; *La Prensa* was expropriated in January 1951. Commissions were established to look into "un-Argentine activities," and espionage, sabotage, and treason took on new and much broader meanings. Civil liberties were severely curtailed and opposition leaders were forced into exile or were imprisoned and otherwise silenced. Paul Lewis describes this period as follows:

The opposition found it difficult to reach the public. It could not broadcast; its press was closed down; and printers were warned not to turn out its propaganda. Local officials often refused to allow opposition parties to hold public rallies, fearing a "disturbance of the peace"; and when rallies were held they were often broken up by Peronist bullies. Opposition candidates were subjected to all manner of intimidation and persecution. During the 1951 electoral campaign the Radical standard-bearer, Balbín, had just been released from prison, the presidential and vice-presidential candidates of both the conservative and socialist parties were in jail or in hiding; and the communist presidential candidate was first jailed and then, after his release, killed when a Peronist mob shot up one of his meetings. Of the 32 Socialists running for the Chamber of Deputies, 23 were either in prison, in hiding, or were awaiting trial.[2]

Reforms for Organized Labour

Perón made an enormous change in the fortunes of organized labour. In particular, he recognized rights for ordinary working people that had not previously existed. He supported unionized labour against the military and against conservatives. His second wife, Eva Duarte de Perón, better known to history as Evita, championed the poor in her short life. Despite all information about corruption and hypocrisy in her charitable organizations, Evita was then and still is regarded as a saint by a large part of the Argentine population. The "shirtless ones" (descamisados), as Evita called her followers, became Peronists with an intensity that is usually reserved for religious movements. The Peróns could attract to a demonstration thousands upon thousands of utterly devoted workers. The steady flow of legislation to bring about wage reforms, improve working conditions, and increase labour participation in decision making were, of course, strongly resisted and resented by employers and more generally by the upper middle class and elite.

Between 1943 and 1946, from the initial interventions by Perón until the end of his first full year as president, trade union membership increased steadily and mightily. In the four following years it doubled, and by 1955, before Perón was ousted, the unionization rate had reached 42 per cent.[3] Meanwhile, membership in the CGT expanded to cover 80 per cent of the organized workforce.[4] Real wages increased steadily after 1942 and as a share of the national income, wages and salaries rose to just under 46 per cent by 1950.[5] Workers gained paid annual holidays, paid sick leave rights, compensation if dismissed or injured in the workplace, and a thirteenth-month bonus at Christmas. Pensions were extended to all workers. These reforms were the result of collective agreements between labour and private capital, with the state acting as the intermediary within a general framework known as the "social pact."

The reforms did not come entirely without a cost to labour, for the unions became dependent on Péron's interventions. They were unable to develop significant independent momentum or democratic procedures. Perón controlled the executive council of the CGT, selected its leaders, shoved aside any nonconforming leaders, repressed strikes, and withdrew recognition from union locals that failed to comply with his directives. Socialists, anarchists, and communists were ousted; indeed, Perón boasted to capitalists that his reforms had saved the country from communism. Under Perón's guidance, the Secretariat for Labour and Welfare expanded into a bureaucracy of over 6,000, and the salaries for social welfare employees steadily rose.[6]

Following Perón's re-election in November 1951,[7] with 60 per cent of the vote, he promised that the syndicalist state would now be implemented. This meant creating a means by which representatives of workers could participate in the legislature and other organs of government. Perón began to implement this experiment in the rural and sparsely populated province of Chaco; there the constitution was transformed so that half the legislature would be selected by the provincial electorate of about 200,000 voters and the other half by the members of the provincial CGT, who numbered about 30,000. Chaco was the only province where this was attempted. As historian Donald Hodges observes, "Although it was still a long way from the goal of a workers' state, if carried out on a national scale it would have given labor a 50 per cent stake in the federal government corresponding to its 50–50 share in the national income."[8]

In 1951, apparently in response to an attempted military coup which had no chance of success, Perón declared "a state of internal war" – something the constitution did not provide for – and claimed that it permitted the government to suspend constitutional liberties. The declaration, which remained in force for the next four years, allowed the government to arrest people without cause, and during that time virtually all political leaders, editors, and many other public figures were arrested. In 1952 the Peronist Superior Council instructed local committees throughout the country to create lists of opponents. The directives included the information that the objective was to undermine the morale of "the enemy."

The National Liberating Alliance, the Peronist paramilitary force, incited mob violence on several occasions. In April 1953 its members burned the Jockey Club, the elite's social centre. They also attacked the headquarters of all other political parties. In June 1955 they destroyed the national cathedral and several downtown churches in response to an abortive coup attempt by members of the navy. Civilians were killed in the fray. Perón encouraged the violence, and in a famous speech in August 1955 he shouted at a mass rally that "anyone, in any place, who tries to change the system against the constituted authorities, or against the laws or the Constitution, may be killed by any Argentine." He promised that for every Peronist who died in civil clashes, five of "the enemy" would be killed.[9]

Relations with the Catholic Church

In the first few years of his government, particularly while Evita was alive, Perón had fairly good relations with the powerful institution of the Catholic Church, which was virtually the state religion.[9] He was careful to express his adherence to the church's social encyclicals; and in his campaign speeches of 1945, when talking to audiences of managers, he referred to Catholic social thought in connection with workers' social rights, thereby trying to provide legitimacy in the national religion for his policies.

In 1947 he enacted a law providing for religious education in state schools. Perón presented the case for this law to the Chamber of Deputies as a means of creating a uniform moral education that would provide cultural and spiritual unity to the Argentine people. Over the next several years, he frequently referred to papal encyclicals in order to legitimize Peronist political interests. Justicialism, the name he created for his political philosophy, was pragmatically attached to Catholicism, and once it became firmly entrenched, it overshadowed the church's version. In the view of a political scientist, José Ghio, the "terminology that had been used for over two decades by the Catholic nationalists was gradually being introduced as a further component of the highly symbolic apparatus of government propaganda. Thus it was appropriated and converted into a National Doctrine." By the early 1950s, the justicialist emblem was everywhere, and schoolchildren were indoctrinated with "the cult of Perón and Eva Perón in school books."[11] By then, justicialism was in conflict with the institutional authority of the church; and Perón, having appropriated the church's social doctrine, was referring to Christianity rather than to the Catholic Church.

This can be understood entirely within the framework of power relations, but it should also be understood relative to the internal schisms in the church. These schisms erupted in full force in the late 1960s and are an important component of the 1970s repression. The Catholic Church in Argentina as elsewhere had a history of internal debate between those who saw Christianity as a social reform movement and those who saw it as a theological doctrine primarily concerned with sin, heaven, and hell. When Perón emphasized the social aspects and appropriated them in his justicialist doctrine, he was essentially dismissing the main body and hierarchy of the church.

The rupture between Perón and the church became more public in 1954, when the president disparaged the church while appearing to defend Christianity. During this famous speech he stated: "I have never been in conflict with Christ. In fact what I have been trying to do is defend Christ's doctrine which, during 1,000 years priests like these have tried to destroy, unsuccessfully."[12] This and other transgressions grew into a major conflict in which Catholic Peronists found themselves torn between two institutional allegiances. Many chose Peronism, and the sacking of the Catholic churches in downtown Buenos Aires was a manifestation of this choice. But the more the people chose Perón, the more the church chose otherwise.

A short word about the philosophical orientation claimed by Perón might be of interest to readers. According to his own writings about his beliefs, he saw history as a series of large-scale and cyclical evolutionary stages punctuated by smaller-scale pendulum swings between individual freedom and state authority. Revolutions might mark the turn of the pendulum or the final movement from one stage of evolution to another, and for Perón the two events coincided when he took over the government of Argentina. His interpretation provided contradictory possibilities. He might argue that the "hour of the people"[13] had come and the socialist revolution was inevitable, or he might argue that the state would necessarily repress popular discontent since otherwise democracy would lead to anarchy. Here he champions the working class:

The French Revolution finished with the government of the aristocracy and gave birth to the government of the bourgeoisie. The Russian Revolution finished with the government of the bourgeoisie and opened the way for the proletarian masses. The future of the world belongs to them.[14]

But championing the working class had its limits. Some of Perón's ideas were rooted in Mussolini's *Doctrine of Fascism*, published in 1932. Mussolini argued that the century of liberalism (synonymous with individualism) was passing, to be replaced by fascism (synonymous with collectivism and the supremacy of the state over the individual). Influenced by Oswald Spengler and Arnold J. Toynbee, Perón also played with the possibility that class struggles and race wars would eventually destroy Western civilization. Labels are important, as Perón fully realized. Although parts of his message were socialist, he called his philosophy "justicialist" even when his followers used the term "Christian national socialists." Socialism was elsewhere linked with atheism, an unacceptable alliance in this strongly Catholic country.

Hodges argues that Perón learned a lot from the thought of José António Primo de Rivera, founder of the Spanish Falange and the Falange doctrine of national syndicalism, even though Perón himself rarely mentioned it.[15] He learned strategy as well from Mussolini and Hitler. Where Perón departed from his mentors was in his willingness to activate populism by actually giving workers a genuine role in government. His reforms eroded the agro-export oligarchy's power, gave the working class governmental capacities, and expanded the opportunities for the professional and managerial middle class in the new bureaucracies of government.

Relations with the Military

Although they had at first reluctantly supported Perón, the officers of the military forces became increasingly hostile, largely because of the changes he instituted. He replaced independent officers and substantially reduced military budgets. At the same time, he attempted to put Peronism on the curriculum of military schools in the same way as he had successfully done in children's schools. He courted noncommissioned officers with pay increases and with improved promotion opportunities, and provided scholarships for working-class youth to enter the military academy. The Peronists he appointed to high positions encouraged the cult of Peronism amongst lower-ranking officers; Peronist party militants gained favours, while anti-Peronists were subject to reprisals. But when Evita Perón seemed determined to obtain the vice-presidential nomination for the 1951 election, even Perón's military supporters rebelled. He stopped her campaign – though by the time he did so, his decision may have been influenced by the news that she was suffering from cancer. After her death, the CGT gave the Circulo Militar (the officers club in Buenos Aires) a gigantic portrait of Evita, hardly a friendly gesture.

By then, the CGT was pushing for an armed militia unit in the workers' ranks, to "defend the revolution." Evita had tried to arm a militia, and possibly Perón had provided weapons and antitank guns – they were in evidence amongst defenders of the government during the abortive coup attempt by the navy in June 1955.[16] Three months later, the military mounted a successful coup.[17]

The Legacy of Peronism: A Summary

The continuing legacy of the Peronist period included a demoralized and politicized judiciary, the absence of due process and the rule of law in daily life, and widespread disrespect for the law and democracy. The mass media had become cowardly in the face of persistent intimidation, and political parties were demoralized and disorganized. The military forces were highly politicized and fraught with internal divisions. But well established by 1955 was a middle class bureaucracy attached to the state. Huge bureaucratic unions, centralized within the state, were powerful institutions. Organized labour and the military were mutually hostile and were prepared to use arms in their contest for control of the state.

The Catholic Church and the Peronists also were locked in a hostile relationship. The church's version of Christianity and Perón's personal populism competed for public support. Both used mass-persuasion methods, the one in the pulpit, the other through the politicized school system and curriculum and every other public institution and venue. A generation of young people had been taught the lessons and cult behaviour of Peronism. Evita Perón was described in schools and popular rallies as a saint. This segment of the population, together with union workers, sustained the faith in Peronism throughout the entire eighteen years of military and quasi-military rule until Perón returned.

ECONOMIC DEVELOPMENT

Guillermo O'Donnell, whose thoughts on import-substitution policies were introduced in the previous chapter, went on to argue that eventually these policies reach an exhaustion limit.[18] The "easy" range of consumer goods that can be created internally has reached its limit, and the country has to rewind its engine to move on. The stagnation, says O'Donnell, is accompanied by a shortage of foreign exchange, alternating brief cycles of recession and inflation, declining fortunes for a disillusioned middle class, and failure to meet the escalating expectations of either the technocratic bureaucracy or the previously active "popular" classes.[19] An economic crisis develops for which there is no obvious solution, since the demands of various segments of the population are incompatible, the populism of the past is no longer workable, and there is no institutional mechanism by which compromises can be reached.

It is debatable whether Perón can be held accountable for bringing about an economic crisis because of his import-substitution policies. He is accused of implementing extreme nationalist policies that stifled the export sector, but some authors contend that his nationalist policies were not consistently applied and even that his economic policies were not especially nationalist.[20] Although Perón ranted against imperialism, he encouraged American direct investment and control in the oil and automobile industries; he enacted a 1953 law granting preferential treatment to international capital; and his "third position" of neutrality in international affairs was lost when he sided with the United States on Cold War issues.

A different argument is that by concentrating on redistribution, Perón's government neglected productive forces and created so many disincentives for production that the pie, though now being more widely distributed, was becoming smaller. Manuel Mora y Araujo argues, for example, that before 1945 there was dynamic economic power with productive capacity; but that under Perón's corporatist state, which introduced forced redistribution and subordinated the economy to political power, there was a general decline in the growth rate of new firms, while the number of distributive associations grew rapidly: "The problem in Argentina was that Peronism blocked the development of capitalism"; Perón neutralized economic power "in order to concentrate all the power in the state, and then set off a distributive struggle as a means of making that state legitimate."[21]

Certain it is that under Perón, the state bureaucracy expanded and, with it, the number of workers dependent on a large and bureaucratic state for their employment. Their demands, together with those of the production labour force, could be accommodated in an expanding economy, but by the mid-1950s the economy was no longer growing. The economic model, whether or not it was as nationalist as claimed, was exhausted.

THE MILITARY STATE

Military rule in Argentina began in the 1930s, and although Perón was elected twice to the presidency and there were restricted elections that provided two other constitutional presidents, the underlying reality included military control or a strong military presence in the state from 1930 to 1973. Military historian Alain Rouquié observes: Through periodic intervention that produced political discontinuities, the Argentine army successively removed from power the middle classes and their representatives (1930), the export agriculture oligarchy (1943), the labour unions and populist parties (1955), the industrial sectors (1962), the traditional political parties (1963), and again the unions and populism in 1976."[22]

This record does not suggest a simple pattern of alliance with any one civilian interest group. The military was always opposed to organized labour, particularly after the fall of Perón, but that did not mean that it would always defend the interests of the oligarchy, whether in the form of the financial and industrial sector or the agricultural sector. In Rouquié's view, the army was never a party of the middle classes or of the industrial bourgeoisie, or of the multinational companies either. He views it as playing the "role of alternator of social currents." Another reading of the same information would be that the army prevented any other interest group from gaining control of the state; it regarded the state as its own.

Having noted the history of military domination since 1930, however, we must immediately add that the military was not united or homogeneous in its interests. Factionalism was rampant and became even more so under Perón and in the aftermath of the 1955 coup. Perón's successor, General Eduardo Lonardi, was deposed by another military coup less than two months after taking office. This and further coups within coups were symptoms of the critical divisions within the military itself. Lonardi was backed by Catholic nationalists and some liberals, but when he tried to create a cabinet of Catholic nationalists, the liberals objected. "Liberal" in this context implied free markets and had nothing to do with political liberties. Military liberals were typically antilabour and had no sympathy for unions. Part of the objection to Lonardi was that he had not yet initiated a crackdown on labour.

General Pedro E. Aramburu came next, and he was more popular with the liberals; he intervened in the CGT and he banned the Justicialist Party. "Intervention" in the Argentine lexicon meant the imposition of a trusteeship on a government ministry, union, university department, or any other public entity which the reigning powers considered unruly or out of line. Intervention included the potential or actual use of military force to oblige elected or current leaders to leave (some into exile), replacing them with "acceptable" persons, and dictating the program or agenda for the intervened organization. With respect to Peronism, Aramburu not only banned the Justicialist Party; he banned Peronism as a word, Perón as a person, and everything to do with Perón and his politics. His legacy continued after his 1958 departure from office. The elections in February of that year and all those until 1973 took place without representation of what was still the majoritarian party, thus reinforcing popular contempt for democracy.

Meanwhile, the Radical Party, which had supported the coup, was having internal disputes, and it split into two factions; the Intransigent Radical Party (UCRI) led by Arturo Frondizi; and the People's Radical Party (UCRP) under Ricardo Balbín. Frondizi won the 1958 election after allowing the Peronists to run their candidates on his ticket, but the military intervened, prevented further Peronist incursions, and ensured that Frondizi lost the 1962 election.

The Colorados and Azules

The two major factions within the armed forces after the 1955 coup, which both factions supported, became known as the *colorados* (reds), who were fanatical anti-Peronists and inclined to favour military rule, and the *azules* (blues), who were inclined to favour civilian rule. In economic terms, the *colorados* were neoliberals, who advocated laissez-faire government and market relations. Marvin Goldwert has described their ideals as "simplistic anticommunism." He quotes a military analyst in Argentina to the effect that the *colorados* wanted a military dictatorship "to straighten the country out, break the back of peronism and achieve real democracy."[23] The *azules* argued in favour of less politicized and more professional armed forces, and defended the corporate interests of the military. Although they appeared to be the more democratic in inclination, at least one analyst argued at the time that the *azules* were in fact intensely nationalistic, Catholic, and pro-Franco; they were legalists when the electorate behaved itself, but in

Table 3
Dictatorships and Governments, 1946–1973

Date	How Power Gained	President
1946–52	Election	General Juan D. Perón
1952–55	Election	General Juan D. Perón
1955	Military coup	General Eduardo Lonardi
1955–58	Military coup	General Pedro Aramburu
1958–62	Restricted election	Arturo Frondizi
1962–63	Military coup	José María Guido
1963–66	Restricted election	Dr Arturo Illia
1966–70	Military coup	General Juan C. Onganía
1970–71	Military coup	General Roberto Levingston
1971–73	Military coup	General Alejandro Lanusse

democratic crises they were right-wing militarists.[24] In economic terms, they were more interested in promoting industrial development than the *colorados* were, though this may simply be a reflection of the amount of shares held by military leaders in industrial holdings and banks. As well, the military still held collective ownership of military factories, which had become a significant component of the industrial spectrum in Argentina.

Throughout the post-1955 period, a major objective of military groups was to ensure that Peronism did not resurface, but both the military governments and that of Frondizi were unable to avoid chronic political instability without the support of the Peronists. Justicialism, though banned, remained the party of the working class, and elections were perceived as fraudulent as long as that party was excluded. Although both factions of the military had agreed on the overthrow of Frondizi, they wanted opposite solutions to the political crisis that resulted from his removal. The *colorados* attempted to take direct control of the government again through a military junta, but the *azules* installed the president *pro tempore* of the Senate, José María Guido, as president of the country, in accordance with the constitution.

Guido's government, however, dissolved Congress, maintained the proscription on Peronism, annulled earlier election results, and suspended political parties. These antidemocratic actions did not prevent military crises. In April 1962 a military confrontation in downtown Buenos Aires concluded with a "win" by the *colorados*, backed by the navy. Within a few months, the *colorados* controlled the key ministries of government. Inevitably, the *azules* retaliated. They had the support of a majority of army generals plus the air force in an armed conflict with the *colorados*. This time the *azules*, led by General Onganía, triumphed. The *azules* then issued a communiqué to the nation emphasizing their commitment to the constitution. The concluding paragraph was particularly significant:

We believe that the Armed Forces should not govern. They should, on the contrary, be subordinate to civilian power. That is not to say that they should not influence the institutional life. Their role is, at one and the same time, silent and fundamental. They guarantee the constitutional pact left to us by our ancestors and have the sacred duty to prevent and contain any totalitarian movement which arises in the country, whether it be from within the government or from the opposition.[25]

Although the communiqué promised that there would be elections, "which will assure to all sectors participation in the national life," no military government in 1962 could possibly allow Peronism to re-surface. An attempt to distinguish between Peronism and justicialism, by way of permitting a Justicialist Party but without the participation of "men who continue addicted to Perón,"[26] failed to still the *colorados'* dismay with the government. Finally, the shaky government under Guido hardened its stance on Peronism and arrested labour leaders and other Peronists. Unappeased by these measures, *colorados* in the navy, with some backing in the army, staged a rebellion in April 1963. It lasted four days and involved some fighting in downtown Buenos Aires before the rebels were defeated.

The navy suffered cuts in staff and budget as a consequence of its rebellion, but the *colorados* had forced the government to take stronger measures against Peronism. Under the justification that Peronism constituted a dictatorship and a threat to the Argentine constitution, all Peronist parties and candidates were outlawed in forthcoming elections. With only 25.1 per cent of the vote and a huge number of blank ballots, a new president, Arturo Illia, was elected in July, 1963.

Illia lost no time in trying to rid the military of its *colorados*. He promoted *azules* to all vacancies in command, but at the same time his government permitted Peronist parties some access to political representation. His error as far as the armed forces were concerned was to fail to appreciate the full importance of the Cuban revolution and of potential communist subversion.[27] By 1965, military voices were again expressing deep fears of a resurgence of Peronism, and in November that year General Onganía resigned as commander in chief of the army, signifying disapproval of Illia's approach to communists and Peronists. Further signs of softness toward Peronists, and even some suggestion of softness in the military forces themselves, led to an escalation of belligerence among *colorados* and finally to a military coup on 28 June 1966. In one of Argentina's many ironies, General Onganía – the champion of the constitution – now became the president in a military government that was backed by a junta of all three armed forces and was dedicated to ensuring that Peronism and communism were kept at bay. As became known more generally in the next three years, General Francisco Franco was General Onganía's model, and the Spanish Falange ideology, as expressed by José António Primo de Rivera, was his rationale.

PERÓN IN EXILE

All this time, Perón in exile continued to influence his followers. He had said on numerous occasions that he opposed violence and that countries that had experienced violent revolutions had suffered for it; if he had armed the workers in 1955, he consoled his followers, there would have been many killed without any certainty of success. But during the years he was out of power and living in exile, Perón brooded over his decision not to fight back against the military coup, and he lost his admiration for moderation and peace. His letters to friends and political associates now advocated violent revolution – especially his letters to his designated spokesman, John William Cooke. "We have to create ... a permanent state of insurrection," he told Cooke.[28] A group of Peronist militants who called themselves Peronist Resistance took him seriously, and under Cooke's leadership they exploded some seven thousand bombs between the 1955 coup and the elections of February 1958. Further encouragement from Perón ignited fires amongst young people ten years later.

Meanwhile, early in 1956, Perón issued a "General Instructions to Leaders." This was a detailed strategy, based on one created by Cooke and others, for fomenting revolution by means of guerrilla activity. It provided a plan for sabotaging public order and the productive process, and it advocated a form of resistance that would encourage massive destruction so that the military government would be immobilized. As well, it recognized the need for clandestine cell organization of guerrilla revolutionaries, and it moved from general principles of destruction to specific targets. The "gorillas" must be wiped out (they being military personnel who had executed loyal Peronists and other citizens during or since the coup). Enemies of the people should be brought to justice in a secret court, and chief among these enemies, said Perón, were General Pedro Aramburu and Admiral Isaac Rojas, who had been responsible for the military coup of September 1955.

Some fourteen years passed before this directive was acted upon by the newly formed Montoneros, but when the Montoneros acted it was in strict conformity with Perón's instructions of 1956.

A few months after these instructions were first issued, a bloodbath was unleashed by the military government; there had been an unsuccessful revolt by Peronist generals, and the government responded with a shooting spree against military officers loyal to Perón, and also against imprisoned workers who had taken part in earlier uprisings against the coup. This brought about an even stronger document, "General Directives for All Peronists," in which Perón said there were no further options: "We must face up to the consequences of fighting for a definitive social revolution destined to achieve its objectives through active combat until the reaction is totally disarmed and absolutely extinguished."[29]

The strategies proposed in this document included civil resistance that would lead to paralysis of the society and, if that did not work, "political action by our mass organizations." But by the late 1950s the potential forces for revolution were exhausted, and although John William Cooke and others continued to prepare for armed insurrection, training their followers in Cuba, Perón was not successful in inciting the masses to revolt during the 1960s. Nonetheless, he successfully blocked the path for his military successors. A decade passed during which the military forces and undemocratic governments tried to repress Peronism, to sidestep or oust the unions, and to take revenge against Perón's supporters. During this time the economy continued to decline, and the social fabric remained torn and tattered.

THE COUP OF 1966

The 1966 coup that brought General Onganía to power was the third military coup since the ouster of Perón's government in 1955 and the sixth military coup since 1930. Under Onganía, the military began to govern Argentina directly, rather than simply intervening through coups and temporary presidents. Thanks to Perón, the military had discarded what remained of its earlier alliance with the agro-export oligarchy, and while it shared the conservatives' fears of communism, it had its own economic and political interests. Indeed, in the period 1966–73, the military had a predominant role relative to the financial elite, since the financial sector and foreign corporations were subservient to it as their government. The military's ability to wield this power came in part from its continued ownership of major industrial enterprises throughout the country. Daniel Poneman estimates that sales from military factories represented 2.5 per cent and in some years as much as 5 per cent of the GDP.[48]

The test of the proposition that the military had achieved independence from the financial elite would be whether the financial class was able to overturn a military government or oblige one to put in power a president of its choice if that were not also the choice of the military; and whether members of the financial class, when in government, could make inroads on the military's control of so much of Argentine industry. On neither test is the hypothesis of elite control upheld. Although the military was far from homogeneous, it was responding to its own power dynamics, not to those of the financial elite. As well, neither Krieger Vasena nor Martínez de Hoz – the economic wizards who managed the economy under Onganía, and then under the military junta after 1976 – was able to privatize the military factories.

Onganía's new government outlawed all political organizations, ousted and replaced members of the Supreme Court, dissolved Congress yet again, and sent troops into the universities. While no longer beholden to the financial and industrial class (the former oligarchy), Onganía created smooth relationships by appointing liberal nationalists to cabinet posts and giving high priority to economic policies that favoured agro-export and other industrial interests. He succeeded in reducing the rate of inflation – indeed, the Argentine peso became one of the strongest currencies in Latin America. The federal deficit declined, and foreign investment increased. Meanwhile, Onganía developed closer relationships with the U.S. military, reorganized much of his own military's structure, and, at an ideological level, emphasized national security and national development.

The military sent out the message that it would destroy the left. Under its neoliberal policies, the workers experienced frozen wages, loss of social benefits, and other forms of reduced living standards. Compulsory arbitration was introduced, and disputes were regularly resolved in favour of management. Unions were hostile organizations as far as the military was concerned, though some factions within the union movement chose collaboration with Onganía for a brief period; but by 1969 there was only hostility. After the workers' strikes in Córdoba (see chapter 5), Onganía lost control.

Relationship with United States

The Argentine military regime under Onganía – indeed, from the early 1960s onward – sought American military aid and sent officers to courses on anti-insurgency methods and ideology. However, the United

States may well have treated Latin American military forces as colonial police, as Argentine military personnel claimed. The United States did not sell the Argentine military top-of-the-range weaponry, and the regime sought better equipment in France. By 1967 the Schneider Company of France was selling tanks to the Argentine military, and it arranged for the manufacture of further arms under licence in Argentina, thus breaking the American monopoly and establishing a national armament industry under military control in Argentina.[31] The independence this afforded became particularly important a decade later when the Carter administration reduced military aid in protest against the human rights violations in Argentina. The military simply abrogated its agreements with the United States; it no longer needed U.S. aid.

VOICE: MARÍA DE LOS ANGELES YANUZZI

This short extract is from an interview with a resident of Rosario, who tells us about the violence in that industrial town in the 1960s.

I was in secondary school in Rosario in the 1960s. We had three presidents, military presidents. People consider the first military president, General Onganía, a very efficient one. People thought that when you have a big problem in society it was better to give it to the military because they were so clever and so intelligent. It was an authoritarian government, but there was this matter of efficiency. People need efficiency, and you are much more efficient if you are an authoritarian because you are the only one who makes the decisions. Congress, and in general this whole society, accepted the coup of 1966, and they were in agreement until 1969.

In 1969 we had the first important demonstrations in Rosario. They were very violent ones. You know, there were protests in France in 1968, followed by a kind of chain reaction in the whole world, including Argentina. This was my first participation in a political event. I had not previously had any political involvement, unless you include a kind of youth association sponsored by the United Nations. We were doing volunteer work in the north of the country, in the slum areas. We began to worry about the social conditions – well, we would not have done that kind of work if we were not concerned. In 1969 we had an important demonstration to show the police that we were opposed to violence. This was because someone had been killed by police in the town of Corrientes, and we were showing solidarity with the people there.

I was in my last year in secondary school when I went to the demonstration. I was not really aware of what was happening. Later, when I joined a political party, I learned that you should not go to a demonstration if you do not have a "control" outside, because otherwise, if something happens to you, nobody will know. We went there without any kind of "control." A "control" was a person who was at the bar, or at a house, and at the end of the demonstration, when you left, you had to pass through the bar, not to talk to him, only to be seen by him, or, if he was at the house, you had to phone him. We thought all the telephones were bugged, so we talked about anything else except the demonstration just to let him know we were safe.

During the 1969 demonstration, one of our protestors was killed by the mounted police. They used swords against people's necks, there were a lot of people who had their necks cut and even part of the head. The day after the demonstration I had to go to the school. Nearby were the headquarters of the army. As well, the CGT building and the provincial police station were nearby. I describe this because generally when there were demonstrations, the army and police stood in front of the school. Sometimes they took over the school as a place to store weapons. So the school was in a difficult place, and I had to go there early in the morning. Someone had highlighted on the wall the marks of the swords, and you could see blood there. The marks were at the height of a man's head, so it was really dramatic. The soldiers and the policemen were at the corners of the school. If you didn't identify yourself, the policemen would shoot you.

The city was under siege because we had martial law. People here were frightened, yet at the same time they were very angry with what the mounted police had done. These police killed people. It was said that they were kept inside their headquarters for several days and even that they were given drugs so that they would be willing to do anything; they were very excited. The public reaction was strong. People said, "We are not going to have any more of this kind of police behaviour." It was a moment of upheaval in Rosario.

During the demonstration, we were in the centre of things, but we were very quiet because it was a silent demonstration. Suddenly a gas bomb was found in the middle of the street, and we ran away. We began to run to Santa Fe Street. I remember running and running, and as I was passing a house someone took me by my clothes and pulled me inside. I did not know who he was, but he took several young people off the street. If he had not done this, we would likely have been arrested or killed.

There were some places where people were so angry with the mounted police that they had strung some ropes from one building to another in order to make the horses fall down, and they also began to throw marbles on the road. Some people threw boiling water at the police in order to stop them, because they were very angry. The newspapers and all official information sources reported nothing, except about one person who had died. Nothing else, but we saw what happened.

At the same time there were the first manifestations of urban guerrillas, and we learned then about the Montoneros. They were a Catholic group, on the right. Another group was the ERP [People's Revolutionary Army]. It was a Marxist group, not so popular as the others. Nevertheless, people here, in society in general, agreed with the methods of these guerrillas. They were happy when the Montoneros or any of these groups killed a military leader. They said, "Oh well, he was really an evil person; they did a good thing killing this man." It was a middle-class reaction to treat the killers as heroes, yet these people would certainly never have done the same thing themselves. It was like this until the end.

I think that perhaps many people did not make a distinction between the Montoneros and other groups. "It was one of these groups," they would say. You might say, "They have killed the chief of the army," and the people would be very happy to hear that. Of course, this would not be said in public, but in the privacy of their houses they would say, "Well, this is wonderful, they have killed Sánchez,[32] this is marvellous, because he really was an evil person." They thought this killing was a solution to all our problems, and this was the same structure of reasoning that people continued to accept after the military coup in 1976. You know, "Someone is going to provide a solution to all our problems." It is true that these groups, the Montoneros, were encouraged by Perón, before the democratic period of course.

In 1970, when I began my university studies in Rosario, it was a very violent period. People complained against the government, and though politics was not allowed at that time, there were many political groups in the university. We had a lot of demonstrations, and we knew that if we went to the demonstrations, we were going to have a fight with the police.

CHAPTER 5

Unionism

Perón's legacy to the unions was a hierarchical power structure centralized in the state. The General Confederation of Labour (CGT) was the institutional mechanism for this power structure, and whoever controlled it, controlled the Peronist labour unions. Competition for power led to manipulation of the slippery rules and could develop into shooting wars. The trading of promises for votes, with rewards on delivery, were commonplace. In a close examination of unions in the post-Peronist period, Daniel James described an election in the powerful Metalworkers' Union (UOM) in 1970 as "a mixture of organized gangsterism, 'el far west sindical' and the highest political manoeuvring."[1]

Union leaders were powerful political figures, and their ability to extend or withhold benefits to others was what maintained their power over rank-and-file members. Beyond ordinary power, there was money. About 20 per cent of a union's finances came from membership dues. These ranged from 1 to 5 per cent of members' wages and were deducted from paycheques by the employers, then paid into the Labour Secretariat, going from there to the unions. As long as the union towed the line with the CGT and the government, its leaders were not closely monitored for their administration of union dues. Ordinary members had no leverage over the use of funds. Investments and levies were an even larger source of funds than union dues and could amount to millions of pesos.[2] Consequently, control of the funds was a source of enormous power and patronage, and of persistent tensions, violence, and corruption.

The boss of the commercial employees' union, Armando March, managed to amass a huge fortune, live in a Buenos Aires mansion, collect paintings, and raise prize dogs before the Onganía government decided to blow the whistle on his diversion of some $30 million from his union's account. He was sent to jail. The construction workers' union boss, Rogelio Coria, also built up a grand fortune; he retired to an estancia in Paraguay until, on a visit to Argentina in the mid-1970s, he was assassinated. José Alonso met the same fate. Union members may have wondered how he had managed to afford a mansion, servants, limousines, a weekend chalet, and other perks on his modest union salary.[3] He was assassinated in 1970. At the end of June in the previous year, his former arch-enemy in the CGT, Augusto T. Vandor had been assassinated.

As these examples indicate, union bosses had the opportunity to steal large sums from their organizations, but they had to live with continued death threats. Keeping bodyguards around was normal behaviour. In all these cases, the assassinations were attributed to left-wing guerrillas. One has to be careful with attributions of this kind, even those that were apparent admissions of guilt broadcast by the Montoneros. The guerrillas built up a reputation as well-trained and strong fighters, a reputation that turned out to be far above their actual capacity, and it was often in the interests of government and military or police groups to sustain this mythology. As well, the rivalries within the unions were crudely acted out, and it was well within the realm of possibilities that one faction might assassinate the leader of an opposing group.

Although the unions by themselves had power, their power was limited by their ties to the CGT. The CGT received dues from union members across the spectrum of industries and regions, and exacted fines and percentages for various services. It was pivotal in establishing relations with the government and jockeying for power on behalf of the entire organized working class within a highly centralized state.

The CGT also had limitations to its power. It was subject to the tacit or explicit agreements of the government of the day, because the labour laws established under Perón's management gave the government the right to grant legal recognition to a union, the right to intervene, and a range of other rights that could be invoked whenever a union staged too many strikes or otherwise irritated the government. Governments throughout the 1960s did in fact invoke these laws, sometimes cutting an entire union adrift for a while or intervening and appointing an administrator. They also played favourites, supporting particular leaders or unions even when they were aware of widespread graft, gangsterism, and general corruption.

The role of government in union affairs obliged the unions to become political in more than the usual oppositional sense. Leaders had to figure out how both to represent their members' demands and to get along with whoever was the secretary of labour. The Peronist unions, moreover, were constantly in touch with the exiled Perón, who maintained a strong directive voice in their affairs. If a union tried to wrest more independence for itself or voted in leaders whose allegiance was not proven, Perón and his loyal followers managed to stop them.[4] In 1965, following political victories in congressional elections, the very powerful leader of the CGT, Augusto Vandor, tried to establish "Peronism without Perón." Despite his powerful position, a rival clique blocked Vandor's aspirations through the creation of what was known as the "sixty-two organizations that stand alongside Perón."

Union leaders and the rank and file both assumed that unions had to go beyond wage bargaining – that unions were essential components in the governance of the society. Indeed, some union leaders, urged on by Perón when he was in power and by his emissaries in his absence, considered that union members were the most important members of society and that their needs should be paramount. Thus it was inevitable that the unions took political positions that influenced events under the many governments from 1955 onwards.

Despite this influence, the fortunes of unions and their members fluctuated over this time, especially during the 1960s. The resistance they mounted against the Aramburu government in the immediate aftermath of Perón's eviction was so strong that the unions were rejuvenated in the process. They were part of the Peronist support for the government of Arturo Frondizi in 1958, as well as being an important cause of its downfall in 1962. But they suffered numerous setbacks over the following years. Daniel James, historian of the Argentine labour movement, argues that by the early 1960s demoralization was setting in and members were becoming resigned not only to defeat in face of the combined pressures of anti-Peronist governments and employers, but also in face of the corruption and deceit of their own leaders.[5] By 1966 the organized rank-and-file working class was deeply alienated from political currents in Argentina.

A large part of this alienation was due to a decline in the traditional economic sectors, along with increased unemployment and widespread underemployment. Labour-displacing technology was disemploying workers in Argentina as elsewhere, but in Argentina few new opportunities emerged to absorb a labour surplus. Most large unions experienced a very large drop in membership between the early 1960s and 1970. The powerful Metalworkers' Union (UOM) had 219,000 members in 1963 but fewer than 126,000 in 1970. The Civil Servants' Union (UPCN) had 190,000 in 1963 but only 50,000 in 1970. The construction workers, woodworkers, bus and trolley workers, food-processing workers, textile workers, and dockworkers all lost a substantial number of members. A few sectors maintained membership – for example, the state oilworkers at 30,000 members – and some new sectors even gained members; telephone workers and municipal workers in some cities (including Buenos Aires) were among the growing unions.[6]

Peronism, far from inciting working-class opposition to capitalism, had always been a major ideological barrier against communism. Communists made less headway in Argentina than in neighbouring Uruguay and Chile, where no similar barrier emerged.[7] Even so, Peronism was a substantial obstacle to liberalization of the economy. Dynamic multinational corporations were being established in the capital-intensive technologically advanced sectors, and they wanted a free (or at least freer) labour force, organized within separate trade unions, rather than gigantic industrial unions. They wanted an end to the power of the CGT, and they wanted market-based wage bargaining. Workers obtaining employment in these new sectors were acquiring greater trade skills, training opportunities, and wages than other workers. In the new industries, led by the automobile sector, employees in the mid-1960s earned some 35 per cent above the industry average and nearly 59 per cent above workers in the traditional and resource-sector industries. The difference had increased further by 1970.[8] The union movement was torn between its commitment to industrial unionism Peronist-style and what was called "modernization."[9]

After the 1966 coup, Vandor was seriously challenged by José Alonso, who had gained the support of the Onganía forces in government. Vandor had the indirect support of business, not because businessmen favoured him but because he represented a more arm's-length approach to the relationship between the CGT and the state. Vandor organized a series of strikes and general strikes in the period following the coup, but his high-risk strategy backfired when Onganía's government reacted with extreme force, suspended several unions, and enacted a law that allowed for the militarization of the labour force in times of national emergency. Says historian William C. Smith: "The message was unmistakable. If the unions and the working class wanted a role in the new authoritarian project, they had to 'collaborate' and abandon militant Peronism and combative trade-union tactics." In Smith's view, the popular slogan that promoted an alliance between the "People and the Army" should have been revised to "The bourgeoisie and the Army *against* the People."[10]

Beaten, the unions had to reach an accommodation with the new government, but they could not agree about the degree of subordination they should accept. Two "tendencies," as they were called, emerged: "collaborationists" and "Vandorites." Vandor's approach at this stage was to negotiate with the state while awaiting more favourable conditions. The collaborationists were more inclined to accept subordination to the state and increased integration into its machinery. Onganía's labour ministry dumped Vandor and developed a patronage relationship with his opponents.

CLEAVAGES WITHIN THE CGT

Although the tug-of-war between the Vandorites and the collaborationists took centre stage within the union theatre, other dramas were being rehearsed behind the scenes. The actors in these tended to be outsiders – leaders of non-Peronist unions or shop stewards who were not in agreement with unionism as it had been practised since the 1940s. In one branch of the dissidents, known as *clasismo*, this tendency was more radical, more concerned with class politics, and more in favour of militant autonomy than the union bureaucracy of either Vandor or Alonso and their cronies. By 1968 this group had gained strength and was able to challenge the CGT leadership, with the result that two union federations were established. Vandor, Alonso, and their followers became the CGT de Azopardo (referring to the location of the CGT offices in Buenos Aires); the upstarts became the CGT of the Argentines, led by Raimundo Ongaro and including Agustín Tosco and his devoted followers. The CGT of the Argentines took a strong Marxist line in public documents and speeches, though it developed no vanguard strategy and in fact was less revolutionary in its actions than in its rhetoric.

Both the state and the union bureaucracy attempted to crush the new union federation, but in June 1968 the CGT of the Argentines managed to create a broad-based civic resistance front that included students, members of the Third World Priests' Movement, small businessmen, and others who were willing to oppose the state and the union bureaucracy. Demonstrations and mass arrests popularized the movement, and it spread into workers' districts.

THE 1969 CORDOBAZO

A strike in September 1968 by militant workers in the state oil monopoly was met by force. Workers were fired and other strong action taken, with the result that workers in other sectors began to see their alliance with the state as ultimately self-destructive. By this time Vandor and the CGT de Azopardo, fearing that the left was outmanoeuvring them, were opposing Onganía more openly. Vandor had ensured that he had explicit support from the exiled but ever-powerful Perón.[11]

The turning point in labour-state relations came in May 1969 in the interior industrial city of Córdoba, when workers in the automobile and other industrial plants rebelled against the government. This insurrection, known as the first *cordobazo*, has been compared to the "tragic week" of 1919 and the Patagonian Rebellion of 1921–22. The first *cordobazo* involved thousands of people and became a movement of mass destruction, rampaging through Córdoba for a full week before being stopped. Barricades were erected against the police. State, bank, and multinational buildings were attacked and damaged. The uprising was eventually quelled by some 5,000 special army troops together with the local police force of about 4,000 men.[12] It had repercussions throughout the country and resulted in the forced resignation of Onganía a year later. His successor, General Roberto Levingston, suffered through a second *cordobazo* in March 1971 and was forced out of office by another military coup.

The labour unrest of the late 1960s was part of a larger social ferment that had been gaining momentum against the Onganía regime. Demonstrations by students, the activities of the Third World Priests' Movement, and occasional bombings and kidnappings by armed insurrectionary groups were all part of the dynamic and increasingly violent situation. In April 1969 students had mounted protests in the provincial industrial centres (Corrientes, Rosario, and Córdoba), and workers had demonstrated in Córdoba and elsewhere, but the uprising in May went far beyond these comparatively limited efforts.

It is generally agreed that this battle took place in Córdoba, rather than Buenos Aires, because Córdoba had a strong working class, a divided and weak bourgeoisie, and provincial politics that were in disarray and widely viewed as corrupt. Industrialization in Córdoba, which had occurred rapidly during the late 1950s and early 1960s, consisted primarily of the automobile industry and its service sector. Ford, Renault, and Fiat had plants in Córdoba, but the head offices were in Buenos Aires. During the 1960s, more and more of the final assembly plants were situated in the province of Buenos Aires, and Córdoba was already becoming stagnant. Because most of the industrial workers were employed in very large plants and most were young, organized labour was more unified than in the traditional industrial centres and was led by younger, post-Perón leaders. An additional factor of considerable importance was that management had encouraged strong shop-floor organization, in contrast to the hierarchial structure of traditional Argentine unions. Shop stewards had become the militant front line in what they viewed as a struggle against capital (rather than a struggle within the state).[13]

Following the 1969 *cordobazo*, the CGT of the Argentines was forced underground and its leader was imprisoned. Yet this did not stop the strikes. They increased in frequency during the early 1970s, and for a short time the *clasismo* tendency became more prominent. Meanwhile, shortly after the *cordobazo*, the leader of the CGT de Azopardo, Augusto Vandor, who had dared to oppose Perón's stranglehold on the union, was assassinated. While the unions were fighting back against the military government, they were simultaneously carrying on a major internal battle for control of the labour movement. These internal battles did not end with the change of military rulers as coup followed coup. Nor did the change in rulers modify the economic crisis. Inflation and the foreign debt had escalated: the military had failed to discover an economic miracle, and its confrontations with labour did nothing to restore investor confidence or brake the soaring cost of living.

In the midst of these conflicts and disasters, the new guerrilla movement, the Montoneros, announced that it had kidnapped General Aramburu. The abduction took place on 29 May 1970. Shortly afterwards, the Montoneros said they had found Aramburu guilty as an enemy of the people and had executed him. They took full responsibility for this assassination, even issuing a press release in which they prayed for his soul. No one at that time questioned their claim, but since then two separate claims have been made. One, by surviving Montoneros who were there at the time, claims that Aramburu actually died of a heart attack; the second states that the kidnapping was arranged and paid for by the Onganía faction to ensure that Onganía's rival, Aramburu, would not regain power. We shall return to this interesting sidelight in the next chapter.

THE (TEMPORARY) END OF MILITARY RULE

General Alejandro Lanusse inherited the leadership but could not rein in his rivals. Catholic nationalists had developed strength under Onganía, and they expressed support for the forging of an authoritarian, corporatist society. Military reformers who had accepted Perón's leadership and were prepared to accept the sharing of power with workers in order to gain social peace were less influential. The *azules* preferred democratic solutions but were willing to accept the banning of Peronism from electoral politics. The *colorados* had settled for the power to set the economic agenda of government while the Onganian Catholic nationalists held political power, but they were less accommodating as power changed hands. While the military factions competed with one another, Lanusse had to confront the possibility of a nationwide rebellion. Violence was rampant in every town and city. There was a sense of anarchy, combined with extremely harsh repression – a concoction that was bound to blow up – yet the military was unable to get its act together and could no longer govern.

Because Peronism was still so much part of the rhetoric of unions and rebels alike, and had in fact gained a mythological status by virtue of being banned as a political party, a possible solution was to admit Perón back into politics and allow for an election that might involve his return to power. The unthinkable had to be considered, and the military accepted it as a possibility.

The electoral rules in 1972 in effect banned Perón as a candidate for president by requiring candidates to have five years' residence. Since Perón had been in exile since 1955, he could not meet this requirement. Lanusse persuaded his colleagues to accept a change of rules to allow Peronists, via the Popular Front (Frejuli), to enter the electoral fray. Perón returned briefly in November 1972, assessed the situation, and, to general surprise, nominated Hector Cámpora as the presidential candidate for Frejuli. Cámpora was nobody's favourite, and a widespread conclusion was that Perón was inviting the military to renege on its agreement to allow open elections. The military did not, however, step back from its decision: it was no longer capable of ruling the country. In May 1973 Cámpora took office as president, the Frejuli (dominated by Peronists) having won the March election.

VOICES IN CÓRDOBA

The autobiographical accounts in this chapter begin in the mid-1960s and early 1970s, and continue through to the end of el Proceso. These excerpts provide a sense of the violence in the industrial city of Córdoba between the military coup in 1966 and the end of the military dictatorship of 1976–83. In the first excerpt, the death of a much-respected union leader and the disappearance of one of his loyal followers are described by the wife of the disappeared unionist. The excitement of a teenager at the cordobazo, followed by a lengthy incarceration, is recalled in the second interview. By way of contrast, the third interview is with a union leader who claimed to have experienced no serious losses throughout these turbulent years. The union movement in Córdoba had the full range of members, from militant dissidents to acquiescent survivors.

Some of the information in these interviews goes beyond the historical periods so far described. Where necessary, very brief notes are provided in square brackets or as endnotes regarding events or persons named. More detailed information is given in later chapters.

VOICE: DALINDA OLMOS DE DI TOFFINO

In 1970 I was thirty years old. I worked in the Córdoba Provincial Electricity Company (Empresa Provincial de Energía de Córdoba/ EPEC), which belonged to the province and still does. I began working there in 1958 when I was eighteen. Three or four years later I became a union representative for my sector and continued in that role thereafter, though I did not participate in the leadership of the Light and Power Union. In EPEC I met and in 1964 married a fellow worker, who was also a union representative for his sector. Today he is one of Argentina's 30,000 disappeared.

In our union there emerged a leader of international importance, who is now dead. His name was Agustín Tosco. He died while he was living in a clandestine way in 1975. Because of his irreproachable conduct, brilliance, and honesty, Tosco was the greatest leader the Light and Power Union had.

On 29 May 1969 Tosco and my husband took part in the *cordobazo*. On 30 May 1969 the military branch of the gendarmerie broke into the union offices and detained Tosco and my husband, along with many other union leaders whom the military considered responsible for the *cordobazo*. They were convicted, not through the legal system but by the Military Council of War, under the military dictatorship of General Onganía.

For two or three days I did not know where my husband was. I looked for him in the military barracks but could not find him. Then he appeared on a list as detained by the military. When his mother arrived to visit him, he was no longer there. He had already been judged, condemned, and transferred, first to nearby La Pampa, then 2,000 kilometres south to the Rawson Prison. My husband was sentenced to four years; Tosco, to eight years.

Our local union was part of the large Argentine Federation of Light and Power Unions, which in turn was part of the national CGT. Although the federation and the CGT went along with the dictatorship, our union wanted democracy and confronted the dictatorship. At the end of the 1960s, we were expelled from the main federation and then, with some other unions, we started another confederation called the CGT of the Argentines, headed by compañero Raimundo Ongaro. The people of the main federation controlled the medical and social services of all the unions. If a union left the federation, its members lost their medical and social services. But here in Córdoba we were very independent. After we were expelled, we created our own social services, managed by Tosco, and our own vacation centres, also managed by Tosco. Tosco persuaded fellow workers to purchase our own hotel in the mountains. We still own it. He also rented a place by the sea for the workers.

Even during his imprisonment, Tosco was still leader of our union. It was not intervened[14] until later. Along with some other unions, we put a lot of pressure on the government to free the people who were detained by the Military Council of War, and in December 1969 President Onganía ordered the release of prisoners detained by that council.

After the second *cordobazo*, in 1971, Tosco was again detained, this time for about two years and my husband for about two months, here in Córdoba. The union was intervened and the building was occupied by the military's appointed supervisor. The union employees remained and continued working. But outside the union, the resistance was organized by those who were left. Strikes and demonstrations, though illegal, were carried out. Of course the police repressed them, and arrested and beat people before 1976, but not to the degree we experienced later under the military. Members of compliant unions were never arrested, but Raimundo Ongaro, our general secretary, was. Tosco, who won re-election as union leader while still in prison, was released in September 1972. Then democracy returned to Argentina in 1973. Peronism won the election and Cámpora became president on 25 May 1973.

When Perón returned later that year, the events at Ezeiza Airport revealed the divisions in Peronism. The extreme right was on one side; the most progressive Peronists were on the other side. The two clashed, and that was the beginning of everything. Most unionists were Peronists, but our union, with Señor Tosco as general secretary, was pluralist. Tosco identified himself as a Marxist. There may have been some other Marxists from minor unions. Tosco never was part of a political party. He had his own philosophy, his thought, and he expressed it. Everybody on the left wanted to co-opt him; he was offered positions, deputations, vice-presidencies, but he always considered himself a worker who must remain with his union because we had entrusted him with our welfare, and that is how he died.

In February 1974 the government in Córdoba was Peronist, the progressive sector of Peronism, let us say. The vice-governor of Córdoba had been a leader in the CGT of the Argentines, the group of unions that had resisted the dictatorship. On 28 February 1974 the chief of police took over the governor's offices and took the governor and ousted him and the vice-governor, Atilio López. The police chief dismissed the democratically elected authorities, but Perón, the president of the country, did absolutely nothing. He did not punish the culprits, nor did he restore the elected authorities. He did nothing. Instead, the province was intervened. The national government put in the interveners. By September 1974, an air force officer and a police chief were in charge of our union and the union was controlled by right-wing Peronists. Then the persecutions of union leaders, activists, and dissidents in the progressive unions began. This especially affected our union and SMATA [Automobile, Mechanical, and Allied Workers' Union][15] at the Renault plant, where police took over the union and imprisoned workers. At this time many of our people began to have underground lives. My husband stopped sleeping in our house, though he continued to go to work. The right wing placed bombs in houses and also bombed and destroyed the building of the only newspaper that existed in the city, La Voz del Interior.

Agustín Tosco did not go to work, and they dismissed him from his job. He was underground already because they were searching for him. In 1975 and 1976 the bombs and the shootings continued, and they began to kill people. In September 1975 Atilio López was killed in Buenos Aires. That same year the Triple A also killed Dr Alfredo Caruchet, a union lawyer from Córdoba who was in Buenos Aires at the time. Well, all of 1975 was terrible, including the climate at work. Yet despite the fear, the resistance organization was restructured and there were clandestine organizations. There was also a mimeographed newsletter for workers.

In November 1975 Agustín Tosco died. My husband had maintained contact with him, so we knew he was ill; our union members had hidden him and helped him. When he died, the authorities gave permission for people to attend the memorial service. They regarded him as their enemy, but they recognized that he was an important figure. It was a historic memorial service for the workers of Córdoba. We knew it would be dangerous, and we were not sure what might happen at the ceremony. We marched from the memorial service to the cemetery, perhaps twenty thousand people. At the gate of the cemetery, members of other unions began to give their eulogies. But armed men had been posted at the church and inside the cemetery, and they began shooting. These armed men were police or from the intelligence services. You can imagine how it was, with so many people running all over the place, the coffin with the body, without the possibility of burying it because of the shooting. Some people were arrested, but nobody was killed. The intention was to terrify us, not kill us. Finally, some compañeros, including my husband, ran with the coffin to the grave, bullets flying around them, and they buried Tosco.

In January 1976, still under the constitutional government of Isabel,[16] the Triple A began disappearing many people in Córdoba. The first disappeareds were two young sisters, both students, fairly activist, who were seized at night. They were very young. The number of kidnappings and disappearances increased from January until the coup of 24 March 1976. Before then, the Triple A had killed in the streets and left the corpses there. Suddenly they began to take people without anyone knowing who had taken them. Alberto Cafaratti, the first person who disappeared from Light and Power, was taken during the day, in front of other people, in front of other *compañeros*. In the case of the sisters I mentioned, it was done during the night. For our *compañero*, yes, in the street, while he was leaving work, in front of all the people. It was done by men in civilian clothing, members of a paramilitary organization that existed in Córdoba. We hoped they would treat our *compañero* as an arrested person and not as a disappeared. Our unionists who had been imprisoned in 1974 were still detained. Agustín Tosco was already dead. And now we had a disappeared *compañero*. That January of 1976, when many kidnappings occurred here in Córdoba, we began to realize that something strange was happening. We began to see that it was probable our *compañeros* had been killed, but we did not know where they could be. Then the coup occurred in March.

I naively thought that the kidnappings would end when the coup came at last – that the things that made life impossible were going to end. My husband told me: "Don't fool yourself. The kidnappings are carried out by the police and military forces together." More of our members disappeared in July, 1976. Some *compañeros* collected money for the families of those who were imprisoned. Hernán Vives was doing that, and they knew it, so they kidnapped him. During all that time, from March to November 1976, my husband did not sleep at home, but he still went to work.

I was pregnant with my youngest child, who is now twenty-one years old, and my pregnancy had a lot of difficulties so I was confined to bed. It became obvious to me how the relationship of the employees with the company, the bosses, and the doctors changed after the coup. My physician told me I had to rest because I might lose the baby. After the coup I went again to the medical service and I told the doctor, an employee of the company, "Here is the certificate, I must stay home and rest." And he said to me, "Things have changed here. A military ambulance will go to your house to take you to the military hospital so that they can say whether you really need to rest." I think he said that so I would answer, "Well, if it is like that, I will go back to work." But I told him, "They can come to my house, then." They never came. But these doctors from the company appeared at my home at any hour to verify that I was in bed. It was because I was the wife of a persecuted union leader.

My baby was born in August and I then returned to work. According to our union contract, a mother could leave an hour earlier than the others when she had recently given birth. So one day in November I left early, and my husband left at the usual hour and was kidnapped in front of everyone. A *compañero* was following him because he wanted to talk with him, so he heard what the men who were kidnapping him said. They presented themselves as being from the federal police. They showed their credentials – they were dressed in civilian clothes. Those who watched the kidnapping recorded the number plate of the car. The next day, as I worked in the computing centre, I contacted some people I knew in the municipal offices to find out who owned that plate number. According to the computer, that number belonged to a man who was known by some of my *compañeros*, but he had nothing to do with all this. The police had simply taken this number; they put it on their car and went to kidnap my husband. They were able to do this because they controlled everything.

So from that day I began the search. Much later, in 1979, some *compañeros* contacted me. They had been imprisoned since 1974 and were released on condition that they leave the country. They told me that a person who had been detained in La Perla concentration camp had told them that my husband had been killed there around February 1977.

I sent letters to the United Nations and to the Organization of American States, giving them to a person who travelled abroad, and I wrote to unions abroad. Now I am going to present the case of Tomás Di Toffino in Spain, where judicial action regarding crimes against humanity is being prepared by a Spanish judge; the mother of Tomás Di Toffino was Spanish. Furthermore, there are the testimonies of the survivors who saw my husband in the La Perla concentration camp.

VOICE: MICHEL ENRIQUE

I can tell you something about the *cordobazo*. In 1969, when I was twelve or thirteen years old, I experienced the *cordobazo* in a working-class district, the "red" northern district, where many factory workers lived, especially workers from the railroad sector. The *cordobazo* was a massive expression of the opposition of workers and students to the military dictatorship of the time. It seemed more than just an attempt by the workers to reinstate the legitimacy of the unions, it was a fight for democracy – headed, without any doubt, by important union leaders.

This was not an isolated or spontaneous act of the masses, rather, it was an organized act of the masses directed by the unions of the time. Among the union leaders was Atilio López from the UTA [Transport Workers' Union], who became vice-premier of the province in 1973 but was murdered in 1975 by the Triple A; and Agustín Tosco from the Light and Power Union, a prominent figure of the left, and others like them. The first dead worker during the *cordobazo* was affiliated with SMATA [Automobile, Mechanical, and Allied Workers' Union].

The *cordobazo* left a very strong imprint on the labour movement of this city. It set back the military regime, and then there was the second strike a year later, what we called the *viborazo*. That was another massive demonstration, and it led to the looting of major supermarket chains. Most of all, these demonstrations were actions demanding the re-establishment of democracy, and they gave the labour movement here an important role in the national union structure. The leaders of the national movement had made compromises with the military dictatorship in the early stages [after the coup of 1955]. We provided renewed leadership to the union movement after the *cordobazo* and *viborazo*.

These events were also supported by the strong presence of the student movement of Córdoba. The students even met together with the assemblies of workers. Their motto was "Labour and Students will struggle together." Students were major participants in the *cordobazo*. Córdoba is a city with an important university and a strong cultural tradition. It was different in Buenos Aires. There, the students and the workers were separated. Students there were very much influenced by the events of May 1968 in France and the hippie movement, in which people rebelled against the system by wearing long hair and not using soap. Our rebellion was also influenced by Che Guevara and his death in Bolivia.

At that time there were two CGTs, two groups of workers, the Argentine CGT and the Azopardo CGT. There was also a group of independent unions, but the main division, without going into too much detail, consisted of the more combative and less combative unions. The more combative were in the Argentine CGT. However, at the time of labour action, all unions worked together. There was no sector left out.

You want to know how I became involved? As a secondary school student, I was deeply moved by the return of Perón. At that time I identified totally with Peronism. The return of Perón was for us the triumph of the Peronist resistance, the triumph of a movement that had been proscribed for many years, the triumph of the motto adopted by the Peronist Youth Movement, "Fight for his return."

On the day Perón was scheduled to return in June 1973, many followers in different groups travelled to Ezeiza Airport to welcome him. Before his plane was due to arrive, the rightist sectors launched an armed attack on sectors of the Peronist Youth and the guerrilla armed forces. Many people were killed. It was the beginning of a period of killings and kidnappings.There were some union organizations, especially their leaders, who allied themselves with the right in this confrontation. At the same time, the young people were questioning the bureaucratic attitude of union leaders of the time. The young saw Peronism as a national and revolutionary movement of the left.

After Perón's return, we, the progressive and popular sectors, became caught up in a struggle with the nationalist right for control of the state. It was almost fratricidal, this struggle between Peronists. It was encouraged and supported by the oligarchy, the right, and the grand Argentine bourgeoisie who were afraid that Perón and the most progressive sectors would form a more progressive government with some of the characteristics of socialism. The right was allied with the intelligence services of the armed forces under the National Security Doctrine of the U.S. State Department and the school of Panama. They all had great fear that Perón, allied with the most progressive sectors, would become the leader of a socialist country.

Well, in 1974 I was a public employee and became involved in the Public Employees' Union of the province of Córdoba. I did not have a strong union role, but in April 1976, during the coup, I was detained under state-of-siege legislation; and I was in jail for almost six years. The reason for my imprisonment was that I was a member of the Peronist Youth. I was not detained because of union activities; I was detained because of political activity. Everyone close to the Peronist Youth organization was detained, murdered, or disappeared. It was enough to be in the movement; you didn't have to do anything. The thing was that with the arrival of democracy in 1973, the Justicialist Party had become legal again. So membership was a public activity, nobody had tried to conceal it. My father-in-law, who was in the Justicialist Party and was at that time a councillor for the city of Córdoba, was also imprisoned.

The logic of repression is sometimes difficult to understand. Why did some people disappear and others not? I still can't find a logical explanation to that. I was detained by the police and the army. I was here in the Penitentiary Unit no. 1 of Córdoba, where thirty-six *compañeros* were killed. Some of them had also been detained under state-of-siege legislation; others with cause. These murders were followed by the information that inside the prison there would be three to five prisoners executed for every attack suffered outside by any policeman or military officer. They took two or three cellmates to the army offices and informed them of this intention, then returned them to prison so that they could tell their friends about it. They even informed them, vaguely, who they were going to get; and sometimes they told them the exact people they were going to select. That was really sadistic. No one knows what kind of judgment was used to determine who they would kill or not kill.

I remember the case of a cellmate who was a member of a union of public employees. One day we were being searched in the patio of the jail. It was a very cold morning, we were naked, and we were being hit with sticks. They hit him and he fell, and then, because he could not get up, the officer pulled out his weapon and shot him in the head. In another case they took the prisoner out of jail and they applied the "law of flight," which means they claimed he was killed while trying to escape. There was a case of a *compañero* being stretched out and beaten all night until he died. This could have happened to anyone regardless of any degree of political participation. Who knows what criteria were in effect? These were judgments made only by the security force.

VOICE: NORBERTO

In 1970 I was thirty years old and already a director of this CGT union. The country continued to hope for the return of General Perón, a man who had generated social justice and had worked for the workers, who had made laws and given us victories. Perón had given us elections, pensions, education, housing, and universities, so the people after that time always awaited his return. They fought hard to get him back, and the unions were the main permanent generators for achieving this, even when we had to deal with different military leaders.

Did the unions have a relationship to the guerrilla groups before Perón's return?

There was no relationship between the guerrillas and the unions. Many times the guerrillas fought against the unions, and there were attacks on union leaders. Where the subversive guerrilla groups attempted to implant a revolutionary system, they were minority groups, and the majority of Argentine society rejected them. Some of our leaders were killed at that time. José Ignacio Rucci, José Alonso, and many others. They were killed by the guerrillas or by paramilitaries. Some of our leaders were killed by them. Our leaders participated in the arrival of Perón at Ezieza, in the welcoming that we wanted to give the general. A million people descended on Ezeiza to wait for the return that had been so desired for so many years. However, some came with arms and many people were killed as armed groups from distinct ideological camps came into conflict.

When he came back to power, Perón was up against international capitalistic interests that wanted his form of government to fail. They created problems by not supplying consumers, by placing financial obstacles in the way of his government. And in some places the guerrillas took hold permanently. Perón was always against violence. He always said that the two extremes are bad. But international guerrillas constantly obstruct democracy in countries, and they do not permit a Latin American leader like Perón to develop the unification of Latin America for mutual defence. Perón once said so, in the Plaza de Mayo, when speaking to a group of young people who had influence with the guerrilla groups, groups who looked to the international left and were very much intimidated by the president of the nation, even though they insulted him because they sought political change. They were a minority group of young people who alienated the great mass of people.

After Perón's death, the country suffered from disorder and anarchy. The military also created dissension and conflict. Before the coup of 1976, the country went through a period of overwhelming social insecurity. Personal security did not exist, because bombs were placed in cinemas and in large central pedestrian squares. We thought they came from both sides, from subversives and from those who reacted to the subversives. The Triple A was fatal for the country. If you did not side with them, they took reprisals against leaders, activists, or students. The country had to live through many painful things during that era.

We did not wish for a coup d'état. We wanted democracy, we wanted to have a government that was elected by the people. Our union tried to negotiate a change of presidents, but not a military coup. After the coup, union activity was practically paralyzed. The unions were taken over, the CGT was taken over, leaders were jailed, leaders disappeared. In Córdoba we had six comrades who were detained immediately after the coup and they did not return for several months. They were detained under military decrees and repressive laws that the military immediately enacted against the workers and union leaders.

My union was not intervened. This was because it was a union that had pacifist tendencies for the workers. It was not a state union in which they were always protesting and fighting against the system, and it was not aligned with any of the extremists. That's probably the reason, and God's will, why they did not touch us. The six detained comrades had political ties; that is why they were detained. One was a deputy in the national congress, and the other was provincial secretary of sports and he was also a Peronist union leader. We were lucky enough to find these *compañeros* alive, and we ourselves were lucky not to be taken over by the military. Also, our union leaders were not fired as others were.

Although we were not intervened, we did not have a free union. They reduced all the union rights, and the union leaders lost all the powers they were democratically elected to exercise. All the unions were under military control, and some comrades who were not detained continued their union work. All were afraid of being detained or kidnapped. We were threatened by the guerrillas and the military – by the guerrillas because ideologically we were Peronists and by the military because we were Peronists. Leaders of extremist unions sometimes had other workers eliminated. Most unions suffered. The more combative unions, such as the Union of Metalworkers, a Peronist union, suffered the consequences, and their leaders were killed.

I think the military made mistakes. They took reprisals against innocents who had no opportunity to defend themselves; there were no explanations. But our union did not share anything with any extremists – guerrillas or unions. We thought that the only way to change the situation here would be to return to a democratic system.

CHAPTER 6

A Very Brief Revolution

Revolutionary movements emerged and proliferated throughout the country in the late 1960s and early 1970s. They were clubs of young, idealistic, middle-class students. Catholic students migrated to the Peronists and Montoneros; others, or Catholics with strong socialist convictions, to left-wing organizations. Superficially, these organizations had the same objectives and similar organizational formats. They sought to overthrow the military government and to create a new society, which they vaguely referred to as socialist. They cared about the poor, about the marginalized, about workers, and they believed they should offer leadership to these populations, helping them and guiding them to mount a revolution.

These organizations were generally authoritarian and hierarchical in form. They were composed of activists – or, as their former members describe themselves, "militants" – even those who were dedicated to literary and theoretical studies. They urged one another on to ever more violent rebuffs to the authorities. Their hero, whomever else they attended to, was Che Guevara (for most, as interpreted by Regis Debray, since Guevara wrote little and was dead by 1967). And for a brief period in the early 1970s, they were convinced that they were invincible.

Their differences were largely ideological. The small left-wing organizations had Marxist or Trotskyist roots and tended to be primarily engaged with theory. Their leaders were dedicated revolutionaries who took themselves to Cuba fairly early on, during the mid- to late 1960s, to learn both theory and tactics from Cuban revolutionaries. By contrast, although the Peronists sometimes called themselves socialists and some of their youngest followers believed they were socialists, most did not know much about socialism. Worse, for some of them, they did know about socialism but realized too late that they were not engaged in a socialist revolution. Whether Peronist or anti-Peronist, all of these movements were influenced by Peronism and by the brief return of Juan Perón to the Argentine stage.

STUDENT EXPERIENCES IN THE 1960S

The social context was violent, as all of our interviewees attested and as all histories of the period describe. For school and university students, there were especially violent events that became important signposts along the way to participation in a clandestine guerrilla organization. These signposts included the closure of literary and satirical magazines, police raids on night clubs, and punishment for girls or women dressed in short skirts. They also included restrictions on student political participation in university affairs, and government intervention in eight national universities during the early 1960s. One outcome was the emigration of an estimated three thousand faculty members and researchers. A particularly grisly memory for many who were students at that time is the "Night of the Long Sticks," 29 July 1966, when mounted federal policemen used truncheons against students at the University of Buenos Aires. As indicated by the account (in chapter 4, above) of the Rosario resident, María de los Angelus Yanuzzi, similar events were occurring elsewhere. In the mid-1960s this situation favoured the growth of Peronism. There had been hostility towards Peronism throughout the universities in the early 1960s, but by 1966, with the attacks on universities that followed the coup, the Peronists began to look like the only group capable of mounting a defence. A list of the various groups, with brief descriptions, is given in the appendix, but here we will follow the activities of the most prominent of these organizations.

REVOLUTIONARY ORGANIZATIONS 1968–73

The PRT/ERP and FAR

Of the several small left-wing groups formed in the late 1960s, the one led by Mario Roberto Santucho was the most active. This was the PRT/ERP: Partido Revolucionario de los Trabajadores (Revolutionary Workers' Party), which had emerged with Ejercito Revolucionario del Pueblo (People's Revolutionary Army). Anti-Peronist and Trotskyist in ideological origins, it subsequently turned to Guevarism. The PRT component was supposed to be the control centre; the ERP was the army. An occasional ally was the Fuerzas Armadas Revolucionarias, or FAR (Revolutionary Armed Forces), which at times cooperated with the ERP in kidnapping and robbery operations before its merger with the Montoneros; but FAR and the PRT/ERP sprang from very different ideological camps. ERP identified Argentina as a social formation within international capitalism and saw Peronism as an obstacle to the development of class-consciousness amongst the workers. FAR took the position that a revolutionary vanguard without followers was of no use and that Marxism-Leninism was not part of the folk experience of Argentine workers and thus would never become the ideology of the revolution. Peronism was the workers' ideology, and through it a revolutionary consciousness could be forged. The two perspectives were hotly debated in the early 1970s, before the members become so involved with the acts and consequences of armed insurrection that debate became a luxury.

Among the assassinations for which these two groups took responsibility was that of General Juan Carlos Sánchez, head of the 2nd Army Corps in Rosario, who was killed on 10 April 1972. On the same day, the ERP killed the head of Argentina's Fiat subsidiary after holding him prisoner for nineteen days.

The 1972 Trelew Massacre   Fighters with the ERP, together with FAR and Montonero political inmates at Rawson Prison in Trelew, Patagonia, attempted to break out in August 1972. A failure in communications with external operations prevented all but six of them from getting to Trelew's airport, where a plane awaited them. Nineteen guerrillas arrived too late, were forced to surrender, and were then shot; sixteen died, including eleven ERP members. Luis Mattini, in an insider's account of the ERP, argues that Trelew was the beginning of the "dirty war."[1]

Kidnappings and Killings after Trelew   ERP guerrillas refused to lay down their arms once elections were scheduled, arguing that the military would double-cross the population anyway and that a victory for Peronists was no victory for the people. Their record of violent acts during 1973 is long, including many of the 170 kidnappings of businessmen that year. They wounded two senior staff of Ford Argentina in June 1973, obliging Ford to pay the equivalent of $1 million for protection money, to be spent on medical equipment for the poor. A branch of the Peronist Youth objected to this "charity," saying that the people's new government could maintain hospitals.[2] Even the ERP's own troops were in disagreement about the wisdom of continuing violence under an elected government.

A splinter group (ERP – 22 de agosto) declared its solidarity with Peronist Youth and accused its former colleagues of sectarianism. Nor were the workers prepared to support ERP guerrillas; when a commando invaded a factory at the beginning of June 1973, the workers drowned out the speaker with cheers for Perón and Cámpora.[3] By July 1973, Cámpora was so sure of his support among workers and the youth movement that he gave a nationwide broadcast calling for an end to anarchy and violence. The ERP was isolated.

Juventud Peronista and the Montoneros

The Juventud Peronista (Peronist Youth or Young Peronists) was an outgrowth of earlier organizations such as Tacuara, a Catholic organization for schoolchildren that was virulently anti-Semitic and anticommunist. This and similar organizations used uniforms and ceremonies, including secret initiation rites, to maintain the enthusiastic participation of youngsters. In the early 1960s the Tacuara split, with various groups taking diverse ideological positions. One offshoot, the MNRT, tried to mount a bank holdup in the name of the working class in 1963; it was effectively destroyed by police shortly afterwards.[4] Another group moved toward social work among workers and the poor, and this group provided the nexus for many of the young people who became Young Peronists and Montoneros.

The Juventud was originally formed to oppose the government of General Onganía. Centred in high schools and universities, it expanded rapidly, and branches formed in workplaces throughout the country. After 1970, the organization became the junior, ideological arm of the Montoneros.

The Montoneros became the militant arm of Catholic youth. Three founding members, Fernando Abal Medina, Carlos Gustavo Ramus, and Mario Firmenich, had moved through earlier youth organizations and had concluded that Argentine society could not be changed through peaceful means. They were joined by José Sabino Navarro, who had previously led his own armed group in Córdoba and was the only member with working-class and lifelong Peronist credentials. Emilio Angel Maza headed a branch of the organization in Córdoba that launched raids on several banks to obtain funds for the movement. Nélida Esther (Norma) Arrostito was the only founding member who had come from a traditional left-wing background: she had broken with the Communist Party in 1967 and had travelled to Cuba the following year, together with Abal Medina, to learn about guerrilla tactics. By May 1970, there were twelve Montoneros, and it was this small group that claimed responsibility for the kidnapping and murder of General Aramburu. In communiqués, the organization announced that it was Argentine and Peronist, and "ready to fight with gun in hand for the seizure of power for Perón and his People," as well as being committed to "the Justicialist doctrine, of Christian and national inspiration."[5]

The name Montoneros originally belonged to frontier *gauchos* (cowboys) who roamed the pampas and, according to legend, defended the country in its infancy. A more sceptical version has them as ragtag armies hired by the *caudillos* (strongmen) who owned the estancias and essentially owned the *gauchos* as well. In legend, the name symbolized nationalism, and it clearly indicated that the new Montoneros were anti-imperialists and "pure" Argentines. Apart from its symbolic connotations, the name had a romantic flavour that was signally missing in the acronym labels of other revolutionary groups. As well, the movement called on the romantic legend of Evita Perón. Evita's claim that "Peronism will be revolutionary, or it will be nothing" and her call for revolution against the oligarchy became part of Montonero folklore. The Montonero official newspaper was called *Evita Montonera*.

Fernando Abal Medina and Carlos Gustavo Ramus died in an ambush in September 1970 (ostensibly in connection with their role in the killing of General Aramburu). Navarro was killed in a shoot-out in July 1971. The movement was then led by Mario Eduardo Firmenich.

Guido di Tella, a Radical Party politician of the later democratic period, has offered this description of the Montoneros:

They had developed an extremely romantic version of Peronism, idealising its past and producing a sceptical reaction even among old-timers. They were very much against the unions, considering them as bureaucratic intermediaries and distorters of the "true will" of the rank and file. They longed for spontaneous communications between the people and the leader, even rejecting the idea of a party in favour of the vague notion of a *Movimiento* in which there would be no bureaucracy, no affiliation and no elections, and where leaders would appear by natural consensus."[6]

This description is probably true enough, but it ignores the deep and violent context within which these young people forged their version of utopia, as well as the fact that, once they were organized, and up to 1974, these Peronist guerrillas were capable of eliciting popular support on a scale that boggles the mind. Tens of thousands of supporters joined them in demonstrations during the early 1970s. In the midst of an anarchic society given to extremely violent repression and reaction, with no group capable of governing, the Montoneros captured the public imagination and its fury.

They came from the middle class, not the class that had supported Perón. A biographer of their movement, Richard Gillespie, suggests that for many of them the Peronist movement was part of an adolescent rejection of parental political positions.[7] Whereas the parents remembered the actual Perón, their children listened avidly to the new Perón, who preached revolution and violence. Now Perón was openly aligning himself with Third World national liberation movements, with the Cuban revolution and Guevarist thinking, and with Mao Tse-tung's strategies. He was casting himself as a major leader in the struggle against U.S. imperialism, and his directives became increasingly hostile to capitalism. He sent audiotapes to his young followers, urging them to mount the revolution and to be as violent as necessary in order to seize power. He was also sending right-wing messages to union followers, but this was not known by the young Peronists until much later.

Montoneros and the Third World Priests' Movement

During this uncertain time, the Catholic Church itself was undergoing dramatic changes. Under the papacies of John XXIII and Paul VI, the Vatican began to revise its stance on the role of the church in caring for the poor, even to the point of suggesting that Marxism contained some acceptable messages. The Second Vatican Council in 1965 went so far as to equate true socialism with a full Christian life. In 1967, Pope Paul VI attacked the profit motive, inequality, racism, and much else of the capitalist societies, in a proclamation[8] that had profound implications for the church in Argentina.

These ideas were quickly disseminated. With the Pope's apparent blessing, the Third World Priests' Movement[9] was born in 1967. A document put out by the "Third World Bishops" critically assessed capitalism. It differentiated between the "unjust violence of the oppressors" and the "just violence of the oppressed," though it criticized Marxism and armed revolution. By the time of the 1968 Medellin (Colombia) Conference of the Latin American Episcopate, this document had the support of many priests. As our interviews demonstrate, the Medellin Conference was a major impetus for the Montoneros as well as for the priests. In fact, it was this movement which brought the two groups together. From its inception, the joint venture had contradictory interpretations of the Medellin position. Juan García Elorrio, a follower of the teachings of a murdered Colombian priest, Camilo Torres, argued that "revolution is not only permitted but is obligatory for all Christians who see in it the most effective way of making possible a greater love for all men."[10]

The alternative was expressed by Father Carlos Mugica: "I am prepared to be killed but I am not prepared to kill."[11] Mugica, in Richard Gillespie's interpretation, adopted Peronism as a young adult because he regretted the church's support for the overthrow of Perón in 1955. This Jesuit priest felt that as a consequence of that event, many Argentine workers identified the church with the oligarchy and the military regimes that followed. This "helps to explain why he adopted an exceedingly naive attitude towards Peronism when he entered the popular camp," says Gillespie. Before the establishment of the Third World Priests' Movement, Mugica met up with schoolboys Abal Medina, Ramus, and Firmenich in his role as spiritual adviser in the Catholic Student Youth organization. He took the boys to shantytowns to work with the poor, and he preached the social gospel. According to Firmenich, he set them on their path.

Eventually, however, the three students moved on to armed struggle as the means of ridding their world of oppressors. In 1967 they linked up with Juan García Elorrio in the Camilo Torres command group, which was now committed to Peronism, socialism, and armed struggle. Elorrio had published the influential *Cristianismo y revolución* (Christianity and Revolution) in 1966. This publication radicalized many Argentine priests and a few bishops who supported the Third World Priests' Movement, and by glorifying militants who had died in revolutionary struggles, it created a culture for young radicals that included acceptance of violent death as its reward. Mugica was killed in May 1974, presumably by the Triple A.

OTHER DEVELOPMENTS

The Execution of General Aramburu, 1970

As noted in the previous chapter, there may have been protagonists in this adventure other than the young revolutionaries. General Aramburu had certainly gained the hatred of the Peronists, and Perón's continuing fulminations against him kept the hatred burning, but General Onganía and his faction had their own reasons for wanting to dispose of Aramburu, for he was conspiring against the regime and making preparations to oust Onganía. This is the backdrop to the argument that the Montoneros were the "recipients" of Aramburu following his abduction and that some deal was made for his detention and assassination. The argument was made by a friend of Aramburu[12] whose source claims that the government paid for the killing by a third party but that a member of the third party doublecrossed the government and called the police. The informer died a few months later, so there is no known living proof for this theory. Part of the theory involves the claim that persons close to the crime say that Aramburu voluntarily left his house with people he knew, not under force, and that the "kidnappers" were older than the Montoneros (for example, Abal Medina, who was killed by police in an attack ostensibly connected to this kidnapping, was only twenty years old). One variant of this theory is that Aramburu was kidnapped by intelligence services and then turned over to a gang that subsequently labelled itself the Montoneros.[13] In his 1982 study of the Montoneros, Richard Gillespie dismisses the theory as improbable, based on circumstantial and weak evidence, and flawed by an erroneous political characterization of the Montoneros.

Later Information on Firmenich
as Double Agent

A decade later, however, Martin Andersen, who had been a journalist for *Newsweek*, the *Washington Post*, and other periodicals in that period, produced some evidence of collaboration between Mario Firmenich and the intelligence services of the army. According to Andersen, Firmenich was working as an army intelligence officer in 1973 and may also have had that role in 1970. Andersen's source was a retired American diplomat who had had direct access to top Argentine army officers at the time and had filed dispatches regarding guerrilla activities based on the information provided by the "handler" of Firmenich, Colonel Alberto Valín. A federal police officer, Alberto Villar, had apparently been unconvinced by the Montonero story and had launched an independent investigation of the Aramburu kidnapping. Martin Andersen obtained information about this investigation during several interviews with a retired federal police commissar who had been a confidant of Villar's. Andersen claims that the U.S. intelligence community took it for granted that Firmenich was a collaborator. He also points out that, within a year, Abal Medina and Ramus had been killed in a police ambush and that over the next few years virtually every other leader was killed or disappeared – yet Firmenich miraculously survived numerous tight situations.[14]

The debate on this matter is crucial to our understanding of what occurred at this time. If Firmenich (and possibly others, as was suggested by some of the military personnel we interviewed) was either an officer in the intelligence services (as Andersen claims) or was otherwise in the pay of the army, then the Montoneros were essentially set up as an enemy and were used by the military to justify repression of the "left." A large number of the victims were Young Peronists who were caught up in the excitement of utopian rhetoric in the early 1970s.

This debate was already in progress in the 1970s because of inconsistencies in the claims of Montoneros about the Aramburu murder, but there is no evidence that the loyalties of the rank-and-file Juventud and Montoneros were affected by such suspicions. The entire structure was built on a "cell" formation, so that many members had no idea who was in the armed sections, and most had limited communication with members outside their immediate group. (This is clear from the interviews with young guerrilla fighters that are reported in later chapters).

Few of the original guerrilla leaders survived the ambushes and raids launched against them in the months following Aramburu's murder. Those who did survive were shielded by Peronists in the general population and by some Third World priests, including Father Carlos Mugica, who officiated at the funeral of Abal Medina and Ramus. A groundswell of popular support surprised the authorities. Contrary to their expectations, the murder of Aramburu and some others elicited praise rather than condemnation from the population. Within that context, other, smaller organizations joined the Montoneros, which eventually included FAR, FAP, and the Descamisados (see the appendix for a description of these groups). Prior to the election of 1973, the Peronist revolutionary movement headed by the Montoneros concentrated on bank robberies and attacks on barracks to obtain funds and guns, but they also planted bombs in the homes of foreign executives and in police stations, and they kidnapped several leading businesspeople and army intelligence officers.

Revolutionaries and the CGT

Whatever may be the truth about the leaders of the Montoneros, the vast majority of young revolutionaries expressed a deep longing for a revolution that would achieve the equality and empowerment of citizens. They wanted to forge links with the working class, but for most of them the working class was an abstraction. They did not belong to it, yet they longed to lead it to a glorious revolution. They were persuaded that if they provided the vanguard, workers would naturally become revolutionaries. But unlike most of this self-appointed vanguard, the workers had families to support and jobs to defend. Those who wanted more militant action had already tried that route, through alternative union organizations. The *cordobazos* were an expression of their discontent, but workers in general were not prepared to tolerate a permanent revolution either in the workplace or in their societies. This attitude was interpreted by the Montoneros as resulting from intimidation by the union bureaucrats.

Apart from the ideological schisms, the mutual intolerance between most of the unions and the guerrillas had roots in a power struggle.

Both groups wanted the return of Perón, but both believed that Perón was on their side, and both were jockeying for a place in government that would outlast the aging leader. Not all the unions, however, were in line with the CGT. As noted in our Córdoba interviews in the previous chapter, the *cordobazos* were not the end of the workers' rebellions. Agustín Tosco, leader of the light and power workers, openly defied the Peronist leaders of the CGT and agitated for revolutionary changes in union organization.[15]

Right-Wing Peronist Youth

Union antipathy toward the Peronist Youth gave birth to the Juventud Sindical Peronista (JSP). Organized by the CGT, these young people arrived at rallies prepared to shout down and fight with their revolutionary counterparts. They were joined by an organization of right-wing university youth, the Concentración Nacional Universitaria (CNU) and the quasi-army that Perón had organized in the 1950s, the National Liberating Alliance (ALN). All these groups, from the extreme left to the extreme right, were contained within the Peronist movement.

THE SECOND COMING

Perón's stand-in, Héctor Cámpora, had won the 1973 election; the military forces were fractured, despised, and in retreat; there was every reason for union members and guerrillas to lay down their arms and plan a peaceful transition to democracy. But the antagonists were unable to take that road, for already there was a power struggle for the succession. The aged Perón was clearly out of touch with the 1970s, and all his followers could see that the future would belong to whichever faction captured his favour before he died.

The competition for power had been intensified by Péron's own actions. In October 1972 he had appointed Juan Manuel Abal Medina (brother of Fernando, but not a Montonero), as secretary general of the party, and had negotiated an agreement that gave the Juventud (effectively, the Montoneros) one-third of all electoral offices at all levels, which meant that their power in the Peronist party would be equal to the political and trade union branches.

Killings at Ezeiza

Perón was scheduled to return to Argentina on 2 June 1973, and a gigantic rally had been planned at Ezeiza Airport. Its chief architect was Perón's former security chief of army intelligence, Lt-Col. Jorge Osinde, together with his current secretary, José López Rega. A private army of more than three thousand men was organized to provide security, and the podium was occupied by the right-wing CNU and ALN, armed with machine guns and other weapons. The apparent objective was to outflank the guerrillas and the Juventud. As Perón's arrival time neared in mid-afternoon, the Montoneros and FAR members marched toward the podium. They were met by machine-gun fire, and for the next two hours and more, Ezeiza Airport was a battleground. An estimated twenty people were killed and four hundred wounded. Perón's jet was diverted to land at the air force base west of Buenos Aires.

Cámpora as Interim President

Cámpora's government was the invention of Perón, and its appointment of provincial governors and federal ministers followed Perón's practice of balancing the right and left wings of the party.[16] One of the first acts of the Cámpora government was to grant an amnesty to political prisoners. The mass-circulation newspaper *Clarín* had argued that an amnesty "could be the starting point for dismantling the vicious circle of conflict,"[17] and there was support for the measure on the left and amongst intellectuals. The Montoneros had announced a temporary suspension of violence, conditional on the creation of revolutionary programs by the government. In May 1973, shortly before Perón's return, they had selected six governors and two cabinet ministers (Foreign Ministry and Ministry of Interior), indicating a substantial degree of power within the Peronist party. Yet Mario Firmenich, when interviewed by *El Descamisado* later in the year, stated that his organization would not abandon force: "Political power comes out of the mouth of the rifle," he said. "If we have come up to this point, it is because we had rifles and we used them. If we abandoned them, we would suffer a setback in our political position. In war there are moments of confrontation, such as those that we have gone through, and there are months of truce in which preparations are made for the next confrontation."[18]

Soon after taking office, the Cámpora government attempted to introduce the "social pact," an agreement regarding the redistribution of income in return for abandonment of strikes by unions. Perón, always guiding Cámpora's agenda, needed the support of the trade unions for this agreement, and he began to woo the secretary general of the CGT, José Rucci. The resulting pact was more popular on the right (which sought a reduction in the soaring inflation rates and hoped this might suffice) than on the left. The Montoneros and the ERP condemned it and named Rucci a public enemy. Shortly afterwards, indeed two days after Perón's election as president, Rucci was assassinated.

Perón pushed out Cámpora on 12 July 1973 and caused the presidency to be given, on an interim basis, to Raúl Lastiri, head of the Chamber of Deputies (and son-in-law of Perón's secretary, José López Rega). New elections were scheduled for September, and Perón was now allowed to be a candidate. He chose his third wife, Isabel, as his running mate. He had met Isabel – her actual name was María Estela Martínez – in Panama, where she had been a night club dancer. Lastiri had been the club's manager.

President Perón Again

President again, Perón removed most of those appointed under the Cámpora government, along with bureaucrats in provincial and national governments whom he distrusted. At the University of Buenos Aires, where Cámpora had installed a left-wing rector, Perón installed a right-wing replacement. He moved against the left-wing Juventud, against army leaders who had been tolerant of left-wing activities, and against supporters of left-wing groups. Since he no longer needed the left-wing groupies, he made little effort to retain their services, and he showed no inclination to be the revolutionary leader they so earnestly desired. Over the next several months, Perón pushed out provincial government leaders who were sympathetic to the left, and by February 1974 he was ready to dump the Montoneros and their supporters. Eight of their deputies resigned after the passage of laws to punish political crimes. The Montoneros issued the following statement:

General Perón himself has often said that violence from above creates violence from below, that conditions of dependency and exploitation stimulate active resistance. Of course, since there is a popular government, violence from above does not exist, and therefore there should be no violence from below. But this is only a half truth, because there are contradictory elements within the popular government. Officials from the previous regime survive, and have allied themselves with reactionary sectors of the Peronist movement."[19]

The last of the left-wing governors, Obregón Cano of Córdoba, was removed in a police action in March 1974. Perón's government did not intervene on behalf of the elected official; a right-wing replacement took office.

With Perón's return came a revival of the corporatist policies of the 1945–55 period, including the "social pact" that Cámpora had introduced. The pact was a proposal to hold prices and wages constant for two years. Controls extended to investment, interest rates, trade, and production, and various new laws began the process of reorganizing a syndicalist if not corporatist society. Several laws gave union officers a range of special rights, including immunity from prosecution. This enabled the Peronist labour bureaucracy to increase its power over the union movement, and it soon began ridding the movement of dissident factions. Some non-Peronist leaders were arrested; others went into hiding, including Agustín José Tosco of the Córdoba Light and Power Union. Offices were raided, and non-Peronist unions such as the teachers' federation (CTERA) were replaced.

Within a year the social pact was abandoned. It had seemed to work for a while in 1973, but the decline in oil prices, the increase in other world-market imported products, and conflicts from both business and workers reduced its ameliorative capacities. By March 1974, strikes were occurring again, and loyal Peronists were not receiving unmitigated approval in union elections. In fact, internal frictions in the labour movement were violent, widespread, and beyond centralized control.[20]

At the same time, kidnappings and assassinations of union leaders were occurring with some frequency. The secretary general of the automotive mechanics' union, SMATA, had been killed in May 1973; and as noted above, José Rucci was killed in September. A number of other union leaders suffered a similar fate, as did many business managers and owners. The perpetrators were variously believed to be (or announced themselves as) the Montoneros, the ERP, or one of the smaller groups, though later studies suggest that some at least were instigated by Perón's own advisers, especially by José López Rega.

The kidnappings of business leaders were more clearly attributable to the guerrillas and were typically attempts to gain funds. Kodak, Vestey, the First National Bank of Boston, Firestone, and Esso were among the targeted companies whose executives were abducted for ransom and who were known to have paid $1 million and much more. The ransoms financed the revolutionaries. Some of the kidnapped executives were killed by their captors, possibly because of the captors' ineptitude or because they were convicted of crimes judged by a "people's court." The climate was unfavourable for further investment, and there was an exodus of companies already established.

PART THREE

Escalation of Violence

CHAPTER 7

The Dirty War

The dirty war began in 1973, under the government of Juan Perón. It was not a declared war, there was no specific legislation addressing it, and there were no rules. It was an escalation of the violence that had marked the whole period since the late 1960s, with the added component of right-wing terrorist groups organized by an agency of the state.

The term "dirty war" was coined by the army for the battle against guerrillas. It is not accepted by all who were harmed by military and paramilitary groups, their argument being that no war was ever declared and that this was, rather, an insidious terror against anyone deemed to be "leftist."[1] We use the term here despite this argument, because during this period there most certainly was a civil war in progress. Terrorists of different political stripes fought one another and also killed noncombatants. Yet it was not a war between equal and clearly demarcated "sides"; rather, it was widespread civil strife involving numerous armed contestants, topped by the state. The state was unambiguously, even if covertly, involved in committing terrorist acts and in using its military and police, as well as paramilitary forces, to kill its perceived enemies.

Complicating our understanding of this period are the many sub-struggles that were in progress: competition for power within the union bureaucracy and between Peronist and dissident unions; competition between young guerrillas or their supporters and union leaders; and numerous other rivalries between leaders of various factions within the Peronist movement. The movement embraced both the extreme right and the extreme left, with both ends in constant battle, and with many casualties among noninvolved moderates as well as extremists. The wounded and assassinated could thus be victims of right-wing terrorists, Peronist groups, guerrillas, or even factions that used the cover of other groups to exterminate their own enemies. Some of the assassinations carried out by the state were blamed on guerrilla groups, and sometimes the guerrilla groups accepted responsibility for them, because this enhanced their image as fearless warriors.

ASSASSINATION SQUADS AND MUZZLING OF THE PRESS

The murders of CGT union officials were attributed to the Montoneros (the ERP, the People's Revolutionary Army, was not a likely contender), but the selective murder of left-wingers could be attributable only to right-wing death squads. Such assassination gangs were unlikely to exist without Perón's knowledge. He had used assassins before, so why not now? The Montoneros called them by a name that Perón himself had used in his letters from Madrid: "the gorillas." But when the media attempted to find out about them, it discovered just how sensitive Perón was to any publicity on that score. When a reporter for the leftist *El Mundo* newspaper asked Perón at a press conference whether the police were going to investigate the fascist death squads, both she and the newspaper suffered serious consequences. She was arrested for "disrespect" and several months later was kidnapped and severely beaten up.[2] A few days after the press conference, the newspaper was closed. The stated reason was that it had carried a report on a press conference given by the underground ERP at which the ERP had said it had been paid a ransom for the release of a kidnap victim. This report, it was argued, showed that the newspaper had "clear connections with the action of illegal organizations."

The *Buenos Aires Herald* then noted in an editorial that it had been under pressure from the government because it, too, had published an account of the ERP conference and had commented on the release of the Exxon subsidiary executive on payment by his employers of US$14.2 million to the ERP. A month later a court overruled the government regarding the closure of *El Mundo*, on the grounds that closure by edict was unconstitutional. But before the paper could rejoice, its premises were bombed.

Attacks on the media were not confined to left-wing organs. The Córdoba newspaper *La Voz del Interior* was attacked by armed men, believed to be police, in reprisal for coverage of a murder done by police. State-owned radio stations dismissed journalists suspected of sympathizing with the left. A bomb threat was made against *La Capital* of Rosario. And so it went on, day in and day out, throughout 1973 and 1974. Some of the bombs and threats were attributed to left-wing Peronists, some to right-wing Peronists.[3] No discernable diminution occurred after the Argentine Press Federation issued a statement on the attacks, "criticising Left and Right, police excesses, lack of legal guarantees, self-censorship by proprietors and the absence of protection by publishers for journalists."[4]

PERÓN'S CLOSING STATEMENT

Two months before his death, Perón chose a mass rally in the Plaza de Mayo to distance himself from the Montoneros and Juventud. The Labour Day meeting in 1974 was a great festive occasion, during which the unions marched into the square and established themselves at the front, followed by the Juventud and the Montoneros with their flags flying high. In a crowd estimated to number 200,000,[5] the young people chanted slogans against Isabel Perón and López Rega. Perón reacted in anger and denounced his young followers. He called them "the beardless ones," and *estúpidos* (a stronger term than "stupid" in English) and told them, essentially, to grow up. The government news agency Telam called it the "excommunication" of the revolutionary tendency. Perón told his audience that the government was committed to the liberation of Argentina from external colonial forces and also "from these treacherous infiltrators who work from within, and who are more dangerous than those who work from the outside."[6]

Union workers then stood up and confronted their erstwhile allies, and the entire rally became threatening. The Montoneros, who apparently had not anticipated this response from Perón, quickly departed. Some participants said they fled; others claimed they marched out with dignity. Either way, this was the end of the truce between organized labour, Perón, and the guerrilla fighters. The Montoneros went underground that May 1974 (though Mario Firmenich actually called a press conference to announce the decision to go underground the following September).[7]

Perón had banked on the continuing support of the union leaders, for whom he had taken such risks, but the labour movement was by now an autonomous force. It could not be counted on to support Peronism, and after the 77-year-old Perón died on 1 July 1974, Isabel Perón classed the unions among her chief enemies.

ISABEL AND LÓPEZ REGA

The violence intensified after Juan Perón's death. Isabel Perón, thrust into the presidency without public support and facing a military coup from the moment she took office, could maintain her government only through force. Civil war was already far advanced as the many factions, both within Peronism and against Peronism, created general chaos in the streets. Isabel declared a "state of siege" to counter the guerrillas, though she did not outlaw the Montoneros or put legal controls on union-employed "bodyguards." These were among the numerous groups engaged in bloody battles. Instead, she directed the armed forces and police to rid the country of subversives, a term that embraced genuine guerrillas but also included students, left-leaning intellectuals and artists, trade union leaders, journalists, liberal lawyers, and various others deemed to be enemies of the state by the government and its organized assassins. Lawyers who defended Triple A victims or their families became targets of state repression themselves.

The Triple A

The Triple A (Argentine Anticommunist Alliance) was a clandestine organization established within, or with the approval of, the Ministry of Social Welfare in Isabel's government. A loose organization of right-wing hit squads, it included some police and some army personnel. The Triple A targeted both known left-wing leaders and others whom its members suspected of supporting subversive activities.

Its chief, José López Rega, was the trusted adviser to the president. A police corporal in the 1950s, López Rega had managed to insinuate himself into Isabel's retinue as her spiritual adviser. By the time the Peróns returned to Argentina from their exile in Madrid, he had gained so much power over both Juan Domingo and Isabel that he became known as "the Sorcerer." In Juan Perón's final months, López Riga, who had been designated private secretary to the president, had already formed the nucleus of the Triple A. In Isabel's government, he exercised control of the state apparatus and used it against contenders for political power from either the left or the right. Because it was both clandestine and loosely organized, the Triple A was hard to pin down. Imitator groups, including other members of the military and police forces, worked independently of the Ministry of Social Welfare but under cover of the same name. Payment for activities was, of course, not acknowledged by the ministry.

Triple A hit-squads established some trademarks: they travelled in Ford Falcons without licence plates; typically, they left corpses shot at close range in ditches and roadways or burnt-out cars; and they boasted of their exploits. Although police were informed, they rarely acted on complaints, and the government did nothing to deter the Triple A. As described below by Osvaldo Bayer, the Triple A was so confident of its immunity from prosecution that it advertised its plans to murder prominent figures if they failed to go into exile within twenty-four hours.

Ignacio González Janzen, in an extended study of the Triple A, contends that López Rega and the beginnings of the Triple A planned the killings at Ezeiza Airport when Perón was expected to arrive there in 1973.[8] Later victims attributed to the Triple A under Lopéz Rega were General Carlos Prats, the Chilean exile who had served under Salvador Allende, and many former governors and union leaders. Others fled when they received the Triple A's "anonymous" warnings via newspaper notices.

In Córdoba, General Raúl Lacabanne, who took over the governor's post in September, launched a policy of complete liquidation of guerrillas. The Democratic Socialist Party, or PSD (Partido Socialista Democrático), which had consistently opposed the guerrillas and supported efforts to subdue them, issued a statement saying that it observed "with horror the excesses and arbitrary actions which are being inflicted on the population of Córdoba by the police, in the guise of fighting the guerrillas."[9]

The repression of leftists was combined with intense infighting within Isabel's government and between its ministers and trade union leaders. The removal of the economy minister, José Ber Gelbard (appointed by Juan Péron), was the work of Lorenzo Miguel, the secretary general of the Metalworkers' Union (UOM) and leader of the Peronist 62 Organizations; in this, he sided with López Rega. But no sooner had their candidate replaced Gelbard than López Rega and Miguel were caught up in various disputes, which resulted in Miguel losing his position.[10] Throughout the months that followed, López Rega undermined other trade union leaders, many of whom ended up in prison under state-of-siege legislation.

VOICE: OSVALDO BAYER

We made a film that won the Berlin prize, the Silver Bear, in 1974. The film was called *The Patagonian Rebellion*.[11] I wrote four volumes, which were published in 1972, and then the film on the rebellion. This caused much uneasiness in the military, and because of that I came to be on the list of the Triple A in the times of Isabel Perón and had to leave the country.

It was very easy to learn that you were on the list. You would be there in the morning having breakfast, and you would read the morning paper and there was the list, in all the papers. The Triple A of López Rega would telephone the newspapers and say, "In the washroom of La Paz café," for example, "there is a new list of those condemned to death." Then all the journalists would go to the washroom of La

Paz café, and the next day it would be published as very important news.

You would have twenty-four hours to leave the country; if not, you were dead. The first persons named refused to go because they didn't believe it. For example, Professor Silvio Frondizi[12] refused to leave the country. The next day they searched for him, and they held him in his house, where they killed him. His body was found on the road to Ezeiza Airport. He had been shot 110 times. That was typical. The corpses were dumped on the road to Ezeiza. It was the terror. They wanted to imprint the terror so that people would leave the country, especially left-wing intellectuals.

I read my name in *La Opinión*. That same day I sent all my family to Germany, but I stayed. For me it was a great injustice because, well, I had achieved the fulfilment of my dream to write about historic themes and to take my work to the cinema. Suddenly, exile meant starting all over again. I appeared on the list in October 1974. I stayed until February of 1975. I was here, let's say, illegally, for four months. I went to live in hidden places. I stayed with friends, with an old Spanish anarchist who had a large orchard on the outskirts of Buenos Aires. I couldn't work, couldn't even go to the bank to withdraw money. And then money became so inflated that finally I had to leave. In February 1975 I went to Germany.

When, at the beginning of 1976, Isabel Perón called elections, I thought, good, this was the moment to return. And I returned alone in February 1976. Four weeks later Videla's coup d'état occurred, and immediately it was impossible to leave the country because the borders were guarded. These were the worst months of the repression. In June 1976 I took refuge in the German Embassy, and they got me out; they treated me very well. But I was the only one they took out. Here there were only two countries that gave refuge to people in danger – Mexico and Venezuela.

Then, for me, began the long exile in Germany, until October 1983, when I returned. Meanwhile, many friends were assassinated. My books were officially burned. The stupidity of the dictatorship was incredible and even included public communiqués stating that the burning of books was done for God, mother country, and home. These were public documents which they published themselves, with pride, furthermore. The libraries were expurgated, especially the university libraries and certain faculties. There is much to be said about the silence of the "intellectual Argentine Parnassus" – the firmament in which the great Argentine intellectuals live. They all supported the dictatorship because they had such hatred toward Peronism.

VOICE: CATERINA

When they killed Silvio Frondizi in 1975, we went to the wake. The military were not yet in power. We don't know how they were identified, but many people who were at the wake were threatened, some by telephone, some by bombs thrown at their houses. Those that were lucky left the country. Others disappeared.

There were thousands of people at the wake, but there were many people from the services who infiltrated the "alumni" in the organizations that came from the university. Inside these armed groups of activists, such as the Montoneros and ERP, there were people who were as criminal as those they wanted to have killed. It was terrible. At that time, however, we did not know all this. There was so much yearning for change that we blinded ourselves. There was such a huge cultural movement then, a revival of Argentine culture – movie directors, sculptors, painters, writers, all trying to bring about change.

VOICE: DANTE

The important events began with the death of Perón, that is, on 1 July 1974, but personally it all began for me when my brother was killed in May 1975. He was twenty-three years old, and I was eighteen. He was active in a party of the left, in a section of the Revolutionary Workers' Party [PRT], not in the armed section but in the section involved with the Internationale in Paris, in the RED faction that was opposed to armed struggle. He was working in the print shop. It was a small shop, three or four workers, just publishing for the PRT. There was an attack by armed forces. They appeared to be federal police. I believe it was a legally sanctioned process – there is a police precinct that has records of the event. For the armed forces, the difference between those who advocated armed opposition and those who wrote about it was not understood. My brother was shot in the forehead, so it was deliberate. In this attack, he and one other died.

VOICE: VERÓNICA

My experience in the 1970s was typical of my generation. In the early years I was a member of a university political group in the industrial city of Rosario. We talked about politics all the time, even when the main subject of discussion should have been our studies. We were obsessed by the problem of poverty in the Third World. Workers had a lot of influence on the students, and we were also influenced by student movements in France and at Berkeley. For people like myself, who came from a Catholic background, the Third World priests were a strong influence. My own entry into political life and into political activism was through Catholic groups. Also, Peronism had a very strong impact. We had reconstructed Peronism because we were too young to have experienced Perón's actual government. We believed that he had provided the workers with better social conditions and dignity. For that reason, there was a certain Catholic, religious mentality that followed Peronism. For a great part of my youth, I was a Peronist. When I started university, I became a member of the Peronist Youth.

We were very young. Many were killed. At first we thought violence was necessary in order to get rid of the military regime. For this reason, when General Aramburu was killed by the Montoneros, well, it didn't upset us at all. We thought of him as being one of the military leaders who were responsible for poverty, for domination over the people.

After Perón's return, there was a struggle between the left and the right within the Peronist movement. We were accused of being Marxists, and we accused the union bureaucrats and right-wing groups within Peronism of being fascists. We thought Perón sided with the left, but he was surrounded by right-wingers. At the great rally in May 1974, in the Plaza de Mayo in Buenos Aires, we came in as columns of Peronist Youth and Montoneros, with nothing in our hands, and then we gradually realized that the buildings around us were occupied by armed people. The place right in front of the plaza was occupied by right-wing unions, and they were armed with chains and steel rods. It was a very tense situation, and Perón had not yet appeared on the balcony of the Presidential Palace. When he appeared, he said, "Those stupid people who are shouting ..." It was us. At that moment, those who were next to us, the unionists, drew their chains and their rods, and we all ran away. I was very frightened. I thought they would kill us.

During the next few years, we were always frightened. I recall one night when I was supposed to meet a friend who was an activist in the Peronist Youth movement. When I arrived at her house, there was nobody there. I saw a car with someone inside a few metres away. It was a green Falcon, the make that the military and police used. I panicked and ran away. No one followed me. But this gives you an idea of how we lived, always terrified that something we were doing was going to bring about our downfall. At night we would pile heavy furniture against the door for fear that armed men would break in, even though we had done nothing.

The right-wing paramilitary force known as the Triple A began to circulate lists of the people it would kill if they did not leave the country right away. My husband, who was a psychiatrist, became afraid. We couldn't tell rumour from truth. There were psychiatrists on the lists. We moved to an apartment where nobody knew us, an underground life. We burned a lot of books and buried others. We burned the books in the kitchen sink because we were afraid that they would come at night – armed groups at first, and then, after the coup, the military. I feel certain that for anyone of my generation during those years, life was very difficult. Afterwards, one could not recover entirely. There are still a lot of bruises.

VOICE: ROMEO

I entered the University of Buenos Aires as a seventeen-year-old student in 1973, in the Faculty of Philosophy and Letters. I came from a small town in the interior of the province of Buenos Aires. It was a revolutionary time and the faculty was very politicized. Before I started classes, I had to go to the university to complete the paperwork and write entrance examinations, so my first exposure was in November 1972. The first or second day there was an assembly. On the podium there were two militants of the ERP, who boasted that they had burned the house of the former dean and showed evidence of his burned weekend house. In fact, there were three people – the man who talked and two guards, who were armed. They said this dean had been condemned because he had informed on several students. I was impressed, but I have to say that the climate there was only an extension of a more general climate, even in my home town with only 20,000 inhabitants.

When I started classes the following March, I can say from today's point of view, there was little that was academic; we had classes about Ernesto Guevara and Mao Tse-tung. I felt very good about this, because I was seventeen, and I thought that I was changing the world and was changing it right now. I had a *compañero* who was a Catholic priest of the Third World Movement. I went to meetings of Trotskyists, Maoists, and Guevarists, but ended up joining the Juventud. I first took part just as a sympathizer, without too much commitment, through all of 1973. But beginning in 1974, I became a more active member. That meant, first, being political in the university. The government of the University of Buenos Aires was composed of teachers and students. In the university elections, each group presented its proposals, and we won overwhelmingly. We had a strong alliance with the rector, who was close to the Montoneros. Our task was to try to implement our political ideas in the university environment. We considered ourselves part of a political-military organization.

We had a logo in the Juventud – a Tacuara stick, which is a spear. The Tacuara spear is what the Montoneros used in the last century.

The spear was crossed with a machine gun. The sign was the V of "Perón Vuelve" [Perón will return]. It was the sign of the Montoneros, and below it said, "Perón or death."

My family was anti-Peronist. My commitment rested on the belief that the national liberation movement and Peronism would help the common people. We talked about the national question all the time. My impression of my relationship with the people in my town was that if I talked to them about Lenin or Trotsky I would not gain any political ground. But one could talk of Peronism anywhere and strive for a different type of Peronism.

So we read leftist theories, but superficially. I read *The History of the Russian Revolution* by Trotsky. The "What to Do" by Lenin. Much was written by the Peronist left to disqualify the Marxist left – which in Argentina meant followers of Lenin and Trotsky – on the grounds that that left failed to understand the common people of Argentina. I believe none of us understood very much. I believed in social change and justice: abstractions. I believed that people could live better. I understood the popular books of Ernesto Cardinal about Cuba better than the texts I tried to read of Marx or Lenin. My *compañeros* and I were fundamentalists, but it was a climate widely shared. We were all for "love and peace." Belonging was very precious, and we felt that we were making the history of Argentina.

In 1974 we stopped engaging in university politics so that we could produce political propaganda in general. As 1974 progressed, it became very dangerous to act in favour of the Montoneros. One of our *compañeros* of the JUP, also in Philosophy and Letters, was killed by the Triple A in 1974 while posting notices labelled "Montoneros." Already by late 1974, to paint slogans on a wall was a more risky task; it was done with senior members of the group, who came armed, supposedly to defend those who painted. Ten people would be sent to paint a wall so that all the street corners could be watched. The operation became more aggressive in 1974 and 1975, when the Montoneros went underground. The times, then, were very complicated for us, for the visible groups.

I took part in the event at the Faculty of Law, where the Montoneros announced they were going underground. When we left the Faculty of Law that night, automobiles passed us which we identified as police cars although they carried no identification. We hissed at them. Already we lived in a climate of violence. A man with a gun stepped from a car. I suppose he shot into the air, since no one was hit and we left running, very frightened.

Our faculties had already been intervened by the Ministry of Education under Minister Oscar Ivanissevich, who was a right-wing

Peronist. So we were occupying the buildings of our faculty illegally, with armed student guards. Cars passed by the buildings all the time. They were unmarked police cars, and their armed occupants threatened us.

I will tell you about another incident to show you the climate of the times. The militants of the JUP supported Adriana Puigros, the dean of the Faculty of Philosophy and Letters. One day when we were at the poster tables, a man came by and asked for directions to her office. I took him to see her. Later, when he was leaving, he told me he was a lawyer from Córdoba who defended political prisoners. The next day we saw a newspaper announcement that this lawyer had been killed by the Triple A, presumably on leaving our building.

It was a very intense life. Looking at it from today's perspective, I am humbled to think that I now have a son of seventeen, and I think that at that age we were involved in an affair that could have ended our lives. Actually, I survived because of an accident. I had to have an operation on one leg. I withdrew from militant activism, and I tried to maintain contact with my friends, but the violence was very strong and I lost contact. I had an operation on my bone, so I went to my hometown for two or three months. When I returned, I spoke on the phone with friends and what was left of the JUP group in Philosophy and Letters. The people I talked with were very frightened. People had been killed. I talked with a female friend whose husband had become a militant. He had had military training in the navy, and he was a good shot. She told me of terrible things that had happened. They lived anywhere, constantly on the move, permanently escaping; and because of her husband's activities, they even had to give refuge in their house to an important injured member of the organization. They told me they had to set up a field hospital in their house. They had an infant daughter. They were very frightened. They felt they had to continue, but it was dangerous. Then I asked, "What can I do?" and my friends told me I must do something but must be very careful. They were going to connect me with a group that penetrated the prisons.

In the end, I did nothing, as I lost contact with them. I lived in the north of Buenos Aires, and I was so frightened one day – I wanted to talk to them, but didn't get them when I called them from my house. I called another person at his place of work, and the man who answered said, "How is it that you don't know?" I do not know what I did not know about my friends, but I was so frightened I hung up the phone and left for my hometown. If I had had more responsibility, I would have been in danger there too, but I survived …

I have had many discussions about why all this occurred. I don't have very profound answers, but I believe that we all sensed the possibility of social change, even in my little town. Many in my generation believed we could create a socialist government. And the program appeared realistic because there were sectors in the armed forces who sympathized with the Peronist left, and there were some priests in the Catholic Church who were in the movement. There were small and medium business people who were sympathetic to our ideals. So we believed we could achieve change.

THE ERP, TUCUMÁN, AND MONTE CHINGOLO

The ERP continued to do battle with military forces and their emissaries even while Perón was in power, but during the second half of 1975 the ERP suffered numerous defeats during assaults on military arsenals.[13] Their major offensive, and it cost them dearly, was the battle for Tucumán in 1975. Tucumán was one of Argentina's most backward and impoverished provinces. Sugar-cane estates had long been its economic mainstay, and these were organized in a feudal manner with workers living in extremely poor conditions and treated as serfs. The sugar-cane industry had had a major slump in the 1960s, and various attempts to diversify the economy had failed. Unemployment and poverty were widespread. Following Guevara's teachings about rural guerrilla warfare, the ERP tried to "take" Tucumán in 1975.

Predictably, estimates about the strength of their army in Tucumán vary considerably. Martin Andersen reckons that there were no more than 140 of them and that they were ill-trained and poorly armed.[14] The military claims there were at least 600, and one of the military officers we interviewed maintained that there were as many as 2,000. The higher number was, of course, part of the propaganda war, which included General Galtieri's claim that the guerrillas were "a threat that loomed over the very existence of the country itself." Andersen holds that the military high command had already succeeded in infiltrating the group with intelligence agents and would have been fully cognizant of the actual statistics. They were aided by ERP propaganda, which (like Montonero propaganda) exaggerated the strength and capabilities of their organization.

On 5 February 1975, Isabel Perón signed a secret decree, Operation Independence, authorizing the army to take whatever action was required to annihilate subversive elements in the province of Tucumán. General Jorge R. Videla, head of the army general staff, not only sent his troops into action but ordered the army's propaganda experts to ensure that the general population was aware of the origins of the decree – namely, the executive branch of a constitutional government.[15]

Backed by armoured cars and helicopter gunships, 1,500 army troops and as many policemen were deployed in Tucumán. The state control of newspapers, together with the isolation of the region, enabled the disparity in numbers to be kept out of the public domain, and this was advertised as a war between equals.

The fallaciousness of the propaganda was underlined by a statement attributed to General Vilas, the commander in charge of the army at Tucumán, who said that once the army had obliged the guerrillas to do their fighting in the urban areas, it was possible to fight "with an economy of means *without having suffered during 1975 one casualty among the legal forces.*"[16] According to later counts by the army's intelligence services, only 226 people were members of the guerrilla force throughout its entire eighteen months of existence in Tucumán, and this number included suppliers, couriers, and sympathizers. If Vilas's boast was true, what occurred in Tucumán was certainly not a war; it was a rout of what amounted to not much more than a gang of young men and women who had no idea of how to conduct even a guerrilla fight.

Important lessons were learned by the military forces in Tucumán, and experiments were undertaken there that were used later in *el Proceso*. Vilas argued that "the teachings of the military college and laws of conventional war, where the formalities of honour and ethics were essential parts of military life ... would have been impossible to carry onward."[17] This, then, was the inauguration of activity carried on by army personnel in civilian dress, driving unmarked cars, and behaving in illegal ways in order to catch those deemed to be guerrillas. The captured people might be killed or might be detained in La Escuelita (the Little School, literally a schoolhouse in the town of Famaillá), where torture was routine. This was possibly the first concentration camp run by the army, though prisons elsewhere – for instance, La Perla and Rawson, according to surviving inmates – had been operating much like concentration camps before the coup of 1976.

Monte Chingolo

The final chapter of the ERP's existence occurred just before Christmas 1975, when some hundred and fifty ERP guerrillas tried to seize a military arsenal in the industrial town of Monte Chingolo, a few miles outside Buenos Aires. An infiltrated agent had warned the intelligence services in advance, and the guerrillas were surrounded in short order. The usual propaganda followed the failed attempt. According to General Videla, there were eighty ERP casualties, both dead and wounded, but by the time the propaganda forces printed their version, the numbers had risen to more than two hundred. The ERP itself acknowledged forty-five casualties. More important than the exaggerated body count was an uncharacteristically frank assessment in the army's *Official Report* of 31 January 1976, stating that the ERP had demonstrated "great organizational and operational deficiencies that revealed little military capacity."[18] Despite this acknowledgement, the army prepared for an all-out battle against the enemy that it had now completely vanquished.

VOICE: ZANETA

In 1970 I lived in Buenos Aires, and I was an activist in what was then the People's Revolutionary Army [ERP]. I worked in a factory as part of the ERP project of proletarianization. Our intention was to begin with politicizing the workers and then to gain political power. The union at the factory was the Metalworkers' Union [UOM]. The ERP was an armed organization, affiliated with a political or intellectual arm called the Revolutionary Workers' Party [PRT]. I did the whole route. First I was in the Guevarist Youth and from there I passed to the PRT and from there to ERP. I started when I was in secondary school.

We were convinced that we could win power. We longed for a different country. We read a lot. They used to give us a lot of literature to read; we used to have political discussions. The experience of being in an armed organization, with military positions, with military categories, with practice, survival practice, everything that was military practice, that is difficult to discuss. I was very young, just nineteen years old in 1970. I was taught to use rifles, even grenades. I was taught in Argentina. I wasn't an important guerrilla. I was a soldier.

I come from a bourgeois family like others in my situation in Argentina. It wasn't the lowest social class, it was an educated class that conducted the revolution. I went to Tucumán in 1976, from December 1975 to March 1976. I was in the armed actions, sabotaging banks, foreign enterprises, commando operations to collect funds, money. We believed that the revolution should be financed by the rich, by the powerful. You can read in the newspapers of the time what we did then. I don't remember the details but – well, we didn't murder people, no. We were soldiers, and our task was to get money for the war. We did a lot of talking; even when taking part in all those actions, there was still constant political discussion.

In quotation marks, other guerrilla groups now call us "the pure ones." This was because we had such conviction and strong ideology. I say "pure ones" in quotation marks because in some way we all made a mistake. We need to review things and do some self-criticizing. Not to do that is a degree of arrogance that we can't allow ourselves. There are those who say that everything we did was good, and I don't think that everything we did was good.

We did the commando practice in order to steal. I'm not saying that there were no deaths. There were. But I didn't have to do it. We stormed factories, enterprises, national and foreign ones, a bit of everything. This was always with the objective of collecting funds or arms. The arms came from abroad, from France, the United States, but I would be lying to you if I told you much else, because in fact I myself was never one of the commanders. I was married to one of them.

I went to Tucumán toward the end of the fighting. At that time, just before the coup, Videla was in control of the army, and there was armed combat. There were many deaths, many deaths because it was the bloodiest period, the cruellest. And that's where my husband died. He died in a battle on 18 March 1976 in Tucumán. It was a very confusing period, where our leaders had notified us that this was the end. Earlier, in December 1975, when I left for Tucumán, I was still convinced that it was worthwhile. But I left the country on 30 March 1976, shortly after the coup. My family and friends got me out with help from Amnesty, through Brazil and from there to Mexico. I went with other *compañeros*.

I had gone to Tucumán because the armed organizations were practically destroyed by 1975. So it was a desperate action. We united various armed organizations – ERP and Montoneros – and we carried out some actions together. The Montoneros had been left without any leaders. It was very difficult. It is difficult for me to talk about this. It was a very confusing time, and we were still very young. I think that Tucumán was a suicide trip in 1975. Some people accuse us of having had a Peter Pan complex, of having acted like children and wanting to be children forever. And in fact we paid for those errors with our lives.

I try to look at the past without arrogance,[19] but we were convinced that the conditions in the country made those battles necessary. We committed the error of not gauging the enemy correctly. And we never thought that things would turn out the way they did – with the genocide that occurred. I don't know if you'll understand this, but some of us used to say, "If they take you to jail pregnant, what can they do to you? Pull your hair, a slap on the cheek ..." Now we know that there are almost five hundred children missing because the military stole them. That gives you a picture of how ingenuous we were. I don't regret what we did, but I would not ever use those methods again. That's why today I'm on a different track. But I'm not going to escape the conversation between us about what that period was like.

VOICE: TANYA

I was nineteen or twenty years old when I became politically active in a leftist organization that advocated armed struggle, the Revolutionary Workers' Party [PRT]. I never belonged to the armed faction, but to intellectual student groups that supported action and engaged in propaganda. We were very concerned with the Third World and Third World movements. We thought that society was divided into two big blocs and that the domination was so powerful that there was no alternative to an armed struggle in order to overthrow the oppressors.

My husband of that time[20] was a more theoretical militant and also more activist than me. One time, walking through the Belgrano neighbourhood – the neighbourhood of the rich – with much innocence I said, "when we have the revolution, we will have to destroy all these houses, because the people who live here will have to live a different style of life." What I meant to say was that the place in which one lives, one's everyday lifestyle, shapes society as a whole. And he answered me, "No way, because the revolution needs all the houses." This signified that everything that was in the public sphere, the city sphere, was going to stay intact. The change brought about by the revolution would be an ideological, economic change affecting those who occupied power, but it would not entail a change in the status of people, of daily practices. My idea of the revolution at that time was the possibility of creating, or struggling for, a different society – not just for a change of positions of power but, in a very idealistic way, the possibility of creating a society of equals.

My *compañero's* platform was that in the revolution, fundamentally, the working class would take power. To him this did not imply a total change in the organization of society. That the leaders of the revolution would occupy the houses of the rich was like getting one's own back, a kind of revenge. The rich were going to die or leave the country, or be stripped of their goods and consigned to hard labour. His idea was of a more just society led by the working class. This was utopia. In the intermediate steps, the bourgeois organization would continue, and only the seat of power would change; proletarians would replace the bourgeoisie. The state would be in the hands of the proletariat – furthermore, in the hands of the vanguard. There were very utopian discussions on this, and we debated with passion.

Before the coup, the Triple A killed people who were very close to us – people we knew, professors we admired. My sister-in-law's husband was imprisoned until 1980 or 1981. He was lucky in that when they broke into his house they took him prisoner under a false name, and they only found a little material. They didn't know he was a militant guerrilla. They put him on trial, they condemned him, but they didn't condemn him for what he had done; just for the books and pamphlets they found in the house. He had false documents, but eventually they found out. His mother went to visit him and made the mistake of using his real name. But as he had had a trial for other reasons, that did not lead to an increase in the sentence. When the military coup came, they made the conditions of detention worse and all legal action stopped. So he was a political prisoner. Nothing more. There was no evidence for anything else. If it had not been for the coup, he would have been freed, and then he would probably have been disappeared. So he was very lucky.

CENSORSHIP OF THE MEDIA

Perón had effectively muzzled the press, and a new security law under Isabel's government tightened the muzzle. Newspapers, radio, and television stations that offended the government in any way or that reported on assassinations and imprisonments without government consent became bomb targets or were arbitrarily closed. *La Prensa*, an anti-Peronist and conservative newspaper (which had once been taken over by Perón in his earlier incarnation), suffered gunfire attacks in several of its provincial offices within days of Isabel's inauguration.[21] The home of Miguel Bonasso, editor of the Montonero newspaper *Noticias*, was bombed a few weeks later.[22] A number of newspersons lost their jobs, were imprisoned, or were assassinated by unnamed gangs.[23] The new security law, which was decreed in September 1974, included an article that promised "prison terms of two to five years" for writers, editors, television directors, or announcers who "inform on or publicize" statements or other actions of guerrillas or other illegal organizations.[24]

After the promulgation of the security law, the violence escalated still further. Newspaper reporters and photographers were assaulted and some were murdered, including a business reporter for *La Opinión* in May 1975. At that stage, *La Opinión* joined *La Prensa* and the *Buenos Aires Herald* as persistent and outspoken critics of the government, the censorship laws notwithstanding.

THE CLANDESTINE
URBAN BATTLE

By mid-1975, the Triple A was winning the clandestine urban battle. Casualties among Montonero guerrillas, as well as among others deemed by the newspapers to be in the "subversive" category, were mounting much faster than casualties among Triple A and other known right-wing groups, though the counts varied. In direct confrontations between guerrillas and the Triple A or military and police forces during 1974 and early 1975, the authorities estimated that 109 army and police officers had been reported killed, along with 137 guerrillas. According to the *Buenos Aires Herald* of 12 September 1975, "left-wing" losses amounted to 248 between 1 July 1974 and 12 September 1975, with another 131 (mostly "left-wingers") killed in gunfights; in the same period, "right-wing" losses amounted to 41, police 75, army 34 (these three totalling 150), and businessmen 19; in addition, there were 35 not politically identified (with another 122 unidentified bodies). According to *La Prensa*, for the period May 1973 to March 1976, the security forces estimated a total of 1,358 deaths from terrorist attacks, of which 677 were civilian casualties, 445 were "subversives," and the remainder were military and police personnel.

The Montoneros were the only remaining revolutionary organization with armed capacity (though remnants of other groups joined them), and they too suffered many casualties at the hands of the Triple A and military forces during 1975. In December 1975 the army's commanding officer referred to the "absolute impotence of the terrorist organizations with respect to their presumed military power."[25]

By 1976 the guerrillas had given up any form of sustained organized combat, though they still engaged in occasional haphazard attacks. Following the military coup of 1976, President Jorge R. Videla (see chapter 9) said that 90 per cent of the subversive organizations had already been destroyed; nevertheless, he escalated military operations against them.[26] In 1977 the guerrillas themselves reported that 2,000 of their own had been killed.[27] They did not recover.

ECONOMIC DECLINE

Economic deterioration did not emerge suddenly under Isabel Perón's government; it had been a continual attendant to military rule throughout the previous two decades. Indeed, many economists attribute it to the import-substitution policies initiated under military rule and then fully established by Juan Perón's governments of 1946–55. There is (of course) debate about the causes of economic decline, but there is no debate about the long-term deterioration that beset the country in the late 1950s and continued through the 1960s. By the early 1970s, foreign investment was already in decline. The automobile industry had substantially reduced its investment even in the 1960s. By the time Perón died on 1 July 1974 and Isabel inherited the mess, the economy was into a rapid fall.

Two weeks before the 1976 coup, the minister of the economy in the Perón government called for a 180-day state of emergency, describing the situation as the "worst economic crisis" of Argentina's history. He said that the per capita gross domestic product had fallen; that exports were down and the balance of payments deficit was up; and that practically no foreign capital had been invested in the previous year. The cost of living in the same period had risen by 335 per cent. There was hyperinflation, massive devaluation of the peso, and widespread unemployment. He proposed a series of drastic restraints on wage and price increases.[28] This announcement sparked strikes and violence throughout the country.

The unions had already become the focal point of opposition to Isabel Perón and her minister of social welfare, José López Rega. In July 1975 the CGT had organized a mass demonstration in the Plaza de Mayo, followed by a national strike. This, like most other events of the period, was due in part to power struggles within the CGT, and these were intricately related to the manoeuvres of José López Rega to control the unions. The methods of control included detentions, which, under state-of-siege legislation, required no court order and no court review. Eventually, union militancy led to the dismissal of López Rega,[29] but by then support for government measures had declined across the social spectrum, and the president found herself isolated. The trade unions gained power within the vacuum, but not for long. The coup cut short their small victory.

CHAPTER 8

Imprisoned under PEN

The state had long had the power to imprison people for an indefinite period without specific charges and without recourse to judicial proceedings. A long-standing law permitted the government to override existing legal protection for individuals during a declared "state of siege" (such as that declared by Isabel Perón and several of her predecessors). This procedure was known as PEN (National Executive Power). Detained persons were supposed to have the "right of option," which allowed them the legal right to choose between exile and jail, but many claimed that they were denied the choice; and although the constitution prohibited the punishment of prisoners, every one of the PEN detainees with whom we spoke told of torture, both physical and psychological. Since the sentences were indefinite, part of the torture was never knowing when (if ever) one would be granted freedom. Some remained in prison for eight or nine years, and many died as a result of injuries, torture, the onset of insanity, or sheer despair. Although relatives were able to find out which prison a detainee was in, they were not informed when prisoners were moved, and prisoners were frequently moved from one region to another.

The sins that brought about incarceration varied enormously. As told by his father (below), one young man was neither a guerrilla fighter nor a union member, but he had hesitated when called up for army duty; he spent the next several years in prison. Some guerrilla members were imprisoned, but so were relatively unimportant members of Peronist organizations. A large number of PEN prisoners were union leaders or prominent members of unions. A higher proportion of those belonging to dissident unions, than those in the more traditional unions were imprisoned in the Isabel Perón period. But after the coup, the distinction between unionists in differing factions was abandoned. By that time, unionists from all factions, together with other persons labelled subversives, were more often disappeared than imprisoned.

As events unfolded, those who were imprisoned in the pre-coup period had a better chance of surviving the next eight years than those who remained at liberty when the coup occurred, provided they could withstand the unrelenting punishment.

VOICE: ALBERTO PICCINNINI

In 1976 I was thirty-four years old and already in prison. I had been a metallurgical worker since I was nineteen. In my twenties, during the Onganía dictatorship, I became active in the UOM [Metalworkers' Union]. In Villa Constitución, province of Santa Fe, we formed part of the union movement called "combative unionism," which had leaders like Agustín Tosco, René Salamanca, and Raimundo Ongaro. They were fighting against the dictatorship, for democracy, and at the same time they disagreed with the bureaucratic union leadership of the time. Augusto Vandor was the head of the bureaucratic Peronist unions. Lorenzo Miguel was the general secretary of the UOM at the national level. And the Peronist party was a strong influence. Not all Peronists were the same; some were for democracy too, but the Peronist unions in general were bureaucratic and not democratic. After Cámpora's departure, the right-wing sectors gained influence. Then, after Perón's death, our union was persecuted by both the national union and the Triple A.

At the end of 1974, we won the union elections in Villa Constitución. These are elections within the CGT [General Confederation of Labour] with seven thousand workers having the vote. We were clearly in opposition to the UOM and the CGT leaders. There was only one centre, the CGT, but we were the opposition within it. When we won the elections in 1974, the other union sections accused us of having relations with armed guerrilla groups. We did not have any relationships with them. We were against the economic measures of the main union body, and against the measures of Isabel Perón's government, but we were not allied in any way with armed guerrilla groups.

On the excuse that in Villa Constitución and the whole zone we were planning a subversive plot against the government of Isabel Perón, the government organized a repressive operation in the industrial strip along the Paraná River, a region of some 300 kilometres between Campanas and San Lorenzo, in the province of Santa Fe. They organized an operation with police forces and with civilian forces, the right-wing Peronist groups. And they had around five or six hundred people. The centre of the repression was Villa Constitución. I was general secretary of the union, representing those seven thousand workers. They detained all directors, the internal commission, and delegates, three hundred

people in all. As a countermeasure, the workers paralyzed the metallurgical industry in that zone for two months in a strike.

The Triple A ended up killing some of our *compañeros*. We were
subjected to repression and persecution. In a little over a year, they
killed twenty-five or twenty-six *compañeros* in the area. The ones who
did this travelled in groups. At first they went by day, like police. They
took workers away, and the next day the workers would turn up dead.
Later they started coming out at night, and the dead would turn up
one or two days later. So the workers organized themselves, and when
these gangs looked for them in their homes the workers defended
themselves with arms, and that led to kidnappings. These were all
illegal activities. But that area experienced the strongest repression
during the period of Isabel Perón. It began in mid-March 1975 and
was still happening after the coup a year later. At that stage, the dirty
work was controlled by the Triple A, fundamentally the police.
According to later information, there was already an entire intelligence
operation in the military. At first they were participants in right-wing
groups, and later, in 1976, they openly took power.

I was imprisoned 20 March 1975, and I spent five and a half years
in jail. They came to my house and they charged me with subversive
plotting against the government of Isabel Perón. They imprisoned me
and my *compañeros* under PEN, so it was a legal process, but they
never had a trial, never officially charged me or took the case to a
judge. In the first year, until the constitutional government ended, I
was in Rawson Prison, in the south. The regimen was harsh, but they
still respected some legal rules. After the 1976 coup, they created a
regime of extermination, torture, and beatings.

Before the coup, they never tortured me with the *picana* [electrical
prod]. They beat me. They would leave me for a few days with very
little food, they would lock me in the cell, "the pig," the dungeon of
punishment. It was a little cell without a bed, without clothes, and
with little food. In the south, where it is bitterly cold during winter,
they put prisoners in the cells, in the dungeons of punishment, and
took away their clothes. They did not give them anything to eat either.
Then after ten, fifteen, or even thirty days in the dungeon, the person
would become ill. It was all a form of torture that would not kill us
but would debilitate us. Sometimes they asked some questions, but
generally it was a regime of psychological terrorism. Many *compañeros* got sick, there were some suicides, and others ended up
having nervous breakdowns because of the continual persecution.
There were arbitrary rules, and if someone made a mistake making his
bed, he would be punished. We lived in a climate of constant pressure.
As well, they punished us by prohibiting visits from our families. We

were supposed to be allowed family visits one hour a day for five days, every forty-five days. And since it was not very easy to get to the south, the families sometimes came only once a year. They chose that time to punish someone so that they could not see their family. So two years passed that we couldn't see our families. My father died while I was in jail.

I had two sons, and I was divorced from my wife a year before I was put in jail. My new wife was put in jail with me because she was a delegate in the factory. She was detained for four months. She was freed during the government of Isabel Perón, and the para-police groups killed her in 1977. I found out almost a year later. But I guessed that something was wrong because, while she could, she used to visit my sister. Then my sister stopped sending me information in a secret way, because the letters were all read, so I started to assume that something had happened to her. But I didn't find out anything for sure until later. The children were with my ex-wife. I didn't see them for four years.

In total, I was detained for five and a half years, and then six months more, almost eight months, under house arrest. I had to be in Villa Constitución, I couldn't do any union or political activities, and I couldn't leave the city without police permission. In 1980 they gave me freedom because there was a great solidarity project at the international level· for the freedom of the union prisoners. And in June 1980 there was a request in the OIT [International Labor Organization in Geneva] for the release of all union prisoners. In response to that pressure, from the OIT and from many unions in Italy (I am of Italian origin), and also from unions in Spain, France, Norway, Canada – well, it worked to free all the union prisoners.

VOICE: FRANCISCO GUTIERREZ

I spent seven years and four months in jail, from the last months of 1975 until December 1982. Then for the next two years I was detained in my home. I was, then, the leader of the UOM in my factory at Quilmes [on the outskirts of Buenos Aires]. Many of my friends were in jail during the military regime. Out of a factory with six hundred workers, seventy were in jail. In addition to those of us who were detained under PEN and jailed, twenty *compañeros* were detained without cause, and four disappeared. They never returned.

The government applied the antisubversive law against the union movement, work organizations, popular organizations, and, above all, armed organizations. And they didn't let me leave the country for fear that I would campaign against Argentina. That was industrial guerrilla warfare at the union level. In 1975 the most combatant unionists were detained, the ones they called leftists, including Peronists. But from 1976 onwards, everybody was detained, almost without difference.

The company where I worked was connected to U.S. capital. After the leaders were rounded up, many others were fired. They removed social benefits and lowered the salaries. They increased production and reduced work breaks. There was a regime of repression against all unions. Internally, within the factory, the military would come and investigate everyone. They would take out all workers' personal items and review them one by one; they checked the clothes in the lockers to see if anyone had anything illegal, or weapons, or anything. And if anyone protested or didn't want to be checked, they put him in jail.

All prisoners were tortured with the electric prod. They tortured us frequently, sometimes trying to get information, or for no reason. They always asked who was the boss. If a *compañero* had asked for a salary increase, for example, or wanted to request a job change in the factory, or wanted an improvement … they might take someone away to ask him who was promoting this, who was the leader? Or if someone had some connection with a political group outside the factory, who was involved? And many times, not only to the *compañeros* here, they went to unionists' homes and stole everything. They took television sets, rings, watches, earrings – everything that was of value.

And there were some cases, my *compañeros* and their families can tell you, where women who had babies put their money and jewellery in the baby's diaper to keep them from being stolen. Once a week they would go to some *compañero*'s house and steal everything, with the excuse that they were looking for some guerrilla, some subversive, and that so-and-so who worked in the factory was a guerrilla, and they would take him away and rob him of everything.

They used to beat the wives of some of the *compañeros*, too. They beat the children. They would say that they were out looking for the father, and they would beat the children so that they would tell where the father was. There were *compañeros* in my factory, workers, who went to Misiones, in the north of the country, because the military were looking for them. They were declared subversives under the constitutional government. Many people went away to the north or to other provinces, and the police or the military went to those provinces to look for them. This went on for more or less seven years. It was a very hard struggle.

Beginning in 1976, any sort of union activity was prohibited. Therefore, if you got together with ten people in the company to discuss any sort of working condition, they interpreted it as union activity, and that was reason enough for them to detain you. In my company, near the end of 1976, workers on the afternoon shift were changing their clothes in the locker room. A group of young men were talking, joking around, making conversation amongst themselves. Then a chief of the factory came to the change room to ask some of the men to do a few hours of overtime. Some started debating whether to stay or not, saying that they would stay if they got paid more. Then one of the men, about twenty-two years old, decided not to stay because he didn't want to do overtime. In their discussion, someone mentioned a television advertisement that the military government had released. It showed one employee who worked, who took orders, who fulfilled the laws, who respected the government and the military. That was the good worker. And it showed another person who was an idler, who didn't like work and didn't respect the nation. One was called Juan; the other, Pedro. The government used to say that we all had to be like Juan and work hard. So this young man who didn't want to work overtime said to another guy, "You're Juan because you're stay-ing, and I'm Pedro because I don't really like to work." That night about midnight, an army patrol went to the homes of both men and kidnapped them. One of those men is still disappeared, and the other spent six months as a disappeared in a concentration camp. Then they let him go. He had not done anything, but he was tortured and even-tually released, blindfolded, in another city.

I want to tell you the case of a *compañero* by the name of Jaramillo, a worker who at that time was probably about forty years old and a very capable intelligent man, who had been a union delegate during the military government. Outside the factory, he was also a music teacher. He was Chilean, and Argentina had boundary problems with Chile. There were workers – I think they were military who pretended to be workers – who tormented him, telling him that he had to leave the factory, that he had to resign because he was a subversive, and besides that, he was Chilean. But the man didn't want to leave. He didn't want to resign from the job, because he was not doing anything subversive. What's more, he had five kids, one of them crippled, so he needed the money.

One day the manager of the company called him in and said, "You have to leave, because otherwise they are going to kidnap you and you're going to disappear." The next day he asked the manager for his money so that he could resign, and the manager said, "Okay, at noon, come by and get your pay. Send in a resignation telegram." At noon, he went to the factory after sending the telegram. They gave him a cheque to cash at the bank. When he came out of the bank, he was kidnapped. With the money. Never again did that man appear; never again did the money appear. The manager of the company was connected with the army. Three years ago that *compañero*'s remains were discovered in a common grave in the cemetery.

Sometimes I find it difficult to talk about these things. Jaramillo was a very good friend of mine. We worked together a long time ago, and it makes me very angry even today to remember that and all the injustice. I was a union activist. I never denied it. I was in politics all my life. I was in the JP [Peronist Youth], fighting for the return of Perón when the earlier military was in power. So – well, I spent the seven years in jail because I was active, because I was a politician, a unionist. But Jaramillo was not.

Even though I was an activist, however, they didn't have reason to torture me or to put me in jail. I hadn't committed a crime. But there was a time in Argentina when to be a union leader was a crime. The army didn't accept that the workers had the right to talk. They didn't accept that. And many business leaders were in agreement with that because they wanted to create a subordinate and marginal working class. That's why the labour movements in Argentina are so strong. The workers were the ones who fought the most for democracy, and that's why most of the *desaparecidos* and the dead were young labourers.

The workers of this factory had built the neighbourhood where they lived. Every time we got paid, the military came into our neighbourhood and into our homes to steal. Finally, the people couldn't stand it any more, and all the women and children went to the headquarters to tell them not to steal any more. Many people had to sell their houses, but nobody wanted to buy in that neighbourhood in 1976 or 1977 because they knew that the military would rob them.

The military classified prisoners. We were labelled in terms of how high up in the unions we were and whether we were Peronists, socialists, Marxists, independents, Montoneros, ERP soldiers, or whatever. Union leaders and members of the left-wing guerrilla groups were sent to the special pavilions called "pavilions of death." I was in a pavilion of death where they killed eleven prisoners. They applied "the law of escape." The guards said they were going to take them to another jail and then claimed that they had tried to escape while being moved and had all died in combat.

They would put us in a dungeon, a little cell, and would not give us clothes or light or food. Later they would put us under a cold shower at around three in the morning and would hit us with rubber sticks until we fainted. They would take us from the pavilions to the dungeons for any little thing. They often beat me so much that I was left entirely black, and that's the way I lived for seven years. They didn't want information. They tortured for the sake of torturing. They called us criminal terrorists not recoverable for society.

Some of us found a clandestine way, from the jail, of petitioning the justice system with the collaboration of some people who worked in the penal system. They collaborated with us in getting us information. Some judges came to the prison after four *compañeros* had been killed in 1977. We presented the complaint, and I was interviewed by the federal judges because one of the appeals was mine, and we told the judges what was happening. We said that we, as prisoners, demanded that the Geneva Convention be fulfilled with respect to the life of the prisoners. I told the judges everything – and when they left, the military men took me to the dungeons to ask me what I had told them.

VOICES: JUAN JUSTO AND JUAN GUILLERMO

Juan Justo: In 1971, when I graduated from the National University of La Plata in mathematics, I was twenty-three years old. I became a teaching assistant in 1969 and was on the faculty by the time I graduated. I had become an activist in the faculty union. In September 1974 important changes took place. About thirty days after Perón died, the minister of education changed, and Dr Ivanissevich was appointed minister of education. Ivanissevich had been a leader in the educational sector under Perón in the 1950s, and historians have now shown him to be a man of Nazi or fascist ideas. Perón managed to incorporate the neofascists or Nazis who took over the Ministry of Education in the very broad Peronist movement. Well, in most universities the deans were replaced, and from then on there was ideological persecution. I was on a yearly contract, and without explanation the contract was not renewed; I was suspended.

The next year, 1975, I entered a competition for a position at the National University of Rio Cuarto, south of Córdoba. I was granted an assistant professorship, due exclusively to my educational credentials. I moved there with my wife and our year-old baby. I worked at that university until 24 February 1976.

One day I arrived home and the police were inside. My family was there. They had an arrest warrant because many years earlier I had been accused of being an ideological organizer of guerrillas. These were the federal police, and this was a legal arrest. I was handed over to the National Executive Power [PEN] and imprisoned in Rio Cuarto, and from there I was transferred to the city of Córdoba. Later I was moved to the prison of Sierra Chica for two years, and then to Rawson for four or five years. In the last few months I was in Devoto, in Buenos Aires. I was not freed until December 1983.

It was a ferocious penal system. For example, starting on the first day when I was arrested, I was tortured for five days. And that's how

I was presented to the judge. The doctor who was there said I was in perfect health, even though I could not sign because they had put electrical currents through my hands. They would ask: "Who are your comrades, your friends? Where do they hide the weapons?" I had nothing to tell them, but they did not believe me. Or they would ask, "Why do you read those books?" So, all along, the assumption was "You are a guerrilla who does not want to confess."

In the period from 1976 to 1980 it was very harsh. Slowly there came a change after they allowed the Human Rights Commission of the OEA [Organization of American States] to visit the prisons. We were watched all day. It depended on which jail you were in. For example, in the Sierra Chica prison we were locked in a cell for twenty-three hours, alone. One hour a day they took us out into the yard for a walk. In the yard you couldn't play football, couldn't do any sports. You had to walk nonstop in groups of three. In Rawson Prison we spent almost all day in a pavilion, but there was a prison guard standing there listening to every conversation. So there was a constant heavy pressure on us from the security guards, who were always watching. The regime was highly militarized. For anything at all, we were sent to the punishment cell, the hole. They would not allow books by liberal authors, never mind leftists. During family visits you could not touch, could not hug your family.

I was arrested one month before the coup and was already in the hands of the judicial system. That is why I was not among the disappeared. But there were others who had been imprisoned but who also disappeared. I think that my friend Juan Guillermo should join the conversation at this point, because our experiences are similar.

Juan Guillermo: In the 1970s I lived in the province of Corrientes. In 1975, when I was twenty-five years old, I was arrested in the town of Villa Angela, in the province of Chaco, and put in prison. I come from a family of Peronists, and my father had always been a Peronist activist. He was a railroad man and had always been involved with what was called the Peronist resistance. When I was fifteen, my father introduced me to young people who formed the Peronist Youth, not the ones who later were associated with the Montoneros, but an earlier group. I took part in all the activities of the youth movements in my province and in the region. That was Argentine political life at that time.

I graduated from high school in 1969 and began to study law in Corrientes. I married and had a son when I was twenty years old, so had to give up my studies. I was at that time a leader of the Peronist Youth in Corrientes. When democracy was reinstated in 1973, Cámpora was president. The Peronists won in Corrientes, and I became a provincial government functionary representing youth. That lasted a year, and by 1974 the contradictions in that great movement were heightened. Then Perón's death accelerated what Juan Justo told you about. Isabel Perón declared martial law and ordered the arrest of various political leaders, especially the leftist Peronists. So in April 1975, when I was arrested, I was part of that process.

Well, then, as Juan Justo said, there were already disappeared people and torture, and there were already political assassinations. Now, what was different after the coup? It's that afterwards there was a national plan for the disappearance of people. There was a specific strategy for that. Those events were not excesses of a dictatorship; they were the first chapters of the subsequent plan. The process of repression began in 1975. For those already in prison, after the coup, you could see a well-defined policy intended to break us, to destroy us personally, both morally and physically.

I was tortured in 1975 when I was first imprisoned, and the nature of the torture changed. At the time of detention the political prisoners suffered methodical torture with electric prods, with beatings, with all manner of humiliations. In my case, we had been arrested with a group of friends from the province of Chaco, among whom were the secretary-general of the agricultural association, representing the farmers of Chaco. For us, the torture lasted a month and a half. Then we were disappeared, in other words, not legally recognized. Everyone knew we had been arrested, but when family members inquired about us, the police said, "No, they are not here."

It was like this. I lived in Corrientes, not in Chaco, and my brother was a labour leader, involved with the Peronist youth associations, and they were looking for him. I helped him escape. They destroyed his house, stole his things, threatened his daughter, his wife. When they couldn't find him, they came to my house, but as a precaution against my arrest, I had gone to Chaco. I was arrested at Villa Angela, where I was going to try to let things cool off before returning to Corrientes. I was arrested in a bar, in a restaurant. They had followed me and they were waiting.

They took me to another city and from there to Résistancia, the capital of Chaco, which is where the cruellest tortures were inflicted on the whole group. It was all illegal. There was no lawyer, no law. A special mention must be made about a famous torturer in Chaco, and in the whole region, who was chief of police, head of investigations. His surname was Tomás. He was called "The Irishman" because he looked Irish, red-headed. A group of police were with him. We suffered intensive torture during the next month and a half. Afterwards, in the years in prison, torture was a permanent experience in the form of isolation and the jail cells, the separation from family, the beatings, the fear.

Juan Justo: For example, they would take about twenty people from the jail to a concentration camp in Córdoba, and they would say it was to coincide with General Videla's visit to Córdoba. And they'd say that if anything happened to Videla they would kill all of us. So we lived in constant fear. We began to feel that the prison was the safest place!

Juan Guillermo: So the seven or eight years when we were prisoners were all like that. We are telling you this because you think, well, once you are arrested, well, fine, it's over, you remain there and have to endure the prison term, nothing more. No! It was much worse. Always there was psychological torture.

This brings me to a point few know about because I think that everyone, without going into details, reached an agreement to keep it from national knowledge out of respect for family and the dead. The point is, and I say we shouldn't spread it, that many friends committed suicide. They died by hanging, by being cut up – they just could no longer stand imprisonment. In Rawson Prison I had a friend whom they took from the pavilion and interrograted. After four or five hours with the military he came back so burdened, so psychologically destroyed, that during the night he committed suicide.

Another friend in La Plata Prison was visiting behind glass with his younger brother, and at one point the prison guard interrupted and cut the visit short, saying, "The visit is ended because your brother is giving you forbidden information." And there, to draw a picture, is this young man, after years of imprisonment, with a great love for his brother who was only fourteen or fifteen. They took him to the hole, not back to the cellblock but to the hole. He was in despair, out of fear for what might befall his younger brother. He went mad. Ten days later they returned him to his cell and there he killed himself.

We do not know why or how we stayed sane. That's why there are so few of us from that period who are still activists, very few. It is understandable. There are many who left there sick and I think, if you follow me, it is because of a warping of conscience, of conviction.

Juan Justo: The policy in prison was to destroy the prisoners. We organized ourselves, however, and we generated a climate and the necessary human relations to help us resist. That is how many survived. Unity, understanding, and the need for affection, we resisted together, and that saved us from madness. I believe they never managed to destroy that. We managed to erect a wall, an invisible wall, a dividing line between us and the jailers.

As for our families – well, in my mother's case, to this day she hasn't recovered. She was increasingly depressed, and now her other ailments have become acute. It was very hard because my parents were poor, they couldn't visit. And anyway – well, my father had a hard time understanding it, because he never believed that the military and prestigious people in society could be responsible for such atrocities. He could not understand my situation. He could not believe the truth about the actions of the repressers. He never believed that the police tortured.

My wife was arrested at the same time as I was. She put our son in the care of a friend. She was in jail for six years, and she had a hard time. In the final month she almost died. And when we got out, we split up. We couldn't stay together because, basically, she had been destroyed by all that had happened to her. Our child is now twenty-three years old and, well, there is nothing to say because our friend's grandmother raised him, and we are grateful that she cared for him as if he were her own.

Juan Guillermo: Ahh, this is hard for me to talk about. My parents were the best example of parents, friends, not just for me but for all my friends, because they were always working with the other families trying to help all the prisoners. My father had a stroke the day the mission was here from the Organization of American States. He wanted to talk with them, but during their visit he had a stroke. He recovered, though, and he was always there for me, giving me strength, until he died two years ago.

I was married, as I said before, and at the time I went to prison I had two children. The boy, four years old, and the girl, two. Then, about a year after my arrest, mid-1976, my wife was arrested. She was accused of collaborating with the families of the detained. We were isolated; we had no contact with the outside. When the military took power, they isolated the prison and no visitors were allowed, no mail. The only thing we knew about the outside was information we got from new prisoners. Well, about two months after she was arrested, some of the new prisoners told me the military had killed my wife. I felt a deep sorrow. I tried to find out more, and next day some other prisoners told me she had not been killed but was collaborating with the repressers. That was the hardest time for me in the eight years of imprisonment. That was in 1978. Out of respect for my children, I wouldn't want details published. I am telling you so you get the broader picture of what we went through ... Well, there is a song with the lines "History is made in a slow fire," and the people know that the teacher is the wind. Now I am a teacher and I remain optimistic about the future. We will someday have an honest Argentine government without corruption, one that cares for education and heals the system and works for all of us.

VOICES: SEÑOR JOSÉ FEDERICO WESTERKAMP AND SEÑORA WESTERKAMP

Sr Westerkamp: We were directly affected by the repression because our son was taken prisoner for political reasons under PEN. That was in 1975. He was twenty-three years old. He was in prison for seven and a half years. He was never charged before a judge; just labelled subversive. That was the generic term. At that time he was in the university, in the first year of economics, and of course he was involved in demonstrations in the university and other places too, like many, many young people. There had been many years of strife.

I immediately presented a habeas corpus and tried to obtain permission for my son to go abroad. The constitution says that when the National Executive Power takes a person without giving him a trial or taking him before a judge, it should release the person or allow him to emigrate. But always the person should be taken immediately before the judges. This did not happen, and two or three months passed. This was during the government of María Estela Martínez de Perón, the constitutional government, but the government was already under the control of the military. Even the minister of the interior, who was responsible for these things, when I went to see him, he himself told me, "I cannot do anything, I am already surpassed by the military." And he resigned, because he could not bear it any longer.

As soon as I could, I went to visit my son. He had disappeared at first, and was disappeared for two and a half days, but finally we found him in a prison, a special section of a police prison for political prisoners. He had been tortured. He still had a swollen face ... My wife saw him and she was horrified.

Earlier he had told me, "Dad, I am not going to turn up for military service because I know of many cases of boys in my situation who have been kidnapped in the barracks, and I don't want it to happen to me." We did not believe that was true. We did not believe it. And we told our son, "No, it cannot be true." So I tried to interview some military people, and through a relative I met with a military chief who was a colonel. I went to see him and I told him, "Look, my son says that he does not want to turn up for military service because he thinks he could be kidnapped, as others have already been." And the colonel said, "No, no, this is not possible, we don't do that kind of thing, tell that boy to come and see me."

During that meeting I noticed that he had a box on his table, as if it were a book, but it was a box, and I asked him, "What is that book?" And he said, "Ah, I have this in case a conscript, a soldier, comes to see me, and sometimes I go into the next-door office and open the box and take out the gun that is inside." He said it was because he was afraid of some of the soldiers.

I told my son that the colonel had assured me nothing would happen to him and that he should go for his military service. He went, then. But we were already worried, so we asked him to let us know immediately if anything happened to him. The day he presented himself he did not come here. We learned, because of a telephone call, that he had been kidnapped, taken in the street that very same day, after presenting himself for military service. We know now that when he went to take the bus near the military quarters, he realized he was being followed. I don't know if it was by people in a car or walking, I don't know. So he sped up to take the bus, but those who were following him also sped up. They stopped the bus and seized him before he was able to get on. They called him subversive, assassin, many other things.

Sra Westerkamp: Some people began to gather in Santa Fe Street, and the policemen saw them. And to dissuade the people, the police began to shout, "No, he is a subversive, a subversive, lets take him." And they took him after beating him up.

Sr Westerkamp: So we immediately presented a habeas corpus.

Sra Westerkamp: Yes. And a relative of my husband, who was a journalist in Government House, told us after three days that they knew where he was. And almost simultaneously we received the notice from a judge saying that our son was detained.

Sr Westerkamp: It may have been because he didn't want to present himself for military service, but we persuaded him, and I had the guarantee of that militar. Or it could have been because my son had been detained three months earlier for three or four days. We were going to go to the United States, I remember, when he was detained. A professor from his faculty had asked our son and another student to help him move to a new house, and when they were there, all of them were detained by the federal police. The claim was that they were engaged in illicit association.

Sra Westerkamp: They said it was because the professor was leftist, as were many other professors. At that time, we presented a habeas corpus. A lawyer for the professor told us not to worry, that he was sure he was going to be released soon. So we were not worried, and we went to California as we had planned. And when we came back, the judge had absolved them and he was free. But perhaps he was already marked.

Sr Westerkamp: I immediately phoned this colonel and asked him for explanations, because he had assured me that ... and he said, "Inside the barracks nothing happened to him, but I am afraid of being killed by the friends of your son."

Sra Westerkamp: Through my husband's uncle we found out where our son was detained. So we went immediately to see him, and we brought food for him. When we arrived there, we said we knew he was there, so they could not deny us entrance. We were allowed to see Gustavo through a window. I was horrified, and I asked him, "What happened to you, Gustavo?" His eyes were black, full of bruises, but he didn't know because he did not have a mirror.

After that he was taken to the Devoto Prison. According to article 23 of the national constitution, during a declared state of siege a person can be imprisoned and can be moved from one place to another unless the person decides to go abroad. When he went to Devoto, and as soon as we were permitted to see him, he told us how he had been treated. He had been thrown on the floor in a place where there were many people passing to and fro. His eyes were covered, and he was handcuffed. Everyone who passed peed on him, spat on him, kicked him.

Sr Westerkamp: We could not do anything. We just presented the habeas corpus. It was the only thing we could do, because he was under PEN. But we got a ruling from the judge – I don't remember when that was, at the end of 1975 or early in 1976 – and the ruling granted permission for him to leave the country. I waited. But ... right after the military coup, that judge was removed. Another judge was appointed. Time was passing, and our son was still not liberated. They did not let him go abroad. The minister of the interior to whom I had talked was not the minister any more. There was a new ministry.

Sra Westerkamp: And the new judge said that although the ruling was firm, it was not possible to carry it out because he needed to ask the executive power to regulate article 23. This lasted seven and a half years. And meanwhile the executive power said that our son could not go to bordering countries. Prisoners could not go to Uruguay, Chile, Bolivia, Paraguay, they could not go there. So all the parents of those detained for political reasons began to ask for authorization from countries where prisoners could go, because they told us that we needed that authorization. So we began to visit the embassies of all the countries. Some of the countries we were in contact with were Holland, Belgium, Sweden. Many of them asked us to tell them what was happening. So all the parents of the politically detained began to explain how things had happened, and we described the treatment of our children and why we were trying to get them out of the country. This is one of the main mistakes the military made, because the embassies informed their governments of what was happening here. But even after that, every time we thought we had cleared a hurdle, another one appeared. Always the appeal was missing something …

Sr Westerkamp: In December 1975 we founded an organization, here in our home, the Relatives of the Detained and Disappeared People [Familiares]. And later that same month we founded the Permanent Assembly for Human Rights [Asamblea Permanente por los Derechos Humanos, APDH]. We were not a very big group, between ten and fifteen. This was shortly before the coup. In reality the military were already in charge. Isabel was a puppet …

At APDH we began working in secret, first in the office of a lawyer, then in a church. The lawyer told us, "Well, come today, but do not come back." So we went to the church. We were there a couple of times, and then the father told us, "Do not come back, please." So we met as we could, secretly. The parents in the group had met in the jails when they were looking for their children, or in government offices where they sought ways of getting their children's release. It was during these meetings that we found out that there were disappeared people. We didn't know that before. We had read in the newspapers that, for example, someone had been shot or executed in the street, no? … We believed it because it was in the paper. Then we realized that it was not so, that it was all a pretense. They were in reality disappeared. They had been executed or disappeared or taken to the ESMA concentration camp for interrogation.

Sra Westerkamp: And the prisoners were moved from one jail to another, and during the moving they applied what they called the law of escape. They said they had tried to escape, and they shot them. And when they moved them, they did not tell us. The parents did not know anything. And when we went to visit them, we did not know where they had been moved to.

Sr Westerkamp: Our son was sent to the Sierra Chica jail in Azul, and in other jails in La Plata, Rawson, and Villa Devoto. At the end he was in Rawson.

Sra Westerkamp: They were blindfolded when they were moved, and when they got off the bus they were bound together and forced to run. There were two lines of gendarmes with their steel sticks, and while the prisoners were running, they beat them. And then they were naked and were made to take a bath out in the open before being taken to their cells. Fifteen days later they permitted us to visit him.

Sr Westerkamp: We tried to help if we could. We organized a whole service of assistance for relatives. For example, many people were from the interior, and we organized it so that their fathers or mothers could come to see them, or brothers. So we tried to get some money. We asked Sweden for money; Sweden gave money to the families. As we are affiliated to Amnesty International, we asked it for money. Amnesty sent some money once in a while to help relatives travel to the prisons or take food or clothes to those who were most in need. This is what Familiares organized.

Sra Westerkamp: I want to tell you that when we saw Gustavo for the first time in Sierra Chica, there was a long line of relatives who were waiting to see their transferred children.

Sr Westerkamp: And there was a small tank, a tank, confronting us, threatening all of us with a machine gun.

Sra Westerkamp: Yes, it was terrible. And the relatives entered one by one. They had to present an address certificate and meet a series of requirements to be allowed to enter. There were people who had come from far away, from the north, two thousand kilometres away – very humble people, very, very poor, who had spent what they didn't have to come and see their children, people with small babies, with sick children, who didn't have the money to stay in a hotel. And some were not allowed to go in because they didn't have an address certificate. They had spent all they had and all the money they had borrowed, and they were sent back.

The line-up slowly moved forward. We were at the end of it with a friend whose son was also there. Then we were called, and they told us, "You cannot come in." At first he said none of us were allowed to go in. And then our friend, who was a commodore, said, "I want to talk to the superintendent of the jail to know why Sr Westerkamp and I cannot go in." Then he (the guard) came back after half an hour or an hour and said, "Well, the commodore can go in, but you cannot." And the commodore said, "I am not here as a member of the military. If Sr Westerkamp cannot go in, I will not go in either." So the guard had to ask again, and they gave us permission to go in.

We met there in the church. We were on this side of the church, with the prie-dieu there, and on the other side were the prisoners, with another prie-dieu in front. We could touch the prisoners, stretching our hands. So we asked them what had happened. Their eyes were black. We told them that the guards had tried to stop us coming in, and they said, "Because we have marks of being beaten and they wanted us to sign a declaration that said the marks were the result of an accident, but we refused to sign." And they said, "The guards invent faults. For example, today we had to use a pencil in this way. Tomorrow, they will punish us for doing it that way and insist it be done another way. Everything is a pretext to take us to the punishment cells." This had nothing to do with getting information. They had already been beaten up. It was inhuman.

Sr Westerkamp: ... and this continued until 1982, until the war in the Malvinas, and after that they let our son go.

CHAPTER 9

El Proceso

The military coup of 1976 had not come as a surprise, for it was clear that the government was in a state of paralysis. During the week preceding the coup, the papers (which had become much bolder) reported forty violent deaths and editorialized about the lack of law and order. *La Nación* printed a large advertisement for a newly formed "Federal Party," which bluntly called the government "dead" and accused it of being killed "by its own mistakes." It went on: "We see daily guerrilla actions in all sectors of national life, but the guerrillas with machine guns are not the only enemies of our way of life. Neither are those who in their offices frustrate the process of development. Now the government itself is the greatest guerrilla. A government that has abused institutionality to become a real soviet on the shoulders of the people."[1]

Shortly before the coup, the army replaced its commander-in-chief, who was viewed as sympathetic to the government. The new chief was Lieutenant-General Jorge Rafael Videla. The military, now unambiguously in command, granted the president a leave of absence. When she refused to extend it beyond five weeks, a deadlock ensued which ended with the military coup of 24 March 1976.

POPULAR SUPPORT
FOR THE COUP

The Nazi experience has recently been subjected to the cold scrutiny of revisionists. Unwilling to accept the explanation that the Holocaust was the work of crazed brutes in the SS force or the invention of Heinrich Himmler and his colleagues, Daniel Goldhagen argues that it represented the expressed wishes of the majority of the German people and was the culmination of centuries of virulent anti-Semitism.[2] The debate over his argument is far from concluded (notably, about whether the sentiments were any stronger in Germany than in the rest of Europe and about the validity of some of the evidence), but his signal and important contribution is the insistence that such cataclysmic social events do not occur without the population's compliance.

Compliance need not imply complicity. It involves acceptance, conformity with demands, submission, but not necessarily enthusiastic participation. In Argentina there was compliance for the most part; and then some complicity. There was not a long-standing ethnic animosity as in Germany; the population was ideologically complicit in a different way. This population had experienced the violence of Peronism and the chaos of the early 1970s. These recent experiences were traumatic, and people desperately wanted peace and order. The coup promised an end to violence and chaos, and it was that promise, more than anything else, that initially bound the population to the military regime.

The military promised law and order, a return to "family values," and the re-establishment of "Christian morals and values." These promises were welcomed, and even those who later became severe critics – and some who shortly afterwards had to go into exile or spent the next few years living frantic underground lives – even they applauded the military coup. The Argentine people were used to having military governments. They anticipated a return to a familiar pattern. And although the young of the middle class objected to that pattern, their elders, much of the unionized population, the church hierarchy, and the business and agricultural sectors preferred military rule and stability to the chaos of life in the early 1970s.

Some of the positive reception, which was especially marked amongst well-to-do segments of the population, was due to the strong anti-Peronist sentiment. As historian and filmmaker, Osvaldo Bayer, noted in our interview with him, many intellectuals so despised Peronism that they were prepared to accept a certain degree of state oppression to rid Argentina of the plague. In their view, if Peronists were targeted by the military, they were getting pretty much what they deserved. Montonero leaders, despite their heavy losses and the lack of support they received from the working class and the poor, publicly rejoiced at the return of the military. Now that they had the real enemy in place, they reasoned, they would gain followers in their struggle.

In addition to those who openly welcomed the coup, there were many – probably the majority of the population – who simply stayed silent and kept their heads down and their senses dulled, saying they had no alternative. For some, political events went by without registering on their psyches; they continued with their daily lives as if the political context did not exist. They may have concluded that personal survival depended on maintaining closed eyes, ears, and intellect, with compassion set on "very low." It was not their fight, and they did not want to become involved. Many middle-aged, middle-income parents dismissed the news of disappearances told by their teenaged children. "Left-wing propaganda," said they. Even when their children were subjected to torture, they found it impossible to believe that the "authorities" could act arbitrarily. Some disowned kidnapped children; others simply refused to believe the evidence of torture experienced by their own adult children (as one of our interviewees who was imprisoned under PEN attested). It was too painful for them to acknowledge that the military forces, in whom they had placed their trust, were responsible for state terrorism.

According to a Venezuelan report on 5 April 1976, the well-to-do of Argentina relished the coup. Reporting on a dinner party of wealthy farmers, middle-aged businessmen, artists, media personalities, and the "idle rich," the (Venezuelan) *Daily Journal* quoted one participant: "My husband is so happy over the coup that he's going to pay taxes for the first time ever." The husband agreed: "All my friends are saying the same thing. We really want to see this Government succeed."[3] This is not idle chatter. Argentina's rich sent an estimated US$82.5 billion to foreign banks during the 1974–82 period, while evading taxes in Argentina.[4] Nonpayment of personal income taxes, according to Peronist government sources, had reached 70 per cent in the 1973–75 period. Tax evasion was a major cause of inflation in the 1970s.

ORGANIZATION OF TERRORISM

The coup ushered in a period of systematic disappearances, torture, and killing of citizens and residents of Argentina. *El Proceso* had been planned well in advance, and torture chambers had been prepared. Personnel assigned to torture duty had been trained for their tasks and were on the job within minutes of the coup. The commander-in-chief, General Videla, was the father of seven children and reputed to be a deeply religious man. Other members of the junta were General Roberto E. Viola, chief of the army high command; Admiral Emilio Massera, representing the navy; and Brigadier Orlando Agosti, representing the air force. The three armed services appeared to be working peaceably together. As newspaper accounts of the time declared, this junta appeared to consist of professional bureaucrats who took their citizenship seriously.

In previous coups the army had been the chief protagonist, with the other forces siding with or covertly plotting against whichever army faction was in control. However, this takeover required the more active participation of other services, and Admiral Massera made it clear that support from the navy was contingent on equality – one-third of all posts going to each service. The country was divided into security zones (based on previous army organization); each of the services, and then each of the units within each service, was assigned responsibility for maintaining security in a designated area within the zones. Far from cooling out interservice rivalries, this exacerbated them; from the beginning, the chiefs viewed one another as rivals, and each service unit regarded its areas as private fiefdoms.

The army, with Videla as president, soon held control of the more important territories and a majority of the subordinate public offices. The three original junta members were labelled "liberals," but the reader, seeing history recycled in this episode, will understand that the term meant favouring military government and a free market economy; also, it implied virulent hatred of Peronism.

Among those who took the most active role in the repression was General Luciano B. Menéndez, head of the 3rd Army Corps. Regarded by many as a fascist, Menéndez was in charge of an enormous zone, which included some ten provinces, the city of Córdoba, and the infamous prison camp, La Perla, on the outskirts of Córdoba. Other leaders were also widely regarded as fascists, including General Carlos Suárez Masón, commander of the 1st Army Corps. Rear Admiral Rubén Chamorro was the director of ESMA, the navy engineering school that was transformed into a concentration camp. Interior Minister General Albano Harguindeguy and Colonel Ramón Camps, the La Plata police chief, became infamous for their enthusiastic participation in the repression and its murders.

Although Argentina had carried on quarrels with all its neighbours throughout its history, a program initiated in 1975 by the Chilean intelligence agency, DINA, had the support of the Argentine junta. Under the name Operation Condor, six Latin American countries agreed to allow one another's assassination squads to move freely around their territories. Thus the military had almost a whole continent available within which it could freely detain or murder anyone who tried to escape its clutches in Argentina. It could count on the cooperation and support of the military and police forces in the other countries.

The plans for organized suppression of subversion involved the establishment of 340 detention and concentration camps. While some of these were holding areas from which detainees were transferred, many were full-scale torture centres, where hundreds – and in the cases of the larger centres, thousands – of individuals were incarcerated, tortured, and eventually killed. Such a vast organization required careful advance planning, and personnel had to be trained. Some training of officers had already been provided under U.S. military auspices in the Panama Canal Zone[5] and by French military officers in Argentina, and further training had taken place under the auspices of the Triple A and provincial police forces in Argentina. The army had about 80,000 armed personnel in the early 1970s; the navy, an estimated 20,000; the air force, between 15,000 and 20,000.[6] These numbers would include draftees, who were not normally deployed in the repression activities. On the other hand, the military forces were supported by provincial and municipal police and a number of other security forces. Their total number may have reached 200,000. The nonmilitary forces were subject to military authority. In addition to personnel, the army had tanks, mostly of French manufacture, and other arms obtained from the United States and France. It was well enough equipped to carry out internal repression.

SYSTEMATIC STATE TERRORISM

The repression was harsh and relentless from the night of the coup until the eve of the world soccer championships in June 1978. With an international audience for the finals, the junta put on its best face and reduced its terrorist activities on the streets. After that, there were fewer abductions, though the murders did not cease. The tempo changed gradually through 1979.

The military objective was to rid the country of subversion, but subversion took on many meanings under the military regime. Obviously it included armed resistance or belligerent action against military controls, and it meant anything connected with communism or Marxism, loosely defined. But as we have seen, it went well beyond these areas.

Military Definition of a Terrorist

General Videla defined a terrorist as "not only someone with a gun or bomb, but also anyone who encourages their use by ideas incompatible with Western Christian civilization." [7] Prior to the coup, Videla had told a Conference of Latin American Armies, in Montevideo, that "as many persons must die in Argentina as are necessary to guarantee the country's security."[8] In a press conference in April 1977, General Roberto Viola defined terrorism as "any concealed or open, insidious or violent action that attempts to change or destroy a people's moral criteria and way of life, for the purpose of seizing power or imposing from a position of power a new way of life based on a different ordering of human values."[9]

Such statements, repeated frequently with minor variations, made it clear that the objective was not merely to rid the state of particular individuals but also to destroy institutions, ideologies, books, and ideas of any vintage or origin that offended or ran contrary to the ideologies and ideas of the generals. Universities and trade unions were major sources of these contrary ideas.

The generals were uncompromising in their view that those who held subversive ideas were not altogether human, and in any event were not real Argentines. Said President Videla: "I want to clarify that Argentine citizens are not victims of the repression. The repression is against a minority that we do not consider Argentine."[10] General Cristino Nicolaides said that "the individual who fought and is committed to subversion is a delinquent, for me, incorrigible."[11] Right-wing terrorists, however, were exempted from this dictum because, in the view of the military, they represented "antibodies" against the "diseases" of the left-wing subversives.[12] With such a broad definition and identification of the problem, it may not be surprising that the military thought the only solution was extermination. Said General Ibérico Saint-Jean: "First we kill all the subversives; then we will kill their collaborators; then their sympathizers; then ... those who remain indifferent; and finally we will kill the timid."[13]

The Disappeared

To catch people with ideas was a very different operation from declaring open warfare on armed guerrillas. Terrorism was a selected method, not an accident. For those who were kidnapped, no charges were laid, no evidence was produced, no trials were mounted to determine what crimes had been committed or whether these individuals were guilty. No records of where or why they were imprisoned were ever available to their families, and the prisons themselves were not publicly identified. Their prison terms varied but typically ended with death. They were known as "the disappeared" (*los desaparecidos*) because their disappearances were neither voluntary nor passive. That is why survivors of that period use a transitive verb when referring to the abductions: "The military disappeared them." These people did not merely disappear, they *were* disappeared.

Harsh as the PEN detentions had been, the disappearances exceeded them in cruelty both to the victims and to their families and friends. Disappearances are very different from arrests, trials, and imprisonments. In a society ruled by law, whether a dictatorship or a democracy, individuals may be arrested and imprisoned for whatever the authorities define as subversion or crimes against the state. The charges may be fair or unfair as judged by others, and the trials may be open or closed, just or unjust, but the arrests and trials are at least publicly acknowledged events; the arrested person, the affected families and friends, are aware of the event. By contrast, to be disappeared is to be put in a state of limbo where one does not exist. There is no record. Family and friends cannot locate the prisoner and do not even know whether this person has been confined or has been killed by state authorities. The title of Jacobo Timerman's book, *Prisoner without a Name, Cell without a Number*, captures well the sense of no longer existing. Identity is erased for the disappeared and for those who knew the disappeared. For the family of the disappeared, there is the agony of never knowing the truth: there is no body, no evidence, nothing beyond the last time the person was seen alive by persons other than their torturers.

Most of the disappeared were never heard of again. Our knowledge of them comes mainly from fellow prisoners who escaped death. Prisoners exchanged names whenever they were able to speak so that others would know who they were and could tell of them if they ever had the chance to do so.

NATIONAL COMMISSION (CONADEP) INVESTIGATION

When the military era ended (hastened to a close by the military's abysmal performance in the Malvinas/Falklands War), a democratically elected government appointed the National Commission on Disappeared People (CONADEP) to investigate human rights crimes. The commission heard from persons who had escaped or otherwise survived the concentration camps, and from witnesses to kidnappings, murders, rapes, robberies, and brutalities imposed on others by military and police personnel. In all, it investigated 8,960 individual cases of kidnapping, torture, rape, and murder, and reported these in *Nunca Más* (Never again). The survivors became the primary witnesses during the trials of the military junta in 1984.

Those who had escaped death did not always escape social opprobrium. If they reappeared after a disappearance, their acquaintances were often afraid to approach or trust them. There was a supposition that they had done something terrible in order to escape. This suspicion was so widespread that some of the former prisoners who testified at the trials of the military in 1984 and 1985 had never before told their stories; some had even hidden from close friends the fact that they had been imprisoned. Thus they disappeared twice: physically for a time, and thereafter with respect to their personal experience and the memory of it.

Typical Experiences of Capture and Torture

The usual procedure was that a family or an individual would be woken in the early hours of the morning by loud noises – sometimes including sirens – by bangings on the door, flashing lights, and demands that the inhabitants of the household let in the police or army. Five or six men, usually not in uniform, would enter the dwelling, and while some of them proceeded to ransack the rooms, one or two would tie up the inhabitants, often inflicting kicks and blows along the way, accusing them of various crimes and finally abducting one or more of them. If the inhabitants were not those particularly sought by the men, they might name an absent person who had to be produced before those present could go free. When this occurred, the men might stay until the missing person turned up, whether this took hours or even days. In other cases, they might take one or more of the inhabitants and seek the missing person on another occasion. Sometimes they killed an abductee immediately, and the body would later be found in a ditch somewhere.

Sometimes the bodies were reported in the newspapers as having been those of terrorists caught in a major gun battle with the intrepid police or army. Although a great many such reports turned up daily in the newspapers – often with remarkable photographs of purported battles and reports of weapons found – most of the people who were abducted from their homes, from urban streets, or from places of work simply disappeared. Blindfolded and handcuffed, they were generally put on the floor of a car, (green Ford Falcons were favoured) and were stomped on by the thugs who had kidnapped them until they reached a detention centre. There they were immediately subjected to torture.

Torture often involved electric prods applied to the genitals, nipples, gums, ears, as well as beatings rhythmically applied to the buttocks and back, with particular attention to any areas where broken bones had resulted from the assault during capture. Many persons were put into the "pits," deep holes in the ground, where they were buried, naked, with only their heads above ground, for several days. When they were extracted, they were covered with insect bites, worms, infections, and their own excrement. Others were made to stand for hours or were hung up against a wall, their arms outstretched and clasped, their legs dangling. Often, in these excruciating positions, they were beaten or given repeated electric shocks. Beatings were always accompanied by insults and threats, so that the prisoner – in pain, naked, blindfolded, obliged to live in his or her own excrement for days on end, and constantly berated – gradually lost all sense of personal identity.

Often, women were raped, repeatedly raped, and mutilated. Not infrequently prisoners would be told that their loved ones were also being held or that a spouse, child, or parent had died. Occasionally a prisoner was brought face to face with an almost dead or raped and tortured loved one. Many reported being asked repeatedly for information that they were unable to give because they did not even understand the demands. They were assumed to be terrorists of some kind, but they were not, and they did not possess the information for which they were being tortured.

Those who were or had been members of terrorist groups were subjected to the same tortures. Presumably, they gave the required information, because the Monteneros – the only remaining group of revolutionaries – were decimated within a very short time of the military coup. Along with them went several thousand young people – high school and university students – who had joined the Peronist Youth and given moral backup to the Montoneros. These young activists had never operated clandestinely and were not trained in the use of weapons. Their sins were those of painting graffiti, distributing pamphlets, and speaking about forbidden topics.

The disappeared included many others who had done things of which the military and police disapproved, in particular, given help – material or spiritual, it mattered not – to poor people who lived in working-class districts or urban slums. This was a sin indulged in by the Third World priests, who were generally on low rungs of the Catholic Church hierarchy, and by young people who followed the priests and believed that their work in the slums was God's Christian work.

Others were condemned by their profession or because of their curiosity: journalists, social scientists, teachers, artists, and lawyers. They did not have to have actually done or said something considered offensive. Their sin might simply be that they read books, were friends with others who read books, or attended plays and other events where intellectual exchanges might have occurred. Ideas were problematic if they were not the ideas of the military. From the beginning of the military regime, whole libraries, public and private, were burned. Of course, those who had said something – discussed the theories of Jean Piaget or Antonio Gramsci, for example – were especially likely to be condemned, along with those who had actually done something, such as providing defence for the poor.

Numbers in the CONADEP Report

Of the estimated 30,000 whose lives were extinguished, most were young people. Among the 8,960 cases identified and described in the

CONADEP report, 81 per cent were aged between sixteen and thirty. Many of the people interviewed for this study spoke of "the killing of a generation," and many of the survivors of that generation are convinced that their generation was targeted. Men were more likely to disappear than women – 70 per cent of those identified by CONADEP were men – so it follows that the primary targets were young men.

By occupation (leaving aside infants and young children who were abducted either alone or with their parents), 30.2 per cent of the disappeared were blue-collar workers (the classification used in Argentina), 21 per cent were students, and 37.3 per cent were white-collar workers, professionals, teachers, journalists, or artists. Self-employed persons made up another 5.0 per cent, while housewives constituted 3.8 per cent; military conscripts and members of the security forces were 2.5 per cent, and members of religious orders 0.3 per cent. As these data indicate, many sectors of society were affected.

The estimate of 30,000 dead and disappeared is only a crude guess. It is based on the number of persons fully identified in the commission's inquiry and on information about others who could not be fully identified, information provided by external sources such as *Le Monde* and Amnesty International, and details compiled by various professional associations about their members. Finally, there was information available at the time of the inquiry on mass burials and the heightened number of burials in known cemeteries during the period of the terror. In 1981 General Roberto Viola, commander-in-chief of the army from 1976 to 1979 and later president, admitted that there had been between 7,000 and 10,000 dead and disappeared.[14]

Babies Born in Torture Chambers

Of the 30 per cent who were women, 3 per cent were pregnant when abducted. The fate of the pregnant women remains a topic that few can speak of without tears. They were generally kept alive until they gave birth, usually in appalling circumstances; in many cases, their babies were removed and given to military personnel and their friends. The film *The Official Story* tells of an adoptive mother's discovery that her child was obtained by her military husband from such a source. An organization of grandmothers (The Abuelas of the Plaza de Mayo, described later in this chapter) has traced many of these children, employing the latest technical developments in DNA mapping and strong legal counsel. During the course of our research, human rights organizations in Argentina succeeded in arguing that the amnesty given to members of the junta did not include the kidnapping of babies. At the end of 1998 and in 1999, junta members were charged with these crimes. Because of their age, they were merely put under house arrest, but the charges were not stayed.

Fear of Reprisals

The commission expressed its awareness that a great many families were unwilling to testify in 1984 because they did not trust any government proceedings and feared repercussions. By that time, some mass graves had been discovered and the corpses exhumed. Genetic and other examinations were being undertaken by forensic anthropologists and medical personnel, and these forensic procedures became more frequent over the next decade.[15] Gradually, other means of disposing of bodies were revealed, in particular throwing drugged individuals (as well as corpses) from planes into the Atlantic Ocean.

Much more information has come to light since 1984, including details of burials in cemeteries where the numbers increased dramatically between March 1976 and mid-1978 (after which the killings tapered off). One of the pilots engaged in flying planes from which comatose detainees were thrown into the ocean told his tale in 1995, replete with the lurid details.[16] This man, Adolfo Francisco Scilingo, was reviled by his former colleagues, and in September 1997 he was caught by a gang of men and his face was severely mutilated by knife wounds.

It is quite possible that if the numbers were to be reconsidered in the late 1990s, the total estimate would be larger. Supporters of the military, however, argue that the commission's methods were faulty and that not even 9,000 disappeared. But as was pointed out to us by several persons concerned with human rights, even one disappearance, one torture, or one clandestine murder by the state is already too many. It does of course matter how many disappeared, but the number itself is not the most important piece of information in judging *El proceso*.

CASE TESTIMONIES TO THE NATIONAL COMMISSION

Of the thousands of events described in *Nunca Más*, the following testimonies are typical:

At 12:30 a.m. on 24 March 1976, our house in Villa Rivera Indarte in Córdoba province was broken into by men in uniform carrying rifles. They identified themselves as belonging to the Army, and they were accompanied by a number of youths in casual dress. They trained their guns on us while they stole books, *objets d'art*, bottles of wine etc., which the uniformed men carried outside. They did not talk to each other, but communicated by snapping their fingers.

The looting of our house lasted for over two hours: before the raid there had been a blackout in all the neighbouring streets. My husband, a trade union official, my son, David, and myself were abducted. I was freed the next day. My son was freed some time later, after being held in the La Ribera camp. Our house was completely destroyed. My husband's body was found with seven bullet wounds in the throat. (File no. 3860: Alberto Santiago Burnichon)[17]

At 4 a.m. on 21 April 1976, several men in civilian clothes forced their way into my house. They were heavily armed and identified themselves as belonging to the Navy and the Federal Police. Their commander said he was Inspector Mayorga. They took away my father, who was sixty-five at that time. The following day my brother Miguel presented a writ of habeas corpus the San Isidro court. At 9 p.m. on that same day they came back to my house, this time taking away my mother, hooded. They took her somewhere she has never been able to identify, and for five days subjected her to a violent interrogation. Following her capture, the members of the Armed Forces stayed on in my house. On 23 April my brother Miguel was kidnapped as he entered. During these operations, which lasted for four hours on 21 April, and thirty-six hours from the 22nd onwards, those involved would not allow anyone to give me assistance, although I am a quadriplegic. I had to remain in the same position without eating or having my physical needs attended to. They were constantly trying to force me to telephone my sister, María del Carmen. At one point the telephone fell to the floor and they brought another one, which is still in my house. When they finally left, they drove off in a Ford Falcon car that I had bought. My mother was set free, blindfolded, two blocks from our house. My father and brother have never reappeared. I was later told that my sister, María del Carmen Núñez, her husband, Jorge Lizaso, and one of his brothers, Miguel Francisco Lizaso, were also abducted, and their flat completely ransacked in the process. They are also among the lists of the disappeared. (File no. 3081: Roque Núñez)[18]

As I was inserting the key in the lock I realized what was happening, because the door was pulled inwards violently and I stumbled forward.

I jumped back, trying to escape. Two shots (one in each leg) stopped me. However, I still put up a struggle, and for several minutes resisted, being handcuffed and hooded, as best I could. At the same time, I was shouting at the top of my lungs that I was being kidnapped, begging my neighbours to tell my family, and to try to stop them taking me away.

Finally, exhausted and blindfolded, I was told by the person who apparently was in command that my wife and two daughters had already been captured and "disappeared."

They had to drag me out, since I couldn't walk because of the wounds in my legs ... (They) threw me on the floor of a car, possibly a Ford Falcon, and set off. They hauled me out of the car in the same way ... then they threw me on to a table. They tied me by my hands and feet to its four corners ...

Then I heard another voice. This one said he was the "Colonel." He told me they knew I was not involved with terrorism or the guerrillas, but that they were going to torture me because I opposed the regime, because: "I hadn't understood that in Argentina there was no room for any opposition to the Process of National Reorganization." He then added: "You're going to pay dearly for it ... the poor won't have any goody-goodies to look after them any more!" ... For days they applied electric shocks to my gums, nipples, genitals, abdomen and ears ...

They then began to beat me systematically and rhythmically with wooden sticks on my back, the backs of my thighs, my calves and the soles of my feet ... This continued for several days, alternating the two tortures. Sometimes they did both at the same time ... In between torture sessions they left me hanging by my arms from hooks fixed in the wall of the cell where they had thrown me ...

At one point when I was face-down on the torture table, they lifted my head then removed my blindfold to show me a bloodstained rag. They asked me if I recognized it and, without waiting for reply – impossible anyway because it was unrecognizable, and my eyesight was very badly affected – they told me it was a pair of my wife's knickers. No other explanation was given, so that I would suffer all the more ... then they blindfolded me again and carried on with their beating ...

One day they put me face-down on the torture table, tied me up (as always), and calmly began to strip the skin from the soles of my feet. I imagine, though I didn't see it because I was blindfolded, that they were doing it with a razor blade or scalpel. I could feel them pulling as if they were trying to separate the skin at the edge of the wound with a pair of pincers. I passed out ... I began to feel that I was living alongside death. When I wasn't being tortured I had hallucinations about death – sometimes when I was awake, at other times while sleeping ... I felt it was impossible to think. I desperately tried to summon up a thought in order to convince myself I wasn't dead. That I wasn't mad. At the same time, I wished with all my heart that they would kill me as soon as possible ...

In the midst of all this terror, I'm not sure when, they took me off to the "operating theatre." There they tied me up and began to torture my testicles. I don't know if they did this by hand or with a machine. I'd never experienced such pain. It was as though they were pulling out all my insides from my throat and brain downwards. As though my throat, brain, stomach and testicles were linked by a nylon thread which they were pulling on, while at the same time crushing everything. My only wish was for them to succeed in pulling all my insides out so that I would be completely empty. Then I passed out ... (File no. 7397: Dr Norberto Liwsky)[19]

The Case of Mónica Mignone

In May 1976, shortly after the coup, Mónica Mignone, the twenty-four-year-old daughter of a prominent family in Buenos Aires, was abducted from her parents' home in the small hours of the morning by five armed men dressed ambiguously in military trousers with civilian shirts. Her parents, still inclined to trust authority, believed the soldiers when they said she would be questioned and then released. Through the many agonizing weeks that followed, they searched everywhere, spoke to everyone, begged, questioned, and followed every possible lead; but they never again saw Mónica. Her case became known throughout Argentina and has since become the signature case for an international community concerned with the disappearances.

Her father, Emilio Mignone, a lawyer, president of a Catholic university, a loyal Peronist and Catholic, became a leader of the relatives of the disappeared and of human rights organizations in Argentina. He also became a severe critic, even while remaining a loyal Catholic, of the bishops who had not only failed the people but had in fact collaborated with the military. Among his subsequent publications was a very strong indictment of church leaders and other elites. He stated there: "Most Argentinians were confused and uneasy, but those who belonged to the well-informed sectors of society – military officers, high officials, diplomats, and political, social, financial, business, and labor leaders, as well as journalists and bishops – were quite well aware of what was going on, and many of them justified it, welcomed it, and even cooperated in it."[20]

Mónica's "sin," he inferred, was that she had worked as a volunteer caregiver in the poor neighbourhoods, together with several priests and six other young people who were also disappeared at the same time. She was a trained educational psychologist and was employed both in a local hospital and at a university:

She went every week to the shantytowns with the priests and other students in order to develop some better conditions for these poor people. She never had the time or the opportunity to engage in military actions. My wife and I often went with her to the shantytowns to help out. Perhaps she cared too much. The military did not appreciate that. They said, "you are only helping poor people. This is materialistic. You should help the rich as well with spiritual development." They said this was a materialist interpretation of the Gospel, of the Sermon on the Mount.

Ever since that ominous May morning, we desperately appealed to all kinds of authorities in order to find out something about Mónica. The same was true for the families of her friends who lost their freedom that same day. I do not know the names of the five men who took Mónica. I know now that they took her to the ESMA [La Escuela Superior Mecánica de la Armada, the concentration camp run by the navy]. They said they were army, but they were navy. They said they would take her for only a short while, but they took her forever.[21]

The Cases of Dissident Priests

While a minority of Catholic priests had been active in the Third World Priests' Movement from 1968 to 1974 (by which time repression and assassinations had silenced them), the official church had no sympathy for subversives, not even for those who, like Mónica Mignone, were simply trying to improve health care and welfare in the slums. The archbishop of Paraná, Adolfo Tortolo, blessed the leaders of the junta before the coup. The military vicar of Tucumán, Monsignor Victorio Bonamín, talked about the need for a dirty war even before the junta launched its phase of repression; he said it was "a war in which God Himself must have been interested, so that He could participate with HIS help."[22] Although thousands of bereaved and terrified Catholics beseeched the church to help them find disappeared loved ones, the church did not act, and its public statements offered no comfort.

Those within the church who did not toe the line were vulnerable. On 4 July 1976 three Pallotine priests and two seminarians were murdered in the rectory of the San Patricio Church in the wealthy district of Belgrano. Written in their blood were the words "For poisoning the virgin minds of our youth" and "Priests sons of bitches." One of the seminarians had been raped. This massacre was attributed to a discomfiting message that had been offered up each Sunday to middle-class parishioners, who included military personnel, judges, and businessmen, obliging them to consider the poor. The murders were originally blamed on paramilitary forces, but testimony before the commission in 1984 revealed that they had been carried out under the orders of Rear-Admiral Rubén Chamorro, head of ESMA. The same task force that killed the Pallotine priests also killed three French nuns (in connection with the abduction of the first leaders of the Mothers of the Plaza de Mayo, discussed below) and an Argentine diplomat who crossed Admiral Massera, Elena Holmberg.[23]

Another murder in the church was that of Bishop Enrique Angelelli of La Rioja, who had dedicated himself to improving the lot of the poor farmers in his province. He was denounced by the wealthy landowners, and those who worked with him were subjected to harassment and imprisonment without cause. When the bishop preached against a military takeover at a mass at an air force base shortly before the coup, the military objected strongly enough to bring about a public apology from Monsignor Bonamín. In July 1976 two of the parish priests were murdered. Finally, in August, Angelelli and his aide, driving to La Rioja from the air force base, were forced off the road in a deliberate murder attempt, which resulted in the bishop's death. The file he had put together on the earlier murders disappeared following the accident. Witnesses refused to testify until 1984, when they spoke before the commission.

Night of the Pencils

The night of 16 September 1976 is remembered in La Plata as "the night of the pencils," when ten children, aged between fourteen and eighteen, were forcibly removed from their homes because they had taken part in a campaign to subsidize bus fares for students. According to the testimony in *Nunca Más*, "The Buenos Aires Provincial Police had decided to punish everyone who had participated in the pro-school subsidy campaign, because the Armed Forces considered it to be 'subversion in the schoolroom.'"[24] Six of these students were tortured and killed.[25] One, Pablo Díaz, spent four years in jail and was then released. He was a key witness at the commission inquiry.

The Case of Jacobo Timerman

Jacobo Timerman, editor of *La Opinión*, was abducted from his home in April 1977. He was interrogated by General Ramón Camps and tortured. The reason provided by the army for his abduction, and that of others as well, was that Timerman had had financial relations with an Argentine banker, David Graiver, who was believed to be a business front for recycling Montonero funds (a charge later acknowledged as true by Mario Firmenich.)[26] Graiver was killed in an airplane crash in 1976, shortly before two of his largest financial holdings collapsed. He was the owner of 45 per cent of the shares in Timerman's newspaper.[27] Shortly before Timerman's abduction, Edgardo Sajón, the printing plant director of *La Opinión* and a high-profile journalist, was also kidnapped. *Latin America Political Report* speculated that Sajón, also suspected of having dealings with Graiver, was killed resisting capture.[28]

Timerman and Graiver were Jews, and General Camps was known as a vigorous anti-Semite; for Camps, Timerman represented an international Jewish conspiracy. The DAIA (Delegación de Asociaciones Israelitas Argentinas / Delegation of Argentiine Israelite Associations) publicized the case, and Timerman became an international *cause célèbre.* Jimmy Carter personally intervened on his behalf. He was released into house arrest a year after his kidnapping. A year and a half later, he was stripped of his citizenship and expelled from Argentina. There is no doubt that his interrogators and torturers were anti-Semitic, but whether he was kidnapped because he was Jewish or because of his relations with Graiver, or because of the small amount of banned information published in his newspaper is not clear: there is more to the story than the capture of one newspaper editor. For what little it is worth, the Argentine Information Secretariat stated publicly that his arrest was not an infringement of press freedom and was not connected with his condition as a Jew; that it was connected solely to his relationships with Graiver.[29]

By 1977 many other publishers, editors, and reporters had been subjected to torture. But amongst editors, there were mixed reactions to the news of Timerman's capture. James Neilson of the *Buenos Aires Herald* was one of the few newspaper voices to speak out strongly in support of efforts to release Timerman,[30] but he later wrote: "Timerman ... helped make Argentina the kind of society in which thousands of people could be made to 'disappear' and prominent newspaper owners could be jailed and tortured without anyone batting an eyelid ... Had he been overlooked by the 'hardliners' he could easily have become one of the most effective propagandists of the 'process' ... That, indeed, was the role he was beginning to assume when he was seized."[31] More consistent with the claimed relationship to David Graiver, Timerman was also accused of having been sympathetic to the guerrillas, though that might have grown out of his strong antipathy to the Perón government prior to the coup.

Timerman himself, in *Prisoner without a Name, Cell without a Number,* argues that he and his newspaper were moderates, opposed to extremism in the military forces as well as the guerrilla forces, and that his was "the only daily newspaper concerned with the disappeared."[32] He believes that he was kidnapped by an extremist faction within the army. He points out that the distribution of responsibilities created a vast range of interest groups, and that while the leaders might recognize the stupidity of kidnapping Jacobo Timerman, other factions – extremists in one form or another, fanatical anti-Semites, or simply groups that did not like the coverage by *La Opinión* – could operate independently of the chiefs. Despite his loss of freedom, his book ultimately defends Videla and Viola, and blames the excesses on minorities and extremists. He argues that these extremists were more anti-Semitic than anticommunist; that they were in fact reconstructed Nazis. In defence of his claim that the perpetrators were a faction within the army, it must be pointed out that the generals did attempt to obtain his freedom; he was held in house arrest and ordered out of the country despite their efforts. As is the perennial case in Argentina, nothing is straightforward.

THE EMERGENCE OF HUMAN RIGHTS ACTIVISTS

One human rights organization existed in Buenos Aires before the coup. The Argentine League for the Rights of Man (Liga Argentina por los Derochos del Hombre) was loosely affiliated with the Communist Party. Its leaders were subjected to imprisonment and torture after the coup. But the coup had an unanticipated consequence: it gave rise to a much stronger demand for protection of human rights than had ever before existed in Argentina. By 1977, parents of imprisoned and disappeared children, together with many others, were beginning to meet clandestinely to develop plans for peaceful opposition. Out of these meetings grew such organizations as the Mothers (Madres) and Grandmothers (Abuelas) of the Plaza de Mayo, and the Relatives of the Disappeared and Detained for Political Reasons (Familiares de Desaparecidos y Detenidos por Razones Políticos; or simply Familiares).

The Madres met in the Plaza de Mayo, opposite the Presidential Palace. From the original small gathering of frightened but tenacious women who started the organization in April 1977, there emerged a mighty force in opposition to the military dictatorship. Each Thursday women met at the plaza and marched in a circle, carrying placards naming their disappeared loved ones. They took to wearing white diapers as scarves and began embroidering the names of disappeared relatives on these. The first leader of this group, Azucena Villaflor de Vicenti, was disappeared in December 1977, when she and a French nun were kidnapped in their homes following the abduction of nine other women from the movement (eventually fourteen women disappeared). The women were betrayed by an infiltrator, the naval officer Alfredo Astiz, and forcibly taken by a gang of men from the church where the mothers were meeting.[33]

The Thursday marches of the mothers at the Plaza de Mayo attracted many foreign journalists, especially during the 1978 World Cup soccer championships. Although the soccer matches successfully distracted the home audience, the foreign audience heard a great deal about the disappearances, along with TV images of the white-scarved matriarchs. Afterwards, the mothers were too well known to external television audiences for the junta to disappear more of them, though harassment continued throughout the junta's tenure – for instance, brutal eviction from the plaza from time to time, the arrest of sixty-eight marchers in 1981, and personal threats. Yet their fame had so grown that unsolicited funds arrived to help them obtain a permanent abode where they could plan tactics and meet outsiders. The new leader of the group was Hebe de Bonafini, mother of three disappeared children. In 1980, when the number of disappearances diminished and the junta began talking about national reconciliation, the mothers split into two groups. One was still led by de Bonafini; the other was called Linea Fundadora. Those belonging to the latter have indicated that they accept that their children are dead, but de Bonafini and her group adamantly refuse to accept this without proof. Their position is that the government took their children away and has yet to take responsibility for what happened to them.

As noted above, the grandmothers emerged in 1977 as a distinct group with a separate mission – to locate grandchildren born in captivity and adopted by military families or by friends of the military. In our interview with them, a spokeswoman talked of the inhuman conditions under which their daughters had given birth before they were killed: "For that reason we are seeking truth and justice for our children and for our grandchildren. We never say they are dead, because we don't know what happened to them. The state should tell us where they are, who judged them, who condemned them, and what happened. It is the duty of the state to give us answers."

The grandmothers tell of how they visited maternity wards everywhere to see if they could find their pregnant daughters: "We were totally disoriented, we had no experience of disappeared children. When we calculated that the birth dates had come and gone, we began to visit hospitals. Still no response. And finally we went to judges. We began to recognize one another in these places, all of us searching."

Initially, they identified 180 infants whom they believed were born in prison. By 1990, the group had identified 215 missing grandchildren. They had to find ways of proving that a child whom they had identified was their grandchild, and in this they were helped by European and American experts in genetic mapping of blood and gene types. Using these methods, they have reclaimed fifty-seven children over a period of nineteen years. Although genetic mapping has improved in recent years, the task gets ever more difficult because now they are searching for young adults. They have always made a distinction between children adopted in good faith and those who were "stolen" by people with full knowledge that the babies had been born in prison. The reclaimed children, however, have been informed of their true identity. Partly as a result of their efforts, but even more because of the passage of time and the growth of the children into knowledgeable adults, a relatively new association has been formed by "Children of the Disappeared," known as HIJOS.

The origins of the Familiares were described in chapter 8, in the interview with Sr and Sra Westerkamp. This group continues to be very active, helping relatives of missing persons, providing a meeting place for the children of the disappeared (the HIJOS group), and putting together detailed dossiers on missing persons of Spanish, Italian, or other non-Argentine citizenship. The dossiers are transmitted to European governments in the hope that they will find ways of prosecuting members of the junta, or identified torturers, for the disappearance of their citizens. In 1997, while we were in Buenos Aires, the Familiares offices were broken into and a batch of dossiers stolen. It was not the first time this had happened. Such events remind everyone that although the coup occurred two decades earlier, many of those who have much to hide for their role in the repression are still free and have not changed their habits.

In addition to these organizations of relatives, there are numerous groups devoted to pressuring the government to improve its legislation on civil rights. These include the Permanent Assembly for Human Rights (Asamblea Permanente por los Derochos Humanos) and the Centre for Legal and Social Studies (Centro de Estudios Legales y Sociales, CELS), which undertake research services, maintain extensive newspaper clippings and libraries on the 1970s dictatorship, provide legal assistance to individuals whose human rights have been violated, and act as lobby groups for human rights.

MANAGEMENT OF
THE ECONOMY

The military junta did not attempt to restructure the Argentine economy through its own capacities. It appointed as its minister of the economy José Martínez de Hoz, heir to one of the wealthiest landowner/industrial holdings in the country and an economist of substantial reputation in his own right. His policies, which at the time were labelled "monetarist" but were called "neoliberal" by many of our interviewees, were forerunners of the international movement to dismantle all national barriers to trade. However, in practice, Martínez de Hoz did not apply free-market policies consistently. He was obliged to shift toward interventionist policies from time to time, in order to avoid either extreme unemployment or equally extreme inflation.

Despite these oscillations, the long-term thrust of his policies included reduction of real wages throughout the economy to a level about 40 per cent below the average of the previous five years. As pointed out by William C. Smith, this meant massive income transfers from lower to higher income earners, and reduced demand for mass-consumption goods. Says Smith: "Pursuit of this goal was at least partially responsible for high levels of 'structurally necessary' repression of the working class, unions, and political parties."[34] Like Guillermo O'Donnell, Smith understands the abiding agenda of the military to be restructuring and argues that this was so in 1976 as well as a decade earlier, but his approach does not require a specific process of modernization as its base.

Smith observes that restructuring inevitably provokes resistance from the subordinate classes, the classes excluded from power, who "bear the brunt of economic policies designed to control inflation and increase savings and investment." Yet he argues that eliminating these classes or their resistance is not the primary task undertaken by military regimes in this situation; moreover, these regimes are as likely to meet extreme rejection by capital. This is because the process involves the "reorganization from above" of capital itself, in the state-led projects: "The identification of the state as the subject, object, and determinant of political struggles and class conflicts, therefore, emerges at the centre of any analysis of state-led restructuring."[35] Resistance may come from other sources too, says Smith: the "struggles within the state apparatus and among the various fractions of capital are equally as important as, if not more important than, the state's handling of the 'threat from below.'"[36]

Finally, military and civilian technocratic elites may resist any return to genuine private-sector economies or civilian governments because they have strong vested interests in the state-centred economy. Thus, the new policies of the military government are not to be interpreted as the directives of a cohesive upper class or the policies of a cohesive middle class even within the military bureaucracy. Indeed, as we survey what actually happened under the neoliberal ministers of the economy, we discover that they failed to improve the economy over the long run. The failure may be attributed to the intrinsic nature of the policies or to the continual resistance mounted by diverse sectors of the population.

Martínez de Hoz removed export taxes on agricultural and livestock products, thus allowing the agro-export bourgeoisie to benefit. He reduced import tariffs substantially and curtailed protection of domestic industries and industries for which there was no comparative advantage in Argentina. The financial sector was to be reformed, foreign exchange markets were to be liberalized, and public-sector prices were to be raised in order to promote efficiency and stimulate entrepreneurial administration of state enterprises. Privatization was a policy, but it was blocked both by the inefficiency of many of the enterprises that would be involved and by the military ownership of many of these entities. Finally, the policy would reduce public expenditures on social welfare. Thus health, education, housing, and so on would all receive sharply reduced state funds.

In practice, the policies implemented by Martínez de Hoz very nearly bankrupted the country. In the first year, having gained the approval of the International Monetary Fund, he saw the foreign-trade balance improve slightly, but inflation continued and the reduction of real wages deepened the recession. In the second year, a major "financial reform" was put in place, but it had the effect of sharply increasing inflation and discouraging industrial investment. By early 1978, according to Smith, orthodox monetarism and the rigour of the "old" Chicago school was being abandoned. New policies were introduced to force down inflation, including restrictions on the inflow of new foreign capital. These policies failed, and they had the unintended side effect of attenuating income transfers that favoured the agro-export bourgeoisie of the pampas.

Finally, in December 1978, Martínez de Hoz attempted another anti-inflationary policy that adversely affected the industrial sector. Called "sweet money," because imported goods could be brought in at far less than the cost of locally manufactured products, an artificially ranked Argentine peso permitted hundreds of upper-class Argentines to vacation in Miami and come back loaded with electronic goods on which they paid no tariffs. Total imports increased and domestic firms lost competitive capacity; by 1980 both nationally owned firms and local subsidiaries of transnational corporations producing for the domestic market were in difficulty, and some went bankrupt. Between April 1980 and March of 1981, seventy-two financial institutions died; a major industrial conglomerate and Argentina's largest agricultural exporter collapsed, leaving a billion-dollar debt; and some 15 per cent of the urban labour force was unemployed. Argentina's economy was in a crisis even more extreme than the one that had preceded the military coup.

As agreed between the three military forces prior to the 1976 coup, General Videla and Admiral Massera stepped down in 1981. Videla was succeeded by General Roberto Viola; Massera, by Rear Admiral Armando Lambruschini. Viola immediately dismissed Martínez de Hoz and appointed a new economic team headed by Lorenzo Sigaut. The peso was devalued, and tariffs were reduced still further, but the financial crises continued through 1981.

In December 1981 Viola was ousted and succeeded by General Leopoldo Fortunato Galtieri. Galtieri represented Catholic nationalists, a faction regarded as even more hardline and authoritarian than the "liberals." His economic "superminister," Roberto Alemann, failed, just as Martínez de Hoz and Sigaut had. The gross national product fell by 11.4 per cent in the last quarter of 1981, and industrial production declined by 23 per cent. Real wages declined by 20 per cent while Alemann advocated "Reaganomics," including the dismantling of the remaining measures that protected local industry or workers and the privatization of state enterprises.[37] From this point on, the rivalries between the generals and the three services, as well as between various factions within the services, became open conflict.

THE MALVINAS ADVENTURE

On 2 April 1982, Argentina invaded the Malvinas Islands, otherwise known as the Falklands, which were under the protection of Britain. Apart from the insanity of this desperate attempt to deflect attention from the economic crisis, the international condemnation of the disappearances, and the internal conflicts within the military forces, Galtieri almost pushed Argentina into international financial insolvency with this invasion. Contrary to his expectations, the United States sided with Britain, and Britain brought with it the economic sanctions of the European Economic Community. Says William Smith: "Even if Argentina somehow had managed to avoid defeat, it would have been impossible to return to orthodox economic policy-making. Neo-liberal economic policies had become anathema to the majority of the population and were no longer palatable to important sectors within the armed forces."[38]

Galtieri and his minister were ousted, and the surviving generals were unable to agree on the succession. The navy and air force withdrew from the junta. The army "liberals" reasserted themselves in July 1982, with the appointment of General Reynaldo Bignone as president. However, the junta no longer existed, and Galtieri negotiated a withdrawal in favour of democratic elections in October 1983.

CHAPTER 10

Revolutionaries and Sceptics

It was a time of intellectual and political ferment, a time when young people felt obliged to commit themselves to causes they believed would save their country. It was a time of great danger for those who did commit themselves – and also for many who did not. This chapter provides accounts by people who were young revolutionaries at the time, and it tells something of the price they paid for their convictions.

These are not heroic stories. Most of the heroes did not survive. And most of the unheroic survivors are beset by doubts about whether the enterprise in which they staked their young lives had integrity. As one of our informants said, "Tell our story, and tell the truth: we were not innocents, we did commit crimes. But we were also up against truly evil enemies." Most survivors were unwilling to consider the possibility that their leaders had been double agents, but they were no longer prepared to believe that the leaders had told them the truth about everything. One of the untruths that was particularly offensive was perpetrated long after the events: it was the surviving leaders' blatant underestimate of the number of Montoneros killed by the military. The lie allows the surviving leaders to escape accountability for putting thousands of young lives at risk when they themselves went underground and, later, escaped to Europe. If their dead companions were so easily discounted, what was the use of the struggle?

VOICE: CRISTINE

At the end of the 1960s, when I was just eighteen or so, I began to understand the political currents in our world. The *cordobazo* was a reaction against the military dictatorship of that time, and it revealed a very strong conflict between the dictators and the labourers, workers, students – in fact, the whole population of the province of Córdoba. We young women began to see a different vision of the world at that time. Until then, boys and girls were educated in separate schools, and our education was traditional. The *cordobazo* was a political awakening for a whole generation. We embraced the idea of changing the world. The story of Che Guevara and all his struggles made a strong impression on Argentine youth; Guevara's struggle was ours. I wanted to be a ballet dancer and I also studied theatre in drama school, but instead, when I finished high school, I immediately began to dedicate all my energy to political activism.

I was from a Peronist family and the Peronist resistance was strong. Behind the Peronist flags was a whole mass movement pressing for the return of Perón and hoping that the Argentine military dictatorship would be defeated in the elections scheduled for 1973. I joined the Juventud Peronista and worked in the slums in Buenos Aires. We worked on many projects: health, literacy, repairs in the ghettos. And all this had a political agenda – to bring people from the slums into our political life. I was not personally involved in armed action, but I was an activist.

When Perón returned, that was a day of great excitement for me. It was also the day that I met my future husband, whom I soon married. He was a Montonero in the political section, not the armed section. Perón had a plan for change in the country, a total change of the structure of society. And for that reason, many people, not just Peronists, put their hopes on the return of Perón. But the next year, on 24 May 1974, Perón gave his speech in the Plaza de Mayo when he told the Montoneros to disband. This was very hard on us. We had been separated from the Peronist party, from all the action – in other words, from our vocation.

Shortly after that, I gave birth to my first son. My husband continued to work with the Montoneros, but now his work was clandestine. I was at his side throughout that time. The military coup was in March 1976. In February 1977 my husband disappeared.

During the year before he disappeared, it was very hard. *Compañeros* were kidnapped every day. We were never completely clandestine, but we moved constantly because any of our *compañeros* who were abducted or imprisoned might identify us under torture. I slept in the street many times, pregnant, and with my two-year-old son, and sometimes friends would come to tell me that someone had been killed. Sometimes we travelled all night on one bus and then, when we got to the terminal, on another bus. Or we had to look for a friend's house or an acquaintance or a relative or a neighbour who would let us sleep there. Or stay the whole day in the zoo, pregnant, and with my oldest son, waiting from morning to night until they closed the zoo and someone would take me to sleep somewhere. It was a very horrible period, very dangerous. Then, on February 20, a Sunday, my second son was born.

The following Saturday they took my husband away. They grabbed him in the street during a meeting with his *compañeros*, with a whole group of militant Montoneros. Then they broke into the house where I was staying. I had just finished breast-feeding the baby. I pulled up my slip, I put him in the crib, and at that moment they suddenly entered. They kicked me, they opened the stitches from the birth, and other things. Then they had my newborn baby on the floor, they grabbed him by his feet, with his head toward the ground, and they put a gun in his mouth. They broke everything, they checked everything, looking for things. They said they were under the authority of the superintendency of federal security. And, well, they had me on the floor. Thankfully, my older son was not there, he was with my mother.

To have to remember that day exactly makes me feel terrible. All the rest, the fight, the pain, it was all crazy. That day, from a personal point of view, caused me many years of therapy, of psychoanalysis to be able to talk about it and tell it. It was very terrible, very frightening. There was a lot of fear, violence, aggression.

When my mother arrived a little more than two hours afterwards – they had left because the neighbours called – I was there with no clothes. I had a nightshirt, and they had torn it all and it was all bloody because the stitches from the birth were open. And my mother didn't know what was going on. The whole house was torn up, everything completely broken, and the baby was also naked because they had taken off his diapers to see if he had anything inside. I didn't know how to explain to her what they had done to me. It took me many years to talk about what had happened.

I went out as soon as I could to look for my husband. Since they had told me that they were from the federal superintendency, that same night I went to the branch of federal superintendency and told them that they had torn open my stitches and that I couldn't walk properly because of how they had left me, and, well, there they told me that they didn't have him, that they had no prisoners there. Later we found out that there were prisoners there, that there was a secret centre functioning there, that they tortured people there, that kidnapped people were taken there.

I never had official information about my husband. Many years later some people we knew began coming out of the secret concentration camps, and others returned from exile. From them, I started to get information about where my husband could have been. And in 1984, I made contact with people who could confirm for me that he was in the navy school concentration camp [La Escuela Superior

Mecánica de la Armada, known as ESMA]. These people had been imprisoned there after my husband died. Then, just last year, 1996, I met a *compañero* of my husband, a Montonero who had been caught together with him in the same place and who had survived. He said that my husband died in the ESMA. He died two or three days after suffering very painful agony caused by torture. Officially I never found out anything. Everything I know has come from this person, who also told me that at that time they were not yet throwing the bodies into the sea; those who died were being incinerated behind the ESMA.

When I was searching for him, I went to various offices of the church. I went to the Edificio Libertad, which is the navy cell responsible for the ESMA. That was where the bishop Monseñor Graceli was. At the entrance to the building, navy personnel demanded that we show our documents. They made notes in an index about us seeking information. Then we would see this priest, who also had an index on his desk, and there he would ask us for information. And he would say to me, "I can't find your husband anywhere. Tell me the name of one of his friends." He always asked for information because he was working for the navy. My husband was already dead.

VOICE: MIGUEL

It is hard to speak about my personal experience, because 1976 was a very difficult time for me. Three years earlier it would have been impossible to imagine that I was going to be involved in those things. It took me a long time to convince myself that this was actually happening. I was twenty-two, preparing for a career in law, and working as a clerk in the legal system. My life was on the right track. I was happy and I wanted to become a judge. I married in 1975, and all was well, yet one year later I found myself without home, without career, without job, living in the underground.

My previous political participation had been limited. You know that in the years 1972–74 there was a great social convulsion here, and as a result of the authoritarian system, human rights were limited. One was, in a sense, forbidden to be young and to have long hair, listen to rock music, or kiss on the street. Participation in unions or in political associations or cultural organizations was limited. This explains to some degree the political radicalization that influenced myself and others during our adolescence. I had been a member of the Students' Centre in the Faculty of Law, but I gave that up in 1973 because I was not an activist and I did not want to be a politician.

Shortly after that, with the democratic government in power, repression was resumed against the people. There were right-wing extremists who were gradually penetrating the democratic government. After the death of Perón, it became much worse. All public activities were marked by violence. In 1975 fascists, supported by the state apparatus, murdered someone every twenty hours. Many of the victims were young people – students, workers, neighbourhood political leaders. They were our friends and acquaintances. Facing such a situation we became aware that the state had completely abandoned its duty to protect its citizens. The state wanted to have us dead. We never asked a policeman for protection because it was the police who were kidnapping and killing.

Anybody opposed to the politics of the government ran the risk of death. No distinction was made between a political and a critical position. The majority of civil opponents were in democratic and parliamentary parties, and they were at risk. This spiral of violence made it impossible for us, at that time, to imagine any kind of political action outside the context of violence. One was prepared to be violent in order to survive.

The violence increased with the coup of 1976. The state removed its mask of legality. The fascist organizations transformed themselves into the armed forces and government. The state imposed a regime of terror that included concentration camps, the kidnapping of unarmed citizens, systematic torture, homicide, and disappearances.

Well, in March 1976, during the coup, I was working in a court that dealt with economic crimes. At the same time I was working in the union uniting the employees of the judicial system. This was the first organization of judicial employees in Argentina. During its formation, less than one month before the coup, some of the leading members of the union were kidnapped and murdered. Knowing this, when the coup occurred, I stayed away from work for a week, waiting to see what would happen. Then I returned, and I found the court surrounded by military forces of the federal penitentiary service. They controlled entry. Employees all had to present their credentials, and some judicial employees were kidnapped even over the judges' protests.

Shortly after my return, two people came to the national court from the federal penitentiary service, asking for me. They were going to arrest me. Luckily, the employees at the front desk informed them that I was not working there any more (even though I was in the other room). The system had such impunity that it could arrest and disappear workers right inside the court.

Immediately, I went to talk to the judge. He said he could not assist me, could not even accompany me to the door. He gave me a card on which he wrote a number where I could reach him in an emergency, but then he asked me to leave. What is the meaning of this action?

The judge could not impede the kidnapping of an employee in the court. He was unable to guarantee my security by letting me stay there. He told me that the best he could do was advise me to hide myself elsewhere, and then, in a brave act, he gave me a card. If I was caught I could perhaps use it as a kind of very questionable "passport."

I believe that the judge could have protested against illegal arrests. But he stayed at his desk. There were many concentration camps already operating in Buenos Aires, and a judge could have reported the existence of kidnapped people in them. One of these camps was less than thirty blocks from the court. Any judge could have gone there and demonstrated that there were people being tortured and murdered. But instead, the judges enclosed themselves in their offices. When the parents of the disappeared presented their habeas corpus and asked for help, the judges said they did not know where the *desaparecidos* were.

I was known within the judicial system as a union activist, though the activism in that system was not very militant. I was actually asking for an increase in salary. Five years afterwards I would have been a functionary of the judicial system, and a few years later still, I would have become a professional, just to give you an idea of how we lived before the coup. I had purchased a house when I married. None of my friends had visited my house, nor had I given them my telephone number, for security reasons. I must underline that I did not live underground; I had my job, my family, and I was a regular student, but at that time no one exchanged telephone numbers or visited others any more. Well, I remained at my house until one of my associates was arrested, and then I left the house with my wife, who at that time was twenty-one years old.

Without any vocation for underground living and without any enthusiasm for any revolution, nevertheless, facing the reality of the disappearance and murder of friends, I tried to figure out what to do. My parents offered to help me leave the country. We did not want to accept this, and finally I decided to become involved with the Montoneros. Something had to be done, and I felt I had to act. So I took part in such activities as stealing documents, stealing vehicles, and transporting people in order to get them out of the country. At that stage, the Montoneros were helping many people get out of the country, and for that they needed vehicles and money. These were anarchic conditions, where all that one could do was so little.

This awful period lasted several months, almost a year. It involved much violence. But, surprisingly, I found myself not fighting to overthrow the dictatorship. I was simply trying to save the lives of a few people, and this cost me a great deal. Our parental families broke off relations with us. There were long periods when I did not see my wife. Without a home or job, I became increasingly dependent on the Montoneros. But that group, too, was so greatly repressed that its structures practically disappeared. The leaders left the country. After a while we became virtual thieves, holding up gas stations and stores. Our contact with the Montoneros was ever more sporadic. Our task was to stay alive, and we were continually seeking information that would let us know who had been caught. The information was unreliable. Our contact people disappeared, and we would frantically seek other contacts.

In desperation, we started to hijack buses in order to explain to people who were going to work that we lived under the dictatorship, that people had been kidnapped, that they could be fired – but they already knew all that. Faced with three armed men, they saw us as terrorists, and the only thing they wanted was for us to leave. And they were absolutely right. This shows you the level of madness of the whole situation.

When this began, I believed that it would be enough to help two or three people get out of Argentina. But then I became so involved that I could not imagine doing anything else. To leave the country would have meant personal destruction, acceptance of military power. Perhaps I would have been more useful working for the recovery of democracy from abroad, because I have more talent for work requiring communication skills than for the underground work of guerrillas. I had always disagreed with violence until I had to confront it.

There are explanations for the violence that occurred in Argentina. It has to do with a particular culture. This culture is based on the assumption that force was necessary to resolve social conflict. The law had nothing to do with consensus; it was the imposition of the will of the dominant class on others, and when the oppressed classes reclaimed their rights they were repressed even more. Argentines do not believe that the state has to operate within the law. Deep down, they believe that the state makes the law. If the state has changed the law once, there is the possibility that the state can remake, change, violate the law again. However, the state continues to be the authority.

I think these ideas began in the Spanish counter-reformation. During the colonization of Argentina and the rest of Latin America, the counter-reformation had reached its peak. In Spain the counter-reformation was practically a state religion. And in Spain the religious battle was not against Christians, as in other countries, but against Jews and Moors, whom the Spanish succeeded in expelling from their country simultaneously with the discovery of America. To have this enormous area available for Christianization allowed the Spanish to justify colonization as fulfilment of the Divine Law of God to Christianize the whole world. The authority of the state and the authority of God are placed together on a high pedestal, and the law of the state together with the love of God are given as gifts to subjects below. When the Spaniard meets the Indian, he does not say, "I am coming to subjugate you." He says, "I am coming to save you." If the Indian does not want to be saved, he or she is killed. These are the historical roots of the repression.

There are also more contemporary factors. From 1955 onward, the ideology of the leaders of the military forces was developed in the context of the Cold War where the enemy was communism. This explains why the military forces repressed their own people. And then the 1976 coup originated with the representatives of agrarian capital. The landowners and financiers needed to control the state. For that, they needed to discipline Argentine society so that people would accept lower incomes.

The minister of economy during the dictatorship was Martínez de Hoz, a representative of the ancient oligarchy. Several months before the coup he joined with the men who were going to rule – Generals Videla and Viola – and gave them the go-ahead for the coup in return for control of the economy. Martínez de Hoz represented the interests of the most powerful economic sectors of Argentina. Now we have the results of these actions: concentration of economic power, privatization of state companies, and alliances with foreign capital.

The armed forces witnessed the collapse of their own morality and ethics in order to facilitate genocide. When the officers lost their ethical principles, many leaders who were conducting the repression enriched themselves by robbing the property of kidnapped people. The military heard what they wanted to believe, the nationalist discourse. I mean that although the coup appeared to be organized for ideological reasons, at the same time it served the purpose of reconstructing the economy. What this meant was that the work they had to do was so dirty, so immoral, that those performing the tasks ended up in crisis. They overcame this only through the prospect of more powerful positions and financial benefits. A similar mechanism has been at work in the case of those conducting the process of privatization since the military dictatorship. The judges and everybody related to the law had to know about what was happening under state terrorism. The same thing happened in Argentina as in Nazi Germany.

Well, to continue with my own story, toward the end of 1978, there was a profound crisis in my life. At twenty-five years I found myself without home, without profession, without job, without future, an authentic punk, and my wife was pregnant. It was a big shock.

Confronted with this situation, I could have abandoned my wife, I could have abandoned myself at that stage, but I decided to try to begin again. I think now that my son returned me to life, returned to me the sensation of being alive again, let me plan for the future. I would certainly have been killed if I had continued to be militant. I tried to find a place to live, a job. I have had many jobs since then ... I was stacking the cans in the supermarket, worked in the metallurgic factory, and finally, after 1983, I succeeded in getting a job using my own name, and I returned to, let's say, a middle-class life. I also worked with human rights organizations, and several years later I was able to resume my studies and my legal career. Well, in personal terms I missed the possibility of a lucrative future, a very low price to pay. I was not in prison, I was not tortured, I am alive. One day when I was taking my two sons to school, I took them by their hands, and after leaving them at the entrance to the school, I could not stop crying. I was alive and my sons were safe!

VOICE: GRACIELA

I became a political activist in 1968. I was studying in Europe on a scholarship. I was married and we already had a baby. We were influenced by the 1968 events in Paris and by discussions going on in Germany. When I came back in 1969 I found all my friends involved in political activities. Here we were discussing Che Guevara and the Cuban situation, and this was happening in all of Latin America. So I joined in this movement.

In my group there were a lot of Catholic activists. There were Third World priests as well. My husband and I became involved with them. An important bishop had married us. I joined the Montoneros a year and eight months after their founding meeting in Córdoba. The Montoneros were a federal group, and our group had its own organization and leadership. By that time I was pregnant with my second child, and I was the only woman with children in the organization, so I was the strange woman; it was not normal in the group. Most others were younger than us or they were not married, so when the kids were young I tried to do everything the fellows did, but they said, "What are you going to do with two kids?" It was very difficult, so I would say to them, "I am a woman, but I want to do the same as you, and it is perfectly normal to have kids. You talk all the time about the workers, and the workers have children – they are not single students – so you have to make room for a woman with children." Besides that, I was a social worker and I had worked in the slums. I knew about working people, poor people. These young people did not know about them. Neither the men nor the women knew, because all of them were single. There were some workers in the movement, but most of the members were in the middle class.

In Córdoba, our objective was to make money, and Córdoba was not so rich. I don't remember any kidnapping or violence. We often discussed the political situation, and we thought the only way to save our country was through guerrilla warfare. We stole cars and we stole money; we discussed every step of violence. We believed that to steal things was completely different from killing people. At the beginning was the money, the transportation, that kind of thing. Later, we started to think about popular justice. We thought about judging people, kidnapping people to judge them. Perhaps it was justifiable to kill some of them.

When General Aramburu was killed, the Peronists were really happy. I felt this when I was with the poor. They remembered the repression under Aramburu, the whole history. The poor people were very supportive. I was not at a high level of the Montonero organization at that time. We were told about the killing, actually about two killings, and we were happy about them. One was José Rucci [secretary general of the General Confederation of Labour, killed in September 1973]; the other was Aramburu. Actually, we were happier about Rucci than Aramburu. Then there were the Bunge Born brothers who were kidnapped for ransom. When Rucci was killed we broke open a champagne bottle. My husband said, "Who is the crazy person that killed Rucci?" and I said, "I think we are, we are very proud of this." Well, this is how it was then. There were people who believed it was okay to clean up the union movement, and now I understand that this was the beginning of our problems, of the first step of the problems – not to understand what the union movement represented in our country. It was a typical class mistake, typical university mistake, not to understand the power of trade unions.

At each step there were some people who did not agree, and those people left the organization. They might say, "I agree with this and that, but I don't agree with killing that person." So those people left. Until 1976 it was easy to leave the organization. Well, no one would kill you. But you lost all your friends. You moved away from the neighbourhood because you would not want to see the same people. It was like a marriage for members; we shared important things.

In your opinion, was the organization democratic in its decision-making processes?

Well, I wish there had been more democracy, but I cannot say they ever deceived me. I started to think about this later, when we were out of the country, but not at that time. In the 1960s we were really close. We could disagree, but we were so close. We had not so much money, we were really very poor. There was a hierarchy, yes, beginning with the military decision makers, then the party and the army. It was a typical revolutionary organization.

Aramburu made no difference to our organization. Nobody made difficulties about Aramburu, but many people had difficulties about Rucci. Rucci was a big name in the Peronist trade unions. No one said anything about Aramburu, he was just a general. A lot of people thought that to kill Rucci was to attack Perón. It was ridiculous, but a lot of people left after that.

After Aramburu's death, I was working in a government office – I was not part of the clandestine operations. I was working in the poor neighbourhoods, and my work was political but completely open. The Montoneros did not tell me about military actions, so as to protect me, and I was spared from being involved. I remember the kidnapping of the American consul in Córdoba, and the manager of the Chrysler company, but I was not involved in those actions. Still, I knew who did these things, and the details.

In 1974 in Córdoba there was a coup d'état against the governor, who was openly a Peronist like the governors of four or five other provinces. Most of the people in this region were Peronist. The perpetrator was the chief of police. After the coup, we who were Peronists had to resign or go to jail, about a hundred of us. We made a declaration and all resigned together. The police came to my home that day, but I was not there. They stole all my things.

We left the city, my children and husband and I, and moved far away. And then, two months later, one morning, friends said, "They are looking for you, you have ten minutes," so we took the children in the car and we left, and the army took the house, and that time we lost everything. We fled to Buenos Aires – I have my family there. So I asked my family for help. We were completely clandestine. We stayed a month with my family, but it was very dangerous. Then we left, and no one in my family knew where we went. The organization tried to help us. I worked in the organization press, the archives, this kind of thing until 1977.

The children were now seven and nine years old. It was very hard. They knew, and they were very careful with the police, and they would tell us, "Watch out, Mommy, the police are two blocks from here," and so on, more than you can imagine now. We moved forty-five times, with the children and the things. In 1976 I was pregnant – the baby was born in November 1976 – and I went to a public hospital under another name. My comrades thought I was completely crazy.

I continued to carry the cyanide pill, and only when I left the country did I stop doing so. I carried it from the time the militars started kidnapping people. At the beginning we didn't understand the concept *desaparecido*. We could understand that someone was in jail, but not *desaparecido*. It was very difficult to understand what they were doing. So we were looking for missing people in jails and police stations, and when we finally understood what was happening, we started to carry the capsule. We were well provided for; the logistics part of the organization was very strong. We had medical doctors.

Once I was standing in the street with a packet of information material and I was next to the police station. My comrade was waiting on the other side of the street. The police came toward me. I had to decide, second by second, whether to take the capsule. I was pretending to be waiting for a bus, I could not turn back or run. I decided, if they are going to kidnap me, I will take it, but maybe they are only trying to frighten me. It was very difficult to decide, and I was frightened. They did not kidnap me, so I survived.

At that time, in 1976 and 1977, I was just surviving. Later, looking back, I realized that life had been a matter of just trying to survive, that was all. But at the time I did not understand so well. We were always running. I started to work with ten people in my group, and when I left the country I was the only one still alive. These things I realized afterwards. Then, I thought only that we had a lot of bad luck in our group. I was so blind, we were so blind. Later, I realized that most of the disappearances happened that year. Yet I believed we just had bad luck in our group. I had completely lost the whole vision of the situation while trying to survive. By then, I had lost most of my comrades.

I started to have a different point of view at this time. I could not allow myself to think about what I would do tomorrow, how I would survive. I would think about an appointment at eight in the morning to give something to someone. If at 8:05 he was not there, I knew he had disappeared. Immediately I would contact other *compañeros*: "Alberto is missing, so please do what you need to survive." We thought only of survival, it was impossible to think beyond that. I would think only of little things, such as: Those people need ten manuals, the other one needs ten documents, and how can I get these things to them? We had once had a complete vision of the political situation in the country, but later I came to the point where I could only understand the little things, no more than that. It was completely stupid. Nothing. Useless. But I didn't know that then.

The leaders got out of the country. Most of them in 1976. They came and went for a while. They had false passports. By the time we left the country, that was no longer possible. We left with false passports, through Uruguay, through Brazil, but nobody got out after we and a few other comrades did. Then the border was closed. Some others were kidnapped in the airport.

VOICE: DOLORES

I was seventeen when the military killed people in Trelew in 1972. At that time being an activist was normal. We all believed that Argentina was going through the same process as that of May 1968 in France and the revolution of 1959 in Cuba. The role of Che Guevara gave us a sense of belonging. For us teenagers it was very important that he was an Argentine. We felt that we were part of the revolutionary history of Argentina. There was no possibility of being young and not being an activist; it was like a destiny. In 1973, when I entered the university, almost all my life had been under military control, so I felt that our generation was part of a critical moment in our history. Also, we thought we were freeing literature in Argentina, because we were reading Marx and Freud and Lévi-Strauss. I joined an activist literature group, at the periphery of the Juventud.

The repression began at the University of Buenos Aires in 1974. Not in 1976 but in 1974 under the government of Isabel Perón. They closed the university from September 1974 until mid-1975. They even destroyed the building where we were studying. We went on with our studies, and we had what was called the underground university. There were several groups studying in a few churches and in students' homes. That was critical when the repression began, because all of us knew each other and could identify one another if we were picked up and tortured. When the repression began, we had no doubt that from this root we had to join the resistance, so I joined the Montoneros. I knew it was a military organization.

My life changed completely, because being part of the Montoneros implied having to work and obey orders, having a special relationship with my family, and being part of a very close security network. After classes began again in 1975, I was responsible for talking with students and being active in classroom discussions, and for this I did not let others know that I was a Montonero. So I had two identities at this time – as a student, and as a clandestine member of an armed guerrilla group. But I realize now that we were armed by the Montoneros for no realistic purpose, unless it was to be killed, because the weapon I had was not used at all. It was just so they could kill me if they caught me. I was taught how to use the gun, but imagine a young girl being armed, making graffiti on the street with two other partners, and a car with three or four armed militars arrives there – imagine, how could we respond to that?

So for me the key to our destruction was on the inside, in the militarization, the progressive militarization, not only of the group but of the activities. In the last two years that I was in the Montoneros, I was just taking security precautions all day long, that's all I did. And I knew by then that the project was wrong. It was not part of the class struggle. But I could not leave the organization because it was more dangerous for me to be on the outside than on the inside.

Our project was a military one. The same was the case with the ERP [the People's Revolutionary Army], but the ERP was different because they were really leftists, and most of them were dead by 1975. We admired them, but we believed that being against Peronism was wrong. If we were going to transform Argentina, we had to go through Peronism. Peronism was the only viable force to create a social transformation. At least the ERP could have thought that they had a revolutionary project in terms of class struggle. We didn't. I remember reading material that we got from the upper levels of the organization, and we realized that. We were students, and very active intellectually, and we realized that the project was not exactly leftist. It was a strong combination of left-wing words and right-wing practices.

The church was part of our military socialization. Most of our leaders had studied at the military school in Argentina. They were from the ultra-right side of our society, from the conservative side of our society, and when they became left-wing people, we thought they had undergone a conversion. When they kidnapped and then killed General Aramburu, we saw that as part of an irresistible process of history. When they caught Aramburu they had to kill him, because he was the person who killed Peronist partners during the dictatorship. It is very important to me to think about the sense of destiny that all of us had during this process, because a sense of destiny was part of the mentality. We couldn't see that there was another way to live.

We had to stay in the organization after the repression began. Actually, I have not met anyone who left the groups and survived. To be outside the groups was to be caught within a week. We had a security network that let us know who was caught and who was not, and who was talking to police. Anyone who was caught, talked. I had several friends who were very close to me who tried to leave the organization at the beginning of 1976. In the next two years they were all killed by the military.

Did the Montoneros ever kill their own people who tried to leave?

I don't know if the Montoneros killed their own people. I know that they abandoned their own people, but I don't know if they killed any.

Being an activist then meant that you worked and gave most of your income to the upkeep of a Montonero soldier. We worked hard, for example, conducting people from one place to another, engaging in publicity stunts, which were very risky and had few results. We distributed flyers to people in a market at noon, people who didn't understand what we were doing, and we exposed ourselves for the sake of a flyer that said something like "We, the Montoneros, will die for our country." We knew it was useless and that it was risky and not social – only risky, not genuine social work – and at the same time we thought that it would be very dangerous to refuse or to leave. I survived because I remained in the structure. I called three times a day to a contact who told me who had been caught and who was still free, so I knew how close they were getting.

Young people like me were known to the military. They knew who we were because they tortured so many others who knew all about us. They knew where I was living, where my sister was living. It was chance that I was not caught. They had massive information available, but they were not always coordinated and some units were less vigilant than others. I was hunted three times and on each occasion was nearly caught. There were different groups involved, with different strategies and tactics, and different ways of handling the information. A woman who was caught but later released told me she saw a blackboard at the concentration camp where she was held. On it were all our names, with all our data – where I was working, where I had been living. And they were torturing people just to certify the information on that blackboard.

The parents of one of the people who had left the group and returned home mentioned her return to somebody. She was quickly picked up, and she gave some names that destroyed a complete group structure.

In 1977 we were told the leaders were no longer in the country. They said they had to leave the country because they were in extreme danger and their departure was in the interests of the organization. Just as people in Vietnam had to enter the jungle, they had to go to Paris. Can you imagine! They used the jungle, Vietnam metaphor, as if they were hiding themselves in the jungle. Some of my friends who had left the country in extreme danger were working for them in Europe. We were still here, though. They said the organization was trying to deal with European governments to try to solve the situation.

Later, when the worst was over and we were beginning to live real lives again, I was able to get to Europe. It was 1980. I learned there that [Mario] Firmenich was meeting with Massera [Admiral Emilio Massera, a member of the junta] in Paris. They used a very tricky rhetorical device to justify that. We knew it was wrong. The speculation was that Firmenich was talking with Massera about [David]

Graiver's money. Did you know about Graiver's money? Graiver was a very important person, part of the financial sector at the beginning of the 1970s, and it was said that the Montoneros gave him the money they got from the kidnapping of Mr Born,[1] but he died in Mexico in an aircraft accident in the mid-1970s, so nobody knows where that money was. We still don't know. Some people say that Firmenich bought some people.

Did you trust Mario Firmenich?

No, I did not trust Firmenich then. The problem was that we thought the organization was authoritarian, yet we were willing to do anything for the movement. That's the contradiction. That's why I left the university and became an activist. I thought that the project was for the people, that we had to do anything for them. I trusted the organization, even if later I didn't trust the leaders. But that is an Argentine problem that you have to think about. We are always thinking the problem is the person we are dealing with and not the whole project.

We did not know about the Graiver money at that time. No, no, I am quite sure Firmenich was not a double agent, because otherwise we would have been destroyed before, in advance, as the ERP was. They disappeared in 1975 when they tried to capture a barracks and they were completely destroyed because they had people inside who were in the army. So I imagine that Firmenich had a very authoritarian personality and had personal, maybe even psychotic, problems, but if he had been paid, we couldn't have survived until 1980. You should realize that killing people in Argentina is part of normal political practice.

I didn't know that Firmenich was talking with Massera at that time, though I knew he was in Paris talking about the survival of the project. I remember that I talked with a friend – well, it was a difficult situation because we were not supposed to have a discussion on the street – but I remember trying to talk with him about that problem, but all we could talk about was our friends, our partners, who had already been killed. We couldn't think about ourselves; we thought about people who were already killed. He told me – I remember it was an important sentence in my life – he said, "The project is wrong." I remember that sentence like an iron sentence in my head.

But at the same time I thought that the only way I could survive was to be part of the situation. I called three times a day to know where I could walk in the city. There were parts of the city where we could not walk. I didn't see my friends for two years, I didn't see my sister, and I only saw my father in an undercover situation. I think that might be one of the reasons I survived, because I was really obsessive about security measures.

Well, one of the reasons I can be sure that Firmenich was not a soldier or paid by the army is that in 1977 the Montoneros were reorganizing, with a plan called Operation Return. I know someone who was in Brazil in 1978 and 1979 who was working in the return organization. So it was impossible that Firmenich was paid by the army; he was planning to come back and revive the Montonero organization. But at the time, the ones who were here like myself were trying to change the front.

I myself, with my first husband, had gone to a working-class district in 1974 to do social work, and in 1977 we returned to that place. There was nobody left. Everybody had been killed, the houses bombed. We stayed there, hiding, but there was nothing left of the district, only the parents of our friends who had been caught. We saw that the project was wrong; if everyone in the neighbourhood had been killed, there was something wrong.

It was the end of 1977. I had an appointment with someone, maybe someone important, I don't know, in the upper level of the organization, and it was in the middle of nowhere. We were walking in the mud, I recall. It was a woman, I didn't see her face – she was a lady in a hat with dark glasses and a scarf over her mouth – so I can't describe her. She told me she was going to dismantle the loop; our group would be disbanded. So we were left in the middle of nowhere. They dismantled it.

Now I think we were fortunate, because friends of mine who were activists in another part of the province had terrible problems because their organization was not dismantled. They knew that it was very dangerous to continue, but at the same time it could be more dangerous to leave. When we were left in the middle of nowhere, we could do anything we wanted, and we were told, "You can do whatever you want but you can't contact us, we won't contact you. Don't contact anybody." We didn't have the control telephone number, which before then had been as important to us as having a place to live, a place to work.

We stayed in that working-class district, hiding, and trying to reorganize our lives for the next two years. Isolated, because we couldn't visit our families. We couldn't do anything else. We were hiding. For two years. And after that I began very cautiously to see my parents, and after a while I found a place to live in Buenos Aires. And after that I came back, and in 1980 I asked for my passport, because I wanted to go to Europe to visit my friends. At that time the military knew everything about me, I am sure they still know everything about me, and they still are in control, but that doesn't bother me any more.

At this point in history there is a gap between two generations, the mothers and the children. That was very clear to me when we had a great demonstration in the Plaza de Mayo and the mothers and others were saying the same things they have been telling us for the last twenty years. The daughters and sons were trying to listen to another statement than that of their parents. And then we realized there is a whole generation that has been silent for all this time. My generation. We didn't talk about what really happened because we didn't produce the material conditions in terms of history and in terms of discourses in order to be able to tell the things I have now told you. I cannot talk about these things here to my friends; I could not tell you these things in public. I cannot say, 'We were in a militia, we were armed, we were not innocent.' Because if I say that, I am saying that my partners, my *compañeros*, were killed because they were armed, and then somebody can say there was a fair war. It was not a fair war.

I cannot say that we were subsumed in an authoritarian organization unless we can find a way of putting our leaders on trial. But the leaders who were most responsible for the situation are now working with the government, with the universities, with the public institutions, and they have been doing this for the last ten years, legitimating history, and we are not allowed to make a counter-history of that. It is for me a curious responsibility to keep the silence.

Some of them think that we were not wrong, that we were right, that we were killed only by a completely mad repression. I agree it was a mad repression, but I can't say it was not linked to the true nature of our activities. I am not being fair with the next generation, with my own students who are the age we were then, if I cannot tell them this. But first I have to understand how we could create the conditions that would allow us to be critical of our situation.

Oh yes, I do want you to tell this story. Exactly. And to say that we were not innocent. That we were really fighting and we were convinced that arms and social work were the way to achieve a better world. That's the problem. And that our leaders were corrupt, were authoritarian, were completely infatuated with power. And that for the last two years all we did was engage in security measures and struggle in a war we couldn't understand but had to fight. That's my task for the next years. All I can do now is listen to young people.

They are more sincere, they are more direct than we are. Sometimes they are very critical of us. They understand that we lived through a struggle, but they can't yet understand that we lived in such an authoritarian society. Since we are not talking about it, there is a gap in understanding. Between the mothers [Madres de la Plaza de Mayo] and the children there is a generation that is staying silent, and it's mine, and that is the problem. People from forty to forty-five. Some of my friends have told me they would do it again. I never would. And when the militars are walking on the streets, how can I create the space to speak? The mothers seem to be caught in a time warp. Everyone is caught in a position and we can't move forward.

In 1992 there was a conference at the university with some of the people who had been leaders of the organization. I went to listen, and one of our leaders said that there were five thousand missing people of the Montonero organization. That is not correct. If they are not going to recognize even the missing people of their own organization, we are not going to have justice. They are wrong, there were many more. It is their responsibility to acknowledge our numbers, to claim our friends and the people we loved who disappeared. With such leaders ... we need to put on trial both sides at the same time. That's the problem. This is a different phase of history. After ten years of the trials, and now living in democracy, we can go through a new stage of the historical process. The question is how to do that, what is the condition in which we can say that. How do we create the conditions that would make that possible?

My friend has told me that some people are saying that Aramburu was not killed, that he died of a heart attack. That is terrible, because that was how the whole project got started – with that death. So if they are now saying such things, they are denying all the people who died during those years – a denial of their responsibility and of death. We are denying history all the time. There are a lot of the former leaders now in the university. [Names several, also in the Ministry of Education.] We were many, many people, at least as many as there are disappeared people. We were a whole generation. And there are survivors, too, all over the world. I have friends everywhere, talking, denying, trying to forget.

VOICES: SABINÓ AND RICARDO

Sabinó: The people who were involved with Peronism, with the Peronism of the left, with the CGT [General Confederation of Labour], half "social Christians," half leftists, and then with the Monotoneros, it all smelled to us of the sacristy. We didn't trust it, because the message with the murder of Aramburu ended by saying, "May God take pity on his soul." It was the first communiqué of the Montoneros, and it told about the death of Aramburu. It signified that God should forgive Aramburu. "We killed him, may God forgive him." That belongs to a Catholic culture. We were anticlerical ourselves. We were not practising Catholics in general. We had sympathy for the priests who had views in tune with ours, the Third World priests. We were with the Third World priests, but we were not believers.

We thought that the dictatorship of Onganía was terrible. In the early 1970s there was a magazine published and sold in the kiosks. It was called *Christianity and Revolution*. Every time we bought it we felt as if we were robbing a bank. That magazine published the messages of all the guerrilla organizations that existed, the discussions, the debates, and the whole chronology of all the bombs they had thrown. That was in 1970 and 1971.

Ricardo: In 1972 there was a film by Costa Gravas, *State of Siege*. It was about the sequestering of Dan Mitrione, an official of the CIA who was kidnapped in Uruguay by the Tupamaros. I went to see that film. Before entering the cinema I was an imbecile. I left the cinema as a revolutionary. Before that, there was an Argentine film that we saw secretly, and once in a while the police would break in and take prisoners. It was called *La hora de los hornos* (The hour of the ovens) by Solanas. Solanas is the one who made *El exilio de Gardel* (The exile of Gardel).

Sabinó: Yes, *La hora de los hornos* was totally clandestine. We had made a copy because when the police came they would take it. There was no video, no satellite television at that time. When I was sixteen I faked documents to enter a cinema where they showed French and Italian films. We saw *The Battle of Algiers* there. And Godard. What we wanted was to go to the cinema, then gather in a café with people to discuss, and to make the revolution. Those were times of great exhilaration. I realized later that it wasn't just Buenos Aires. These same things happened in Bogotá, for example. What was later known as the Montoneros was not original. Very similar to the Montoneros was the LM-19 in Colombia. We admired the Tupamaros, but those of the LM-19 we didn't know.

As for the Montoneros, there is a mystery about them which we could talk about all day long. I don't know if it wasn't an invention of the intelligence services in origin. There was a struggle between factions of the armed forces. I am not saying that the Montoneros were a creation of army agents. The founders were some kids who had gone to Cuba – at the time when there was no tourism in Cuba, of course. They had gone to Cuba to receive military training. They were Christians. In the years 1968 and 1969 they were twenty-something, and some not even that old. Before 1968 the Montoneros did not exist. The FAP [Peronist Armed Forces] existed. With the kidnapping and death of Aramburu, the Montoneros appeared, suddenly, as if from beneath rocks. Those of us who opposed the regime were still the minority. There was a communist party, but it was Stalinist and shameful. For example, at the death of Che they celebrated with picnics. They were pacifists. We made fun of them.

Ricardo: The Trotskyites were also ridiculous. They painted on the walls: "Proletariats rebel against the perfidious surplus" ... Juan García Elorrio edited the revolutionary left's journal. He was a man who lived a good life. He was a Christian but not a Peronist; he was from a Christian sector that had defeated Perón. In 1971 someone ran over him with a car, and it was never known if it was an assassination. The suspicion always remained that he was assassinated. The journal was prohibited.

Sabinó: There were members of the FAP, FAR, and Guevarists who ended up in the Montoneros, but the exceptions were the ERP and the Descamisados. In my particular case, I was so wary of the sacristy smell of the Montoneros that I went to the FAP and the Descamisados, who were small groups of high school students. The FAP had been split into two: those of the left, and the Peronists. We didn't want to go to the Montoneros, but we ended up there. The Montoneros had the most beautiful name; that helped them. Then, when Cámpora won the elections, Perón named Rodolfo Galimberti as the chief of the Peronist Youth without knowing that Galimberti had arrangements with the Montoneros. Well, this facilitated the unification of all the anarchist small groups – similar to rock groups – with Galimberti and the Peronist Youth. Thus the Montoneros became the leading group, and they linked up with the Peronist Youth.

We disdained the word democracy because, for us, democracy was something they taught in the schools during the eighteen years when free elections were prohibited. For us, therefore, democracy was a trick of the dominant classes; and in any case, it had to do with the democracy of the Greeks. There were two hundred Greeks who enjoyed democracy and ten thousand who had nothing to do with it, who had no rights.

We were very young. I had entered politics at the age of fourteen. There was an uprising in Córdoba. The government was at death's door when the Montoneros killed Aramburu. The government fell, and at that time many banks were robbed. These revolutionary groups had to make money – they were all anarchists really, the FAP, the FAR, the Descamisados, the ERP. I knew it was they who robbed banks, both because they talked about it and because newspapers reported this.

Sometimes we placed a bomb at night and then stayed in a café, awake, to wait for the papers to come out, to see if the news had been printed. It was from this that some members ended up in journalism! The papers said that we had a sophisticated organization. It was all lies. They said we were financed by Moscow, as if that were possible. With all that, we did help all the unions that went on strike in 1969, 1970, and 1971. In particular, there were three unions that helped us with the printing we needed; we worked closely with them.

The Montoneros were created with the symbol of the FAP; the federal star of eight points was the symbol of the FAP. Even the word Montoneros had been used by the FAP. There was a detachment that had already been called Montoneros October 17. The original Montoneros had been the resistance force in the interior of the country during the last century; they had resisted the exploitation by the people of Buenos Aires. By 1972, the Montoneros were joined by other groups, and they decided to open Peronist locals. At the time, I was a member of the Descamisados, a more democratic organization because it had small groups of about two hundred people. But in 1972 there was an explosion in numbers. Most members were only high school students. There were perhaps a hundred or a hundred and twenty militants in the group. All the leftist groups began to merge with the Montoneros.

I was by now in the army, doing my military service. I tried to hide my affiliation with the revolutionary groups. I had lots of luck, because ten months passed and they didn't know about it. When it came out, I tried to fake a suicide. Then, a little later, I became aware that the militants of the Triple A wanted to kill me. There were four officials who told me they were going to kill me. They had found out that I was a Montonero. I made out like I was crazy, the "little sissy." I would put on rock songs, I wanted to pass as a demented person, not as a guerrilla fighter. And that's how I escaped from the barracks, and that ended my military service.

Meanwhile, I warned my comrades that the Triple A was going to kill them. There were several indications. To begin with, they gave us specialized military instruction. They would say, "We are not going to teach you how to use bombs or artillery because you would just use them against us." Those who entered after me, the following year, were given a different treatment. They took black and white photos of them dressed as soldiers. They took colour photos of others dressed in civilian clothes. Already they were investigating us. I left the Montoneros in 1975 for a more left-wing organization. Until 1975 or 1976, if you were not in accord with them, you could leave. In fact they wanted you to leave. I was sad to leave, in a way. I had left my home at sixteen. I lived alone. All my friends belonged to the Juventud and the Montoneros. They saw me as a traitor, as a liberal (to say "liberal" was an insult). An individualist.

In January 1976 I went on vacation with a large group of these people who continued to be my friends and loved me – they were childhood friends. I tried to convince those who were going to enter military service that they shouldn't do it because the militars or the Triple A would kill them. I told them the militars were already investigating and were in a state of alert. They had already investigated my parents' house, the family – the whole bloody group. They were preparing for the coup. I didn't succeed in convincing my friends. And the two I most wanted to convince were killed while they were soldiers. I didn't convince them to desert, to leave the country or the army. The army does not depend on civil authority. It is very easy to kill someone.

The organization I had joined in 1975, Palabra Obrera, was a communist organization. It was smaller then the Montoneros and much less violent. What distinguished it from the Montoneros when I joined was that they wanted to avoid the coup d'état. The Montoneros did not want to avoid it because they thought they could ride it out like the previous military coups. They believed it was going to have a radicalizing effect that would benefit them – that the polarization would radicalize people. And I, who was coming from inside the army, realized that they were crazy – that the army would crush them. I tried to tell them not to confront the army, that they would lose, because the difference in power was terrible. But the majority of the people in the Montoneros were euphoric. They hated the military, and they said that if there was a coup, they were going to fight them. They had lost all common sense. They had two hundred very well armed people. But no more. The rest had handguns of low calibre.

What occurred is that, beginning with the death of José Rucci in 1973, they had gone crazy. In the Montonero meetings they didn't speak about politics any longer. They talked about logistics, bullets, hunts. In reality the leaders were ignorant. The Montoneros had people who weren't ignorant, but they were not leaders.

Many of the leaders died. And those who stayed alive were a disaster. Mario Firmenich, Fernando Vaca Narvaja, who is now the secretary of industry of a Menemist municipality. They all suck off the government. Roberto Cirilo Perdía, who was military chief and was called "the loser."[2] These are the ones who were left from the first line. They are alive and they are three smooth bastards, with different shades. Firmenich is more tolerable than his words would imply. The rest died. They were good people.

Vaca Narvaja was the son of the minister in the government of Frondizi. He was thrown out of military school because he was a nationalist. He was not a coward in physical ways. At the age of twenty he put a bomb on a railway line, and his documents fell out. Then he became a fugitive. From 1970 to 1973 he lived in hiding and robbed banks. In 1973 Peronism won, and everyone gathered in the Plaza de Mayo. Cámpora released the prisoners. And suddenly this man, Vaca Narvaja, spoke on a microphone before 50,000 people. What did Vaca Narvaja think? That the 50,000 people had gathered there because he robbed banks and was valiant?. It was madness. The people had gathered because they were Peronists. Peronism had won after eighteen years of proscription. The people saw Vaca Narvaja as a combat soldier of Peronism. The applause was not for him. But he thought the masses would follow him, and he became a leader of the Montoneros. He was not an intelligent type.

My brother and I are the only ones of our high school group who stayed alive. The rest died or left the country. It is not a merit staying alive, but it is a prize, this longevity. My brother was in prison for eight years. I survived because at the end of 1976 I left Argentina, and I lived in Spain for eight years. I completely left the Montoneros the day they attacked the barracks at Formosa. For me, they had gone crazy. Formosa is on the border with Paraguay. They had no political support there, yet they attacked this barracks and then hijacked a plane. And with a blue uniform with a red star, Levi jeans which they had stolen, hikers' boots, Montonero shirts, and heavy weapons! About twenty people died. This was madness. Imagine how the soldiers saw this! The soldiers were half illiterate, and I imagine that when they saw that those who attacked were dressed in blue, with uniform, they must have thought it was a Hollywood film, that the Third World War had started. The worst was that the Montoneros actually believed those soldiers would join them. The Montoneros were not even taking drugs, they were just crazy without drugs. The Montoneros caused the death at Formosa of friends of mine. And I said that these people were completely crazy. Then I got drunk and left.

CHAPTER 11

Tucumán

The province of Tucumán was an impoverished backwater, left behind by a sugar industry that had collapsed, and with no immediate prospect of economic improvement in the mid-1970s. Its infamy during the dirty war rested not on anything its own citizens had done but on the invasion of revolutionaries who believed that this semi-tropical mountain region met the appropriate conditions for starting a revolution.[1] It soon became the testing ground for the strategies of state terrorism which the military later used throughout the country.

The revolutionaries were quickly defeated, but the small population of dissidents, student leaders, journalists, and Peronists were caught up in the vortex of the storm. General Antonio Domingo Bussi, who was associated in the 1974–75 period with Operation Independence, created one of the most notorious killing fields at the camp called Arsenales. There were also many other concentration camps in the province of Tucumán. Few who were kidnapped survived. We interviewed their loved ones; also, some of the tacit supporters of the regime in the capital city, San Miguel de Tucumán. We were mindful that our interviews took place during a period when the same General Bussi was the elected governor of the province.

VOICES: NELLY DE BIANCHI (RIZO) AND SR RIZO

Nelly: I have lived all my life in the town of Tucumán, where I was born in 1923. Before this happened, I knew absolutely nothing about politics. I was told "Vote for this," and I voted for this, altogether innocent of what was happening in our country. Most people were like me, we didn't know anything. Only the bosses, the big owners, the powerful ones, the ones who had the money, they may have known what was happening. Of course, the military coup was done with a reason, it was not casual.

In the 1970s when Perón came back to Argentina, left-wing organizations began emerging. Our son entered the university here in 1973 and then, about 1974, he joined the Peronist Youth. Everything, everything emerged from the university. He was studying biochemistry, and he had a disagreement with the administration. I don't understand what it was about. But he was not then heavily involved in politics. In 1974 he joined the political sector of the ERP [People's Revolutionary Army]. In Tucumán the ERP had a small group of 180 guerrillas, no more than that, including both the armed and political sectors. That was when Perón was in power.

It was in 1975 when the big trouble began. President Isabel Perón came to Tucumán and gave precise orders to annihilate the guerrillas. With that very word, "annihilate," and they took it literally, the military. They annihilated. The president said she did not mean to exterminate them; she said they should be annihilated in a way that I do not understand, to leave them without weapons or something. I think she did not mean that they should be killed. I believe – I want to believe that.

My son was still here studying in 1975; he was not with guerrillas in the mountains. What the students wanted were improvements in the university. That was their struggle, that is why they rebelled – because they wanted to improve the university. For example, they wanted the state to provide eating places at the university. There were many youngsters who did not belong to any political party, who were not communists. I don't think my son was involved in any armed actions, though he never told me anything about his political activities. He was trying to protect me, I guess. Then in 1975 he told me, "Mom, I am going to get married while I can, because they are going to kill me." He married, and then he disappeared shortly after the coup.

On 15 April 1976 at 2:15 in the morning we were awakened – I, with a gun like this to my head, and my husband as well. My husband was pulled from bed and forced to lie down with his face to the floor. They kicked him, violently. Ten heavily armed men came in. They were disguised, the cowards, so we could not recognize them. My son was not at home.

Sr Rizo: They said they were from the police. But they were from the military, except for one policeman we recognized, who was later killed by his own comrades. I think the others were military because they spoke in a southern accent. They sounded as if they came from Buenos Aires. When we say "south" here, we mean everywhere south of Córdoba. After they had subdued us, they began looking for things all over the house, and they robbed us. They took Nelly's rings and our daughter's necklace. I worked as an electrician at the university, so from my tool case they took pincers, lanterns, and other items. They found my salary cheque made out to me, and they took it too. It was later cashed.

Nelly: Yes, it was cashed. They were all involved. They emptied the fridge. They ate all the food we had in the fridge.

Sr Rizo: I was taken out of the house in underclothes, blindfolded, with my hands tied behind my back. I could not walk because they had hit me. They put me face down on the floor and they put the safety belt around my neck, and they stepped on me, trying to make me talk about where my son was.

Nelly: Before that, they woke up my eleven-year-old daughter also with the gun to her head.

Sr Rizo: Then they put me in a car where another blindfolded person was sitting. He was a student from the same faculty as my son, and they were friends. I recognized him because he had respiratory problems and I could hear him trying to breathe. The man who was driving the car did not know Tucumán city, so one of them who was beside me wanted me to take them to the house where my son lived with his wife's family. I know the city. Every day I passed through that zone, so I was counting the blocks as we were passing them. Then we arrived at the house of my son's in-laws. I stayed in the car and they entered to take him. They put him in another car, and the cars began to follow each other. I think there were three cars.

Nelly: The next day, very early in the morning, because I had not slept and because I did not have a phone, I went to the house of my son's in-laws to see what had happened. There they told me that all of them – it was a large family – had been made to lie on the floor. The mother was an invalid and could not move, but nevertheless they treated her badly, they hit her, they forced her to lie with her face to the floor. There were eight persons in the house, including my son. My daughter-in-law was five months pregnant. They put a plastic bag on her head and left her. There was a telephone in the house, but they cut the line.

Sr Rizo: They took the radio, the tape recorder ...

Nelly: They stole as much as they could. They stole and ate what they found. Bedspreads, blankets, whatever they could, they stole.

Sr Rizo: After they had taken my son, they took me to Patillejo, about fifteen kilometres from here. There, one of the fellows with a southern accent asked, "What do we do with this old man here?" Then he opened the door and threw me out. The car was moving and my hands were tied behind my back, and my face was bandaged so I couldn't see. That is all I can remember.

Nelly was in a very bad condition, she was petrified. Some days later I tried to lay charges with the police, but the police told me not to do that. They said I was not going to gain anything and I would lose my job and everything else. The person who took my charges threw the paper away. We did not have any idea, we did not know what we could do. There were no lawyers, no one wanted to be involved. After that night, it took me a very long time to be able to do anything because I had a lot of trouble walking. I was unable to return to work for almost a month. Then there was another problem with Nelly because she was very bad all the time. We had her on Valium.

Nelly: Doped, I was doped for a year. Even so, when I could wake up I went to the command post. I tried to find out what had happened, and I filled out an accusation form at the military command and also at the police station. I went, but I was in a very bad condition, very bad. Then, when they saw that I was so bad, that I could not walk, I could not eat or sleep or anything, then I got some treatment with a psychiatrist, but I had already lodged my accusation in the Command of the Fifth Military Region by that time.

General Bussi was the man responsible for this operation. Antonio Domingo Bussi is the one responsible for all our disgraces. He is responsible for thirty-three concentration and extermination camps in the province of Tucumán, especially the one in Arsenales. Those camps were all prepared by the time of the coup. The report by CONADEP, the separate report on Tucumán, talks about that.[2]

When I recovered, I began to have contact with other mothers whose children had been abducted. We were a group of mothers, fifteen of us, and we met because our children had been fellow students and all of them had been taken as part of the same operation on that night of 15 April. They took the Romero boys – they were two brothers – they took a boy named Medina, they took my son, they took others. We did not know then that they had been disappeared. We knew only that they had been kidnapped.

We went to the episcopate, all fifteen of us, and we began bothering them so much that they sent us to the Church of the Holy Heart, where we were given a meeting place so that we would stop bothering them in the episcopate. We went there every day after that. Otherwise, the Catholic Church turned its back on us and was an accomplice of the military. I am a Catholic because I was baptized when I was a child. I went to see Pio Laghi in Buenos Aires, in the nunciature. He was also an accomplice of the regime. All the Catholic Church was, except for very few people. Yes, there were exceptions such as Monseñor Jaime de Nevares, and Padre Lalo Amate Pérez here. And one in La Rioja who was assassinated by Harguindeguy and another one in Patagonia. And another, who was also killed on 4 August, Angelelli, I think. We always asked for help from others in the church, and they refused. They did not want to undertake anything. They received us and they prayed the Lord's Prayer for our children. That was the total interview – that they would pray for our children. It was very difficult for us to understand how the church acted.

And we also tried to see Governor Bussi at Government House. He never had the courage to receive a mother. Never. At Government House nothing happened. Nothing, nothing. We were standing there for hours, and nothing happened, so we went back to our homes. All through that year, and while I was recovering, I went to different places: I went to the episcopate, I went to the church – from the church to the episcopate, from the episcopate to the church – and in that way 1978 arrived. In that year a delegation of twenty persons went to Buenos Aires, and there we learned that there were other mothers, the Mothers of the Plaza of Mayo, and we joined them. We met with different human rights organizations, SERPAJ [Service for Peace and Justice], then the Permanent Assembly for Human Rights, the one to which I belong now, and with different shepherds from several non-Catholic churches. They attended to us, they opened their doors to us, they gave us spiritual help. These memories move me because all these people were so good. Their human quality, their solidarity, all these move me when I remember it.

The Mothers group was officially founded in Tucumán in September 1981. Before that, our group had been dominated by four or five mothers who were communists. They had information they did not pass on to us. Altogether there were about four hundred Mothers in Tucumán, all looking for lost children. We were a flock of sheep. So the ones who first decided to form a separate group and work together with the Mothers of the Plaza of Mayo were a friend of mine and myself – we were two mothers. And then other mothers began to separate from the other group and join us ...

I believe that everything was politically structured, because as the discontent of the people grew, it was necessary to stop it. When the constitutional government fell, there was a witch-hunt to exterminate all who were fighters for the people. Bussi was in on it from the beginning. He invented Operation Independence. With that began a well-structured plan to begin the witch-hunt, to begin disappearing people. It began in 1973 or 1974, I am not sure. There were disappearances from 1973 onward, before the dictatorship. And General Bussi was already involved. He already had the detention camps prepared. The most horrible camp was Arsenales. Almost all who were taken there were killed. It was a very big extermination camp. About ten blocks into it they dug six holes, each six metres deep. Every ten to fifteen days, those condemned to die had red bands put on their arms and were taken to the edge of the holes. They were made to kneel down, and Bussi shot the prisoners there. They put things that would burn into the holes, and the prisoners were thrown there, sometimes half alive, and the officials were made to participate in this massacre. The numbers killed varied depending on Bussi's mood for genocide.

I learned that my son was there from a prisoner who survived and because later it appeared in the magazine *Página/12*. I know that he was there because a young man who had been there told me some ten years later that he and all the group from biochemistry were there. He had seen one of my son's friends there.

Now we have to live again with Bussi as governor. This man lied and did not keep his promises. The need is so great here, there is such poverty, yet it is the very poor people who voted for him. They are not fascists, but they are mistaken. What I think is that our children should not have died for this, for these people.

VOICE: MARTA OFELIA VALOY

In 1976 I was studying and working as a teacher in a secondary school. I had completed my studies at the Faculty of Philosophy and Letters in the University of Tucumán. I had not been involved at all in politics. However, my younger sister's involvement affected the life of my family. She joined the Peronist Youth movement, first at university and then outside it. Now she is disappeared, both she and her husband. Our family did not know the details of her participation in the Juventud. We knew only that she was an activist and had been one since secondary school. She had moved by then to Buenos Aires. She disappeared in May 1977 when she was twenty-seven years old.

They left a baby. He was one year and three months old. We eventually recovered the child about two months after my sister was disappeared. An uncle who was a militar told us that he had the child, but he never told us how the baby had arrived at his home. So we went to take him, and now he lives with me. Until my uncle contacted us, we did not know my sister was disappeared. I thought she had escaped and had left the baby with him. He told us that the baby had been left at the door of his apartment with some clothes and a note asking him to take care of it, because my sister was going to be away for a long time. That was one version. Later he told us that my sister herself had left the child. We do not know the truth. Later, much later, in 1984, we talked with some witnesses who were in the concentration camp then, and we learned that the child had been kidnapped as well as both parents. My sister was kidnapped first, then her husband with the child. She was tortured in front of the child, and they tortured the child in front of her.

We learned this from a survivor of the concentration camp. My sister's case turned out to be one for which there were witnesses in the trial of the military commanders. Her case appeared, her kidnapping, but the details of the torture of the child do not appear in the CONADEP report. We were able to verify it on the basis of the child's behaviour. When the boy arrived here he was one year and three months old, and he could not lie down in a bed, nor could he bear to see anyone wearing a uniform. Uniforms were worn by the torturers. So if he saw a nurse, a doctor, or a stretcher, he had a nervous attack.

I was a teacher, but I was kept on part-time basis and was not able to get more time or be promoted. The authorities refused to look at my credentials. This procedure was established by the minister of education. I think it applied to anyone who had disappeared relatives: we were marked. We were also discriminated against socially. There were many people, many former friends even, who did not see us any more, who did not talk to us any more. Some neighbours also discriminated against us. We were helped by human rights organizations, and we came to know other people with disappeared relatives.

Our neighbours knew about my sister because when she and her husband left for Buenos Aires, some information appeared in the newspaper stating that leftist militants were fugitives, and her name and the name of my brother-in-law appeared there. They knew that my nephew was the son of my sister. It would have been difficult to hide how he had arrived here. Besides that, we did not want to hide him. Many people, people we know, concealed the fact that they had disappeared relatives. They denied it and did not look for them, afraid of being marginalized. They were not afraid of something happening to them, but of being marginalized and not being allowed to make progress in their profession. For example, there is the case of a lawyer friend of mine who wanted to become a judge, and she knew that if she had a disappeared brother it would be impossible for her and, well, she denied it. They never looked for him. They considered him dead.

When General Bussi won the last election in Tucumán, the human rights people suffered a lot. There is a Madre of the Plaza of Mayo who died from a stroke. When she knew that Bussi had won, that he was going to be the governor, she had a stroke and she was in a coma until she died. The people suffered very much, morally, those who were affected by the dictatorship, because Bussi had been in charge of the repression here in Tucumán. My two children and my nephew suffered a lot. For them it was a crisis. This happened in many homes. It was a tragedy! It was like a mourning, a terrible mourning. And since Bussi took power, things have not gone well.

There is no simple explanation of why people voted for him. One reason could be the bad governments of the other parties, and probably the people wanted to punish them. There was a lack of organization in the administration, and Bussi appeared as a promise of order. Another reason could be that this Tucumán society has a very authoritarian culture. The most conservative church in the world is in Tucumán. The Catholic Church here is almost Nazi. And the other hypothesis is what is called the Stockholm syndrome, that people vote their own ... They seek their own repressers, as a sickness.

In Tucumán there were about four hundred disappearances, and there were others from here, as in our case, who were disappeared outside Tucumán. There were others who were never claimed. Yet even with so many families affected, to have disappeared relatives was seen as being left-wing, as being a terrorist or the relative of a terrorist. Many people justified the repression, and they still believe that the disappeared were killed and tortured because they had done something and deserved punishment, and that they were a danger to society.

In Tucumán, the Catholic University was always protected. Even more, the Catholic University collaborated with the repression. They kept a list of whoever was on the left; we learned about this later. The Catholic University was very, very reactionary, and besides that it was at the forefront of the repression. Its leaders admitted that they maintained lists, and they even threatened some people saying, "We are going to include you in the list." The person who directed all this was a prior of the Dominican Order, a person who was very close to the army. He was in charge of the order and of the Catholic Church during the repression, during the 1960s and 1970s, and with the arrival of democracy he left Tucumán. He returned recently for a visit and went to greet his great friend, Governor Bussi. After he left, people discovered secret agreements between the military and the Catholic University of Tucumán regarding the takeover by the Catholic University of the affairs of the National University of Tucumán. Afterwards, this man was transferred. He is in Argentina but not in Tucumán.

These agreements were published in the newspapers. The first rector of the university after the arrival of democracy discovered and denounced this. The lists with the names of the leftist students were also discovered and published – and many of those students had disappeared. They also found lists in the archives of the National University of Tucumán. The rector of the National University had been appointed by the military of that time, so the same policies were in place for both universities. He was an ultra-Catholic. The agreements showed transfers of information, the sharing of tasks between the two universities. There was an intelligence service within the university directed by the rector. People were openly identified as monitoring activities of students. Many ex-officers of the armed forces were at the university as administrators and teachers. There was no attempt to hide their identity and there was also surveillance on the unions. In those lists of students, there were notes about the political and labour affiliation of each one.

Within the National University a whole intelligence service directed by the rector was established. Furthermore, there were people openly appointed to watch the students, to give information, to infiltrate themselves. I mean, they did not have any other specific task; they did not hide it. Although they did not say, "This belongs to the intelligence service," they made no effort to disguise who they were. In general at that time, many former army officers began to work at the university as administrators.

Before the coup, in 1974, but especially in 1975, not only were students persecuted but union members were too. In 1976 the leader of the sugar cane workers, Atilio Santillán, was assassinated. [His murder has been attributed to an ERP gunman.][3] As well, Isauro Arancibia, secretary general and a founder of CTERA [the teachers' union], was killed the night of the coup. He was murdered in his own house, and they also killed his brother who was there by chance. It was done by police and army under the orders of General Bussi.

At the time all of us were afraid. And we did not know who exactly the enemy was – the enemy was hidden. A *compañero* could be the one who denounced you. After my sister disappeared, I felt that those who had a disappeared relative were marked and marginalized. We did not understand the full dimensions of what was happening until at least 1978. For a lot of the time we believed that there were imprisoned people who were transferred from one jail to another, but we did not imagine the horror of the concentration camps and the torture. We learned about the torture when the OAS came in 1979.[4] We suspected some things, we knew what was happening, but until then we had not realized the full horror of it. We believed that the people were still alive. Until 1980 or so, we still had some hope that they were alive.

VOICE: PADRE RICARDO FUMARO

In about 1970 the sugar industry fell into a crisis situation. The sugar refineries in Tucumán were, in general, obsolete structures. They maintained the old tradition of a dependent population residing near the refineries. When the refineries fell into crisis, all these people lost their jobs ... This was the situation of a small province with grave economic and social crises, high unemployment, a subtropical jungle, and two large roads which crossed it. The subversives believed it was the key place to establish themselves. They thought they could influence the population. They had come from Córdoba, Santa Fe, Buenos Aires, La Plata, generally university people ... and also some Chileans, some Bolivians ... I do not remember any Cuban. Cubans, no. But this was the configuration.

The rural people from Tucumán did not support them. Tucumán was a province of the ancient country with a strong religious popular culture, a Catholic culture. The workers in the sugar-cane fields and refineries did not support the guerrillas. The people who supported them were university people. It was ideological, no? In Tucumán city, the university became a centre of subversive ideology. Connected to the subversives in the university were some people from the church. But those people did not join the groups in the jungle; they were from the city.

There were complicated negotiations between government agencies, the sugar-cane owners, the refineries, and the sugar-cane workers' union. The presence of subversives, rural as well as urban, created insecurity. The military government of that time, the government of General Lanusse, was not able to solve the economic and social problems, and finally, when elections were called and the democratic government was re-established, the political parties did not have appropriate leadership. I would say that they had a second-rate leadership.

The people who could have provided better leadership, who were better able to help, did not want to commit themselves. Many left for Buenos Aires. They were afraid of the guerrilla issue, and they watched from a distance rather than taking a role themselves. Those who had a lot to do with the refineries' owners stayed away. The university leadership held a leftist ideology, and the labour union leaders were fighting for political rather than economic power. The church was split internally because there were some very leftist priests, and the common people of Tucumán did not understand a thing.

I was working in a university at that time. We tried to maintain an intellectual environment, to stay clear of political alignments. There was a period when the National University was almost transformed into a centre of political and ideological power and was not an academic centre at all. The Catholic University was less affected by politics. It did not witness any book burning, and no one was dismissed for political reasons. That university belonged to the Dominican Order, and the priests were devoted to the church.

Let me distinguish between the poor as ideology and the poor who are real people. It was when the church concerned itself with ideology that it was mistaken. It was a very complex and difficult situation in the 1970s. There was a subversive civil war here. I opted for a difficult course – to stay in the country, to stay and teach, and to be part of the process of re-establishing peace. Many who talk about these issues were outside the country – Paris, Madrid, etcetera. They brought arms to the young, and they left the country and then returned as saviours of human rights. And those who stayed here and reorganized life were sometimes treated as if they were the traitors.

The United States under President Carter was advocating human rights and considered itself the judge. It began to examine the human rights of everybody else, completely forgetting its own situation. The United States took two important actions which provoked the fall of the Russian empire. On one side was the armament industry, which weakened Russia. At the same time, Carter focused on human rights in order to weaken the Russian power internationally. What I'm saying is that President Carter adopted human rights as a priority of U.S. foreign policy in order to weaken the enemy.

I want to say that in no way do I share the idea that anyone should have been killed here. I think that the armed forces made a great error. First, because they made a Leninist analysis of Marxism, and they saw the issue of subversion in terms of the Marxist-Leninist armed struggle. They did not realize that the Marxism that was developing was not Leninist but Gramscist.[5] It is the type of Marxism that focuses on reform of the culture in order to obtain political power. So they chose a mistaken strategy, and they transformed it into an armed struggle when it was a cultural struggle. I do not think that the strategy of the cultural struggle can be dealt with by the armed forces. Our young country did not recognize the crisis. This emerged because the people never felt incorporated into the political fabric of the country, and that resulted in the great institutional crisis.

In Argentina, neither the university nor the church managed to achieve political power. I would say that this was the great intention of Peronism. It arose as a popular movement, embodying the great values of the national culture, and that is why it had force. But because Peronism had a good doctrine but bad execution, it could not succeed. Nevertheless, it survived because of this spirit. This is very difficult to understand in Argentina. The politicians have not understood it. And the militars have not understood it one bit, because they have presented themselves as an alternative, which they are not.

To an outsider, it seems that one of the problems here has been an inability to deal with pluralism, to avoid intolerance.

Well, I think that the world "pluralism" is a contemporary word. Argentina has always been an open country. My grandparents are Italian, Spanish, English, and Argentine! In 1825 an Englishman visited the country and published a book about his impressions of Argentina, and one of the things he said was that he was impressed by the openness with which he was able to move freely in Argentina despite the English invasions of a few years earlier.

Yes, openness between ethnic groups, yes, but I mean between ideas.

Look, what happens is that if by "pluralism" we mean a reduction in the exercise of an individual right, I mean, the liberty of expression, that is preserved in the national constitution. But beyond pluralism, which is the personal freedom that each person has, a political community should have a conscience, a memory of its cultural patrimony, and one does not negotiate that, that is not pluralist, that is so. That is why we talk of an Anglo-Saxon culture, a Hispanic culture, a French culture, or we talk of the culture of the Slavic countries. Those are values that cannot be pluralist.

As to the tolerance that you associate with pluralism, I think there is a mistake in your conception, because the armed forces should not have a dialogue with subversives. They are an institution of the nation, and they acted in compliance with a decree of the president of the republic, approved by the national Congress, which ordered the armed forces to repress subversion. That was the 1975 decree of Isabel Perón. That is why the armed forces acted as a national institution. What failed was not the dialogue between the armed forces and the subversives. The dialogue failed at the civilian level. The national institutions were not able to talk to each other. The armed forces are not there to talk, they are there to fight. The crisis was a civilian crisis; it was civilian, not military.

I think that what we need to clarify here is whether the political institutions were capable of helping people of different persuasions work together, or whether the people who had the obligation to lead the institutions were able to carry out their obligation. I think that the great crisis of contemporary Argentina was the crisis of the institutions formed in 1880, when the national state was constructed with the big institutions – the university, the armed forces, the political power, and the parliament. These institutions did not develop the capacity to respond to the challenges of their times. They were conceived as part of an international politics which looked at England, because England was the centre of international political power until the First World War. When this centre moved to the United States, the institutions of our country remained constituted as if nothing had happened. And the Second World War came, and the country continued with the same arrangement. And this has caused the crisis in the institutions. In the end, the institutions have failed.

It seems to me that what is still lacking is adequate political leadership. People do not yet have confidence in politicians, and they feel that they are not represented by their deputies, by their senators. The Argentine community, because of these institutional problems, has not developed ways of embodying the common good. And this lack of a sense of the common good complicates the exercise of politics as the architecture of the common good. So the civil society displaces the political society through the pressure groups, and this generates a kind of social anarchy although it is not expressed in the formal power structures. I think that this is the most difficult issue for the country now. The people need to believe in a political society. And this is the great challenge for the political people of today. If they are not capable of achieving this, I think that there is not going to be any solution, and I think this is also a great responsibility for the educational institutions.

VOICES: A GROUP OF BEREAVED WOMEN

The following excerpts are from a discussion with several women who had come together to speak with us about their experiences in Tucumán.

Bianca: The governor of Tucumán is a retired general, Antonio Domingo Bussi, who was exactly the same governor of Tucumán in the time of the military government and was responsible for eight hundred disappearances in the province of Tucumán. He was elected by popular vote. We keep trying to find an explanation for this frightening development.

Anna: Eight hundred declared cases of disappearances were reported in the bicameral report for Tucumán, but we think there were about three thousand people who disappeared or were killed in Tucumán. They didn't give any reason for killing them. I lost five family members: father, mother, sister, brother, and my sister-in-law who was pregnant. They were all together at the same time, during the siesta. Why they were selected – well, we think it was because the younger ones, my sister, brother, and myself, we had political experience. We were Peronists. My sister and sister-in-law were student activists and I was in the press union, and we think it was because of that. Those were enough reasons to pick somebody to be kidnapped. But why were my parents selected? There were no reasons. No one can give us a reasonable answer.

Starting with their coup d'état, that was the beginning of the arbitrary actions. We think that the difference between this and other coups that occurred in Argentina is that this experience was organized against the people. This is what happens when they make their national security doctrine a reality.

Gabriela: It's putting into practice what in a certain way started to develop in Brazil, Uruguay, Chile, Bolivia. The Americans were not directly involved, but some of the officers were trained in Panama. For example, General Bussi, who was the governor of Tucumán at that time, was trained in Panama. Bussi had some experience in Vietnam as well. We lived in a dictatorship under state terrorism. This terrorism established that there was a pact of silence in society.

Bianca: Silence because of fear and also because some people shared their views. In society in general, fear dominated more than complicity. The church and other institutions were complicitous.

Gabriela: As an institution the church had, I think, a McCarthyist consciousness, fundamentalist. It came to think that this was a form of crusade against international communism. It transgressed the message and the essence of Christianity. In my opinion, that is one of the causes of great corruption that exists today in society. Because, in reality, this complicity was immoral. To me personally, it brings a lot of pain, because I am Catholic. My husband graduated from the Catholic University of Chile, and from a very young age was a Catholic leader. He was committed to the principles of *Populorim Progresium*, the message of Pope John XXIII. We were very influenced by some of the most advanced thinkers, those who were committed to helping the poor.

My husband was president of the League of the Humanist Students of Tucumán, and he was a brilliant student. We had great international teachers. He was abducted on 21 July 1977, and the same day another student leader also was taken. The other one was a Marxist. So the province's two most important leaders in the university disappeared on the same day. They were political adversaries in the university, and there was no relationship between them. This coincidence makes me think that his kidnapping was the result of a plan to eliminate all young leaders. Today, the absence of leaders makes it seem that our disappeared ones are present by their absence. Permanently.

A man who had been in the jail of Villa Urquiza, who was able to see my husband with another disappeared person, gave testimony to CONADEP. You, as a foreigner, and in the international community, what do you think one can do today for this situation of crimes against humanity that are without resolution? Can one do anything?

Luisa: The people were the victims of this kind of terrorism. They were terrified. There were some institutions, the military, the church, but the political parties too – especially the political parties, even the Radical Party, and the Peronistas – who did not act. For example, while Isabelita was still president, they put through the Independence Law, which said that subversives must be liquidated. That was in 1975, and the Peronists, the Radicals, they all signed the law. Later, the military did the kidnappings in the name of that law. That was in the democratic period. Party leaders were complicitous. And they even said it was a very necessary thing to do, to kill. For the first time, people were kidnapped and other people didn't even know, but somehow the leaders of the parties said it was necessary. That is how they were complicitous.

There were a lot of newspapers which wrote that things were all right – well, they said it was necessary. Maybe the newspapers couldn't speak, though. There were more victims among journalists than any other group. About one hundred of them disappeared, and they were a small group to begin with. The state owned and controlled many television and radio stations, so they controlled mass communications. Also, many newspaper publishers agreed with the military. But others could not act.

Anna: I write now for newspapers. I have to live with the sadness that the democratic government did not act. The general who is now in power and others who participated in the crimes control the government. It is immensely painful having to live with the elected authority of this society knowing that they were implicated in abhorrent crimes – to direct oneself to this person, General Bussi, and the people who participated in those crimes. It is essential that those who perpetrated the crimes do four things. First, they must publicly acknowledge the truth of what happened to so many people. Second, they must publicly repent of those crimes. Third, they must ask the forgiveness of the relatives and descendants. Fourth, as a public restitution, they must retire from public life.

They are now protected by the laws of impunity. Those laws protect them. They were pardoned by [President Carlos] Menem, and the Law of Obedience protects the others. The majority were not judged, and those who were judged were pardoned by Menem. In view of the pain of today, these characters should at least withdraw from public life, because today it is immoral that they continue; furthermore, a terrible example for the next generation.

Bianca: They are assassins.

Gabriela: This General Bussi was elected by democratic elections with 48 per cent of the vote. He was governor during *el Proceso* and he participated in the genocide.

Luisa: I cannot understand it emotionally. I can explain it rationally, leaving aside the horror that it caused us, the pain. Evidently, the other political parties did not provide a valid alternative.

Bianca: How does one explain the people's vote for an assassin? The governor before Bussi deceived the people. He was someone one voted for thinking that he could take Tucumán out of the chaos and economic disaster it was in. Its leader was a singer, Palito Ortega from Tucumán, a Peronist of very humble origins, a worker in the sugar fields, who had become popular in the 1960s as a singer and guitar player. Suddenly he presented himself as a candidate for governor of Tucumán. For many people he represented the possibility of leaving the chaos and disorder they lived in, but the government of Palito Ortega was fraudulent and corrupt, a disaster in every sense. It was a great deception. So he had to be ousted. But when the chance came, the other parties offered no serious candidates, and Bussi captured the vote. I have heard people of sound intellect say that perhaps Bussi would bring order. We replied that he was going to bring the order of the disappeared.

Anna: This is one reading. There are others. This is the one of "punishment." Another reading could be that the authoritarianism in Argentine society did not disappear. It is part of the conduct of people. Because our democracy is only in diapers, just born, it is not mature. There is no democratic conduct. It is primitive. And that is like the historical tendency to search for the saviour in the military. We have had more military governments than civilian ones.

Bianca: I think this would not happen again here, because the international community would not support the military now. But it is for this reason, and not for internal reasons. I think that they could still come to power with the popular vote. Democracy hasn't brought people what it promised.

Luisa: I agree with Bianca. I just want to clarify that President Carlos Menem took out of his top hat a Tucumanian of humble origin, but one who was successful as a singer – a man who actually lives in Miami – Palito Ortega. I support the Radical Party, but I voted for Palito so that Bussi would not win. In my opinion, offering Ortega as the Peronist candidate was a deliberate intervention, a way of ensuring the victory for Bussi.

Anna: And, one thing I would like to clarify, with reference to whether the military could return, is that I think they are not necessary any more because the role they assumed as guardians of the powerful economic interests of this country is now being performed by the democratic president.

Luisa: The present governor, Bussi, was going to win in the previous election. And the population voted for Palito so that he would not win. They even say that there was fraud so that Palito Ortega would win.

Anna: Bussi looks after the economic interests of the rich. But he was also supported by very poor people. Many of his votes were from the poor sectors. In our popular mythology he is general and is called Domingo, which is of course Péron's middle name as well as the name of the holy day [Sunday]. He is the representation of General Perón.

Gabriela: We know the disappeared are dead, but we want to know where they are. Our disappeared were kidnapped. They did not have the right to speak, and their honour was stained, then and for always. My husband did not have a chance to defend himself. Even the most atrocious criminal has a right to defend himself. But our disappeared could not defend themselves. And society does not comprehend this, because when I say, "My husband disappeared," the question that follows is, "And what was he in? What wrong did he do?" In the love of the father of my children, I must defend my husband, I have always defended him; and for the sake of my children, who have to know that he was innocent and could not defend himself. But also I want other people who were not affected to realize that he and all the thousands like him were denied ordinary human rights. I want our people to commit themselves to human rights now. I think this is the only thing that would ensure that this does not happen again.

Bianca: Something that still happens to us teachers, to those of us who were teachers in that terrible time, is that we saw our students disappear. We would note that someone had failed to come to class, and we would ask about her (most of our students were women). Suddenly, no one knew where to find her, and she didn't show up, and then either she would appear in the lists of those officially detained (those called "Detained by the disposition of National Executive Power") which did not signify that they were protected by the law, or we simply never learned about her and never saw her again. It became our responsibility, those of us who had chosen to stay here and not leave the country – I made that choice, to stay in the country – to try to help these young people, to protect them if we could. But we had the ethical problem, which I still have with my students and my children, of what to say – how to educate them about democracy without putting them in jeopardy. To do that is our duty. As a teacher, it is my duty, which I will never renounce, to educate them to respect the other. But at the same time, we had to teach them to be careful so that they did not become one more disappeared or one more tortured person.

By profession I am a professor of a foreign language, and that gave me an opportunity to resolve this ethical problem. I did it by teaching about cultures with democratic spirits – very solid ones ... like that of the French culture – mostly through the medium of literature, through literary texts, which were prohibited here. Camus was prohibited, Sartre, even Saint-Exupéry. These authors' books were prohibited by the National Executive Power. We took the books out of the library because the authors were prohibited, all the French ones, from Anatole France on. We took them all home and distributed them among ourselves so that they would not be burned. I will never forget that. They burned books from the university's central library. So we came, four or five professors of the French Department, I still remember, and took the books to our houses. In this way, we could preserve what we thought was a patrimony, and we could continue teaching. It was a risk. If we had been caught, they would have detained us or we would have disappeared.

Many of our colleagues were dismissed ... the dean of the faculty, for example. There were what we called black lists. Black lists had the names and also activities of people, departments. The Psychology

Department was closed because it was on the black list. Throughout the country, sociology departments were closed – they were closed in Buenos Aires and La Plata. I confess that still, in spite of not fearing for myself – and I wasn't frightened at the time – I feared for the young people. I always tell my children and my students that if a similar situation presents itself in their lifetime, they must always work closely together in organizations. This cannot be fought alone, because the terrorism of the state is impossible to face alone.

The state has power. Unfortunately, we are in a pseudo-democracy. It is a government that is constitutionally elected by the people, but the relations between the powers of the state make it impossible to achieve democracy or justice. There is an executive disguised with a power that is almost absolute, and the administration of justice is subject to the executive power, is not independent. Well, the majority of the members of the Supreme Court follow the ideology of the executive power because of the last constitutional reform. The number of judges in Menem's Supreme Court of Justice was changed to ensure that the court follows the executive ideology. Menem has the power to elect judges because he has the majority in Congress. They have their positions for life. So the courts follow the executive ideology – except in the case of a political trial, which is determined by the Congress of the nation. So social change is very slow, very slow.

CHAPTER 12

The Media and the International Context

The *Buenos Aires Herald* expressed a widespread view in this editorial on the 1976 coup:

The entire nation responded with relief when it was realized that firm hands have taken over the reins of government ... It is impossible not to admire the style of these reluctant revolutionaries ... This was not just another coup, but a rescue operation. These are not men hungry for power, but men with a duty, which they have stated with seriousness. By their first actions, the country's new leaders appear to have won the confidence of the people ...

The government's laudable moderation in both its language and its actions has created an atmosphere which gives the country's problems a different perspective. The moral, economic and social decline of the past year and a half is daunting. It will not be easy to achieve the country's renaissance but the first steps have been taken in the right direction. The junta appears to have created the conditions in which it can expect genuine cooperation at home and help from abroad.[1]

Spanish-language papers, though generally supportive of the coup, were more sceptical in their editorials. *La Nación*, which became virtually a mouthpiece for the military as their reign continued, was supportive but with reservations:

The crisis has ended. There is no surprise in the nation at the fall of a government that was dead ... Instead of surprise, there is an enormous expectation ... Precisely because of the magnitude of the task being undertaken, the most important condition is that the armed forces guarantee the cohesion with which they have acted till now. The country has valuable reserves of confidence, but terrorism also waits in ambush.[2]

Support and, in many quarters, euphoria continued for the next few months. On the face of it, the armed forces were acting with restraint, sobriety, and integrity.

Toward the end of April 1976, the government prohibited "information, comment or reference to themes related to subversive activities, the appearance of bodies and the deaths of subversive elements and/or members of the armed forces or security forces in these happenings, unless they are reported by an official, responsible source. This includes kidnappings or disappearances."[3] This might have sounded the alarm in a country less beleaguered by kidnappings and assassinations. But it was taken in its stride by Argentina's press, as was the official explanation that "this is a country at war." Censorship had never been absent in Argentina and had intensified under the government of Isabel Perón, so the actions of the military were regarded as moderate and necessary.

In fact, the military directives did not actually use the word "censor"; instead, they encouraged the media to censor itself. Some guidelines were presented, entitled "Principles and Procedures to be Followed by Mass Communication Media." These provided a vague directive to "foster the restitution of fundamental values which contribute to the integrity of society; such as, for example: order – labour – hierarchy – responsibility – identity – honesty – etc., within the context of Christian morals; Preserve the defence of the family institution ... Take firm and consistent action against vice in all of its manifestations," and other such moralistic advice.

In addition, the press was given a set of "procedures," which included such dicta as "Do not enter fields which *are not for public debate* [underlines in original] because of their effect on audiences which are not prepared (educated) or because they are unsuited to their physical and mental age; Eliminate all mass propagation of the opinion of persons not qualified or without specific authority to give opinions on subjects of public interest. This includes interviews and/or street polls."[4] These vague orders were soon made more concrete as reporters and editors began to disappear and newspaper offices were bombed.

Self-censorship became even stricter than the official decrees, and most of the press in Argentina became the silent witness to a new form of state terrorism. This was partly caused by fear and the experience of repression in previous regimes; but also, at least in the early stages, by support for the military takeover in a situation generally defined as chaotic under the government of Sra Perón.

The publisher of *El Día* of La Plata, Raúl Kraiselburd, whose father had been abducted by the Montoneros and killed in a police ambush in 1974, provided the model when he told the Inter-American Press Association on 5 April 1976 that "it is premature to judge the situation of the freedom of the press in Argentina." A year later, however, he told the same association that the Argentine press was suffering from "collective intimidation."[5] In April 1977 *Le Monde* of Paris reported that seventy-two journalists had been killed, detained, or disappeared in Argentina since the coup. By March 1978, *Le Monde*'s count was forty disappeared, twenty-nine killed, and seventy arrested or imprisoned.[6]

It became impossible to know which of the media's reports were true. Reports of antiguerrilla activities increased over the next several months, and several Spanish-language newspapers thrived on pictures of "caches of arms" said to have been uncovered in police and army raids, or of dead bodies said to be guerrillas who had been stopped while engaging in warlike acts.

According to Andrew Graham-Yooll, who was then the political editor with the *Herald* but was editor-in-chief at the time of our interviews in 1996, "In Argentina, there is only a tenuous dividing line between censorship dictated by succeeding governments and self-censorship in the media."[7] By the end of August 1976, Graham-Yooll's own columns showed less self-censorship than most of the press. At that time he was noting (though still cautiously) that despite the government's assurances of its concern for human rights, a distressing number of persons had been "abducted or otherwise disappeared"[8] and that guerrillas were "on the decline," hinting that government references to "war" were overstated.[9] Graham-Yooll went into exile in London the following month. The *Herald* quietly continued to print news of disappeared persons, alone in its defiance of censorship at that time; and the editor-in-chief, Robert Cox, continued to publish restrained (but no longer laudatory) editorials.[10] On 22 August, in an editorial headed "Frankenstein's Monster Again," Cox came very close to accusing the government of the disappearances of, among others, leading members of political parties, and of the murder of the parish priests of the Irish Pallotine Order:

Decent people have been trying to comfort themselves with the belief that the murders that cannot be attributed to the subversive left are vengeance killings ... For the majority of ordinary people – hoping against hope that the deaths and disappearances that could not be blamed on the subversive left will eventually be explained in a way that will not outrage their natural sense of justice – the moment of truth came with the slaughter of [the priests]. From that moment onwards, it became increasingly clear to every law abiding person in Argentina – unless blinkered by prejudice – that some mindless Frankenstein's monster has gone berserk. From then on it was no longer possible to blame all the murders of innocent people on leftwing subversive delinquents. In yesterday's communique the interior ministry came closer to identifying that monster than it ever has before when it repudiated "this

vandalistic episode only attributable to the dementia of irrational groups."
But we have yet to see a single member of these demented irrational groups
fall into the hands of the security forces.[11]

Cox left Argentina on 16 December 1979, after repeated death threats
against his family.

The following interviews provide the views Maximo Gainza, who
was then publisher and owner of *La Prensa*, and Andrew Graham-
Yooll, leading political editor before he went into exile in 1976.

VOICE: MAXIMO GAINZA

Gainza is the former publisher and owner of La Prensa.

La Prensa was one of only two newspapers that published the names
of about 6,000 people who had disappeared, together with the document that the human rights organizations had presented to all the
newspapers in Buenos Aires. This was a two-page advertisement
brought to the newspaper by Dr Pérez Esquivel [who later won the Nobel
Peace Prize for his work in defence of the detained and disappeared].
It was paid for in cash. The reaction to that information was that we
lost 10,000 readers. People did not want to know what was happening.

I don't care if it is 30,000, 40,000, 6,000, or one. In no civilized
country should people disappear. But to understand what happened
here, you have to understand that the armed forces were just a state-
run corporation. And we know how bad state-run corporations generally are. The first thing about this bureaucratic group of armed,
uniformed men was that they had the power that the guns gave them.
The guns were superior in power to law. People started disappearing.

It is like a lawyer losing all the paper relevant to a court case that
he might lose. Then everything has to be redone, and sometimes that
is impossible. This is what these armed and uniformed people did.
They thought as bureaucrats much more than as crazy men. There
were crazy men there too, but the majority were pure bureaucrats with
uniforms and guns. They thought the best way of solving the problem
was having it disappear. And that is what they did with human beings.

One of our top correspondents wrote a piece in our paper. He said
that if those people were guilty, the so-called terrorists or guerrillas,
whatever, they should be judged, and if they were found guilty, then
according to our laws for kidnapping and murder, they deserved the
death penalty.

There are now some 53,000 retired and active army, navy, and air
force officers; they generally retire at forty-five to fifty years of age.

The army now comprises a total of 15,000 soldiers, including some women. There is no longer a draft here; these are professional soldiers. Of the 15,000 soldiers, 10,000 are in bureaucratic jobs! The navy was instructed by the English, the army by Germans, the air force by Italians. Perón, who was a military attaché in Italy, especially admired Mussolini. Hitler had a more bureaucratic style – demanded orderliness, consistency – but Mussolini was a demagogue who changed according to what was convenient.

Before the Second World War, at the university, we were divided into two groups – the pro-Nazis and the others. The pro-nazi group favoured Franco in the Spanish Civil War because Franco was Catholic, and Argentina is a Catholic country. Communism cannot get power here because the people always return to Catholicism. Perón was all-powerful, the absolute boss. And if there was any union man who got too powerful for General Perón, he was killed. Some tried that. They were shot, they were killed. Like Rucci.

What did La Prensa *do to try to help the people understand the situation after the military came in?*

So many editorials. But you come to the conclusion that when the country doesn't feel well, it's like when you don't feel well and suspect you may have cancer. Some people go to the doctor immediately, and if they have to be operated on, they have a chance of being saved. Other people don't go to the doctor, they don't want to know what is wrong. Here the same thing happens. They knew that the armed forces were killing people, and people were being taken out of their homes in the night and so on. They didn't want to know. When we published the habeas corpus of those who had disappeared, people didn't even read it. Why was that?

The paper was always respected, but eventually they just took us over. Why don't I have the newspaper now? Because we couldn't live with it, we couldn't be a decent newspaper in an indecent country. We were first taken over by Perón's government in 1951. We got it back four years later, in 1955, under President Aramburu. But no government ever liked us – La Prensa's independent position. They respected us, or they tried to make us change. For instance, the monopoly of official advertising was not Perón's doing. It was done under the government of Onganía. He created an agency with a monopoly on official advertising. Don't forget that in those days when the airlines were national, and the railroad, and the gas, oil, and electric companies, there were nine hundred corporations that were under the government, and their advertising was very profitable. They didn't want to support independent newspapers. You can write all the brilliant editorials you want, but the least-read part of the newspaper is the editorial. Horoscopes are read more often, and we never had a horoscope.

Which other newspaper published Esquivel's list of the disappeared?

La Opinión, Timerman's paper. He was the owner. We published the same thing. In those days Timerman was on the side of the guerrillas. He changed. Most of the good writers from the left went through *La Opinión*, and left-wingers are generally better writers than the right wing. I don't know why, but they do write better. They do write well.

But you were not a left-wing paper, obviously, and you were publishing this information. Were you ever threatened?

Once a secretary from the Information Bureau phoned and just told me that we could not publish any news about guerrilla movements or fighting or things like that. I asked him, "Is this advice, or is it an order?" He says, "It's an order." "Well, then tell your superior to write it out for me." He says, "You are not allowed to publish any news about people being wounded or killed by fighting against the guerrillas." So I put that on the front page. At least our readers knew why there was no news about what was happening. But the same day there was a violent shooting nearby, and we followed the news of the shooting. Nothing happened.

So why were the other newspapers so frightened?

Because they had been frightened for so many years back, they continued to be frightened. They couldn't change. The Gainzas are Basques. They are very headstrong people. So we couldn't change. The revolution that overthrew Isabel Perón in 1976, well, we knew that the revolution was bound to happen. And we had information that it would happen tonight. What did we do? We kept the presses waiting, and we got six editions out as we were getting more news of what was happening all over the country.

Next day, I found out that the other papers did not have a single line on the revolution. Because at a certain hour, the new military government had called all the top men in the news departments and given them strict orders not to print anything about the revolution. And when the whole thing ended, he said, "Where is the man from *La Prensa*?" But there was no man from *La Prensa* there. Why? Because we were not on the list of people to call when they wanted to get their news out! So we were the only paper. They were doing the bureaucratic thing. The people didn't have the list with the telephone numbers of the papers they didn't usually want to contact. They didn't have the name and address of the man from La Prensa who has been covering things for years.

The left wing never speaks of the two pages we printed, but I received an award in New York, given by the American Foundation, and the award is for having continued to fight against a dictatorship ... and for printing the two pages of the 6,000 names of the disappeared. You ask people here, "Did you see those two pages, two full pages?" They didn't see them, says the left wing, because they don't want to honour something published by their enemy. You know, even if you are an enemy, you respect your own enemy and what they do; that is the honourable thing ...

People fear you, because they know that some day they might ask a favour that is against the law, and we will not do it. And they claim that we are helping the enemy. It is not helping the enemy to publish the names of the disappeared. What could we do? We used to publish the whole thing of habeas corpus and the judge would intervene but many of those people, young people, nobody knew. But when that double-page came out, it wasn't a case of one habeas corpus, it was thousands of people who had disappeared.

VOICE: ANDREW GRAHAM-YOOLL

Political editor of the Buenos Aires Herald *in the 1970s and editor-in-chief in the 1990s.*

When you have a whole generation, a very active generation, debating politics, and you have a general who says, no more politics, parties are banned, and he sends mounted police into the university, the first effect was that a whole generation of lecturers said, "Well, we're leaving the country," and they did. Students were suddenly left without politics and without their teachers. And by the way, this is not an apology or an excuse, or even in sympathy with the guerrillas, but in my mind, when you find all doors closed to political debate, you go for your gun. It might not happen in Canada. It might not happen in England. But it happens in many other places. Violence is the only way you have left for expressing yourself. And this is what happened to my generation. The leader of the Montoneros was two years younger than me.

The young guerrillas were people who came from nationalist groups, from Catholic groups, from left-wing groups, and they all met, really, not around an ideology, but they met around the gun, and we have brilliant people. I recall a friend, he was really one of the leading poets of his generation, a little older than me; he died in a shootout. Well, that is the beginning of the guerrillas. The Montoneros, it's important to bear in mind, were twelve people when they started. When they kidnapped and later murdered General Aramburu, they were just twelve people. Of those twelve people, only one or two survived. I knew some of them before that. I met Mario Firmenich later, much later – I met him and interviewed him before the kidnapping of the Born brothers.

Did the Aramburu event change your relationships with any of them or your views of them?

My views have always been the same. You do not go around killing people, not even for a political ideology. I don't know what would have happened had I been in Germany under Hitler. But I was in touch with these people, they came to the paper, they trusted me. The one who didn't trust me was Firmenich. He ordered me killed because I had insulted the memory of Eva Perón.

How did you manage to find out that he had ordered you killed? You are obviously still alive.

Because one of his henchmen was an Anglo-Argentine who had gone to St George's College.[12] And he said, "No, no, you can't kill Andrew." Some of those men were taking a grenade to the *Buenos Aires Herald*. The idea was to leave a hand grenade on the metal desk with the glass top, and if you leave the pin hanging over the top of it, then when someone opens the desk – well, I kept ties and clips and papers and everything else in there – so that when you open the drawer you pull the pin, and it blows up. On their way to deliver that bomb, this other fellow said, "You might not like Andrew, but don't kill him." The order was withdrawn.

I think the reason Firmenich wanted me killed was because of two things. First, there was a book by a friend of mine, one of the earliest books on the life of Eva Perón, called *Notes for a Biography of Eva Perón*. I have it in my office. I lost it in one of the police raids, and then I found it in a second-hand shop a month or two months ago. I reviewed the book in 1970–71 – it was after the Aramburu thing. They became angry and wanted to kill me. They tried to kill the author too. But what made it worse was that we also reprinted a review from the *New York Review of Books* about V.S. Naipaul's

History of Eva Perón. It was a bit later than that, in 1972. And then Naipaul himself came to Argentina and wrote a very long essay called "The Body behind the Iron Gate" about Eva Perón. We reprinted that. As I was political editor, the Montoneros assumed that I was responsible for it.

So the review of the book, plus the reprinting of Naipaul – those were heinous and vicious insults to Eva Perón, the two things that prompted them to decide to kill me. Naipaul said Eva Perón was the typical Argentine macho's woman whose fleshy red lips inspired the fantasy of fellatio within the Argentine male. We reproduced that article, and a Montonero said to me, "You can't call me a cocksucker!" That is why they wanted to kill me, but the order was countermanded. ·

Their people had built up a fantasy about Perón. This was because Onganía wanted to bring history to a standstill. Iwakawa didn't invent anything; the end of history was invented by Onganía. He wanted to bring politics in Argentina to a complete stop, and he banned parties. Perón had been a complete failure. His economic policy had failed five years before. But now, suddenly, young people in their twenties were raving Peronists, and you know, it was the product of fantasy. If you shut all the doors and have no political activity, you see, it is like godfathering religious sects. These people created their political fantasy around Juan and Eva Perón.

I've read your account of what happened with the Born brothers, and that very curious incident where they handed back Jorge Born.[13] In light of the charges that Martin Andersen made in his book,[14] about Firmenich being an intelligence agent, do you see him any differently now than you did then?

Well, Firmenich was in command by default, because earlier leaders were dead. I've always disliked him. And I tried to disguise that, later on, during his trial, because the lawyer could have argued prejudice, which it would have been and it was. I disliked him intensely and he tried to kill me. Had they asked me, "Are you against this man for any particular reason?" it would have completely destroyed my testimony against him. Since they didn't ask, I didn't have to say anything. That's the way justice works.

But Martin Andersen argues that Firmenich was playing both sides.

I don't know if Firmenich was playing both sides. It wouldn't surprise me. I've given you my opinion of him. If he were playing both sides, well, at the end of the day, like the famous terrorist Carlos, it was money that decided what he was going to do with his life. And Carlos, after all his spectacular exploits, he said it was not for politics, it was for cash. I think Firmenich settled for cash.

That reminds me, I happened to meet up with the mother of a dead Montonera at the French Embassy, and I said to her, "I deeply regret your daughter's death. But she had a shit for a leader. He was completely protofascist, or neofascist." And the mother became very annoyed. In her tragedy I grant you that she was right to be very annoyed. But to me, that was it. At the end of the day, he sent all these young troops to their death. The mother said, "No, it was an individual decision to come back from exile to fight the military," and I couldn't say this to the mother, that the dead woman, who died for her beliefs, well I wanted to say, "I'm sorry, Madam, but your daughter was a bloody fool, and that's why she's dead." Well, you couldn't say that to people.

In 1974 I had the experience of going underground. I had to change houses every night for ten days of my life. I mean, it takes an enormous strength of character, ability, and presence of mind to operate underground. You don't just go underground. I was alone at that moment, so I could decide for myself how I was going to play things for ten days. I didn't go to work, I just changed houses every night. You have to know where to go, you have to know who will accept you, you have to know who will be your host without feeling endangered or fearful and then give you away. And Firmenich suddenly declared that because the Montoneros were being persecuted, he was going underground. He left a whole surface group so that he could go underground. You're telling Andrew Graham-Yooll to play his own game, you're telling a large segment of surface folks who go home to their parents every night or their wives or their children ... and they ... how? Well, it's really complicity in their murder. You don't do that.

Now, to go back to Andersen's argument that Firmenich was playing both sides, I don't know. There is no proof. But there were strange things. The house where Born was held and then released, where I played that short role as a journalist witness, had been infiltrated by a colonel who eventually found it very profitable to take part in the kidnapping for ransom, so he joined the Montoneros. He was a double agent. I don't remember the colonel's name. He went to prison, he was sent to prison, he was a very easy target in the end. If you have that one way, why shouldn't you have it the other way? No identifiable military authority has come forward and said, "Firmenich was a double agent." It is all hearsay. Andersen does not quote any direct, shall we say, contact who might have been Firmenich's minder. But I wouldn't put it past him. He also tried to negotiate with Massera. Massera tried to negotiate with Firmenich. Massera was a perfect shit. Firmenich was, is, they both are.

That was later, though, that was in Spain, when Massera was looking for support. There are people like Galimberti – who is now Jorge Born's security advisor – in arms, whatever. And there is a poet who broke away from the Montoneros in Spain, accusing Firmenich of megalomania for sending his troops back to Argentina to fight a battle in which they would be killed for sure. But even they, they are not prepared to say that "this guy was a double agent." And they are like *cucarachas* ... Things simply worked that way ...

I was the main witness against Firmenich. I was a journalist. So the prosecutor and the judge gave me the files of other people's testimony, which they shouldn't have shown me. I saw Galimberti give a very clear explanation in his testimony of how the money was managed within the Montoneros. And at no time does he say Firmenich was a thief. You know, the whole process of money management was very clearly set out.

In your opinion, did the money that you were engaged in negotiating, because of your particular role in the handing over of Jorge Born, actually go to the Montoneros?

Oh yes, oh yes. I think it went to the Montoneros, and part of it was in Cuba. Cuba was the bank for most of it, Cuba didn't keep the money for itself. It was argued by the prosecutor that Cuba has it, but I don't believe Cuba has kept any of the money. I was offered – no, I wasn't offered, I was told – when Firmenich was already under arrest, that he had six million dollars available to change my testimony. I would probably have received $600 by the time everybody took their commissions. A lawyer friend of mine phoned me in London and said, "$6 million are available to change your testimony." But by then I had already testified. So my children always tell me ... "We could have been rich ..."

I left Argentina in 1976. France offered me asylum, but I don't speak French. It was Giscard d'Estaing, who was a conservative right-wing president, who ordered Air France to get me out of Argentina and my whole family quickly. It was signed by Giscard. I've never met the man, I've never seen the man in my life. He was told by Amnesty International that they ought to do something to get me out. It was Air France that actually provided the tickets and the hospitality to get the whole family out. So that was 1976. I was very grateful to the government of France for saving my life and that of my family, but I wanted to go to London, where I could speak English.

I was very lucky after that and obtained work at the *Daily Telegraph* in London. Then I worked on the *Guardian* until 1984, then edited a magazine in London, and in that year I came back to testify against Firmenich. I came back at Alfonsín's request. He was very explicit. When he took office in December 1983, he issued two decrees, one ordering the trials of the military juntas by their peers, in other words, to set up a court martial. And the other decree ordered the trial of the guerrilla chiefs, but there were no guerrilla chiefs available. A few months later the military court martial said there was no case against their peers. There was no reason to go on trial. And Alfonsín was under tremendous domestic and international pressure to be seen to be doing something, so he needed to put the juntas under federal law, and he in fact had decided to order a trial of Videla and company, Videla, Massera, and ... and he was told, quite obviously, you can't put the military on trial if you don't have at least one guerrilla on trial, and what followed then was, some of what was, judicially speaking, an illegal aberration.

Firmenich was in Brazil and he was protected by Brazilian authorities. And he went to the consulate for his passport and then he was taunting the authorities. And the governor of the state, who had protected Firmenich under pressure from the left, suddenly lifted his protection, said he was no longer responsible for Firmenich. So Firmenich was promptly put on a plane and brought to Argentina under arrest.

The legal proceedings, the visible legal proceedings, were that he could be charged with a criminal offence but he could not be charged with a political trial, so the criminal offence was the kidnapping of Born and the murder of Bosch, Born's manager. The thing is that what they used in the sham legal proceedings was a translation from my book. They had no other legal document to justify their expedition. So this is why it was judicially an aberration. It's illegal. I don't know, it's a legal nothing, it's a translation from a book. The translation was done for the ministry, and the prosecution filed extradition proceedings.

Firmenich was sent back. The arguments were that Firmenich wanted to be arrested, so he allowed himself to be caught, and he negotiated, thinking that he would come back, be charged, and immediately be released. Alfonsín couldn't afford that. So Alfonsín concocted this extradiction, which I say is a legal aberration. However, he got me to come back and testify that the chapter in my book was mine and my own experience. And then it became more complicated after that. The courts demanded a confrontation between Firmenich and myself, so it became legally more respectable.

You were under police guard all this time, you must have been. Have
you been guarded since then? I mean, Firmenich is free and ...

No, no. A friend phoned me and said, "Don't go to the hotel, the
government wants to kill you. Come to my home." This was quite a
responsibility for him. "Come to my house, I'd rather you came to my
house." And he never quite explained why he said that. I mean, I
wasn't sure, or what. He just said, "Come home." So I went with
twelve bodyguards. Then I recognized the head of my bodyguards. I
said, "Hey, I know you. Yes, you were the guy who tried to kill me
in 1975, when you came to raid my home." He said (slapping his
thigh or the equivalent), "Doesn't life change!" And so he was. In
other words, I was protected by previous potential killers, but now I
was in the home of a friend, and my friend argued that I was safer in
his home than in a hotel where anything could happen. All the bodyguards knew where I was, and if I wanted to cross the street, the
traffic was cut all around here and it was Operation Street Crossing.
And this continued for a week, a bit long. Then I returned to London,
and I did not come back permanently until 1994, when I was
appointed editor of the *Buenos Aires Herald*.

There is just one other thing I should tell you. In 1976, when I was
already in London, there was an article in the *New Scientist* by an
Argentine scientist telling what was happening to science under the
military. A military officer wrote to the *New Scientist* saying, "It is
absolutely untrue. That is ridiculous. The military has never done
anything like that." And I saw that. The *New Scientist* is not my
breakfast reading at all, but I happened on that – somebody showed
it to me. I then wrote to the *New Scientist* and gave them chapter and
verse of one book burning in Córdoba, how it was done, what day,
that sort of thing. You see, journalists were invited to see this. There
were book burnings in Córdoba; we had considerable book burnings
in Tucumán; we had raids and book burnings on publishers. And that
little letter of mine became virtually a classic, telling the world what
was happening here.

INTERNATIONAL OPINION
AND INTERVENTIONS

The explanation given by the military forces for the repression was
that they were saving Western, Christian civilization from subversives
and communists. During our interviews with civilians, we heard a
parallel explanation: "If they (the military) had not taken over, we
might have ended up like the Soviet Union or Cuba." From a Canadian
who visited the region on business, we heard pronouncements about

how the USSR had been fomenting subversion and subsidizing guerrillas right through the 1970s: he claimed to have this knowledge from sources inside Argentina. If there was evidence that Western, Christian civilization was indeed in dire danger of subversion at that time, this might be treated as a serious hypothesis. Some of those whom we interviewed would still argue that the danger was real. They point to the numerous guerrilla groups that had formed in Argentina during the late 1960s and early 1970s, the violence of some of these groups, and the influence of Cuban revolutionaries on young Argentines.

Although beliefs need not be based on truth in order to induce many people to act on them, we might divert the discussion momentarily to assess this rationale. First, is there any evidence that the Soviet Union or Cuba was involved in Argentine politics? The USSR was certainly engaged in supporting allies such as Cuba and infiltrating other regions from time to time during the 1950s and early 1960s. However, after that time, its direct influence in South America declined. Contrary to the general expectation that if it intervened it would be on behalf of the guerrillas, there is undisputed evidence that it was a strong supporter of the military junta from 1976 to 1983, and there is no evidence at all that it ever supported the guerrilla groups. As noted below, the Soviets' need for wheat and the Generals' need for markets were stronger than Cold War ideology. The Communist Party of Argentina, invariably taking its cue from its Soviet comrades, never entered the fray against either military or capitalist forces; on the contrary, it was well known as a thoroughly conservative (and very small) party that could be counted on to support the most traditional and conservative policies of military governments.

With respect to Cuba, the Argentine guerrilla forces were enamoured with the Cuban revolution and Che Guevara's methodology for warfare. Some protorevolutionaries went to Cuba in the early and mid-1960s to learn how to conduct guerrilla warfare, and Cuba became a safe haven for some exiles during the military regime. However, there is no evidence that Cuba as a country took any action outside its own borders to strengthen the guerrillas in a struggle within Argentina. On the basis of current evidence, Cuban forces were not active in South America after Guevara's death in Bolivia in 1967. No other sources of communist insurgency have ever been shown to exist. Thus, there does not seem to be any evidence of a threat of communist attack from external sources in the mid-1970s.

The United States and the Cold War

The belief that communist subversion was a genuine threat in Argentina was related to the United States (and, to a lesser extent, European)

fear of communism, and to the mentoring role played by the French
and American military to Latin American armies and police. These
countries had pivotal roles in training the Argentine military forces
and police from the 1950s through to the early 1970s, and some
Argentines blame the advent of state terrorism on French and U.S.
pressure, infiltration, and training. They point to the fact that
although the French army lost its colonial wars in Indochina and
Algeria, it boasted superior knowledge of antiguerrilla tactics and provided its expertise to the military forces of other countries.

The United States, seemingly obsessed with its national security
interests in the Western Hemisphere and with the potential for communist takeovers, especially after the Cuban revolution of 1959, also
became a mentor in antisubversive methods for army officers. Along
with the military training, the United States provided instruction
against communism to police and military officers from Latin America. The International Police Academy in Washington, D.C., originally
called the Inter-American Police Academy and located at Fort Davis
in the Panama Canal Zone, is reported to have provided training to
the police forces of Latin America, Asia, and Africa.[15] This fact was
frequently discussed during our interviews. Summarizing such material
as this, political theorists Raymond Duvall and Michael Stohl observe,
"One might be tempted to say, without too much exaggeration, that
the superpowers govern their empires indirectly, in part through the
support of Third World state terrorism."[16]

The United States government, military, and CIA had strategic reasons for training other countries' military forces and employing agents
to engage in secret and unsavoury activities; presumably, their objective was to protect the economic interests of American capital and the
political interests of the American state. The participation of these
groups in Chile at the time of the coup against Salvadore Allende's
government has been well documented, and we know that a number
of North American mining and other companies also were involved in
the preparations and conduct of the military coup against Chile's
elected government in 1973. The economists known as the "Chicago
boys" were involved in General Pinochet's Chile, and Pinochet's objective was to restructure the Chilean society with a monetarist "free
market" economic base. Thus, the explanation that rests on global or
American capital and American military or covert CIA intervention
is plausible.

However, Chile and Argentina are two separate cases, and while the
evidence is substantial and acknowledged in the Chilean case, there is
no similar body of evidence about American intervention in Argentina.
As far as is known, Americans played wildly divergent roles in Argen-

tina under the presidencies of Jimmy Carter and Ronald Reagan, and while both sets of policies need examination, neither involved direct manipulation of local politics or an active part in state terrorism.

Indirect intervention is a more plausible theory for Argentina. There are a number of variants on the general theory that the southern cone countries of Latin America were subjected to monetarist controls by the International Monetary Fund and other international lenders, and were persuaded by international capital that monetarism was the escape route from the persistent debt and inflation problems they experienced. Interviewees frequently cited these theories or offered their own variant, usually pointing the finger of blame at the United States and the "Chicago boys" who provided the rationale for monetarism and extreme free market economies.

One theorist, David Pion-Berlin, contends that the military became enamoured of the belief that monetarism, as established by the "Chicago school" in Chile, was a policy capable of saving Argentina's economy. In his view, "not only do economic ideas generate their own maps of reality that define how the costs and benefits of productive and allocative decisions should be distributed within society; even more significantly, they render judgment on current and past economic affairs."[17]

Judgments involve attributions of blame against anyone who might jeopardize economic growth. If economic growth is viewed as a *sine qua non* for social development, it becomes possible to view opponents as evil and to conclude that their elimination is justifiable. Pion-Berlin argues that the particular content of the monetarist ideology is central to an explanation of the terrorist strategy. The content includes downsizing the unions, decreasing social security for the poor and unemployed, and getting rid of left-wing opposition. We shall consider this argument further in the concluding chapter.

Amnesty International

Whatever international capitalism and external military forces may have been up to, Amnesty International acted consistently as a voice of conscience against arbitrary imprisonment and disappearances. Amnesty became a persistent voice on behalf of PEN prisoners and the disappeared under military rule. Called "Marxists," and "naive" by the governments of Latin America, Amnesty volunteers publicized the violations of human rights in Argentina and petitioned for the release of "prisoners of conscience." As Iain Guest points out in his detailed study, *Behind the Disappearances*, "terrorists, to Amnesty, were common criminals,"[18] whereas governments had to be accountable for acts of terror. This distinction was not appreciated by the military government in 1976 when Amnesty visited Argentina. Human rights were on the agenda in the United States at that time while Jimmy Carter was running for president, and stories of events in Argentina were reaching the American public.

The military junta agreed to Amnesty's investigation, aware that Amnesty would not protect ERP or Montonero members because it steadfastly refused to intervene on behalf of those who had advocated violence. Although the Amnesty investigators gave no information to reporters, newspaper accounts were produced, presumably by publicists for the junta, that were inaccurate and highly damaging to Amnesty. A demonstration by a group of young people called the National Patriotic Movement was mounted outside the hotel of the Amnesty investigators, even though demonstrations were illegal. While police took no action, the youths screamed epithets at the investigators and distributed a communiqué against "these foreigners who offend our national dignity [who] should know that we are fighting against Marxism: so that we can continue to believe in God; so that the family can continue to be the center of Argentinian life; so that fathers can continue to be the main educators of their children."[19]

The remainder of the visit by Amnesty included "security escorts," who photographed anyone bold enough to talk to the investigators. Two newspapers provided thoughtful discussions of the Amnesty visit – La Opinión, then edited by Jacobo Timerman (at that time a supporter of the coup, though he later became one of its victims), and the Buenos Aires Herald, edited by Robert Cox. Other newspapers printed the "news" that was provided by the junta. La Prensa, then the leading newspaper in Buenos Aires, editorialized: "Whose rights are they defending? Only those in prison? Apparently, the rest of society has none. Amnesty remains indifferent to the brutal killing of innocent people. It cannot hope to inspire confidence and sympathy in our country."[20]

The Amnesty report came out on 23 March 1977, one year after the coup, and it provided the details – names, dates, and places – of disappearances. It was a major public relations setback for the junta, but it did not stop el Proceso.

ILO and Other Interventions

Six months after the coup, the International Labor Organization published a list of detained and disappeared trade unionists. This had no immediate effect but eventually pressure from the ILO and member unions brought about the release of many unionists, as attested to by some of the survivors interviewed for this book.

The international community was also alerted to Argentina's plight by expatriates such as Argentine lawyer and former ERP activist Rodolfo Matarollo[21] (who was already resident in Paris when the coup occurred) and by two organizations that had been established in Argentina before the coup but moved into exile in 1976: the Argentine Human Rights Commission (CADHU) and the Argentine Information and Solidarity Center (CAIS). Two of CADHU's leaders, Gustavo Roca and Lucio Garzón Maceda, gave testimony before the U.S. House of Representatives Subcommittee on Human Rights and International Organizations. Although CADHU disintegrated, other organizations of exiles emerged throughout the world, and their members mounted a sustained campaign to alert the world community to the abuses in Argentina.

Three released women from the concentration camp ESMA,[22] all of them subsequently exiled in Europe, put together a detailed dossier of prisoners they had encountered there. They counted 4,736 persons who were detained in that camp between 1976 and 1979, and they concluded that fewer than 100 had survived. They released this information to the French National Assembly in October 1979, and it became a major document in the fight against the junta.[23]

American Policy under the Carter Administration

Under Jimmy Carter's presidency, the United States had become more aggressive in its policies toward countries with unsavoury records on human rights. The U.S Congress passed laws cutting U.S. military aid to governments with "consistent patterns" of human rights abuses. A major reason why the junta conducted its abductions and murders secretly was to avoid precisely such sanctions as were incurred by Chile.

Patricia Derian, U.S. assistant secretary of state for human rights in the Carter administration, aggressively pursued change in Argentina, and the United States strongly pressed for an investigation by the Inter-American Commission on Human Rights (IACHR), an arm of the Organization of American States (OAS). After many delays, the IACHR visited Argentina in September 1979. Despite the disappearance of key witnesses belonging to Relatives of the Detained and Disappeared (Familiares), despite the raiding of offices that contained testimonies, and despite other unambiguous threats and blockages set up by the police and armed forces, the IACHR attracted thousands of courageous Argentines who made their allegations. The investigators received 5,580 allegations, observed bullet-riddled corpses in burial grounds, and saw other evidence that the disappeared were being buried secretly.[24] The OAS report, published in December 1979, denounced the junta for many crimes, and though the junta would not release the report in Argentina, Dr Emilio Mignone was able to smuggle in some five hundred copies to give a psychological boost to the relatives of the disappeared.

Argentine Military and Soviet Interests

The junta was much more successful in avoiding scrutiny at the United Nations. A full-time Argentine ambassador to Geneva, Gabriel Martínez, managed to keep Argentina off the agenda of the U.N. Human Rights Commission through 1979.[25] Among Argentina's principal allies was the Soviet Union, which had two vested interests in the case: Argentina was a major source of wheat during a period when the Carter administration had imposed a trade embargo; and the USSR was keen to keep violations of human rights off all international agendas. Argentina was prepared to ignore the grain embargo, and the USSR reciprocated by ignoring Argentina's human rights violations.

It was the OAS report that finally provided the momentum for advancing the case of Argentina on the agenda of the United Nations. A "Working Group on Disappearances," established under the U.N. Human Rights Commission, compiled a documented case against the Argentine junta in December 1980, based on testimony from released or escaped victims of the concentration camps and also from some of the torturers.[26] By this time, the junta was decreasing its use of disappearances as a method of governance and was instead talking about "reconciliation."

Contradictory Policies of the U.S. Government

Although Jimmy Carter's government pursued human rights violators and imposed sanctions, the various components of the U.S. bureaucracy were not consistent in supporting this policy. Just as it had done during the 1943–45 period, the U.S. government said one thing but did another.[27] The events of the 1976–80 period indicate strong statements by Patricia Derian and actions taken to back them up by Jimmy Carter, yet at the same time the Eximbank continued to provide generous funds to the junta. Early on in the period, the State Department vetoed the financing of hydroelectric turbines on the grounds of human rights abuses. It was immediately besieged by the company that was to produce these, as well as by the Chamber of Commerce and many other lobby groups whose members would lose either employment or profits if the deal were cancelled. The State Department abandoned its stance, and Eximbank continued to operate in Argentina. After this failure, Jimmy Carter's human rights policy, in the view of Carlos Escudé, who studied these issues in depth, "never had an economic-sanctions dimension. The popularity of Argentina's economics minister, José Martínez de Hoz, with U.S. business and with the Treasury Department, probably also had an impact on this result: after all, the Treasury is less politically minded than the State Department, and the minister, who had many influential friends, engaged in almost permanent lobbying in Washington."[28]

In fact, it was not only the Eximbank that continued as usual: the World Bank awarded extraordinarily large loans to the junta during its tenure. Further, the United States listed Argentina as one of the "principal beneficiaries" of the U.S. Generalized System of Preferences. In 1980 Argentina exported a total of $231 million, duty free, to the United States, a sum that could not possibly be justified in terms of protecting the U.S. trade balance[29] (a usual explanation for U.S. export credits where human rights abuses were noted).

The Reagan Years

In rhetoric on human rights, the United States abruptly changed direction after the 1980 election. Ronald Reagan immediately removed Patricia Derian from office and essentially stopped U.S. action with respect to human rights violations. The U.S. embargo on arms sales was repealed in due course. For Reagan's government, any violations were ignored if the cause was the cessation of communist subversion. The United Nations finally pronounced its verdict of guilty on the junta, but too late for the disappeareds of Argentina.

A Possible Explanation of International Inaction

The simple explanation for the United States' contradictory policies is that the multinational businesses (and their unionized workers) who sold goods to Argentina cared not a fig for human rights. Reagan's approach was to ignore human rights violators if they were anticommunist. The same unions, however, were pivotal to gaining international attention to the plight of unionized workers in Argentina, and there were not that many American multinational businesses still operating in Argentina by the time Reagan assumed office in the United States.

Unfortunately, one other explanation has to be contemplated by any honest observer: a majority of middle-class Argentines, even as late as

1980, were less concerned than external witnesses about human rights violations. Buenos Aires taxi drivers of that time, along with many private car drivers and any others who could display slogans on their belongings, sported stickers saying, "Los argentinos somos derechos y humanos" (Argentines are both righteous and humane – a play on words) as a rebuttal of the denunciations of foreign human rights activists. Escudé cites data from Gallup archives showing that "in March 1980, approximately 64 percent of the population considered that living standards were *stable or rising*, while 62 per cent considered that the family economy was in *equal or better* shape than in the previous year" and that "67 percent considered their incomes sufficient for their basic needs."[30]

For those who were unconcerned and untouched by human rights violation and who were, in 1980, the beneficiaries of economic policies under Economics Minister Martínez de Hoz, any pronouncement from the United States about internal affairs in Argentina was offensive. Although Carter and Derian did much good for the morale of the families of the disappeared and were responsible for the release of occasional prisoners such as Timerman, their pronouncements produced anger and resistance in many Argentines, rather than concern for the disappeared. Such reactions supported the population in its continued compliance with the military dictatorship. Says J.S. Tulchin, in a study of U.S.-Argentine relations: "The majority of the Argentine people was disposed to accept the ... regime, with its horrible repression, as the best possible alternative. For the acquiescent majority, external pressure on their government prompted a hostile reaction and self-defense."[31]

PART FOUR

The Central Institutions of the Repression

CHAPTER 13

A Deeply Divided Church

The Catholic Church of the 1970s and its offspring, the Third World Priests' Movement, were as far apart from one another as the same church had been from Peronism in the 1950s. The ideological divide was similar, though the priests had no political agenda akin to that of Perón. The Third World priests were concerned with the poor, and their agenda was to eradicate poverty. The church hierarchy was concerned with its traditional theological interests – sin, the soul, salvation – and regarded the priests' movement as subversive of the true mission of the church. This great division was not new, nor was it unique to Argentina. It runs through the entire history of Christianity. But in Argentina of the 1970s, the conflict between these two ideological groups was strong and deep – so deep that they took opposite positions and allied themselves in opposite ways with the military on the one hand and the guerrillas on the other.

Emilio Mignone, a stalwart of the Catholic Church as well as a lawyer famed for his outspoken defence of human rights, and father of Mónica Mignone whose disappearance so shocked Argentina in 1976, published a scathing attack on the leaders of the church in the mid-1980s. He blames the leaders of the period, not the institution. In his view, the leaders were in league with the dictatorship.[1]

Archbishop Adolfo Servando Tortolo and Cardinals Juan Carlos Aramburu and Raúl Primatesta comprised the Executive Commission of the bishops' conference in 1976; Tortolo, then located in Paraná, was vicar for the armed forces and president of the Episcopal Conference. In their search for Mónica, Mignone and his wife contacted Archbishop Tortolo, only to be told that there was nothing he could do. Later, together with other parents of disappeared children, Mignone again sought out Tortolo and challenged him, pointing out that he, of all the church fathers, was in a position to influence the military to obtain freedom for the disappeared. But Tortolo was uninterested, and in October 1976 he stated publicly, "I have no knowledge, I have no reliable proof, of human rights being violated in our country." Later he affirmed his support for the military regime, saying that it was necessary and the armed forces were "carrying out their duty."[2]

Mignone had similar experiences with Bishop Victorio Bonamín, the vicar for the army. Mignone went to the bishop's office and was informed by his secretary that the provicar did not deal with questions of disappearances, arrests, and layoffs, "because he did not want to interfere in the army's course of action." During a speech he made in Tucumán in October 1976, with General Bussi in the audience, Bonamín stated, "Providence entrusted the army with the duty to govern, from the presidency all the way to intervening in a union." He later said, "Christ has entered with truth and goodness" when discussing the military carrying out repressive duties.[3] He called the military struggle a defence of "morality, human dignity, and ultimately a struggle to defend God ... Therefore, I pray for divine protection over this "dirty war" in which we are engaged."[4] He told a university audience in December 1977 that the world was divided into "atheistic materialism and Christian humanism."[5] When Tortolo and Bonamín retired in 1981, their places were given to others of similar or even stronger views.

Cardinal Aramburu became the next president of the Episcopal Conference in Argentina. In reference to the discovery of mass graves at a cemetery in the province of Buenos Aires (eventually 4,000 bodies similarly buried were found in different graveyards), the cardinal told a news reporter in Rome, in November 1982, that these could not be disappeared persons: "I don't understand how this question of guerrillas and terrorism has come up again; it's been over for a long time ... Things should not be mixed up. Do you know that there are some 'disappeared' persons who today are living quite contentedly in Europe?"[6]

Several of the case reports in *Nunca Más* state that priests of the church cooperated with the military to the point of inviting prisoners to confess everything in order to serve their nation. Numerous survivors tell of fruitless searches for their loved ones, in which officers of the church refused help but passed on information given in confidence. When the Mothers of the Plaza de Mayo sought support and a place to meet, the churches in the centre of the city were unable or unwilling to accommodate them.

Inevitably, with much evidence to support it, the claim against the church tends to stick: it was an accomplice. It is important, then, that we listen to the church for an explanation. Readers should be aware that obtaining interviews with members of the church hierarchy is not a simple matter. The papal nuncio in place while we resided in Buenos Aires told us in no uncertain terms that he would not give us the time of day for an interview and that he believed no one else would do so either. A very high-ranking bishop agreed to an interview but declined to permit it to be taped. An even higher-ranking individual promised an interview but failed to be available when we arrived. We have not included a couple of interviews because the biographies could not be rendered without identifying these priests, and they did not want to be identified.

When the hostilities were drawing to a close and the church, like the society, was preparing for the new democratic era, the church convened an episcopal conference to discuss its social role. This was published as *Iglesia y comunidad nacional* (1981). Other documents followed. The bishops said that they (or their predecessors) had occasionally objected to human rights abuses by the military. Indeed, there are letters, now public, to General Videla. Perplexed readers might have much difficulty finding any reference to abuses in them; they are, let us say, subtle. But as the millennium draws to a close, the pope's instruction to church leaders throughout the world to acknowledge past wrongs, and right them if possible, has had a moderating influence on pronouncements by the Argentine church in the 1990s.

The three interviews reported in this chapter represent diverse positions within the conservative Catholic Church. The first of these interviewees, who occupied a priest's role in a very traditional seminary, exhibited no sympathy for the victims of military terrorism when he discussed the matter with visiting Canadians in 1997. The second, in a much more politically sensitive position and concerned about the church's public image, carefully chose his words while defending the church hierarchy of the 1970s. The third represents those priests who tried to steer a middle course in the turbulent years, though he condemned the guerrillas and had personally experienced their viciousness during the Juan Perón period.

VOICE: PADRE SANTANO

During the 1970s there were problems within the church. Prior to that time, there were two major Catholic currents of thought in the Argentine church. One current could be called more Hispanic, nationalistic, Tomista[7] in its structure. Between the 1930s and 1950s, this current was dominant. After that a new, more liberal current developed, along the lines of a Christian democratic style, which brought about a division in the Argentine Catholic way of thinking. This current, Christian democrat in nature, grew in importance in the university halls. The priests were parish priests of university student groups. Then in the 1970s, to put it briefly, due to a derivative of that current, there was an intrusion of certain philosophical Marxists into the church.

Initially there were ideas that sprang from liberalism, but then Marxist ideas infiltrated the world. Some priests were unable to totally accept the church's social doctrine, and they were confused about state power. They thought that because the church was opening up to the world, as was said in the Vatican Council of 1968, that meant that priests should be more concerned with politics and with the poor. This thinking was Marxist. Everything that in Europe might be termed technological progressiveness, here, due to the lack of technology, became progressiveness in the social sphere. What in Europe led in some cases to the negation of Christ's divinity – more doctrinal themes, more theological – here led to the negation of the church's social doctrine and other social themes. Over there, the debate was more theological; here it became more social.

It was then that two guerrilla movements appeared in Argentina. One was the ERP, which is of complete Marxist extraction without any Catholic influence. The other was the Montoneros, which had certain Marxist tendencies but the members were Catholic. Many of the members came from Catholic student groups. So the ERP was belligerent, and the Montoneros had a mixture of Catholicism with more mysticism.

In the ecclesiastical sphere there was the emergence of the Third World Priests' Movement. Many of them were parish priests. They created disquietude among the youth and conveyed it in terms that took young people into the battlefield. They flung the kids into war, and they stayed behind in their parishes. Well, in some cases I believe they did go into battle. A military man told me that in one skirmish he was laid out on the ground and nearly killed by someone whom he later recognized in a newspaper photograph as a priest. I know his name, but I am not going to tell you. This was not uncommon. What was more unusual was for them not to fight.

There was a case in which all the students of a school course died fighting years later while they were in university, but they had been educated in a Catholic school. They died in combat or they disappeared. This means there was a strong influence on the students. Sometimes the educating priests would say, "No. No. You haven't understood us. You went too far." And the boys would say the opposite: "We followed the line you drew for us."

In your opinion, those priests who had so much influence among the
students, were they mostly influenced by the Vatican Council of 1968
or more influenced by other worldly things?

Half and half. But I don't think that was the only reason. The preoccupation with the poor was combined with a very myopic idea that it
was necessary to fight in an armed rebellion. It was myopic in the
sense that they temporalized the evangelical message. Their only theme
was the social theme. Grace, sin, eternal life, heaven and hell were not
talked about. The supernatural theme disappeared bit by bit in favour
of the temporal and social themes.

Then – I don't know exactly if it was 1970, 1971, or 1972 – the
Episcopal Conference, presided over by Monsignor Tortolo, bishop of
Paraná,[8] brought out a document condemning the Third World priests.
The main criticisms he levied at them was that they insisted unilater-
ally on the social aspect. A lay Catholic called Sachelli wrote a book
called *The Clandestine Church* in which he even named names, along
with the activities of certain priests in the country. He was a professor
in Canada; he taught six months here and six months there. He was
murdered by guerrillas. I'm not saying by the Third World priests. He
denounced them.

During that time, between 1971 and 1973, were you involved in that
debate between the two currents within the church?

Yes, I would have to say yes. I wrote some things denouncing that
situation in some articles. I participated in the seminary of Monsignor
Tortolo, the bishop of Paraná, who became the archbishop in Buenos
Aires. Long ago, Monsignor Tortolo brought Eva Perón there, then
Isabel Perón, and he had dealings with the military too, as he was the
military's priest. He travelled the whole country in that capacity. I also
had some contact with the military, occasionally arranging for meetings and giving talks. However, it was not an alliance thing, no, it was
cordial and correct contact. But yes, in the war of the Malvinas (the
Falklands conflict) yes, then we helped a lot. When someone was
killed, we went to his home. In addition, one of the priests was a
chaplain in the Malvinas.

The whole country was relieved when the revolution of 1976
occurred, although they now deny it. At that time we all thought the
government was off track. More because of corruption or inertia, or
for having lost the reins of power. Then, when the military took
power, with the desire – as in various previous revolutions – of merely

bringing about order, there was no clear purpose of what needed to be done. They did much work, building roads and bridges. They did not want to do more than that, it seems to me.

Their enemies attacked from two vantage points: from the military angle, fighting, and from the cultural angle, in the universities. The military made war in military combat, but they did not engage in the cultural combat. So culture remained in the hands of those militants, although they got rid of many, but it was not a total change in the universities despite the fact that they placed deans in the universities. The people who were not dismissed by the military were later "judged" for having remained. I was in favour of the military, then.

It is said that the armed forces used very strong methods when they came to power, including torture, death, disappearances. Were you aware at that time that these were the methods of the armed forces in government?

It was rumoured, yes; that is, I was aware, though not through inside information. But it was rumoured, yes, that the armed forces used strong methods when they were in power. I learned of this around 1978 or so. Well, I don't remember exactly when I learned of it. What I do know is that they were told that if someone had to face a firing squad it should be done in public, after a trial. It was not officially discussed, but their response was as follows: If they had a public firing squad, right away the rest of the world would say, "Don't shoot! Don't shoot!" – and we cannot fight that way.

Who made the comments about the legal firing squads? The people, the priests, who?

Those who objected were friends of the military who disapproved and said it had to be done correctly. But the problem was that there were subversives who even wanted a separate nation, and wanted recognition from the United Nations. Therefore, for those in the military this was a patriotic defence. The guerrilla methods were terrible, so the military started to imitate those methods because they could not see how – in Algiers something similar had occurred – to act differently, and that resulted in injustice and needless violence.

Some of the objectors were in our church, our order. Yes, it is so. Some, since Pinochet – not directly because of Pinochet – but some had recommended doing it like Chile because that way ... but there were others who said it was not convenient; they said, "You don't understand war."

Did the church make any public appeal to the military to cease clandestine actions?

I don't know if the church ever made direct appeals to the military to have public trials. Not that I know of in public, no, but in private, yes.

In your opinion, why didn't the church denounce the disappearances, the imprisonment of children?

I don't know why the bishops did not denounce the disappearances. I know they denounced them in private, and in many cases they saved the disappeared. They would talk to the military and were sometimes successful. Other times, not. It occurs to me that perhaps the intervention wasn't public because that might have encouraged the Marxist enemy. What I mean is that the idea would be one of a just war, although there were unjust methods. A just war is when there is a right to do that. Thus, without wanting to stop the war itself, the church did criticize the methods.

You've used the word "the enemy." Who was the enemy of the church?

The enemy was Marxism. Marxism in the church, let us say, and in the mother country – the danger of a new nation. I don't know if all the people who were killed were Marxists. Well, not the children; if they were little, they knew nothing. I don't know. The Marxists had many followers. These are the excesses of repression.

Looking back on that now, would you still call those people the enemy?

Yes, to the degree that they maintain their conviction, yes. Marxists were the enemy, and people who were thinking like Marxists.

I want to make sure I'm clear on this. The problem was Marxists. People who were thinking like Marxists. It wasn't just armed guerrillas?

That is correct. It was not just armed guerrillas. There were some leaders who later joined with others, because of their hatred for the military. Not all of them were Marxist thinkers entirely. The general line was Marxist. But possibly there were allies who were not.

Do you believe that most of the dead or disappeared were Marxists?

I don't know what to say. I think not, but the main ideologists, yes.

In your opinion, was the military successful? Did they achieve their objective of doing away with the Marxists?

The military did not, however, achieve their objective of doing away with the Marxists, because of what I said earlier. Because, if in certain ways they were victorious in the armed conflict, it was not the case with the cultural objective. The cultural objective, as expressed by Gramsci[9] – they won that.

Did the army have a cultural objective? During el Proceso, *many books were banned and burned. New math was considered pernicious in the schools, and Jean Piaget, who is not normally considered a Marxist, was banned. Why were his books banned?*

Because they believed it necessary. I don't know the problems of Piaget and Freud, but they contributed somewhat to the undermining of the Christian and traditional concept. Catholic intellectuals who have nothing to do with the process wrote books against Piaget and objected to Piaget and Freud for reasons that were unrelated to the military theme. I myself was unaware of the burning of books; it must have been minimal. I know some university publications were taken out of circulation, but there were many new books to replace them.

Did I understand you correctly? Are you saying that you did not know about the burning of books until this moment?

No, no. Taken out of circulation, yes. Some in the military were stupid, one can see they were not well advised. Somewhere they may have burned a book by Marx in order to refute it.

When the military prohibited and took out of circulation books that did not fit in with the Christian religion, were they complying with the church's request?

If by "church," you mean the hierarchy of the church, I do not think so. However, there were many Catholic militant ministers who perhaps were in on this.

Looking back on el Proceso, *do you think that that was the best way to solve the problems?*

No. I must say no. It was done so badly that the military junta was brought to justice. When the anti-military won, the military were judged. They did it very badly. They did not manage it like Pinochet, who remained on top, or as in Uruguay, they delivered themselves fully to those who would take them to the tribunals, without conditions. They also mishandled the other task; they did not eradicate the problems.

When you say "they" won, to whom are you referring?

Well, in a way, to the groups that defied the military prior to their fall, to the ones who allowed the guerrillas to do what they did, the ones who opposed the military authorities, the ones who did not agree with the eradication of the guerrillas. In other words, the ones in total opposition without mitigation. You see, before the military regime fell, there were people who had looked kindly on subversion, without themselves being subversive. They are the ones who gained power after the military departed. The military government was unable to create a community. They tried to follow Pinochet's example, but it was a disaster. They did not know how to do it as Pinochet did; he formed a party. Here one was created by General Massera, but it was a disaster.

Do you think that, culturally, the Marxists won?

It would be cruel to say that. The ones who won were the ones who didn't see the need to fight Marxism. Alfonsín was not a Marxist; he was a social democrat.

Within the first part of the military regime, were some Third World priests murdered?

I believe so. Let's see. Ah yes! Father Mugica, but in that case they say that the comrades killed him because he got too close to Perón and Perón ousted all of them. No one knows. The Montoneros approached Perón before Perón came back. When General Aramburu was killed, Perón congratulated them. When Perón came back, there was a big affair in the Plaza de Mayo. All the Montoneros were there to greet him, and it was apparent that he was, as Perón used to say, a "herbivore," in other words, tame. Then Perón ousted them. I think Mugica stayed with him when the Montoneros left, but I am not sure. What I mean is that not all the Third Worldists who were murdered died at the hands of the military; there were also internal fights amongst Peronists.

There is also the issue of Angelelli, the bishop of the province of La Rioja. I have been assured that his death was an accident. And as proof, he was with a priest who has since left the priesthood and lives in Córdoba. Had it been murder, both would have been killed. I cannot say for sure one way or another.

But *el Proceso* did not destroy the Third World Priests' Movement. No, not at all. No, in no way. The process did not attack the Third World priests. That was an ecclesiastical problem. They annoyed the church. The church had to deal with this. Later, they re-emerged under another name, but when communism fell, they disbanded. Although they say they are not Marxists, what is objectionable is that their analysis is Marxist. They don't accept the whole Marxist doctrine, but, yes, they accept some parts of it. The movement is less of a problem for the church than before. They don't attend congresses as they once did. That mentality is latent in many of them, but it is not as evident.

Some American and European writers suggest that the hierarchy of the church cooperated with the military to eliminate some of the Third World priests and students. Do you think that is true?

This is an infamy. I totally deny it. What Tortolo did for them! I am personally aware that many bishops did much good in the prisons they visited.

The role of the church in Chile, under military government, was it different from the role the church played in Argentina?

Yes, it was different, and I believe that is because the hierarchy was more in favour of the party line; in other words, the clergy there were more leftist. The reverse was true here. In Argentina, most were against what was favoured by the majority in Chile.

Today, I think that the church hierarchy and also the leftist sectors are confused and not sure what to do. The pope insists on spiritual themes. You will remember that the Third World priests insisted on temporal issues. The bishops, those who do not want to disobey the pope, have little leeway. But in Latin America there have been many changes. I would say the more traditional currents have become weaker. Most of the bishops have chosen a middle line; in the middle there is little room to manoeuvre, save for a small group that remains more leftist. The rest do not get involved much. They are in a more contemplative mode. Now, when I say social concerns, I don't mean that the traditionalists were against social concerns. They were against that specific solution to social problems. For example, the differences between Medellin [1968] and Puebla [1979][10] illustrate the little episcopal changes in Hispanic America due to the pope's influence. Medellin was much more like the Third Worldists; Puebla more like a cooperative: "You must insist on the importance of God and Jesus," the pope said. He was worried about Medellin and its consequences, so in Puebla he gave a speech to halt this tendency and disconnect it.

On a different matter, I would say that currently globalization in Argentina is causing many devastating effects in the church and the country. For example, the youth who were in the guerrillas, in combat, today they are disbanded, without ideals, even if those ideals were bad. They now carry guitars and nothing more. Che Guevara is seen as a folk hero. It's a sceptical youth, not at all idealistic, almost worse than before.

VOICE: MONSEÑOR MORALES

I wasn't a bishop at that time [referring to 1976–83]. The church has many voices, and the bishops from the time of *el Proceso* are not the most important. Today's bishops have reviewed the whole period, but it is not easy to examine it because not all the bishops of that time are still alive.

The period was difficult after Isabel, because in the previous period there had been a lot of confusion. There were many military coups in Latin America, and one lived according to the historical moment. Historians have difficulty because they take one side or the other, but there were two different perspectives, and it is important to appreciate both. There were excesses in both groups. Some say that the Argentine state had to be defended against the guerrillas, so this justified excesses. But on the other hand, the guerrillas – well, those who did combat – do not talk today, even though the Montoneros are returning from exile. The Madres de la Plaza de Mayo say that they do not forgive because the state took their sons' lives without giving them a trial. They say that the state should have followed due process with trials, not killed them. There were meetings between military personnel, priests, and lawyers at the time, but with a fear of bombs and attacks they could not get very far.

I think the guerrilla movement was a very bad thing. These groups were a threat, like the left-wing Peronists. They justified themselves – the kidnappings, for example – saying that they were defending the poor. The chaplains claimed that they were dealing with this situation, but they didn't know what it was all about. When all the disappearances began, many bishops talked, intervened, but they did it as a way of trying to make sure that this did not get any worse, trying to ensure that it did not become public knowledge. They did not want to break the dialogue with the government. Always within that context. Other bishops always spoke in opposition, becoming more and more critical. There was nothing else hidden, but it had a lot of connotations.

In a recent document, the bishops have asked for forgiveness for their omissions. They say that they should have done more for the members of the left-wing groups because many of them were Catholics. Now they say, "Maybe we were not clear enough in our understanding." So they ask forgiveness for two things. The journalists say, "It is not sufficient to ask forgiveness, because the church actually consented to the events." Judgments have been made about these events because so many people died. Those that live, like [former archibishops] Primatesta and Aramburu, say that they were never accomplices. They are men with a long history in the church.

Former Archbishop Aramburu is on record as saying that the disappeared are all living in Europe.

Yes, that is true, but he tried to find disappeared priests. There were cardinals going to visit the jails. Aramburu met with everyone.

Many people see Marxism as being very close to Catholicism when it deals with the poor. Montoneros developed their concern for the poor in the church. Why was the church hierarchy so opposed to people who said they were Marxist but were in the church?

There was no Marxism here. Peronism was not Marxist even though it maintained support of the poor. It wasn't Soviet Marxism. It was giving food to the poor. So these priests were educated in the church. These groups were not democratic in their ideas; they became activists who responded with force.

But I understood you to say earlier that the church was very concerned with communism, including that which was espoused by Christians?

Yes, but some parts of the church worked in the slums. They say these groups were used to form revolutionary groups. Marxism is not the same as Catholicism, but an antagonism was created between the two groups that nobody could stop. That's why democracy was important. The church hierarchy did not have any other path but to protect the people. There was also terror.

According to testimonies in Nunca Más, *many people went to the church to ask for help in locating the disappeared, and many people said they didn't receive help from the church. What is your opinion?*

I think maybe not everything was done that could have been done, but a lot was done because the concern about talking with the families was real. They took their names. A newspaper in Rome has written something against the papal nuncio of the period, Cardinal Laghi.[11] He was a very personable man, he was close to young people. He developed a connection with the government, and there were people who left the country with his help. But some say, "How did he find the people if he didn't know they existed?" It was a constant battle. What was not known was that there were tortures. Many were in prison. One saw that they were taking people away, but it was not known what was being done with those people. Some bishops spoke out, but others say that they should have done more. But you must realize that there was a climate of fear. They would kidnap you or they would shoot you. The important thing is democracy, because it allows for the expression of ideas without violence ...

The voice of the church can be heard in historical documents.[12] We must not see history through the voice of just one bishop. Let's look at the church through the whole context. If one permits secularism, euthanasia, those are bad positions. The church is not opposed to the death penalty, however.

At that time, did those who were killed by the military deserve the death penalty?

For many people, yes, because they were very bad. That's why the military kidnapped them.

When Nunca Más *was published, were you surprised by what it recorded?*

Yes. I didn't know about a lot of that. Many people did not read *Nunca Más*. We wanted to get over that period with forgiveness and dialogue. And if it's possible, to pay our debts. To pardon is to say that nothing happened. The pope, when he was shot, forgave the criminal, but the process continued. The church wants to advance. It is impossible if that is not recognized.

VOICE: PADRE BERTRAN RAFFINI

In 1970, I was teaching at a Catholic university. The church was polarized between the Third World priests, about four hundred in all, and very conservative priests, especially the group that was associated with the military (known as the Castrense). There were those who justified the violence of the left, and those who justified the violence of the right and the church. I tried to take a position, which was unusual in the church, in favour of democracy and opposed to both the church hierarchy and the guerrillas.

The guerrillas were all in favour of violence. Their objective was to take over the government. They didn't believe in democracy. They were Che Guevara, they were Fidel Castro, they were Marxists. The people who directed the church at the time had a corporate view of society as an alliance of business interests, Peronist unions (no socialist or communist unions), the military, who were Christian, and the church, which occupied the cultural sphere, especially in education. Many thought this institutional arrangement was the formula for development.

We thought of the Brazilian epoch with its military government, and of the Peruvian military government, and then we saw the experience of Salvador Allende in Chile and found it essentially frightening. That was the culture of the time, you understand. The first time the church produced a document in favour of democracy was in 1981, it was called *The Church and the National Community* [published in 1984].[13] There were two reasons for our fears about Chile: the information that we obtained from both the media and the Christian Democratic Party in Chile, and the arrival of exiles from Chile. We saw a form of socialist radicalism with atrocious economic consequences.

Allende was democratically elected, but with only 38 or 39 per cent of the vote. He hadn't a strict majority. And in the second place, even the Nazis had a majority. It's not a question of majority, a democracy. It's respecting the rule of law, and Allende didn't respect the rule of law. If we are speaking of 1970, we must remember a certain context. In 1967 Che Guevara was killed in Bolivia. In 1968 [Robert] Kennedy was killed in the United States. It was the year of the cultural revolution in China. So this kind of radicalism was very strong here.

In 1973, when the Peronistas arrived in the government, I lost my position in the university. At that time, the Jesuits were completely in favour of the Montoneros, and they were powerful in that Catholic university. The students took very radical stances, and they were supported by the Jesuits. So the moderates had to leave the university. Through violence, that was condoned. I arrived one day at the faculty and found signs denouncing me, and the door of my office was closed by two wooden bars. Later, several of my students disappeared. We were teaching people who were in the guerrillas. I was trying to teach them civilized ideas, democratic, republican.

I think the teaching staff, the Jesuits, were divided. But those who were at that time in charge of the university did not stop the violent ones. On the contrary. Many faculty resigned at that time. We thought we could not teach in that context. At least 50 per cent of the faculty in the social sciences resigned. This included psychology, sociology, economics, and political science. For the next two years I worked in various ways, and then finally I obtained a teaching post at another university ...

In my opinion, the church was an accessory to the violence because it did not strongly denounce the violence of the military; but it did not strongly denounce the violence of the left either. There were members of the church on both sides. They would kill each other. And I think that until now the Argentine church has still not come to terms with this fact. As a church we were responsible, because the Montoneros came out of the Catholic Action Movement and from Catholic schools and universities. I think the fundamental reason for what happened was that our political culture was not based on respect for human rights and we did not have liberal political institutions.

There is a very strong antiliberal ideological strain in Argentina. It is not by chance that we have no democratic party. What was strong here was social Christianity, typical of the Peronistas. I think most of the church was more intent on seeing what happened with the government – the effectiveness of government but not the origin of government. It is a difficult distinction, but it is important to the nature of political culture. They only began to consider this in 1981. I think many bishops voted for the 1981 document without knowing very well what they were voting for. However, in any case it was courageous, because at that time the military were not in any mood to call for democratic elections. Elections came only because of the Falklands War.

I think that in 1981, with this document, the church finally came to terms with two questions: first, the issue of the constitution, of democracy; and secondly, the acceptance that Argentine society is a pluralist society, it is not a monolithic society. This is explicitly recognized in the document. The church also has to work with the poor. The work of charity is done out of a theological conviction, not only from a Red Cross mentality. I mean, if Mother Teresa did what she did, it was not because she was a member of the Red Cross. She saw Jesus in the poor. Well, I think that here, at the moment, more or less 400,000 people are eating thanks to Caritas, which is run by the church, though it also has government subsidies. Earlier, priests who cared for the poor were accused of being Marxist. That has changed.

The principal criticism of the Third World priests was that they had a political and ideological point of view. The majority were of the Perónista kind, and they said, well, the poor people here are Perónistas so we have to be Perónistas. And Perónistas are Catholic, they are against socialism, against the communists, they are the people, and they tended to have an equation – that the people of this country and the people of Peronism are more or less the same. I was strongly critical of the Third World Priests' Movement because I thought they hadn't done their work in political science and sociology. They were not experts at all in social sciences, in economics and politics, and they took one theory or two from other places without any effort to see whether this was compatible with the Christian outlook on life and society. And as you know, at least 50 per cent or more of these priests are out of orders now. I would say most of them lacked a priest's vocation.

CHAPTER 14

Third World Priests' Movement

Padre Carlos Mugica was killed by machine-gun fire outside a church in Buenos Aires in May 1974. In the period immediately before his death, he had clashed with his former disciple, Mario Firmenich, and had told associates that the guerrillas might want to kill him. But at the same time, he was an outspoken critic of López Rega and the policies of the Ministry of Social Welfare.[1] Firmenich strongly denied the killing, expressing his "affection and gratitude" to Mugica. The killer was later identified as a federal police corporal acting under the cover of the Triple A; he was a member of López Rega's personal bodyguard.[2]

Three Pallotine priests and two seminarians were killed shortly after the junta took over, in July 1976. An outspoken critic of the relationship between the church and the military, Bishop Enrique Angelelli was killed in August of that year. There were others, some of whom were outspoken members of the Third World Priests' Movement, but some were simply engaged in pastoral work in the slums. The movement was initiated in 1968 and lasted only until 1974, when murders and threats finally extinguished the possibility for priests to meet under its auspices. At its strongest, it had only four hundred members. The interviews in this chapter are with priests who sympathized with the work of the Third World priests or were themselves associated with that very small band of reformers.

VOICE: PATRICIO RICE

I came here from Ireland in 1970. I was a priest, and at that time I was with the Little Brothers of Charles de Faucauld. I began working in the Chaco and then, in 1976, in a shantytown in Buenos Aires. In October 1976 I was arrested and tortured, but the Irish Embassy in Buenos Aires[3] petitioned on my behalf. I was kidnapped at first. About a week later, I was put into official detention. And then I was expelled after two months and told to leave the country. I finally returned to Argentina in 1987, when I began to work with the Ecumenical Movement for Human Rights [MEDH].

Looking back to that time, a Catholic priest had a conflict. The church really is a state church in Argentina, and that produces a particular type of reaction, especially from those who are deeply rooted in the Roman Catholic tradition, which is almost antistate. That created for me a certain conflict at the beginning. I found it difficult to be asked to go to a civil ceremony, to give the blessing or to hoist the flag with a definite religious connotation. Well, here, very openly, the church represents state power.

In the 1960s, especially in 1968, with the Vatican Council, the whole system was being questioned in Argentina; maybe more than in other Latin American countries. At that time a lot of new dioceses opened up, and many new priests came from the lower-middle and middle classes. The bishops began to send them to Europe to be trained, and they became a very well-educated clergy. In 1968 the Third World Priests' Movement was born. For a while in each diocese there was a nucleus of very open, progressive, and articulate priests who questioned a lot of what was going on. Then the persecution began, with a series of repressive actions against these priests. It was even becoming common for priests to be imprisoned, for short times. In Rosario in 1968, forty priests were all imprisoned at one time. So this was already a divided church when I arrived in 1970. There were reactionary bishops who are still so, and there was a structure that was very reactionary. Naturally, there was conflict.

There is always the question of how to interpret the political history of this country, especially the history of Peronism. A sector of the church had been persecuted under Peronism, and one had to recognize that. But that does not explain the persistent refusal to include members of the progressive movement amongst the bishops. It was exceptional for a progressive bishop to be nominated, so you never had more than four or five progressive bishops. Actually, fewer still were progessive when they were nominated; occasionally they became more progressive after they were ordained. The episcopal conferences were controlled by the apostolic nuncio.

Part of the problem is that by custom, unlike other countries, bishops here are often nominated in gratitude for favours. So there are German, Italian, and Spanish bishops that have probably been ten or fifteen years in the country, who were nominated because they had money, or they had done something "good," as the church perceived it. It is still quite common to go to a diocese and not find a native-born bishop. You will find Argentine priests, but you won't find an Argentine bishop. In Venezuela, it is obligatory to be born a Venezuelan in order to be a candidate for bishop, but not in Argentina.

Now, that doesn't mean that the foreign bishops are all conservatives – they probably are not. But it does mean that there are many very good priests, good, decent Argentine priests, with a long history of social commitment, who are still in the same position as when I knew them twenty years ago. They are still parish priests, they retire as parish priests, yet they would have been excellent bishops. The internal policies of the church have kept them back.

During the repression, the structure of the church in Argentina was like that of the 1930s. The archdiocese of Córdoba, the archdiocese of Buenos Aires, and others were always very traditional. No Archbishop in Argentina would be progressive or open. On the contrary. And it was those people who dominated clerical policy, and took the leading role in the bishops' conference.

I think that the conflict, as the bishops began to see it, in the period of repression, had to do with the stability of the country. They thought that the military was needed for stability. Also, the Argentine military always had a strong affinity with a certain interpretation of Catholicism, which was largely a right-wing falange type of Catholicism. The military persuaded the Vatican, or had sufficient leverage with the Vatican, to bring about the creation of a separate diocese for all the military chaplains. So the bishop in charge of the military had a separate jurisdiction. The military did not integrate with local Catholics and instead had their own structure. And the military bishops were the real crusaders who justified abuses, the violence, and everything else. And they were capable of intervening in any diocese. Many people believe that the conservative bishops were complicit with the military regime, that they actually identified people who became victims of the repression. It was not because the church was aloof or too busy with other things. The right-wing church was closed to the suffering in the world and actively supported the military.

There was an historical opposition to democracy amongst Argentine bishops. I remember that when I first came to Argentina in the 1970s, one of the big concerns was that under nineteenth-century democracy, the church had lost control of schools; the government had got rid of religion in schools. It went back to the last century, but the religious community still saw politicians as enemies. Then, in the 1970s, the Montoneros had come from the church. And the Third World priests came from the church. Bishops allowed these facts to be used to justify the intervention of the military in the church, in church affairs, such as the banning of the Latin American Bible in 1976 or the control of catechism in 1977.

The priests who were imprisoned were treated worse than others because we were considered to be traitors, betrayers of our faith. They felt that we were supposed to be on their side, and we were acting as if we were on the other side, so there was particular anger against us. Twelve of us were in the prison in La Plata. We were treated with a lot of hostility, somewhat similar to the Jewish prisoners.

We ask ourselves, How do church people justify the violence, the torture, the murders, and participate in it, and continue to be bishops or priests? It was not just that they did not know. It is a question which has been haunting the church and Argentine society: it is a reflection on the society as well. That does not reduce the responsibility, but it may help to explain. It was not only the church people that participated and supported the repression. It was the whole society; it was a society that had become paralyzed. Even in 1976, I remember people who were working in the municipal graveyard telling me that they were burning bodies. I mean, it was quite openly said they were burning bodies in graveyards.

Well, there was the official version that people had to be sacrificed. There was the saying that in order to get stability some terrible things really had to be done. President Jorge Videla himself, in November 1975, announced that in Argentina all the people must die that are necessary in order to get stability. That quotation was published here, and then some people said, "Well, you know, the guerrilla movement is strong and so the military has to do battle with it." But actual confrontation was minimal. What happened was the installation of state terrorism.

Last year our society remembered the twentieth anniversary of the onset of the military dictatorship. People were particularly critical of the church, and the church has lost a lot of its prestige, a lot of its moral authority because of its support for the military. The pope published a document for the millennium, recommending that local churches repent, take a look at their history, clean the slate, so to speak. The Vatican was requiring a self-critique. Well, an attempt was made in 1995. We proposed that the church should support truth. That means that if the military or church officers have information that is part of our reconciliation process, they should be encouraged to tell the truth to some type of commission, which we were trying to get set up in the parliament. It has not yet been set up.

We addressed letters to all the bishops on the matter of truth – it was a five- or six-page letter on the question of truth. We said that a society that does not face up to its own reality will never be at peace. Finally, toward the end of the year, a document was approved, but then it was rejected by the more right-wing sector. A compromise document finally appeared in March of last year [1996], but this document focuses on the failures of others and does not criticize the bishops. It gives a reading of Argentine society which suggests that it was total combat between two extremes, with the church in the middle. There was some discussion at first about that document, but finally the debate ended. The pope was much clearer than the Argentine bishops' document. Our original document aimed at what the pope said – that the church accept its errors. But the Argentine church does not acknowledge its responsibility.

VOICE: PADRE DOMINGO BRESCI

I was a priest in the Third World Movement and was active in various roles from its origin, on 1 May 1968, to its end in 1974 or 1975.[4] The social convulsion underway in Argentina and the beginning of the military repression, these obliged us to close our movement. We were active in confronting authorities and trying to achieve social change. That disturbed the conservative and military people, whether they were inside or outside the church. Our members suffered from the same persecutions as social, political, and labour union activists. Sixteen priests were killed; others were imprisoned and tortured, or exiled. We were finally obliged to abandon the movement because we could not meet, just as the labour unions were not able to meet. In the same year, 1974, on 11 May, Padre Mugica was killed. He was the most representative and publicly known of our movement. We have recently published documents about the persecutions, the attacks against the movement, and the defence we mounted.[5]

The external pressure that prevented us from meeting also prevented us from carrying forward the debate between different currents that had been formed in an environment of fraternity, an environment of respect for different ideas. The movement itself had been engaged in an internal debate. Politically, some agreed with Perón; others did not. Some were allied with Marxism; others were not. Some denied the church as an institution; others did not. It was the debate of the epoch. What was the implication of Marxism? It had to be debated, for it had profound implications for the church. We debated the political commitment of the priest and the priest's relationship to armed organizations. Everything had to be considered. Was it more necessary to act than to think? There was not enough time to think. The action pushed us to constantly make choices. When we got together, it was to discuss what to do to confront this or that. And so the movement was fundamentally a movement of action, of support, of accompaniment for all the social demands of the whole country. Demands of every kind – strikes, demonstrations, popular works, fastings, protests. The arrival of Perón confronted us with a new political situation, as did the crisis of Peronismo after his death. Isabel Perón signed the order to annihilate subversion, as an order to the army, and we were considered to be subversives.

The hierarchy of the church at that time also considered us to be subversives. The president of the Episcopal Conference, Monseñor Tortolo, was the vicar general of the armed forces, and he morally supported the ideological position of what was called "the national security doctrine." Monseñor Tortolo tried to excommunicate us using a document in which he stated the mistakes, the heresies of the movement, and we replied to him with a document of seventy-five pages, in which we demonstrated that what we were doing was consistent with what Jesus Christ wanted and was within orthodox theology. There we explained what we understood as subversion, as revolution, as armed struggle, as property, as liberation. At that time, within the church, the difficulty was that this was political action. We believed that political action was necessary because we were emerging from eighteen years during which the most popular political party and the ideology of Peronism had been proscribed. Together with many other social groups – in the middle class, amongst professionals – we were rediscovering the values of Peronismo. In 1973 and 1974, with the revival of Peronism, we were permitted to vote. The population was allowed to express itself for the first time since 1955. We said "Enough! We need a political option!"

Well, from outside the church, the intelligence services of the army included us on the list of those who wanted to destroy the nation, the Argentine tradition. They said that we were part of an international communist subversion. In those conditions dialogue was impossible. They never tried to talk with us; they just labelled us. In those circumstances, there was very little we could do. We struggled to maintain contact with one another and to seek support within our communities. We were helped by a few, very few, bishops – not more than five or six out of seventy or eighty. We continued to speak in public until 1974, then we had to stop. All the country began to darken, and we too, as part of the country. After the death of Perón, the military were already preparing for the coup. So there was censorship and persecution.

About four hundred out of Argentina's five thousand priests were in the Third World Movement. They were all over the country. Few from Buenos Aires, just fifeen out of seventy or eighty activists; more from the interior and from the province of Buenos Aires. Every priest who had a social commitment was called a Third World priest. Even nuns said "Third World priests" to name those who went to the poor and working-class neighbourhoods to work with the people. We were a movement, but we had minimal organization, no structure or lists. It was a current of thought and action within the church, with a very strong social commitment. So all who had that commitment were called Third World priests, even if they did not belong to the movement. There was no membership requirement, and the meetings were public, open, not clandestine. Well, of the four hundred who might be called members, I think that two hundred were persecuted in various ways during the repression. I myself was threatened and advised to leave the country.

I received warnings indirectly from the church itself. What did not exist was protection. I had to look after myself. When the coup began, I decided to stay here, in the same school where I am now. Then the military was in control, chasing after everybody. There was a list of priests, and all who had been involved in some public activity were on it. As we were not clandestine and as we had signed the documents, had talked, had supported social activities, our names were known. In the past, it was the army that overthrew governments, but this time it was all three armed forces, because they wanted to oblige all the armed forces to share in the decision to liquidate everybody. It was a pact of silence that continues today.

I have been asked several times, I and some others, how it was possible that we survived. First [laughter], because God did not want me to go. Second, because they did not dare to take us all. It was infernal what they would have done. Eliminate us, well, I do not know whether the regime could have afforded to eliminate a hundred priests. Third, some communication was established between the armed forces and representatives from the episcopate, who periodically discussed the situation of the members of the church. The military went with the list, with recordings, writings, denouncing priests for their preaching or their subversive action. And this commission of the episcopate told them, "This person is not subversive." For them, subversive was to be part of an armed group; it had to be something illegal.

This commission of the episcopate consisted of three delegate bishops. They required that the armed forces demonstrate that the priest had done something illegal. The episcopate said, "If you do not demonstrate that the priest is doing something illegal, like being part of an armed organization, then he is not a subversive." I was not part of any armed organization; they could not demonstrate that, because I never did it. If they had kidnapped me, it would have been because they did not like me. This was a limit that was set up by the episco-pate. But the episcopate did not take care of the priests who had any relationship with the armed organizations. They were kidnapped and killed.

Once I was called before an ideological inquiry of the Federal Coor-dination of the Police. They extended a favour to me. Instead of taking action against me, they gave me the chance to explain what I thought. I did not know if they were going to let me out. I was put under an ideological interrogation. They asked how was it that I, as a priest, sustained certain opinions. Did I realize that I was doing harm to the people? They said that what we did was taking people into commu-nism, to death.

Were you criticized for not being available for the spiritual support that the generals required?

No [laughter]. That was something. And then again, when they came to tell me to leave the country, they sent someone on behalf of a priest who was a friend of mine, who, I found later, was chaplain of the armed forces. To help me, he sent someone who told me that I was on the list, that maybe I was going to have a car accident, and that it was better for me to leave the country. There were many "accidents." Monseñor Angelelli was one.

I stayed. You see, when I was told someone was coming to see me, I did not know who it was, if he was friend or enemy, or if, through the conversation, he was going to find out something that I did not want to reveal. It was very difficult. That was the mechanism. If I had said, "I am leaving," it would have meant that I was involved in something. If I said, "I am not involved in anything. I preach what I believe, and I do what I have to do," I would put myself at great risk. I was offered the passage and everything, the documents. The chaplain offered these through this lay person whose name I did not know. If the priest had talked to me, I would have been very careful, but at least I would have known who was talking to me. But if an unidentified person comes to me, then I have no way of knowing whether what he says is true. "Ah, thank you for coming, really," I finally said, making no commitment. This encounter lasted twenty-four hours altogether.

So you stayed. You did not get run over, obviously. You did not stop crossing the street?

I looked first [laughter]. This is nothing compared to what happened to others. Other priests did not have this chance. They had to hide, or they were imprisoned and tortured. The bishop excluded them from the diocese, or they had to leave the country. In my case, curiously I think, I was saved. But there were many priests very committed to the movement, and that, we think, was one of the reasons they did not dare kill us. They would have had to kill many priests. That is why they killed Mujica selectively.

In your opinion, who killed Mugica?

The Triple A of López Rega.

Did the Vatican have any influence on what happened?

There is a debate about the role of the papal nuncio, Pio Laghi. He helped some priests and laypersons escape. But what could the Vatican say? It was the responsibility of the Argentine episcopate. Pio Laghi said that: "Do not ask from me what the archbishop and the other social or political institutions do not do!" There was a tacit agreement with much of what the military did. The concrete acts of the repression were not well known. When some of the others said that some persons had been kidnapped, killed, many people did not believe it. Cardinal Aramburu said that the subversives were living in Europe, the disappeared were in Europe, and that it was a lie that there were communal tombs with NN on them.[6] And having to choose between the cardinal's words and mine, most people believed the cardinal. The Vatican also listened to the cardinal.

You said, Padre, that the attitude of the nuncio was under discussion. Where is it under discussion?

There is an interview given by him in the Italian newspaper *Il Regno*, published in Rome in 1997.[7] The headlines read "*Di bisogno di fare di piu*," meaning they should have done much more. The episcopate defends itself saying that it talked about repression, that it talked in favour of the prisoners, but it did very little. It did not accompany the talk with action, as the church did in Chile, in Brazil. The reason was that in Argentina the conservative church leaders shared the view of the armed forces! It was stronger than their religious vocation. I believe that they shared this view and they approved of what the military did. The vicar general and some chaplains theologically justified the torture. It was a holy war against international subversion, against the atheist communism which they believed would destroy the church.

This is a very Catholic country and the church had a lot of power over the minds of the people. Why, here in this country, were the church people not more progressive? And how did you come to see things in a different way?

There are several studies about that. From its origins, the education, their lack of sensibility, a lot of causes, their fear, their popery. They are more papist than the pope. My views differed from theirs because I was formed in a seminar that had its origin in the times of the Second Vatican Council in the 1960s. We were formed in that climate. And in Argentina there was a real social change in the 1960s. We had great expectations. In the panorama of those times in Latin America, there existed a revolutionary atmosphere. I think that the sensibility to understand without prejudice, without sectarianism, was developing. But in the episcopate they were more concerned with anticommunism.

VOICE: PADRE BERNARDO
(PATRICIO TOMÁS HUGHES)

I was the parish priest at Santa Cruz church in 1970. I was almost forty years old then, and for me those were beautiful years, because in Argentina and in almost all of Latin America we shared the dream that something different was possible, the possibility of participating, the possibility of justice. Our country had experienced many dictatorships and military coups. And because of that there was a surge of hope, especially among the rebellious youth. Also at the level of the church, after the bishops meeting in Medellin, there was hope for what we called "the new man."[8] In 1968 eighteen bishops of the Third World wrote a letter, and many priests from Argentina joined them. From this emerged what later was called Movement for the Third World.

The main preoccupation of the movement was much more the relationship of the priest with society than the relationship of the priest with the church. The people were socially and economically divided, but within this parish there was a lot of strength, a lot of enthusiasm. The church hierarchy, of course, did not agree. But the youth, especially university students, had two new experiences during that time. First, many of them went with priests to the poor areas of the country, and others worked in urban slums. One of their leaders was Father Carlos Mugica, who was murdered by the Triple A. In the slums we hoped to help the people obtain the essentials of life: food, health, education, organization, and employment. We realized that the church had its centre in the middle and upper classes. Just look at where the churches are located! Most people were marginalized, yet they were Catholic, they were believers.

In 1955 the church had a big conflict with Perón, and this created a rupture between the people and the church. The people kept baptizing children, but they rejected the church. So the Third World priests approached the people and tried to create a common ground between the church and the people, or between church doctrine and Peronist doctrine. Well, then the guerrilla movements emerged, some of them of Catholic origin. From the faith, they participated in missions to the interior and to the slums, and this led to the events of 1973. The military power emerged with what was called the Triple A. They were already active in 1973, but stronger after the death of Perón. It was a confusing time, and there was much corruption in the political process. But the majority of the youth did not see that. They believed in Cámpora's election and then Perón's. Not only the young people but also the priests, we were not very sceptical.

During that period there was one very nice thing that happened. The peasants, who traditionally were not organized, formed an association. When the leadership began to develop, some exciting cultural, sports, and other activities were organized. The church was an important part of this process. Later, they matured and became independent of the church. They organized themselves as a union. And they were very close to the guerrilla groups.

It seems to me that the guerrilla groups began as groups engaged in reflection. It was after they concluded that change was impossible, because of the repression, that they became guerrillas. Some people think that the guerrillas emerged fighting against democracy, but they are unwilling to recognize that, before the guerrillas existed, we had so many years of repression, of silencing.

What was the relationship between the Third World priests and the more conservative church?

Well, the bishops prefer a submissive priest who gives them no trouble. The Third World priests were tolerated in Buenos Aires. There were a few who supported the priests and the rural movement, but not the majority. The priests were a minority of the priesthood, maybe about two hundred altogether, but they were not necessarily the only ones who thought that way. For example, I did not belong to the movement, but I thought like them. The government and the police called them "Third World priests" for what they said in their preaching if they talked about justice. Well, not only about justice; if they talked about reality. A priest was considered good if he talked about heaven, about virtue, no? The Triple A murdered Padre Mugica.

Many Third World priests went to live with the poor. And this is a very significant experience for the priest. The daily and palpable experience of injustice, of the death of children, provokes sometimes a violent reaction. For one who is distant, like me, this may seem exaggerated, but it explains the strength of their commitment to the people.

Well, in 1976 I had the feeling that we were going over the precipice and were not able to stop. Just before this happened I thought that the politicians, those who had power, the church, none of them reacted. The violence was terrible, violence in the streets. Yet they did nothing. It would have been possible to judge the president and to put a civilian in as interim president, call elections, do something, rather than have a military coup. I feel the same experience some days now, seeing all the corruption ...

Well, faced with the violence that existed before the military coup, some people welcomed the coup. Many people thought it was a solution. And the military thought they were the saviours. I felt very differently. I felt frustration that we had not reacted as a country. Some months later I was sent by my order to Puerto Rico on a study course for five weeks. At about that time, on 4 July 1976, members of the Pallotine community were killed: three priests and two seminarians. And in August Padre Angelelli was killed. So they phoned me and told me not to come back. I did not know what was going on here. The military called at the church, and they said that I was going to be killed, that I was a subversive. There were threats against me; they were searching for me, and I was warned not to come back.

You were not formally a Third World priest. What made you a special target?

In this parish we always had a great concern for reality and we were criticized because of that. The authorities claimed that we were always involved in politics. We had cared for Chilean refugees, and that was regarded as a serious crime. Then there was the killing of General Aramburu by young people from the Catholic movements, and a priest from this parish was accused of having been involved. This priest was almost blind, and he would not have been capable of participating in such an operation. On two occasions, while he was imprisoned during the early 1970s, we celebrated the mass for him. There were more than forty priests here. When we did that, the police surrounded the church.

How did they know you were celebrating the mass for him?

They knew everything, they infiltrated everywhere. It was impossible to work in secret. We worked in the light of day. Half a block from here are some offices of the State Intelligence Services [Servicios de Inteligencia de Estado, SIDE].

I was the most senior priest here at that time. There was criticism of our order, and of the people who came to mass, of the faithful people. Some people left the church because of our activism. Others came because of it. We were suspected for anything at all. If you had young people in your group – well, any young persons were suspect here in Argentina. If he was young and had a beard, he was more suspicious. If he was young, had a beard, and was a university student, he was even more suspicious. And if he was young, had a beard, was a university student, and worked for the poor, he was clearly a subversive. Do you understand this? It did not have any logic. Did Hitler have a logic, eh? It is the same mechanism ...

I went to Spain and did not come back until December 1977. One night, when I was returning to the church around midnight or so, I found graffiti all around this place: "Communist priests," "Guerrilla's cave," and such words. We could not know why they wrote this. Anyway, there were many young people here. That is what was happening, no?

I can tell you an anecdote to describe it a little bit. One Saturday afternoon I was performing baptisms. A short-haired young man came and told me that he wanted to speak with me, and I told him to come when I had finished the celebration. He was waiting at the door. He told me, "I am sublieutenant of the army of Jesus Christ." I said, "This is the first time I have heard that Jesus Christ has an army." He responded, "Yes, I belong to a high specialized squadron to fight against the communists, the guerrillas, the drug addicts, the Jews, the atheists, against everybody." I told him, "There are guerrillas who are also Catholic." He said: "That cannot be true." I told him, "Yes. As you say that you are from the Jesus Christ army, and I did not know it existed, there are guerrilla people who, for their Christian faith, have chosen to be guerrillas."

"If I find a guerrilla, I'll kill him. If you tell me that such person is a guerrilla, I'll kill him. If I kill a person, I kill only the body. The soul I give to Jesus Christ." And then he told me, "Ah, now that you say there are Catholics who are guerrillas, I remember I had two prisoners, two young ones, a girl and a boy, tied on the floor, and when I was going to kill them I heard them praying. Ah, so they would have been Catholic." He said that he had killed them with one shot. This was in Tucumán. It was such madness. Of course, the guerrilla did insane things too. Imagine, let's suppose that a priest was a guerrilla who was making bombs in the parish – it is not very logical, it is as absurd as the other thing.

The police never disrupted our meetings, but sometimes the police-men were inside. We knew who they were. And some nights, after a meeting, the policemen were at the door, watching, and then they, in their cars, would follow people who were walking home. Or they would get out and walk behind them. There was a lot of fear. The objective was to frighten them. None of them actually disappeared, the ones who were followed.

Well, back to my own story. I stayed out in the country at first, during the worst period. They went twice to the church to find out if I was there. My superiors told them that I was not at that moment in the house. I did not meet them. Others were taken at that time. I think the Pallotine priests were taken for several reasons. First, because they were in an upper-middle-class neighbourhood. The upper middle class was quite happy with the coup. Also, many military lived in that zone, military who were married to our oligarchy. And many of the young activists were with the Pallotines. And finally, there was their preach-ing, one in particular was too strong for them. And they felt that he was criticizing them instead of the guerrillas. He was critizing injustice and violence.

Were the young people there, the ones who worked with them in the slums, children of the upper middle class?

Yes. They were afraid of young people because young people think. And they are free to give their lives. Older people are very attached to life. The grown-ups make war, but the young ones die in it.

Were not some of the soldiers also very young?

I do not think soldiers who were only nineteen years old were the ones who tortured. What we know is that soldiers disappeared within the army. The boys that were there for a year only, no? They disappeared. Argentine young people were not communists. But they wanted a different society.

I think that the military were not intelligent enough to have a vision. I believe that the military were made to believe, made to believe – they were convinced that they were the moral reserve of the country against communism, which was seen as the destruction of the nation. And above all – another sin of our western and Christian culture – com-munism is against our style of life as Christians, you see? So they took the flag of the country and of religion. If you want to be a militar, you must be baptized.

Can you help me gain some insight on why the church seemed to support the military against the people?

It seems – I say it seems to me because I respect very much what others think and on this topic it is very difficult to have an absolute idea – that the church was not focusing on the economic aspect, but it was afraid of these leftist movements, of these revolutionary movements and of the questioning that was going on within the church. The Argentine people are Catholics, but the consumers of the Catholic religion are the middle and upper classes. They go to mass, they baptize their children, they marry in the church. The military are there. And the church has priests within the military, the chaplains. So the military and the church are two institutions with a lot of weight. They are conservative on principle. And I say that some chaplains, some chaplains inside the military, end up being more military than priests.

Note on the Church of Santa Cruz

The church where Father Bernardo resides provided meeting space for the Mothers of the Plaza de Mayo. It was in the courtyard of this church, on 8 December 1977, that several leading members of the mothers were pointed out to militars waiting there by the naval lieutenant Alfredo Astiz. Astiz had infiltrated the mothers' movement, claiming to be in mourning for a disappeared brother. On that day and the next few days, fourteen members of the group, including two French nuns, disappeared.

CHAPTER 15

The Military Defence

Most currently employed military officers will not speak for the record. In the air force and navy, they will not do so as a matter of explicit policy. The notorious naval officer, Alfredo Astiz, who infiltrated the Mothers of the Plaza de Mayo and pointed out its original leaders to his *compañeros*, who then abducted them, was finally punished by the navy for doing the one thing disallowed: he boasted to the press about his prowess as a killer.[1] Early in 1998 he was jailed for a short period and scheduled to lose his status as a retired naval hero. Several of the navy and air force personnel whom we invited for an interview claimed that they were not actually forbidden to speak, but they were expected to "allow their superior officers" to do the speaking for them. Their superior officers declined invitations or failed to return calls.

We did, however, speak with four retired senior officers of the army, two of whom are represented in the interviews in this chapter. The other two, and two junior army officers who felt sufficiently secure in the kind of army that their new chief-of-staff was creating, gave the interviews in the next chapter.

Chief-of-Staff General Martín Balza is on public record as having expressed regret that the military dictatorship behaved as it did. He has spoken strongly about the need for armies to accept civilian control. And he has expressed liberal views more generally with respect to the role of armies in modern democracies.[2] For this he has been roundly condemned by members of the other forces (and most publicly by Astiz, who called him "a cretin" in the same outburst that caused him his jail sentence). Despite this liberal leadership, the everyday reality for junior officers makes frank discussion with outsiders a risky choice.

One of the unrepentent repressers of the period was Miguel O. Etchecolatz, director general of the investigations of the police in the province of Buenos Aires from 1976 to 1979. He conducted operations against the guerrillas (whom he called terrorists). Etchecolatz was among the few who were charged, imprisoned, and then released in the general amnesty after the military dictatorship. He has re-emerged as the author of a book that condemns the investigations of the National Commission on Disappeared People (CONADEP) and attempts to justify the repression.[3] His argument is that the subversive forces were a very real threat to society and that the police and military forces were engaged in a full-scale war. For him, the CONADEP investigation systematically failed to examine the subversives' activities while pointing the finger of guilt at the military and police. In his opinion, the commission produced a wildly exaggerated estimate of the number of persons affected by military action and also underestimated the number of victims of the terrorists, 711 of whom he lists by name and occupation.

Another defence, one that was often put forward in conversations with persons whose sympathies were neither with the repressers nor the subversives, is the "two-devils" theory. This has it that there were two forces, both insanely belligerent, who between them created a battle, and that the rest of the population was held hostage while they fought it out. This theory ignores the difference in the military capacities and numbers of the two sides and fails to explain the outbreak of the "insanity." It allows its believers to ignore the social conditions that spawned the guerrilla forces as well as the economic and political interests that were defended by the military of the period.

A more persuasive argument is put forward by Ramón Genaro Díaz Bessone[4] in a lengthy and detailed account of what he refers to as "the aggression" and the army's "defence of the national society." This book, published by the officers' club, is a carefully documented argument for el Proceso and was cited frequently by our interviewees.

The first interview reported here is with an officer who held an important position during el Proceso. He accepts the possibility that some of the military's actions were indefensible but argues that, on balance, they acted with reason and justification. Our second interviewee denies that anything happened. These interviews are given at some length because they articulate the defence for state terrorism.

VOICE: COLONEL LORENZO

I entered the army in the mid-1940s and retired as colonel before the end of the military government. I had command responsibilities in an infantry regiment in Buenos Aires during the epoch of the subversion. This allowed me to participate in this fight. So I cannot say that I saw it from outside. I saw it from within, and as a regimental chief I had to participate in all the responsibilities related to my position.

I want to clarify that the subversive phenomenon did not begin in 1973. In 1959 and 1960 the first guerrilla manifestation in Argentina occurred in Tucumán, with the so-called Commander Tuturunco,[5] who tried to establish a small guerrilla base. Then, in 1964, there was another guerrilla group in Salta, which also failed. But the guerrilla really emerged with extreme violence in 1968 [sic], with the assassination of General Aramburu by the Montoneros. At that moment the guerrilla movement exploded with all its force. So the guerrilla was not born in 1976 with the military government; nor in 1973 with the Perónist governments from 1973 to 1976. It was born before these events. Its antecedents are in the previous decade, and they all failed.

In your estimation, how many guerrillas were there?

It is very difficult to know how many members there were in the guerrillas because they were organized into cells. Only the top leaders of the guerrillas knew how many combatants there were and how much logistic support they had. Our intelligence services had information about numbers and logistics, but I was not in those services. I can give you a number that happened to come to me some days ago. It happens that there is a legal charge made by a lawyer against Isabel Perón's government because of the deprivation of liberty and the disappearances of people during 1975–76, before the military coup. He says there were 908 persons. So this was a former guerrilla who charged the Perónist government with similar conditions to those of the military government that began in 1976.

President Raúl Alfonsín's government[6] decided to judge the events that had occurred from 1976 to 1983. But everything that happened before then was not included. Many of the disappearances and deaths of the guerrillas happened earlier, and the government of Isabel Perón did nothing to avoid it. On the contrary, she proclaimed the decrees and the directions to organize the repression of subversion. So this accusation is against the Peronist government of 1975 and the first three months of 1976, for the deaths that, according to this lawyer, happened in those years. The Perónist government should be judged the same way as the military juntas were judged, taking into account the principle of equality before the law. This lawyer also asks for the trial of Alfonsín's government for concealment and delay of justice, because Alfonsín had objective information from the [CONADEP] commission's investigation which showed there were disappearances and deaths before 1976. The lawyer says that it is a continuous crime, which in an arbitrary way is said to have begun in 1976. So he accuses all the members of the Peronist government of those years, as well as Alfonsín's government and all the judges who judged the junta and who knew that there had been disappearances before.

I mention this because of your question about numbers. This lawyer argues that these authorities had to take charge of a war and to confront organizations of thousands of combatants who had widespread influence. One of the few remaining survivors of high rank in the ERP, Luis Mattini, according to the report published in *La Nación* [12 January 1997], admitted that the ERP had around 600 armed men and had influence over 8,000 persons who collaborated with them, lent them houses, and provided information. All this happened in 1975. On their part, the Montoneros had 2,000 armed people and others who were under their influence. If their ratios are the same as for the ERP, then the Montoneros would have totalled 26,600 people. So it is very difficult to know, not only who were the combatants but, fundamentally, who provided the logistic support, the intellectual support, the media support, etcetera. In any guerrilla phenomenon it is said that for each combatant there are a lot of people who provide support.

How many men were there in the armed forces at the same time?

I cannot give you a precise number, but I think that, putting together the three armed forces, it could have been a total of between 70,000 and 80,000, including all ranks, officials, subofficials, and soldiers. The most numerous was, of course, the army. Half of these 70,000 I am mentioning belonged to the army, and the other half to the air force and navy. But this is very compartmentalized because there were the combat elements, the service elements, and others. So it is very difficult to know exactly who were combatants and who were not. What one can truly say is that we had a significant numerical superiority with respect to the guerrillas. I think it was ten to one. That is more or less a normal relation in guerrillas' fights all over the world, where in effect the regular forces are superior to the subversive forces.

Precisely because of this, guerrilla warfare is terrorist. They cannot confront the military forces in open combat, unless the revolutionary subversive movement grows to the point where it can mount regular forces. The revolutionary doctrine establishes the phases of a revolutionary organization, beginning with small cells. Each time there is an increase in supporters, they increase their fighting force, with the intention of forming a regular revolutionary army, such as that of Mao in China. Mao finally fought in a conventional way against the army of Chiang Kai-shek because he had achieved complete development.

The Argentine guerrillas tried, but failed, to constitute regular forces. The strongest effort to form regular forces was the fight in Tucumán. There were organized guerrilla companies; they had uniforms; they had banners; they had a military discipline. Although they conducted combat as guerrillas in the mountains, they were organized in a way similar to the armed forces. This gave rise to Operation Independence[7] during the years of the Perónist government. This was when Isabel Perón ordered the liquidation of the guerrillas. The armed forces engaged in the war in that rural environment and annihilated the guerrilla companies in the mountains of Tucumán.

The guerrillas wanted to create what they called a liberated zone in Tucumán. The army succeeded, and the guerrilla forces disappeared; they stopped existing as combat forces. Here it is important to clarify what is understood by "annihilation." This is a concept which comes from Clausewitz.[8] Annihilation is not the destruction of the life of all the opponents but the destruction of their combative capacity. Now, what did many guerrillas do? Not all of them died, no way, but they dissolved, they went back to their houses, to the city; they escaped, and the organizations were annihilated. I believe that was the ERP.

When the military took over the government in March 1976, did they still think they had a major guerrilla force against them?

Of course, because the guerrilla has the characteristic of fighting with all available means, all imaginable methods, and in all kinds of terrain. It is a multifaceted and multidirectional subversive phenomenon. As a consequence, when their effort in Tucumán failed, they understood they were not yet able to fight an open battle. So after that, they concentrated their efforts in the cities, where they mixed with the population. This was a more difficult situation for the legal forces. In Tucumán the fight was in the open field, even in the jungle, so things were clearer there. The guerrilla was in the mountains, the armed forces were outside, and the fight was between them. Civilians were not involved, except those few who lived in the mountains. Thus, it was a clean fight, more defined, between combatants. When that failed, the fight was transferred to the city.

Was the army struggling against ideas or against arms?

Both. The president of the Circulo Militar has reproduced all the documents of the guerrillas in a book.[9] These documents show very clearly that the purpose of the guerrillas was to change the political system in Argentina. They wanted to take power, to establish a socialist and Marxist government like the one in Cuba. All of them were big followers of Che Guevara, and Guevara wanted to establish a similar thing here. Guevara went to Bolivia, but Bolivia is very near to Salta in Argentina, with many mountains and jungles, and it is very difficult to control. So it is a very probable zone for guerrillas to establish themselves in Salta and Bolivia, and to organize operations in Argentina from there. That is why there was an attempt to create a zone in Salta in 1964.

So the fight was against the revolutionary ideas which they wanted to implant, and they wanted to establish socialist, Marxist governments in the region, not only in Argentina. And it was also against the arms which supported those ideas. Now, if your question is whether the fight was against leftist ideas, then the answer is no, because the left can be peaceful or terrorist. When the left is peaceful, nothing happens, because each person can have the ideas he or she wants. But when the left wants to impose its ideas through the use of arms and terror, the left wants to change the political system of the country, and then the fight is not against the ideas but against a political project that is different from the political project of Argentina. This means that the fight was against the ideas of the guerrillas – subversives, terrorists – who wanted to impose through force a regime different from the one Argentina had had and wanted to have. Argentina wanted a democratic government.

In 1976, when the military took over the government, the methods used to fight the guerrillas included disappearances and deaths. I would like an explanation of why those tactics were used.

Well, the first clarification, as I have already said, is that it did not begin happening in 1976. This happened within the constitutional government of Isabel Perón. Now, why was this procedure used? Maybe the most important explanation is that the justice system and the politicians in Argentina had previously neglected to put up a serious fight against the guerrillas. And I am going to explain why.

During the revolution in Argentina – not the one of *el Proceso*, but during the revolution of 1966, of Onganía and Lanusse – that was when the guerrilla movement expanded. In 1968 they assassinated Aramburu, while Lanusse was president. [The colonel errs in the dates here. Aramburu was assassinated in 1970. Onganía was then president. Lanusse was president 1971–73.] From there the guerrillas began to be a burning problem in Argentina. This government wanted to fight legally against the guerrillas through the existing justice system, but it was impossible to undertake investigations and procure sentences, because of fear, of terror. Why is that? It is very simple. A judge investigates a terrorist act – an assassination, a bomb. The only thing the terrorist has to do is phone the judge or his wife saying, for example, "You have a daughter of such-and-such age and she goes to such-and-such school and makes such-and-such journey each day – well, be careful." Because of terror, fear of personal attack, the ordinary judge found himself unable to fight against this form of terrorism. So, since the regular justice system had no success in investigating and sentencing the guerrillas, the government had to create a special organ, a special federal system, with judges who, for different reasons, were ready to put their lives at stake, their tranquillity, to investigate, judge, and sentence the guerrillas. In this way they managed to imprison many people.

When the Argentine revolution ended in 1973 and the Peronist government came in, the one of Cámpora, the first thing done by the government was to free all the terrorists who were in jail.[10] These were the antecedents that led to the takeover of government by the armed forces. If the justice system could not sentence terrorists – or if it did sentence them, could not keep them in jail – what was the solution for the guerrilla problem in Argentina? The answer was "We need to destroy them."

So terribly harsh procedures were used for several reasons, and a main reason was that the legal processes, the justice system and the politicians, were not up to their responsibilities. And for many reasons – fear, ideological conformity, or any other reason – this was transformed into a game in which the armed forces, the security forces, put their lives at stake fighting against the guerrilla in order to capture him, to put him at the disposal of the legal instruments, only to see him later go free even if he was judged to be guilty. So the tactic of the armed forces in response to the guerrillas was absolutely military, because it was clear that the justice system or the politicians would let them go free.

Cámpora's government was a leftist government, very close to the guerrillas. During that time there were bloody guerrilla attacks against military quarters such as the one in Azul,[11] where the commander of the regiment and his wife were killed. Perón had to replace Cámpora, and the main reason was that Cámpora's politics were very close to the guerrillas. So the same Perón who, in the last instance was also a militar and was not a communist, began to have very intense social concerns. He could not tolerate Cámpora and his government working with the guerrillas. That is why, when Perón died and Isabel Perón took power, she began the fight with the characteristics that you are asking me about. It was a total fight in which one side was going to win and the other one was going to lose. We lived it as a war. And in a war – in any war, even a conventional one – in order to win, procedures that are against human rights are frequently used.

We just need to think about what happened during the Second World War and in many other wars. There are very few wars in which relatively civilized procedures have been respected. Look at military history and you'll see how many civilians, women and children, have been destroyed. So there came a moment when the army recognized that it was engaged in a civil war in which, once and for all, the guerrilla problem, which had begun many years before, had to be ended.

But surely the largest group of armed guerrillas had already been defeated at Tucumán?

No. The guerrilla force in Tucumán was small compared with the urban guerrilla force. In Tucumán there was a company in the mountains which had one or two hundred people. And for the armed forces, one or two hundred people localized in a geographical sector pose a relatively small problem, because sooner or later the superiority in numbers and the clear definition of the enemy make it a not very difficult battle. The problem is when those two hundred guerrillas are mixed in with the population. Because it is terribly difficult to know who is the guerrilla, where he is, and what is he going to do. The most dangerous guerrilla is not the one in the mountain but the one in the city. Besides, according to the numbers that I gave to you, if there were two hundred guerrillas in the mountains, the number in the cities, in all the country, was much larger. By the way, making a very quick estimate between combatant guerrillas and active, logistic, intellectual and media support, and all of this, there were no fewer than 30,000 or 40,000 guerrillas.

The methods that were used included torture, and torture of pregnant women and teenagers. Why was that necessary?

Torture is a desperate method that is used to try and win when there are no other ways of doing so. The experience I have, because of what I have lived through, is that young people with a gun in their hands kill, just like an adult with a gun. It means that the subversive war, the terrorist war, has very different faces. It is difficult to understand, but in this war, young people, pregnant mothers, and sometimes even children have to die. The question is, Why does someone convince another person – a pregnant woman, a child or youth – to participate in a war in which one kills and one dies? Who is responsible for taking a child, a youth, or a mother to the war? What should we do with that child who plants a bomb? Do you know what happened with General Cardozo, the chief of the federal police? General Cardozo had a daughter, the daughter had a friend, and the friend put a bomb underneath Cardozo's bed. She was just a young girl.

But in Nunca Más, *the commission reported on nearly nine thousand cases of torture and disappearances. It is true, of course, that you have cause for argument on the other side. But nine thousand cases! That is a very large number of cases, and many of them report on disappearances of people who were not combatants, who had never had arms, who were ordinary people working in ordinary places, and pregnant women who were not combatant. Why did these people get picked up? Why were they part of the war?*

This is a matter of belief. I know few cases of delinquents of any kind who admit to being delinquents. My life experience, not as a military man but as a civilian, tells me that most delinquents of any kind deny their participation in the events. So how do we know that 9,000 or 8,000, according to the references of these reports, were innocent? Because they said that? The report says they were innocent because the persons – well, I think we have to accept that among the detained and disappeared people, there were probably some who were innocent. What nobody can know, and probably never will know, is what the real proportion of innocent people was, because one of the main characteristics of a guerrilla organization is that it is compartmentalized. There are secrets and, as a consequence, no one really knows whether any individual was a guerrilla. It is terribly difficult, which means that the possibility of a mistake exists. Probably there were fallen people who were just and innocent, and this is one of the unfortunate consequences that the war – I would say all wars – has. I insist, I do not think that there are wars in which only those who are guilty or those who are actively participating die. And in a terrorist war, this is something terribly difficult to determine, especially when it has the magnitude that it had in Argentina.

According to the Grandmothers of the Plaza de Mayo, and Nunca Más, *some babies were taken from their mothers right after they were born, taken and adopted after the mothers were killed. Is this true and, if so, why did it happen?*

Yes, I think it is true because, objectively, there are cases that demonstrate it. I don't know what the proportion of these cases is, but there are some cases that demonstrate it is true. I think that it was a mistake, a very grave error, in the cases when there was any possibility of locating relatives. But if a mother stays with the guerrillas when she is pregnant and has her child in captivity, two things can happen. First, nobody knows who her relatives are, because she is using a war name. In these cases, it is a humanitarian act for someone else to take the children. But if there is a way of knowing who the relatives are, it is a crime to appropriate the child. It should not be permitted.

One other thing that is reported in many of the histories of the period is that the military forces or the police looted apartments when they went to apprehend people. Did this happen?

Yes, it happened, and it is a crime, and they are delinquents, and they are sanctionable, and they are despicable – and many of them, during *el Proceso*, not after, were imprisoned. To rob makes no contribution to the achievement of victory. It is a crime. To achieve the objective of liberating Argentina from terrorist delinquents, sometimes violent events happened that can be critized *a posteriori*. But certain things were done to achieve the objective, and they have some explanation and some justification. Robbery has no connection with the achievement of the objective. It is a crime and, as such, it is despicable and should be punished.

On a different matter, during el Proceso, *many books were burned and banned. Ideas, certain kinds of ideas, people could not talk about in public. To an outsider this is very puzzling. Could you explain it?*

I do not have much information on this. It seems that guerrilla propaganda was banned because subversion is fundamentally a mental and not a military process. What is really subverting the system are ideas. The ideas by themselves are not the problem, but rather the ideas when they are joined to violence. You can think whatever you want, and I can think whatever I want. Your idea, as such, should be accepted, should be respected, should be talked about, should be discussed, accepted or rejected. But the moment you take a gun or a bomb and want to impose your idea on me, your idea is no longer a clean thing. It is a dirty thing. It is an idea that comes associated with death. It is an idea that someone wants to impose on me. So the ideas that are associated with violence, those are the ideas that are and were criticized, not the ideas unattached to violence.

If you have, for example, a guerrilla, a guerrilla leader who attacks people, and you have a person who, with ideas, argues in favour of the one who has committed the attack, both the one who thinks and the one who does are the same thing. Then, what is the sense of fighting against the one who carries the weapon but not the one who puts the weapon in the hand of the criminal or the murderer? This is a very complex process which cannot, I think, be analysed in a partial way. Why did we have to combat the ideas? Because they were associated with a revolutionary, criminal violence, which was filling the country with blood and death and destruction, and that, besides, was held by people who wanted to change in the system. Those are the ideas.

Now I can listen to journalists who were Montonero leaders supporting the ideas of the guerrilla and of the subversion. I can now hear people, very intelligent, very capable, a large proportion of the youth, who treat Che Guevara as an idol and a saint – words used by Ernesto Sábato[12] on TV: "He is a hero and a saint." Che Guevara was a man who went to Bolivia with weapons in his hands, ready to fight, to make war, to impose his ideas. But today I can hear this, and I do not go to kill Sábato, and nobody goes out to kill Sábato, but this is not a war environment any more. These are ideas disassociated from violence.

As a consequence, if it is an idea, and although it is extreme and, from my own point of view, mistaken, it should be respected. The bad thing is when the idea is joined together with the revolver or the gun or the bomb. That is why it is important to put things in context, in the situation. That is why it is so difficult, *a posteriori*, to sanction, to criticize events, because they are out of context. The dead ones are far away, so today one can analyse academically, juridically, the events that occurred in a war. But at the time they are happening, things are not so clear and differentiated.

Let me take you back to 1976. We have asked you general questions about what happened. I wonder if you could tell us in a more personal way how you saw your own actions at that time, until about 1979. When you were in these roles, did you think that you were fighting a war? Did you think that you were getting rid of subversives? Did you think you were saving the country?

In 1976? Beginning in 1976 there were two basic projects. One was the political project, the way of thinking in a nation that had certain characteristics. And the other was the military project to eliminate the guerrilla. I don't know if you are referring specifically to how the political project of the *el Proceso* was seen, or to how the military project of the destruction of the guerrilla was seen.

The military process against the guerrillas.

Well, I thought, and I still think, that there were – that it was necessary to destroy the guerrillas. That we had the bad luck to be forced to fulfill our military role in a war that no military wants, a war with very strong civil connotations, a war against brothers, a war with an undefined front, with an undefined enemy, in which it was very difficult to maintain the clarity and moderation of ideas. But the persons, the military, did not choose the circumstances in which to live. I had to act at a time when what was demanded was to participate in this unwanted war that was imposed on us, that we did not choose. Nor did we choose the moment or the place or the characteristics – nothing. We had to accept the war in the terms set forth by the guerrillas. The guerrillas chose the bomb, assassination, destruction, threats, and crime, and we were forced to respond to them with similar weapons, because it was the only way to defeat them.

The guerrillas in Argentina were a very large phenomenon which cannot be compared with what has happened in other countries. It is impossible, it is a mistake from my point of view, to compare the guerrillas in Argentina with those in Italy or Germany. There, by imprisoning forty or fifty persons, sixty, a hundred, the guerrilla war was over. It was a very small phenomenon that had not spread to the population, that had not penetrated the institutions.

In Argentina the phenomenon was much more widespread. All the institutions were infiltrated, even the military forces and the police. It had been prevalent for many years, constantly increasing its power. It had so much power that during the first part of the Peronist government of 1973–76, the guerrilla and the government had a very close relationship. So it was a phenomenon that deeply compromised the foundations of the nation, of the state, of democracy in Argentina. I say this knowing that it may not sound believable from someone who participated in a process that ousted a constitutional government. But among the many paradoxes that occur in life – which is not always black or white but is black and white and basically grey – although this may seem paradoxical, *el Proceso* was intended to make possible a better democracy in Argentina.

However, the form in which it was carried out deformed the original purpose, and it failed. And I think it failed in such a way that never again should the armed forces try to lead a political process in the country. Because it is not useful to rearrange the country or to rearrange the armed forces. It is prejudicial for everybody. Now, if it were to happen again – though I do not think it possible that a guerrilla movement in Argentina of the kind that existed would re-emerge, and I emphatically insist that I do not think this is possible, in no way – but if it did happen, then I think we would need to consider our experiences very carefully. We would need to be clear that a guerrilla movement that wants to impose its ideas through force must be defeated. The procedures probably would need to be modified, but everyone who wants to impose his ideas through violence must be defeated.

In this sense I believe that the armed forces, at great cost, fulfilled their mission to save the country from a Marxist government, socialist, that was not wanted by the majority of the country. With all the pain, all the cost, all the suffering for those who died, for those who remained alive, and for those who were imprisoned.

Someone once said that it is very difficult to interpret history until twenty or thirty years after the event. And I believe that when history is made about a civil war, the protagonists and their children have to disappear so that maybe, maybe, the grandchildren can begin to view what happened with more tranquillity and objectivity. It is very difficult to be objective, not only for the direct participants but also for the observers. And even if they are positioned as observers, they are also participants. Because many watched the tragedy from outside, marginalizing themselves but observing the results. In the theatre all participate. The actors and the spectators ...

It is impossible to be totally objective. For some reason I went to the theatre; for some reason I went to see this play; for some reason I went to see this author. The issue of objectivity is a very important issue. I believe that objectivity is more an attitude of the spirit than a result, because every act is charged, in a way, with ideas, with feelings, with prejudices – with everything. But this is life and that is what we are. This is life, and we need to put up with ourselves.

Very well. I do not know if this is going to be of some use to you. That period is very complex, and it cannot be simplified. It has many angles. Everybody who was associated with it is right to some extent and everybody is in error to some extent. And I believe that the error is committed when one part is demonized or when someone thinks they have the right to demonize others. I say this because here in Argentina we talk about the theory of the two demons. One demon would be the armed forces, and the other would be the guerrilla. I think that outside the context there are also some demons that influenced both of us and in a way used both of us. So I think that this is a problem which should be seen from many perspectives, with a lot of breadth.

Who were the other demons? Do you mean international forces, or what do you mean?

Yes, there are international forces, and I am going to mention the United States. The United States was facing a war against communism that could have led to a holocaust, to suicide. I don't know if you are familiar with Mao Tse-tung's theory of the Chinese revolutionary war. Well, according to this theory, the cities should be surrounded from the field – that is how he achieved victory. When it arrived at a world level, communism wanted to surround its enemies – the United States and Europe – from the field. The field was the Third World ... So Russia developed the communist guerrilla in the Third World as part of its fight against capitalism. So this was a fight between two Colossuses which brought this subversive war to Latin America and the Third World. That is why Russia supported the guerrilla movements. And because of that, the United States supported the military regimes that fought against the guerrillas. And when this did not happen, as in Chile where there was a socialist government with Allende, the United States participated in its defeat. Russia used the guerrilla movements for its own purposes of world domination, and the United States used the military regimes to fight against the guerrillas.

When the war was over, Russia and the United States would not have anything to do with it. From there on, the ones sanctioned were the military regimes that had fought hard to do their part in this war, which the Latin American countries experienced as a world war. It was a war that affected their own countries. This guerrilla conflict in Argentina was inserted into a world conflict. And we were pawns, we were pieces of a big chessboard manipulated by Russia from one side and by the United States from the other.

So, in a way, we feel we have been betrayed, because having participated in good faith, up to the limit, in this fight to stop communism from owning the world, the main critics to the way in which we fought now come from the capitalist countries on whose side we played. They take advantage of the results, but they don't want to assume any of the costs of the war that was fought. There are a lot of demons in this world, and not only those who had to fight openly, frankly, and hard.

In blaming the United States, do you have any concrete example of how they encouraged the Argentine military to undertake this war?

Well, to begin with, by giving political support to the military governments. And the French, with their experience in Algeria and Indochina, came here to Argentina, to the war school, to teach us how to fight a war against revolutionaries. In the case of Chile, I believe that it is historically proved that there was U.S. participation in the creation of a military government.

I want to clarify something. I use the word "demons" because it is a term that has been around for some time. Well, in that sense, there are many demons in the world, including the United States and Europe. What I really think is that none of them are demons. What happens is that each one defends its national interests in what it thinks is the best possible way. The United States understood that it was defending its own interests by fighting against communism and supporting the Latin American governments that were fighting the subversive guerrillas. And they were making use of the right that each country has to try to do the best for itself. I am not scandalized that the United States used Latin American countries to defend its interests as allies in this political struggle, this world fight. What I do not accept, or what it is difficult for me to accept, is that in this world of interests, of violence, of war, in this world of conflicts, the end result is that the only ones who are punished or morally sanctioned are the Argentine armed forces.

There are few countries that can feel proud of what they have done during wars. In the Second World War, the United States destroyed a large number of German cities, and the army was not there in those cities. There were children, pregnant women, old people, women, and they should have known that dropping tons of bombs, as they did, would kill innocent people. And when they dropped bombs on Hiroshima and Nagasaki, they knew that innocents were going to die. So there are very few nations that, having lived through a war, are able to say, "I never touched an innocent, I never committed a barbaric act." It is difficult for me to accept their right to point at us as if we were barbaric, as if we were demons.

Were you, were the officers actually trained by military forces from the United States or France? Did you take courses from them?

From the French, yes, for sure. Because I attended the school of war here in Argentina, and there were French officers as advisers in the revolutionary wars. Everything I learned about the theory and practice of counterrevolutionary warfare, I learned from the French, from the experience they had obtained in Indochina and Algeria. I can say that because I attended the school of war with French instructors and advisers.

Did anyone worry at the time that the French had lost the wars in Algeria and Indochina? Did they worry about whether the French actually knew as much as they said they knew?

What happens is that, as I have told you, each generation, each individual, each society always exists in a context – it exists at a specific time in specific circumstances. At that time, the ones who had more experience in the world of counterrevolutionary warfare were the French. So at that time the Argentine military could not consider all possibile advisers, because the ones who had the experience in revolutionary war were the French. Furthermore, I believe that war is a complex phenomenon that is not only military. Often, wars are lost politically before there is a military defeat because politics has initiated a war in unfavourable conditions. So the military war was lost because it was first politically lost. It was lost at the political level because international politics did not create winnable conditions.

So I believe that France lost in Indochina and Algeria because, politically, colonialism was a lost battle. It is impossible for a colonial power to fight against a people who want to become independent. So France lost these wars because they initiated wars that could not be won politically. The French lost Indochina because they had to lose. The United States did not lose in Vietnam. The United States is the superpower, and it has all the nuclear and military power, but politically it was caught in a lost war. So the armed forces were not the ones responsible; the armed forces were obliged to fight in unfavourable conditions. And this was because war, as Clausewitz said, is the continuation of politics by other means. Because it is politics that leads to a good war or a bad war, to a won war or a lost war.

Suppose you were to think of the guerrillas as just young people who were influenced by ideas of a better world. If you think of them that way and realize that only a fraction of them took up arms, then, looking back on it, do you think it would have been possible to have controlled it in a different, less violent way?

I think that with all the defects it has, the republican democratic system is the best political system because it includes everyone, includes young people, in such a way that they can realize their ideals, their utopias. And as I think Churchill said, the democratic system is pretty bad, but there is nothing better. I think that the mistake committed by the young people was to think that an absolutely antidemocratic system, communism, could better achieve their ideals than a democratic system. So this is the main mistake committed by the idealists and also by many intellectuals of the first rank – to think that through real communism, real socialism, it was possible to arrive at that ideal world of equality, liberty, fraternity, etcetera. I attribute to the intellectuals and to the young people a confusion about the possibility that real communism, Marxism, and socialism could achieve their ideals. When socialism was born in the nineteenth century, or communism was born with the *Communist Manifesto*, they were not working toward democracy. And after 1917, in Russia, when the communists took power, and in 1960 or 1970, there should have been very few people who remained confused with respect to what was happening there. Unless they wanted to be confused and did not want to know the reality. And after Castro took power in Cuba, I think there was enough information to know that those ideals of democracy were not achievable through socialism.

I believe that these idealists were mistaken with respect to *el Proceso*. I don't understand an idealism that is based on force. I think that the idealism of youth or the utopias of age are essential to be able to progress, to have a better horizon than the current one – today, yesterday, and tomorrow. But never if it is imposed by arms. Because if they want to impose it by arms, there is going to be an armed reaction. And when the reaction comes, with it comes crime, homicide, destruction, and there is no possible exit. I don't understand the position of a young idealist, or whoever, who decides to go to the revolutionary war, to use terrorism, knowing what that involves, and then when it comes their turn to lose, they cry and complain.

Argentina lost the Malvinas War. Have you heard any military person complaining because of the deaths we suffered, because of the defeat? These are the risks of war. One goes to war, wins or loses, and does not cry afterward. But here, the subversives go to war, kill, destroy, and then believe that there will never be a reaction, that their turn will never come. So they act in a military way, through military violence or pseudomilitary, and then they protect themselves under civilian laws. It is a cheating game: I kill you, but when you react and hit me, I appeal to human rights and civilian laws. In this way it is difficult to lose.

The range of uncivilized behaviour that can be accepted from young people has its limits. It is true that young people are not mature yet and as a consequence they are disrespectful, they are more irreverent, they are more violent, they shout more, etcetera. We need to accept this because they are young, as we once were. But when this young person takes a gun and shoots someone in the head, it does not matter if this person is eighteen, twenty, fifteen, or fourteen, this person is a criminal.

VOICE: GENERAL FALCÓN

The war against subversion occurred in two parts. The first was from 1973 to 1978, when the war was at its peak, its maximum violence. And then from 1978 to 1983 there was a transition period toward a democratic system. Of course, after the coup the armed forces were the national government.

To explain this we must realize that Cámpora's government relied on the support of left-wing Peronism, and the population was very restless at that time. He opened the jails and let out all the terrorists, and after that there were terrorist organizations in everything, in the university as well as in the state. Because of this, one month and a half after assuming office, Cámpora was forced to resign by Perón. Then, in May 1974, five or six months later, Perón dismissed the Montoneros from the Plaza. Then these terrorists were left without political support, and the revolutionary war began, the struggle for power through violence. But then Perón died and Isabel took charge, and after that there was a crisis, so there was pressure on the armed forces to assume power, which they did in March 1976. The pressure came from the press, business groups, and citizens in general. Even the political leader from the opposition, Ricardo Balbín, publicly said that there was no other solution for the Argentine problem.

Between Perón's death and March of 1976, were the armed forces involved in antisubversive activities?

Yes. There was a decree in 1975 that ordered the armed forces to take action against subversion. It ordered the annihilation. It was signed by all the ministers from the Executive Power and by the provisional president, Dr Luder, because the president was – well, I don't remember what was happening. She had two or three absences, one due to sickness, the other – Well, from that moment, the Military Junta of Government took control, in March 1976. It took over without any kind of resistance. There was not even a strike, nothing. And from there began the Process for National Reorganization, whose main objective was, of course, the fight against subversion. The fight against subversion began then, in 1976, with virtually the same procedures as had been used earlier. The only difference was that the government was in military hands.

Who developed the procedures?

Isabel's government. The country was divided into zones, and each zone had, in addition to normal political authorities, a military authority that was responsible for the fight against subversion. Then each zone was divided into subzones, and each subzone into areas. So the whole territory was controlled in a geographical arrangement. The three forces each had control in their zones. But in reality, the army had the primary responsibility because it commanded the major zones.

The fight against subversion was practically over by 1978, because subversive activities had notably diminished. Then the government tried to find a political solution. The government wanted to move toward a democratic system, because the first objective of *el Proceso* was to install democracy in Argentina. In 1981 we had a change of presidents, from Jorge Videla to Roberto Viola, and later that year Leopoldo Galtieri took control. In April 1982 Galtieri, or the junta, ordered the recovery of the Malvinas, and you already know what happened. Then there was an election. But this is history.

Going back to the year 1976, the war against subversion resulted in the disappearance of many people. Why did the army choose this method to fight subversion?

That is really a question. I cannot answer it because I don't have evidence of the existence of disappeared people. I have read about this, but I don't have evidence. There was no method to disappear people. No such order or method existed as far as I know.

But people did disappear. How did it happen, that some people just disappeared?

On this topic, what can I say? At that time I was only a lieutenant colonel, and my mission in the war against subversion was to control one area through patrols. We did not have any kind of operations except those established in the regulations, and as a consequence of those operations nobody disappeared. We checked cars, we checked people, and if we found something suspicious we turned it over to the judicial authorities or to the police. So because of our activities no one disappeared. We had patrols that all day travelled over the area to avoid attack. We had control over the population and checked their houses to see if they had weapons. All these operations were done wearing official uniform in plain daylight, without any kind of, let's say, concealment or anything unusual. So there could not have been disappearances or such strange things happening.

Were you aware of the fact that there were disappearances in Argentina in those times?

No, frankly, I only learned of that after 1983 when the famous book *Nunca Más* appeared, but I still don't know whether this is true or is propaganda.

When you found something irregular, you said you took those persons to the police?

Of course, they were arrested and ...

Who had control over the police in those days? Did they depend on the army?

The army had only operational control over the police. What does that mean? It means that we had the cooperation of the police if, for example, we needed a patrol; or if we wanted to have a search operation and needed to take twenty blocks and search the people who were there, request their documents, and see if they had weapons. But the police had its own authority system, and it had its own regular job to do. It did not depend on us. We had operational control over the police only when our units were in the area, and it was only operational control for the kind of activities that I've described.

When you controlled your area, searching the houses, were you in uniform?

Yes, yes, we wore uniform when we did control operations, and also when we searched houses and when we did civil actions. Civil action means, for example, taking doctors to attend to people. Those controls were done in the marginal zones, so sometimes we brought whole medical clinics with doctors and dentists to them. It was always done in uniform. The people went to the clinics; they were attended to by the physician and the dentist. We checked them. We sometimes stayed in one place for a week or so.

According to the testimonies in Nunca Más, *in some cases the houses were robbed by military personnel. Do you know anything about that?*

I do not have any evidence because we never did anything like that, and I do not know that those things were done. I do not know that anyone did that – so no, no.

How did you consider the subversives in those times? Were they communists or what were they?

We considered subversives to be organizations that wanted to take power through armed struggle. Of course their ideology, well, they had different kinds of Marxist ideologies; the Montoneros were very different from the ERP. The Montoneros had more nationalistic roots, and ERP's roots were more Trotskyist. But the important thing was that they were two organizations that wanted to take power through armed struggle, terrorism, and subversion.

In your opinion, how many people were involved in those subversive organizations?

I have a very general idea, I do not have a precise idea, but I think there were approximately 25,000 Montoneros and around 2,000 or 3,000 from the ERP. This was in the year 1977, more or less. But you should talk about this with intelligence specialists.

If there were around 30,000 subversives, out of a population of 30 million, why was it was necessary to enter everybody's home looking for arms?

Why did we have to enter people's homes? I don't know why, but we had to stop them. What happened is that they did not operate like a regular army; they infiltrated the population.

How did you learn about how they operated?

Their methodology was very simple. They planted bombs and killed people. They kidnapped people, they robbed banks. Besides, they announced when they had done something.

So your information about them came from their public actions? You did not have any special study about their methodology?

The methodology was that, very simple.

Were there people in the armed forces who specialized in subversive warfare?

There were people who studied the topic, for example, a general who wrote a book on this.

Did you receive some preparation, some education in this area?

Really, I can't tell you that. I am not sure, but I believe that the Argentine doctrine in the war against subversion originated in other countries, probably in France and the United States. They have doctrines of this kind. Our military doctrine is usually based in the doctrine of other countries.

Subversive groups formed in many countries of the world during the 1970s, but only a few countries engaged in a full-scale war against subversion. Why did Argentina engage in such a big counter-offensive?

Because subversion had grown a lot in Argentina.

More than in other countries?

I think so. More than in the European countries, for sure. For example, in Tucumán, some zones were occupied by the guerrillas. So there was a real danger of the country being fragmented. There were zones occupied by the guerrillas – they controlled the routes, the paths. It might seem that they were few people, but we are talking about 28,000 combatants. And there were many more if one includes all their supporters and everything else. They had logistic support, ideological support, propaganda, all of that; it was much larger.

In your opinion, at that time, why were there so many subversives in Argentina?

Subversion had grown so much because during these four years everything – well, from 1973 onwards, subversion had infiltrated many places and had increased in the universities and in working-class districts.

Why did it grow so fast?

That happens all over the world when governments are not successful. Isabel failed. That created an opportunity for the development of subversion.

Going back again to 1976, now some years later you know that there were many people who disappeared ... How would you explain those disappearances?

I cannot explain them because I did not participate. I cannot explain how it happened.

What did you think of el Proceso *when you read the report of the commission or when the trials of the junta took place?*

I insist. Personally, I do not have any evidence to know whether the accusations were true. No, no no, I do not have the knowledge to be able to judge the commanders.

Do you think the trial was fair?

The trial in reality had a lot of vices from the legal and constitutional point of view – vices, errors. I am not able to explain them because I am not a lawyer, but I have read studies that identified grave mistakes in the whole process. Constitutional mistakes.

You have said that you cannot comment on the disappeared people. Can you comment on the number of dead people?

At this stage, I am not able to give you a number. Twenty years have passed. But I am sure you will find it in the book by Diaz Bessone.

In your opinion, was it unjust for people to dislike the military after the Malvinas and the trial?

Was it fair or unfair? I think the people did not understand us. We made some errors in the military government, and the Malvinas was another error, not the Malvinas as such but the way it was handled afterwards. Also, there were economic problems. It was understand-able that people were disgusted with the government after it had ille-gitimately held power for six years.

Why do you use the word "illegitimate"?

Because the government was not elected. And besides that, there were institutions, like the Congress, that were not working. That took away the political sustenance.

Why did the military shut down the Congress?

I don't know. I think that, well, yes, there could have been other solutions. Some other military governments have coexisted with their Congress, like Bordaberry in Uruguay. But I don't know why. I think that those who organized the coup and *el Proceso* thought they could not govern with a Congress.

They also used some illegal methods; they kidnapped people, kept them without access to the legal process, without a trial. Why did they feel obliged to use those kinds of ...

I cannot answer that because, in the level I was working at, those methods were never used. And I have no evidence that those methods were used by others.

You said that the subversion declined by 1978. How did that come about?

It never finishes, but it had begun to decrease by 1978. I suppose that was because there were fewer options, fewer possibilities for the subversives by then. Besides that, the news said that the kidnappings and bombs and terrorism had stopped. There was more security in the country, that was clear.

But many of the subversives had been killed by then, by 1978. Would that be a major reason for the decline in their activities?

No, but all the leaders of the subversion had left the country – that is something everybody knows. They left because they realized that if they stayed in the country they would be imprisoned. And when in any organization the chiefs run away, the organization collapses.

But you see, I have this problem. All the reports that I have read, international reports and Nunca Más and historical studies, said that there were many people who disappeared and were killed.

Yes, but you would need to check that with the authors of those reports, because in my particular case I do not know of any case of disappearances. I have never seen and do not know of any case of disappeared people, so I cannot talk about them.

Looking back at that experience, do you personally think that the armed forces did the right thing for the country?

I think that our major mistake was to take over the government in 1976. For the armed forces, taking the government is always a bad experience because it wastes the forces. I think that they should have thought of a way of dealing with the problem while maintaining a constitutional government.

But besides the actual process that the armed forces undertook to reorganize the country, did they do the right thing?

The objectives were adequate. What I cannot say is whether the implementation was good or not, or if it could have been a better one. It is a very difficult thing. If we had not acted, what could have happened? Argentina could have become a socialist republic, because the subversion had grown a lot.

Would that have been a terrible thing?

It would have been terrible because it would have been imposed by force, that would have been terrible. It would have happened not because the people wanted it but because a very small group would have imposed it by force – the terrorism, the violence – and then it would not have been possible to go back again.

This is a different kind of question. Did the Catholic Church have any influence on el Proceso?

Not a decisive one. The military authorities were Catholic, as are 95 per cent of the Argentine population, but I don't think the church had any relevant political influence.

Did you think at the time that the church supported your actions?

I would say that the whole population supported the actions. It is impossible to fight against a terrorist enemy without the support of the population. And I would say more: the coup of 1976 occurred because of a very strong pressure from the population.

I just want to ask once more, when you read the current accounts of what happened and read Nunca Más, *how do you personally feel about it?*

It is very difficult for me to believe these reports because I never saw anything like that, and it is difficult for me to believe things that I never saw.

CHAPTER 16

Other Military Perspectives

Senior officers who were involved in the repression of the 1970s generally defend their actions, though Colonel Horacio P. Ballester, author of a scathing attack on the army he served for many years, told us in our interview that some of his former colleagues had turned to drink or religion, and others had chosen suicide. He himself had chosen to rebel and had paid a heavy price for it, as he recounts in *Memoirs of a Democratic Colonel.*[1]

Colonel Ballester established the Organization for a Democratic Military (CEMIDA) after being forced out of the army he had served for most of his life. The office where CEMIDA met was bombed in 1984. The area destroyed by the bomb was clearly visible when we visited. Of the five hundred members who had joined, half ceased to participate after the bombing. Said the colonel: "We did talk, and that's why some disappeared and others were put in jail. Colonel Perlinger was in jail for seven and a half years without any formal process against him. I was punished with house arrest several times. Others were frightened away." In his view, the junta had obeyed the people's wishes but also had undertaken an international service by introducing neoliberal policies under repression. We include here a brief excerpt from our lengthy interview with him.

There were army officers who rationally considered their personal alternatives at some point during *el Proceso* and chose retirement. These individuals may be found in many other occupations today. They are knowledgeable about events instigated by or affecting the military, and they are not disloyal, but they have a critical edge that few of their former peers can afford. Such is our second speaker, Major Villegas. The major pursues a line of thinking introduced in the last chapter by Colonel Lorenzo regarding the importance of French and American instruction in revolutionary wars, and the Cold War mentality of the armed forces.

As suggested in these interviews, there is ongoing debate within the services about the events of the 1970s. The most frequently expressed view is that the forces did what the population wanted – namely, rid the society of its communist subversives, re-established law and order, and paved the way for democracy – and they feel they should suffer no blame for that. Some say they feel that they should have been feted and honoured for their heroic work. Many express the belief that the society has shown hypocrisy by first demanding that the armed forces take on the dirty task (thus the lingering phrase "dirty war" for the entire episode) and then spitting on them for doing it well.

But there are other voices within the services. In particular, there are new voices, officers who were too young to be burdened with responsibility for the coup and the repression, who are able to look on those events with fresh understandings. Under the more open organization of Chief-of-Staff Martín Balza, the two majors whose interviews are reported as the conclusion to this chapter spoke frankly about the past. Two separate interviews were recorded, one with Major Carlos Bobbio alone; the other with both Bobbio and his colleague, Major Ernesto Bultras. As is evident in these excerpts, new insights and published information on the events of the 1970s are part of the culture for a new generation of officers.

Readers who have followed the debate about the relationship between leading Montoneros and the army intelligence services will find these interviews particularly intriguing. Was Mario Firmenich an intelligence officer, a double agent? Were other leaders who escaped the country in 1977 also cooperating with the armed services? Was General Aramburu captured by army insiders and given to the newly established Montoneros? Indeed, did he actually die of a heart attack before the Montoneros were invented as his assassins? These all seem like conspiracy theories concocted by enemies of the Montoneros, and indeed, one reader of this text suggested that the army might have "planted" the information for that purpose. However, there seems to be a fair body of evidence to support the hypothesis of cooperation, and the stubborn fact is that Firmenich and a few others who miraculously escaped in 1977 are still alive and well, while thousands of their loyal followers are among the disappeared. If the information about the double-agent role for Firmenich was deliberately planted by the army, then the military forces had sufficient knowledge of their enemy before the coup to have stopped subversion without causing a bloodbath. If we believe that they planted the information, then we also have to believe that their motivation from the beginning was to kill a large number of people, irrespective of those people's relationship to the subversives. That is a possibility; but why would they boast about it twenty years later?

Equally intriguing in these interviews is the discussion of the kid-nappings and deaths authorized by powerful people, including at least one member of the junta, for their own political purposes. According to our interviewees, Admiral Massera thought he could become the successor to Perón – but first he had to kill off the potential compet-itors. Thus, authority was given to abduct and kill Peronists who were not otherwise on the enemy list.

Finally, we learn that the intelligence service (SIDE) had gained so much power in every institution of the country that no one in the government had control of it. Its insidious methods were gradually destroying all organizations, including the armed forces. This is a feature of state terrorism that Hannah Arendt identified as central to the whole enterprise.[2] The sorcerer's apprentice was as dangerous in Argentina of the 1970s as in Nazi Germany of the 1940s.

VOICE: COLONEL HORACIO P. BALLESTER (RETIRED)

Under the military government, military officers occupied positions related to the repression itself, not positions that were concerned with the country's future such as the Ministry of Economy and the Ministry of Foreign Relations. I do not justify the military conduct, but there was a lot of civilian participation in that government. There were many politicians who knew that they would never win through elec-tions, and they used the military coup to get into power. Then they said to the military: "The country is calling you, the country needs you, these robberies can't go on, this shame can't go on, we have to put a stop to it." And there's no shortage of stupid people who believed those calls.

The military were flattered, and they were trained to do what they did; even in the School of the Americas in Panama. They believed it was the defence of their nation, the defence of the traditions. Also, the ruling powers – I am not trying to make the United States the bad guy here – but they also, in their schools, they taught methods of torture, murder, extortion, kidnapping. It's only a few days ago that some of the regu-lations of the School of the Americas in the United States were done away with. That's the official education that Argentine officers received.

VOICE: MAJOR ADOLFO VILLEGAS (RETIRED)

The major first discussed the conflicts and tensions of the 1960s and the crisis under Isabel Perón's government. He said that at the end of the 1960s, "French colonels came to instruct Argentine army officials on the basic doctrines of revolutionary war." The question that precedes the next section was, "Why the French?"

First of all because the French are the inventors of the theory of revolutionary war. Remember Indochina and Algeria. They lost those wars but they conserved the doctrine of the revolutionary war. According to this doctrine, all antisystem activities, all are in some way responsible for the Soviet enemy in Indochina, or the anticolonial enemy in the case of Algeria. This point of reference was transferred to the Argentine officials in an a-critical way. That is very important, because it practically formed a generation of Argentine officials in a permanent way. They were still in the Cold War. All events occurred within that mental framework, and it explained revolutionary war.

The revolutionary war, or the antisubversive scheme that was to come later via the Americans, is fundamentally a ground problem, and that means it is a primary concern of the army. It was superimposed on the U.S. security doctrine, above all in the Kennedy period. Think about Kennedy, the Green Berets, etcetera. This is very important for an army that is always looking for an adversary, an enemy. This is common to almost all armed forces. And the revolutionary war uses an unorthodox methodology for fighting. The intellectual formation of the officials is very important, and it included the doctrine of the revolutionary war ...

The prime objective of the military government was to destroy subversion, as it was called. Secondly, it tried to organize the economy, to reestablish the institutions of the republic. Always, at least ideologically, they promised or they believed, I don't know, that they had to restore the institutions of the republic. No military coup says, "We are going to create another political style." This fight against subversion used the methodology that had been learned from the French and from the Green Berets in order to reestablish the institutions of the constitution.

They learned the lessons of the Green Berets from American missions that came regularly to Argentina in order to transmit their principles and teach their methodology – sometimes in Argentina, other times in Panama or elsewhere in the School of the Americas. The general idea was that when the enemy uses one means, you have to use the same one. If the enemy has nuclear weapons, I also have to use nuclear weapons. The basic military idea. You can't reject any means that are used by the enemy, because that automatically puts you in an inferior situation.

Up to this point, the guerrillas had used assassination and bank robberies, but is there any evidence that they also used torture?

Not massively, no, but yes individually. Many prisoners of the guerrillas were tortured. In other words, neither of the two sides respected human rights, and that is not good because the military represented the state and Argentine society. I am not trying to excuse them; I am trying to explain why they thought in this way. In general terms, all antisubversive, anticolonial fights are dirty fights. There are very few cases in which bad methods were not used. Even the good Dutch used bad methods in Indonesia in confronting anticolonial groups.

It is important to note something about illegal methodology. I use the word "illegal" as a euphemism. In the same air force that used this illegal methodology against subversion, when the same people were fighting in 1982 in the Malvinas War, they respected all the laws and all the international treaties. The Malvinas War is a textbook example of a conflict in which all the norms were respected by both armed forces. This is to support the hypothesis that it is the logic of the conflict that leads to the use of illegal means.

In a subversive war, the principal problem for government forces is identifying the enemy. Once identified, the military power of the government is far superior. In this type of war, the important thing is military intelligence. The principal objective is to look for, identify, and locate the enemy. And that is where torture can play a key role.

It should also be remembered that our police have always used illegal methods. During the war against subversion, the police were acting under military orders, and they contributed to the transferral of that illegal methodology to the military. This illegal methodology, even apart from the moral and legal problems, has the defect that when you use criminal procedures, normally you have to commit other crimes to cover up the first one. If you kidnap someone and submit them to interrogations with torture, later you have to cover up those previous crimes, and many times the way to cover them up is to kill the person. In that period of euphoria, the armed forces and the police thought they were invincible. That also explains why a criminal methodology spread ... Always, when illegal procedures are used, the notion of what's criminal and what's not gets lost. Therefore, to take things that do not belong to the state, that belong to the prisoners, sometimes was thought of as a kind of war booty. It is important that you point out that difference.

Did the military in 1975 know how strong or weak the guerrillas were?

I cannot say precisely, but there was a lot of fear of growth. In other words, it was an important enemy. Subversive war cannot be measured with the same methods as conventional wars. Guerrillas have fewer military means, but they have the capacity for attacks, murders, and kidnappings, and they could have a big impact on public opinion and government. That is their objective.

It was never thought that society was going to call for an accounting. If the military government hadn't lost politically, maybe it would have been much more difficult to call for an accounting from the people who committed the crimes during this war. For example, you can see that it's much more difficult to call the Chilean armed forces to account for their actions, because they gave up power from a position of strength. The Argentine military had to give up power after a military and political defeat. They were in a situation of absolute weakness from which they could not negotiate terms.

When the defeat in the Malvinas occurred in July 1982, the collapse was very rapid. Even the politicians and the unionists were surprised about the speed of the collapse of the military government. That's why they now say, "How obedient the Argentine armed forces are to the civil power!" They're obedient because they come from an extremely weak political situation. They suffered a loss of self-respect because of their defeat in the Malvinas. That reflected on their professional capacity as soldiers.

For the majority of the military men, the demands for accountability in the war against subversion were unjust, because they had fought to defend Argentine society. Within the armed forces, there is great moral cohesion about the need to defend the military institution. And that cohesion has drawn the attention of various North American investigators. Pion-Berlin, for example, called attention to it. He asked, "Why are there not more divisions, more ruptures?"[3]

The few who have spoken out, like Adolfo Francisco Scilingo and a few others – there are five or ten – have been expelled from the armed forces. Many of them have committed crimes, and not honourable crimes, like swindles and theft of money. That's Scilingo's case. And in some way they are trying to get revenge on the armed forces. What they say may be true, but it probably isn't.

But during the trials of the generals, one of the defences was that there had been excesses among the junior people that had not been ordered by the senior officers. Wouldn't the junior people resent that? Why would they accept blame?

That brings me to the subject of the rebellions during the government of Alfonsín [1983–89]. I don't know if I am going to be able to make a long story short, but Alfonsín had a political scheme with respect to the crimes committed during the war. During his election campaign he said that we have to distinguish between those who gave the orders, those who obeyed them, and those who took them to the extreme, which theoretically was a good distinction. You know the difficulties that Alfonsín had. He had to try to make the military judge one another. He tried for almost a year to get the superior adviser of the armed forces to condemn the military, but because of that same cohesion that I spoke of, he was not able to condemn the military and he had to take the military cause to a special civil tribunal.

But it's precisely that cohesion within the armed forces that produced the following reaction. First, there were officials who had not participated. This was also the case in the navy, even though it had played an important role in the procedures against the guerrillas. In the army there were some soldiers who said, "We are not going to participate." Others said, "We will participate because our superiors have ordered us to." They also said, "All that military action was in defence of society. Why are they asking for accounts and explanations now of actions that were military – actions that I carried out because there were military plans and there were military people to do it?"

Always remind yourself of the French colonels and the Green Berets. As you know, Alfonsín was faced with three rebellions. And he tried, always through the law, to put this principle into practice – to distinguish between those who gave the orders, those who obeyed, and those who exceeded them. And he tried, through the law of obedience, to separate the youngest from the oldest. Finally, through successive changes in the legislation, he ended up playing the members of the military juntas or some superior officials against the police. He ended up dealing with about thirty people, which solved the political problem of the military insurrections.

This situation ended with the condemnation of various members of the junta, who went to jail. Then President Menem, who followed Alfonsín as president, gave a general pardon. Somehow the legal problem got lost in the shadows in spite of the fact that President Menem made one last attempt in December 1989. Alfonsín never pardoned them. He punished them. They were in jail. The government of Dr Alfonsín had to litigate and spend large political resources on all this process. When I speak with my Radical Party friends, they say that Alfonsín "had to dance with the ugliest woman."

His situation was very difficult, considering that there was still the possibility of a military coup, something that has now practically disappeared. However, at that time we believed that military politics, or politics related to the organization of the armed forces, could not technically be brought to the forefront again. It was almost impossible, though so much of the ministry's energy and time was directed at this problem. Only after the pardon could Menem create a military policy and a reorganization of the armed forces. However, his military policy was simply to reduce the budget and maintain the armed forces in a state of hibernation. The violation of human rights comes up periodically in newspapers and television. But here, in politics, that doesn't have much effect. Of course, the people who have lost a husband or a son are never going to forget. While they live, their ideas and their grief will continue.

Has there been any attempt to engage military personnel in discussions about human rights?

I think there has been, yes, some change in military thinking. They are not somewhere else, on the moon or on Mars; they are living here and are influenced by the society. The public statements by Chief-of-Staff General Martín Balza have indicated, in a very indirect way, the responsibility of the army for the disappeared. But the subject of responsibility is not an important one for the army. Right now, they are all fighting to survive on limited budgets. Anyway, people forget, and politicians also make mistakes and become corrupt. So at the moment, in public opinion surveys, the military is in the middle of the scale of public appreciation. Union leaders are much less popular. You have to remember that in 1976 the immense majority of the population and of the politicians either supported the military or they remained silent. The military then was doing the dirty work for many politicians.

Was that true right up to the Malvinas War, or had they lost support before that?

The Malvinas War was the beginning of the end for the military government. It was already wasted. The war against subversion was really finished by 1978. Then the politicians, the businessmen, and the church began to lose their fear. They became more critical after that.

The CONADEP estimated a death toll of some 30,000 people. Is that accurate?

It's the same as if they had killed six or if they had killed thirty. The tragedy, with subversive wars, is that you can't know who the subversives are. Maybe three innocent people suffered for every one found guilty. It's terrible.

VOICE: MAJOR CARLOS BOBBIO

Major Bobbio began his army career in 1974 at the age of seventeen. He provided us with his interpretation of the 1960s and early 1970s before continuing with the following discussion of the Montonero leadership.

I've told you I came from a Peronist family. The army, when it got into power, repressed the Peronist left and the Peronist right. The Peronist right did not have any human rights organizations to speak for them, but it had many deaths. Then there's another phenomenon which the Montoneros acknowledge: their leaders supported the coup. I believe Firmenich was an army man. It's my personal opinion, based on reading I have done, that the death of Aramburu was provoked by the army itself, because of internal army struggles. The Montoneros agreed on the fall of Isabel. Firmenich and the other first leaders left the country.

Were other leaders also in the army, or just Firmenich?

These were very secret links, but it is certain that when Firmenich left, when the leaders left, the second line of leaders began to work with and were in the service of the army, in order to save their own lives. That's why there are so many dead young people. Those leaders denounced their subordinates right down the line. And then there's another phenomenon: the power struggle within the armed forces, between Emilio Massera and the army. And that caused many deaths that were attributed to the repression. It was a society that had lost all rules.

Massera had his own political project, which was to capture Peronism. He killed many Peronist leaders in order to achieve this. He was a sinister person. The problem of the military government was also the fragmentation of power. Every leader in every place did whatever he wanted. The methodology of the disappeareds was a system for which the commanders took no responsibility. If you ask General Videla now, "How many dead?" he does not know. Our chief did not take responsibility. In a hierarchical institution like the army, this is terrible ...

My generation did not fight, but I was in the military school when Perón made his last visit at a meeting of my cadet class. He said to us, crying a little, "May God help you for what you're going to have to experience." We didn't understand anything then, but now I remember his words and I think he knew what would happen in the near future. [Note: Major Bobbio's first posting was to Tucumán.]

... The army tortured, but we never studied how to torture. I was in the military college, and nobody mentioned torture or anything of that kind. They prepared me for conventional warfare. This fight was a struggle between factions of the middle class. The majority of the Argentine people did not participate in the armed organizations. The guerrillas were the radicalized children of the middle class. The military was the other faction, the repressers. The lists presented in the report by CONADEP say that this war produced approximately 5,000 [sic] dead on the guerrilla side and about 200 on the other side. It was terrible. But the 30,000 that the Madres de la Plaza de Mayo claim do not exist. Do you know why the Madres say 30,000? Because they took one day in 1976 and they projected that number to the whole country for a certain amount of time. It was an extrapolation. And the lists they presented are something else. I want to say that what happened was terrible from any point of view, but it was confined to a sector of the middle class. The confrontation was between sectors of the middle class, especially those engaged in the arts and the professions, and then there were tremendous repercussions and impacts.

But we still have to explain why the armed forces chose to conduct their new government with such strong repression. Whether it was 8,000 dead or 30,000, the main question is, Why did the military think it necessary?

It's difficult. I believe that, in Argentina, violence increased from 1955 onwards. Bombings in a plaza full of civilians, shootings. The guerrillas engaged in the violence. I would like to remind you of the death during those years of a captain and his daughter in Tucumán and the shooting at several military bases – something I could never understand, because if the guerrillas wanted to fight against capitalism, why did they have the unions and the military bases as their targets? In 1975 the guerrillas took two military units and they killed everybody. In Formosa they killed soldiers who were drafted, conscripts. This produced tremendous resentment and hate, which lost them support ...

General Balza, our current chief-of-staff, says: "We made the mistake of believing that by copying their methods, we could fight against them, without taking into account what the law said. Now, we must not use methods that are outside the law."

Did the army believe or have any evidence that the guerrillas used torture?

Yes. There is a lieutenant colonel, the most famous case, who was stuck in a well for nine months. He weighed 25 kilos when he was found dead. There are many cases.

How many guerrillas were there?

I believe that the Montoneros had many members; it was the biggest guerrilla organization in South America. It's very difficult to know the exact number, but I think at least 10,000 Montoneros. The demonstrations got up to about 50,000. The army believed they were a serious opposition. They thought that they and their families were in danger; there were dead comrades, sons of comrades dead; there was conflict, there were confrontations, and they felt wronged. If we go to the objective reasons of why there was this violence, I don't think that the military of 1974–75 looked back to the proscription of Peronism in 1955 as something that could have brought them to such a state. The Montoneros went underground during a democracy! They didn't just fight against the dictatorship. They ended up working against their own government, confronting their own constitutional government.

Some writers say that the armed forces saw themselves as the saviours of the nation. Do you think that is true?

Yes, I share that view. Between the beginnings of Argentina, around 1800, and 1930 there wasn't a single military coup. However, the state was delegating important functions to the military. In 1910 "the universal and obligatory law of the vote" put the armed forces as a guarantor of the transparency and legitimacy of the electoral process. In 1920 the state delegated the development of petroleum to the armed forces because of their technical abilities. Whatever the state couldn't deal with, it delegated to the military. During the 1930s the state delegated the implementation of a high-technology holding company. In 1940 the army developed a "government project." The consequence of all this was to involve the armed forces in matters that were not their proper sphere. There were many problems in Argentina. Why do you suppose the universal and obligatory vote was installed? Because fraud was a regular practice among politicians. They were much more corrupt than the military. Between 1930 and 1983, the problem of electoral fraud continued, and it is still not solved ...

Returning to the problems of the 1970s, if Firmenich and the leaders were employed by the army, then the army must have known how many Montoneros there were.

In 1970 the military had no interest in such a small group. After that, the Montoneros changed very much. Then they became united with the FAR. The FAR had Marxist origins. The first Montoneros were one thing; the next, different; and the third, yet another. They changed.

But in 1976, if Firmenich was in the army, he should have been able to give them information.

I don't know if there was a contact in 1976. I suppose there was a coincidence of interest to break the government. The real contact was an intelligence activity ... From the end of the fifties, there was the idea that some military officers were attending the School of the Americas in Panama. Many people believe, erroneously, that the military doctrine for confronting the guerrillas was from the United States. The Argentine military was influenced much more by the French Algerian doctrine. There is a good reason why that is so. The Montoneros appeared after the 1970s, and the United States was a failure in Vietnam. At the Colegio Militar we read novels by Jean Latarguy, especially *The Centurions*, about which a film was made, with Anthony Quinn – *The Battle of Algiers* it is called. With this French doctrine, we learned that in order to win the war, the army has to be among the people like a fish in the water, a phrase from Mao Tse-tung. It was necessary to understand the culture. Vietnam was a failure – much napalm, many deaths, without results.

But the French lost Algeria, too.

Yes. But more romantic.

For you yourself, how did the army change after 1975?

The guerrillas ceased to operate in the country. They were absolutely defeated. I believe that the problems I mentioned about the reorientation of the country began to play a dominant role. During the military government, the Russian presence in Argentina became the greatest in all of Argentina's history. It's paradoxical!

How much preparation did the army have for the Malvinas War?

It's a long explanation! The Malvinas problem started in 1962 with the military's internal fights. The infantry in the Malvinas didn't have

real war preparation because they didn't have the necessary arma-
ments for a war. This situation was the result of public relations in
the army in the 1960s. In the 1960s the cavalry, with Lanusse, was
the strong branch. The infantry was stripped of equipment and left as
a fighting unit of the First World War. It could fight, in this context,
in the mountains and in urban battles, but to carry out a conventional
war it lacked the doctrine and the means to fight.

*With the coming of democracy what, in your opinion, is the role of
the army?*

Like that of any armed force in a normal country – provide the country with an instrument to maintain its territorial integrity, and to
provide the state with a negotiating element with other states. It
should be under civilian control, yes, of course. Because we made
mistakes and fell so low, and because we were defeated in a war, we
are the first to be convinced that subordination to constitutional government is essential. We are not saviours of our nation. We are an
institution within the state, with a specified role, and the worst that
can happen to us is to pervert our natural role.

VOICES: MAJOR CARLOS BOBBIO
AND MAJOR ERNESTO BULTRAS

Carlos: The problems in the 1970s were to some extent common to
the lower classes of all Latin American countries, each with its own
peculiarities. These were structural problems, which were worked out
through armed organizations and were broadly influenced by North-
South relations and the Cold War. In Argentina, the United Kingdom
and the Vatican have been the dominant influences, more influential
than the United States. England was always more important in Argentina than the United States, at least until the 1980s. Just to give you
some facts: pressure on Argentina about human rights came from the
United States, France, Italy, and Mexico, while Russia defended
Argentina, which shows that all this is more complex and paradoxical
than people generally believe.

At a world congress of communist parties, the Argentine Communist Party declared that the Argentine generals were progressive and
said it supported General Videla. It is interesting, because the armed
organizations of the ultra-left then branded the Communist Party a
traitor. The Communist Party here was a very direct representative of
the Russian government. One can also see that commercial trade was
not at that moment interrupted. Even during the blocade ordered by U.S.
President Carter against selling grain to the Soviet Union, Argentina

sold grain. There's more. Argentine-Soviet business achieved its highest level during *el Proceso*. And that, too, is paradoxical because the struggle against terrorism was carried out in the name of the anticommunist struggle. The important guerrillas here, the ERP, identified themselves as Trotskyists. And the Montoneros eventually acknowledged they were Marxists.

Ernesto: I don't think the Montoneros were Peronists, but I do think they were a product of Peronism. Peronism was a very broad way of understanding politics, very broad. I believe it was not at all inconvenient for Perón to have them close to him, to describe people like the Montoneros as Peronists. Those very deep contradictions which Peronism has demonstrated are one of the most important characteristics of the movement. Consider the context of the repression. On the one side, the Cold War; on the other side, the reaction of certain ideologies facing the military governments.

In Argentina, since 1930, the institutions were permanently sustained by certain situations of power, but they did not sustain themselves. We cannot speak of democracy in Argentina; we cannot speak of republicanism in Argentina; we cannot speak of Argentina – at least, of the Argentina before this so very violent struggle – as a country with a strong tradition of established institutions. If we understand politics as the economy of violence, then conflicts are resolved through institutions that make it possible to live together without coming into armed conflict. In Argentina, politics of that kind did not exist.

Unlike Carlos, I was brought up with the idea that Peronism was the demon in Argentina. My family were identified as Allies [i.e., pro-Allies], that is to say, in the polemics of the Second World War, "allied and neutral," and in addition, anti-Peronist. It is certain that the persecution that Peronism suffered was one of the most important factors in the explosion of the early 1970s ...

There was a song sung by Che Guevara which goes: "Spain, England, and also Portugal, and now there are the Yankees who wish to run us." So our history was seen as one of continued domination. That, in the 1960s, was reinforced by a new ideological condiment, the dependency theory of Gunder Frank,[4] which was important here. Our perception was that the Soviet Union was not an alternative for the people, but Ho Chi Minh was. Yes, it was Ho Chi Minh, yes, it was Algeria, but no, it was not the Soviet Union that was the point of reference. Nonetheless, the peripheral countries, the countries of the Third World, responded against imperialism. This 1960s ideology, combined with the nearby experience, the Cuban revolution, suggested that, with struggle, a peripheral nation can defeat imperialism.

Carlos: Ideas from the European left were taken on here by nationalist movements. That is, they were taken and decodified in different ways by national movements. The church was to the left of the left and to the right of the right, but it never remained outside. The church channelled ideas. For example, the United States helped introduce Protestant sects or other religions into Central America, yet these same churches provided some leadership to anti-American movements. There was always anticolonialism in Central and South America. One can clearly see the influence of Christian churches in anticolonial movements such as the Zapatistas ...

These struggles were not primarily about poverty. I believe if one analyses the economic situation of Argentina in the 1960s, the conditions were relatively superior to those of today. In the 1960s polio was eliminated, the endemic diseases were pushed back, illiteracy was reduced, and life expectancy increased to about seventy years.

Ernesto: A number of things coincided. I was speaking of the external conditions that gave legitimacy to the armed struggle. For example, the *cordobazo* happened in a place where the working class was the best paid in Latin America. There the economic conditions may have been an influence, but I don't believe they were the most important. And furthermore, the development of the guerrilla movement – when it tried to go into the countryside, to go into Tucumán, to go to the poor provinces – it never had support.

Carlos: The people rejected it.

Ernesto: When they went to do battle, they were resisted by the population.

Carlos: When they tried to spread into rural zones, the poor of the interior resented them.

Ernesto: An officer who was in Tucumán in the armed battle told me that when the guerrillas began the armed subversion in Tucumán, they encountered resistance from the people long before the army came into the fight. The people themselves, without the army, rejected them.

Carlos: You must understand something about armed struggle. Tucumán was chosen because, it is said, the objective conditions in Tucumán were right for guerrilla warfare. The guerrillas chose to go there, but the guerrillas did not begin in Tucumán. The guerrilla was a product of forces outside Tucumán. Guerrilla warfare was the product of the "focus" concept of Guevara, and its members were fundamentally university people of the middle class of Córdoba, a few from Tucumán and Buenos Aires, who decided to go to the mountains. They believed that from there would develop a "focus" that would bring about the revolution. But the guerrillas were basically a middle-class phenomenon, a university, urban phenomenon. They saw themselves as the Jacobite vanguard. There were no representatives of the poor, no expression through a political party that promoted socialism; it was not a movement of the people. There was no relationship between poverty and the existence of a socialist movement.

In Tucumán the situation was not produced by poverty but because the government of General Onganía decided to close the sugar industry, and that generated a major social problem in Tucumán. He shut down the sugar mills and launched a promotion drive to get other industries. This created conditions of instability and antagonism, as much within groups that were economically dependent on the sugar industry as within the unions, but it was a special situation. Well, the guerrillas interpreted this situation as ripe for their revolution, and they lasted there one year. We know the history of what happened; they were defeated in very simple battles.

From what I have read, the number of people in the army who were sent to Tucumán greatly outnumbered the guerrillas, and most of the ERP army was killed. Is that reading correct?

Carlos: Well, the army strongly repressed them, yes, that's correct. I can make an observation about the organization of the mountain company. I was in Tucumán. In February 1975, the first military encounter was an ambush by the guerrillas against the armed forces. It was a success for the guerrillas. Three or four officers and some NCO's were killed. After that, the guerrillas assembled all of their "actives," about a hundred men, to attempt an attack on the military command in Tucumán. As they were marching on their way, the company met a group of soldiers who were working in a school in the rural area, and they became disoriented because they didn't know how many soldiers there were. They tried to attack the school, and they failed; they failed because they were badly trained. They didn't throw the grenades – not even without pulling the pins! They fled, they left, they retreated in disorder. That, I tell you, that failure shows the level of guerrilla organization.

They had actually encountered ten soldiers, and not even one officer: two NCOs and the rest soldiers. Months later, in Acheral, in a zone called Acheral, in Tucumán, the army detected a change of command in the guerrilla company and attacked it. In this action the brother of their leader [Mario Roberto] Santucho died. This was the last important action in Tucumán, all in the year 1975. There were, I believe, sixteen guerrillas engaged in that action, but they were all the chiefs, the leaders. Through its intelligence, the army knew that this was the place where the guerrilla leaders were changing "shifts." During that meeting, when they were changing the leaders, the army, through its intelligence, became aware of it and brought in two regiments of men who successfully attacked. So in Tucumán we encountered few guerrillas, badly trained, and the army sent large forces and eliminated them. But don't underestimate this; it was a great effort by the army and many people died. It was our first battle in this century.

Ernesto: It is not something to be underestimated. But I don't believe that is the point. The point is that what raised the violence to such a degree was the repression at other levels or in earlier episodes. For example, the violence in the rebellion of 1955–56; the 1956 shooting of Peronists; and, later, all the actions of the military governments, the steps they took to proscribe Peronism, to prevent Peronism from getting into power; the repression in Córdoba in 1969, and in Rosario during the same year, when the police even came to kill a student who was protesting; in Corrientes, also, another student was killed by the police. And later, with the government of Lanusse, there occurred an event that was also very important – the "escape from Trelew." This episode generated as much hatred and violence on the part of the guerrillas as all that would happen in Tucumán. All these events, in one way or another, closed off the openings for expression by the various political sectors, and they were closed off by the military government or the government of the day, let us say. Well, it was military governments that brought on this reaction.

Carlos: ... We have discussed how, when the leadership of the Montoneros decided to get out of the country, the second command line approached the intelligence organizations in order to save themselves. These people informed on their subordinates in the chain. That is why there were so many deaths of people who were of no importance, no importance in the "actions." Miguel Bonasso has written about this.[5] Well, in the midst of this, the armed services themselves were engaged in an internal power struggle. The three services were trying to control every institution. For example, there were military personnel in all positions within the Ministry of Education. In the internal struggle for power between groups of teachers, if I wanted your job I didn't go to your boss, I went to the intelligence services and said that you were a Montonero. In this way, the armed organizations were being changed by the methods of the intelligence services. There came a time when the internal issues of every institution were "demonized." Any internal issue of whatever connection, within the union, within the university, within the armed forces, was dealt with by the "special" groups, that is, the intelligence services.

It's a little like this: the methodology implemented by *el Proceso* gave the intelligence groups absolute power. No one controlled them. A general in Córdoba did what he wanted in unions, schools, universities, by using the methods of the "special" groups. It was this non-government that produced the great number of deaths without reason. Many deaths could not be credited to any ideological issue. I have Peronist friends who were killed though they were profoundly anti-Montonero – had fought the Montoneros – and still they were killed. No human rights organizations have asked about them because they were army personnel. What started out as a fight against subversives was extended until every group in the population was threatened. So this was state terrorism.

Let me tell you about General Actis. There is a book about this. General Actis was the organizer of the World Cup soccer championships here in Argentina in 1978. It seems he disagreed with Admiral Lacoste about what type of colour television would be used. He was killed in 1977, and the claim was that it was by a Montonero commando; but everyone accused Admiral Lacoste of being the instigator of that death. Then, in 1978, Sr Soldate, the director of the Buenos Aires electricity supply company, was killed. It was said that a Montonero commando killed Soldate and the navy killed the Montonero commando. But at that time there were virtually no Montoneros in the country! There is another accusation, that Martínez de Hoz was behind the death of Soldate – not to mention the later death of Ambassador Hidalgo Sola – in the struggles for power between people of the navy and the army.

I was in Tucumán when the top union leader of the sugar industry workers, Atilio Santillán, was killed in 1977. [The major errs in the date here. Santillán was in fact killed on 22 March 1976.] Gorriarán Merlo, the most important living leader of the ERP, who is in prison now, a man who has admitted that he killed Anastasio Somoza in Paraguay, the same man who attacked the army post La Tablada in 1989, this man admitted that the ERP killed Atilio Santillán. The ERP believed that Santillán, a much-respected leader, was setting back the revolutionary conditions. The paradox is that Santillán was one of those most firmly opposed to the economic model of Martínez de Hoz and of *el Proceso*. They killed him. The guerrillas killed him, yet the only beneficiary of this death was Martínez de Hoz. The charge against Gorriarán Merlo was always that he was a mercenary. The Sandinistas accuse him of being a traitor. He was active in Nicaragua and was later expelled from there. He killed Anastasio Somoza in Paraguay in a very strange way – that is, with remarkable impunity – and he was always free to be anywhere. Many say that he had also worked for the CIA.

Ernesto: But I don't think the United States had an interest in seeing Somoza dead. Another matter: The left in Argentina maintains that economic power became more concentrated during *el Proceso*, that the military government exercised control over society so that economic policy could be advanced, a policy that allowed those groups to consolidate their power.

The military government, it is my impression, did not have much of an idea about political economics. But those who assisted the military government imposed a minister of the economy who could implement that policy. Military repression on one side and, on the other, the imposition of that policy. Now we call it neoliberalism. Martínez de Hoz abandoned tariffs, and that destroyed the small and medium businesses and ended up causing a tremendous indebtedness, which was what finally brought the nation of Argentina to collapse. Then there was privatization.

Carlos: Petroleum companies, steel companies, aeronautics; automobiles also. Basically, if we could speak of capitalists, it was those who had sufficient economic power to, let's say, change the situation of the country. Why? Because already at this time one could see the difficulty of sustaining the welfare state. We had terrible inflation, and we could not maintain the level of welfare that we used to have. We were in economic crisis from about 1975 to about 1978. The policies used to solve the economic problems then led to greater concentration of economic power.

Ernesto: I don't think we can talk about this simply in class terms. I believe that what was most weighty at that time, in the whole constellation of power, was the state. The state acted as an arbiter and inclined itself toward one sector or another; that was how the direction of economic policy was decided. The middle class and the working class had a pact with the state under Peronism, and then, at other times, the state inclined itself toward the economically dominant sectors – sectors which, comparatively, had no importance because at this time there were no fortunes of more than $300 or $400 million here. Today, one of those who initiated the process of appropriation,

Gregorio Pérez-Companc, has a fortune of $4.5 billion. The concentration of economic power began with the privatizations of Martínez de Hoz. At the very beginning they were small – a hotel in Corrientes – but later they were more significant, for example, Italo, the electricity company. But I don't think foreign powers were directly involved. The process began with the petrodollars from oil in the Middle East. Capital went to the United States and to Europe and from there as loans to Latin America.

Carlos: All groups felt, after the death of Perón, that we were in a situation of economic chaos, a power vacuum, and there was fighting between elites, the guerrillas, the Triple A, and some other marginal groups, which, as I told you, were opportunists and moved from one side to another. We had high inflation and many other problems. All that created a generalized consensus that a military coup was necessary. Everyone expected that the military would take over power and establish order. When the coup occurred, everyone applauded. And at first everything seemed fine, but the military had conceptions about their obligations, notions of their destiny; they came into power to save the country.

Ernesto: Save the nation. But they converted that into a disaster. That military generation was the least qualified of the century. Very low intellectual level and low professional level, a great institutional decadence in all the forces. The hardliners triumphed. Those economic groups tried to just get on with their business. You should realize that compared to what happened more recently under President Menem, the privatization of that time was small stuff. I say this because privatization here has just reached $120 billion. At that time, they were talking about $85 million.

Privatization. Well, it is a big business. When the military government softened the repression, the confrontation with guerrillas, then the majority of the population abandoned the government. Then there were the beginnings of serious confrontations with the unions, which until then had been controlled by repression and co-optation. A more combative class began to emerge. And General Galtieri invented the recovery of the Malvinas as a way, shall we say, to keep his power.

Carlos: I think Galtieri would have thought that winning the war would solve internal problems, but I think the cause of the war had more to do with Galtieri's realignment of Argentina with the United States. Galtieri was received in the United States with honours. He gave a speech to the Argentine army saying, "We belong to the Western world." I believe that someone led him to believe that the United

States would back him if he invaded the Malvinas. I am not blaming the U.S. government, it was how he interpreted it. General Galtieri was not very intelligent.

Ernesto: Ignorant.

Carlos: An absolutely limited person.

Ernesto: A real idiot.

Carlos: Yes, a real idiot [this leads to further discussion of the politics of the Malvinas War] ... The act of recovering the Malvinas was a manifestation of how little ability those commanders had to understand the world. And they made a mistake which cost us dearly, very dearly, which even today we cannot overcome. It happened, in my opinion, because the military recognized that they had lost support. And they were in conflict with one another as well.

Ernesto: The breakdown within the armed forces was built in from the beginning. This agreement that each armed force was to have 33 per cent of the action was a strategy to ensure the spread of responsibility for what was going to occur. Previously, it was General Onganía or General Lanusse who held the power. Now it was the armed forces, which is like saying all or no one. It is not the same when I, General Videla, order a shooting, to say the armed forces are carrying out this *Proceso*. In reality, there was not that much apportioning of power. The government was being carried on by the army. The navy tried to gain more power, making its own policy, its own repression, and the air force went along with those aspects that were convenient for it. But this division of power never actually functioned.

According to today's edition of Página/12, *former Minister of the Interior Harguindeguy said there were archives on the whole repression. Do you think they will come to light?*

Carlos: No. What he said is that he left archives for his successor. He doesn't say they exist. He says he left them. It is probable they did exist – not one archive, not just one, but millions. In each operations centre there surely was a collection of papers. But it is also certain that at the moment the government changed, the papers were destroyed. Harguindeguy was General Videla's minister of the interior. In his ministry, the prosecutor was Dr Estraceda, who later was the person who judged the commanders. He was also the prosecutor of the junta.

But Harguindeguy, the minister of the interior responsible for the internal policy of the country during the time of the worst repression, in 1976–77, was not tried. The trial was absolutely discretional.

At the discretion of whom?

Carlos: Alfonsín.

Ernesto: Alfonsín had a strategy, but the "discretion" was not because of the strategy. The strategy was to judge according to three levels of responsibility: those who gave the orders, those who complied with them, and those who exceeded them [discussion continues regarding Alfonsín's strategy and outcomes] ...

Carlos: I would like to return to the issue of Mario Firmenich and the origin of the Montoneros. I would like to clarify the issue of the relationship of the intelligence services to Firmenich. The military government of General Onganía was composed principally of nationalist military men who opposed General Aramburu. On the whole, they were army officers, but there were also air force personnel who opposed General Aramburu. These people greatly resented Aramburu because in 1955, on replacing General Lonardi, Aramburu had discarded nationalists in the army, even those who had participated in significant ways in the overthrow of Perón; and because in 1956, in an attempt to gain power, Aramburu had shot military men who were not even Peronists. These military men who were thrown out by Aramburu in 1955, who had comrades killed by Aramburu, were in the government of Onganía. Ideologically they were nationalists, and they shared certain anti-imperialist ideas. They surrounded themselves with a group of young people, many of whom later became Montoneros. An example, to name one, is Horacio Verbitsky.[6] After the *cordobazo*, the ousting of Onganía became the topic. And to promote a transition to elections, General Aramburu appeared as the possible leader of the changeover. The kidnapping of Aramburu occurred within this context of people who had a deep hatred of him.

The first group of Montoneros comprised twelve members, none of whom were of Peronist origin. They were nationalists. The name taken by the unit was Juan José Valle, after a non-Peronist general who was shot by Aramburu in 1956. The first leader of the Montoneros was Fernando Abal Medina, who was part of a nationalist group that was working with a nationalist leader, Sanchez Sorondo (who is still alive), and they published a very important periodical at that time called *Azul y Blanco* [Blue and White].

The kidnapping of Aramburu is a strange and mysterious event. It is said that when Aramburu was kidnapped, he left his house accompanied by people he knew. He was not taken by force from his house. So there is the possibility that the intelligence services took him – people he knew – and that these services later delivered him to this Montonero group. The people who were seen with Aramburu when he was leaving his house were people much older than the Montoneros were at that time. Abal Medina was twenty or twenty-one years old then. That's what is said by Aramburu's people. Different authors suggest different possibilities.

Aramburu's people claimed that Onganía's government was behind the kidnapping. A little later, the Montoneros claimed responsibility. But at first they did not identify themselves as Peronists. The actual existence at that moment of the Montoneros is doubtful. Well, these Montoneros then had to achieve a military action to prime their existence, and they carried out the occupation of a city in the province of Buenos Aires, which ended badly. This was the city of Garín. It's said that this "occupation" had to be carried out to dissipate the political pressure from Onganía's government, which was staggering from the effects of the case of Aramburu. The Montoneros came up with the Garín raid to give political space to the government.[7] A few months later, Fernando Abal Medina died in a confrontation with the police while going to collect money for the death of Aramburu.

Pay for the kidnapping?

Ernesto: Yes, clearly. But what happened? A businessman who was supposed to deliver the payment did not come. Instead he called the police, and these two, Ramus and Abal Medina, were killed.

Carlos: Well, here is the explanation. The accusation made in all these books, the two books from different political sectors, is that it was the government that was paying money so that these people would leave the country. As they couldn't pay it directly, they paid it through a third party. One member of the third party betrayed them, called the police, and that's when Ramus and Abal Medina died. This businessman was killed by the Montoneros a few months later, a crime that has never been explained since then. Why? Because the person who killed him committed suicide after the killing. And he was one of the members of the twelve who first formed the Montonero unit. His surname was Cruz.

A very important fact is that before Aramburu's death, the Montoneros had no contact with Perón. It was fully a year later before they had the first contact, and what is certain is that until 1974 the army did not treat Aramburu as a martyr to subversion, as a military man killed by the subversives. It was all very strange. The Montoneros emerged in 1974 with an account of the death of Aramburu. They spoke of a death, of a trial, and of Aramburu dying with total dignity. They confirmed that it was they who had killed him. Then the army said that the first death in the struggle against subversion was Aramburu, and they gave the name Aramburu to several army units. The Montoneros needed to reaffirm that they existed, and the army needed to reaffirm a martyr in the struggle, in the struggle against the subversives. But the versions of these books say, on the contrary, that Aramburu died of a heart attack in a military hospital. It is not so surprising. The nationalism in the military had a way of thinking that was very similar to that of the first Montoneros. They have the same ideological origin. They aren't Peronists. They are nationalists, and there is an identity of interests, especially in the case of Aramburu. Those ties continue, and there were always contacts between the army and the Montoneros.

On each occasion, as when Carlos Gustavo Ramus died, Firmenich left, running. He ran before every battle. When Abal Medina entered the bar and was killed along with Ramus, somehow Firmenich saved himself. Some time later, Firmenich was having coffee with Carlos Capuano Martínez, another of the leaders of the first group of Montoneros, and Firmenich left to go to the bathroom, and the police arrived and killed Capuano Martínez. In a short time, all the first leaders died except Firmenich and Norma Arrostito. She was killed at the ESMA several years later. After that the FAR joined the Montoneros, but by that time none of the original leaders remained. Later, there were contacts between Firmenich and Massera in Europe. These generated a type of peace treaty which they signed in 1978 ...

Today most of those who participated in the repression are out of the army. Contrary to what happened in the navy, the army retired everyone who was accused of human rights violations. In the navy, those "with a taste for Masserism" still have power. And here comes the problem of Adolfo Francisco Scilingo. When two members of the navy were to be promoted to admiral, Congress blocked the promotions because of their human rights records. Then these two officers presented themselves before Congress and said, "The navy acts in an institutional way. If they deny us the promotion, all of those who are admirals today are as responsible as we are, and more, because they were our superiors." The head of the navy then withdrew the request for the promotion of those two captains.

And then Scilingo appeared with his story about dropping live bodies into the sea, which he told to the journalist Horacio Verbitsky.

What do I think? I think that internal affairs in the navy provoked the following issue, which is what Scilingo illustrates: "We know many things that could be prejudicial to all of you. If you don't let us be promoted, we will tell all we know." The navy deceitfully authorized a charge against Scilingo for fraud, and Scilingo went to jail. But Scilingo made his accusations to Verbitsky. After this, all the human rights organizations began to offer money to "repenters." For example, a retired army sergeant who was getting a very low salary says, "I saw this happen ... in that place," and for that they pay him. Someone pays him, and he comes out talking.

But actually, the accusations about human rights and of CONADEP and the trials covered practically all the cases of human rights violations there were. The army made a public declaration of self-criticism about the procedures it had used in the 1970s. General Balza made a public apology for the methodology used.

CONCLUSION

CHAPTER 17

Conclusion

Argentina's generals had undertaken the war against communist subversion with messianic fervour. Apparently convinced that they were at the front of a Third World War, and blessed by their Catholic bishops, they turned counterrevolutionary war into a Christian crusade.

Theirs was not a haphazard attack against enemies, nor was it the work of madmen: it was a carefully planned, very well organized, even bureaucratic, response to a perceived threat. The killing of subversives was an exercise in logistics, so much so that excellent minds were put to the task of finding improved means of disposing of bodies. Throwing comatose victims from planes was a rational solution – the technological counterpart to gas chambers in the Nazi regime. The gathering of intelligence was a vital component of the battle, and torture for the purpose of obtaining information was an essential part of the process. Once the enemy was identified – young men and women, union members, and their allies, who had subversive thoughts, read subversive books, exchanged subversive ideas, met with one another in subversive collaboration, wore clothes or haircuts that were immoral – then it was simply a matter of capturing them and eventually putting them away so that society would not suffer any further from their existence. They were enemies; they were not people. This was war, a dirty war, and in war nasty things are necessary.

As the army officers attested, a revolutionary war necessitates the use of unusual methods. Soldiers are not organized, supervised, or made accountable in the way they are during a conventional war. They are, instead, thrust into entirely new situations where the rules are unclear and the rewards ambiguous. Stealing from victims is more profitable if the victims have something worth stealing; thus, the net widens. Killing subversives is fine, but there is no clear definition of who they are; so the net widens further to include all possibilities. Torturing people can become addictive. Once the initial hurdles are passed, what is to prevent a torturer from doing all manner of things that could not be done in civilized society? Rape and sodomy become commonplace. Finding new ways to demean and psychologically destroy captives is perhaps more entertaining. Controlling a woman as she gives birth, killing her, and then giving the baby to "better" parents might be viewed as generous behaviour by minds already twisted either by blind faith in the cause or by the ugliness of their profession.

As has happened in so many other cases of state terrorism, an intelligence service emerged that could not be controlled by its political masters. Indeed, as the informants told us, it killed soldiers and priests as well as known revolutionaries. Anyone whose job was coveted could be accused of subversion, and the intelligence services were eager to find new victims, since their very existence depended on the propagation of the belief that subversion had infiltrated all institutions of the society.

Into this concoction yet another ingredient was added: personal ambition. The original agreement within the armed forces was to kill subversives. But from the very beginning, the junta members were dealing with the ambitions of their various members and the conflicting ambitions of three armed services plus the police. When someone with huge ambitions is in a powerful position, as was Emilio Massera, it is not surprising that he uses the intelligence services and clandestine torture chambers to rid the country of personal enemies and potential competitors. Thus it is that a campaign that ostensibly had a straightforward political objective supported many other agendas.

NECESSARY BUT INSUFFICIENT CONDITIONS

The historical record that we examined in the first several chapters, together with the explanations and revelations provided by interviewees, have informed us of a number of contextual conditions that were important to the course of events, but they are not in themselves explanations of what happened.

Above all, it is obvious that state terrorism of the kind witnessed in this society cannot occur unless there already exists an armed force that is physically and organizationally capable of governing the society and imposing terrorism. A society without such a military establishment might engage in all manner of violent behaviour, but state terrorism is not among the options. Most of the literature on state terrorism takes such armed force for granted, yet if one tries to explain societies that have not been subjected to similar state terrorism or even state violence, the lack of military capacity becomes one apparent reason. Further than this, we would be wise to consider what was the normal function of military forces in the 1970s. They were trained to kill enemies. But Argentina had not had any actual battles in the lifetime of the personnel then employed in the military services. Their raison d'être was at stake; if they did not have an external enemy, they needed an internal one. As it happened, they had many times targeted internal enemies, so in this respect the situation was not novel.

The history of Argentine society forms a backdrop to the events of the 1970s. It is a violent history, a history in which the military forces played a central role as enforcers of sometimes arbitrary law. A strong civil society never emerged. Between the state and the extended family there were few institutions. The Catholic Church became a state church, never genuinely independent, though its fortunes vis-à-vis whoever controlled the state varied from time to time. Universities were never fully autonomous; one government after another intervened in their affairs and even in their curriculum. Agro-business was embedded in the state, and small businesses were continually under the thumb of the state. Even unions became centralized within the state, bargaining through the state rather than in independent economic forums. Before the coup there was one human rights association and scarcely any other independent nongovernmental voluntary organizations. Political parties were not well developed organizations, and the full spectrum of political opinion was never represented in those that were active. The legal system, too, was weak, and what existed was gutted under the many military governments and under Peron's midcentury governments. Finally, the mass media were notably intimidated by the violence of many governments. In short, civil society was weak in Argentina in the decades prior to the 1976 coup, and this implies that there were no organized, durable sources of legitimate dissent.

Immediately before the coup the society experienced political anarchy and economic turmoil. These conditions, combined with violence and the lack of institutional stability, were fundamental reasons for the consent of the governed to a military coup. Our interviews and the excerpts from mass media that we included in this text clearly indicate a high degree of general public support for the imposition of military rule. A substantial part of the population expected the military forces to create personal security, stop the guerrilla war, and establish conditions for economic recovery.

These, then, were the preconditions. The military force took over with the consent of the governed under conditions that were otherwise intolerable for most citizens. These were necessary conditions for what happened later, but we cannot explain state terrorism in contrast to, say, state authoritarianism or even state violence, on the basis of these preconditions. More than this was involved in the development of a terrorist regime.

EXPLANATIONS BASED
ON THE INTERVIEWS

Our interviewees provided four possible explanations beyond attributing the events to a general historical predisposition toward violence:

1 This was a holy war: from the military perspective it was necessitated by the militancy of revolutionary groups who threatened the welfare of the entire society.
2 The objective was to impose economic restructuring. Restructuring required defeat of the union movement, downsizing of the labour force and its wage claims, and elimination of opponents. One variant of this theory is that neoliberalism was imposed on the society by the dominant national class together with external powers.
3 This was a displaced war between the Cold War powers, with Argentina being used as a testing ground for the Third World War.
4 This was a struggle for power between fractions of the middle class, with the state at the centre.

Let us consider each of these explanations in turn.

Holy War

The military saw themselves as saviours of the nation. They had been called on many times, and to their way of thinking, they had always come to the aid of their country. As noted, they had never participated in military battles, so the only function they had had over their entire institutional lifetime was to quell internal subversion. Their assumption of sacred duties was supported by an authoritarian Catholic Church. Since the guerrillas played at being Marxists, the stage was set for the military forces to rid society of enemies of Christianity as well as of capitalism.

The military and the church officers understood that this was an ideological war. Our interviews make this very clear: it was Marxists, not just people with guns, who were the enemy. We encountered a curious anomaly in the interviews. Church and military interviewees mentioned Antonio Gramsci, the Italian philosopher who was imprisoned under Mussolini.[1] They told us that they believed the students were fighting according to principles enunciated by Gramsci. But in fact the students rarely mentioned Gramsci. Students told us that they read Lenin, Trotsky, and Marx, together with scholars who are not elsewhere considered to be left-wing revolutionaries, such as Claude Lévi-Strauss and Sigmund Freud, or the poet Pablo Neruda. But not Gramsci, whose ideas about cultural hegemony and revolution had no recognizable impact on the youth of Argentina in the early 1970s. One student alone bordered on a Gramscian idea when she said she thought that the revolution should totally change society and social relations. But her husband of the time, a more powerful revolutionary leader, pooh-poohed her naiveté. In his view, the revolution would merely reverse the hierarchy, and it would be the workers' turn to dominate – certainly not a profound insight from Gramsci.

Gramsci argued that intellectuals can play two roles: as justifiers of the capitalist system or as its critics. Where most cooperate in the system, they contribute to the hegemonic culture that sustains it. Only by attacking the cultural context can workers and their intellectual allies gain the strength to overcome capitalism. For Gramsci, the objective was to destroy capitalism, not merely to gain better working conditions within it. This, then, was a cultural rather than economistic version of both capitalism and revolutionary opposition to capitalism.

The possible explanation for the stronger attachment to a Gramscian explanation amongst the military and church interviewees than amongst the former guerrilla members may be that the military and church leaders sought out a communist theorist who recognized that battles of this kind were ultimately ideological, and that they landed on Gramsci even though there was no evidence that students of the time had read his work. Gramsci was among the proscribed books – but so was Saint-Exupéry. An alternative explanation is that this view is relatively recent, a retrospective rationalization. The current theory might be that they, the military, had engaged in a military battle against forces they then perceived to be armed combatants; and that had they known what they now know, they would have recognized that the more important battle was cultural, in which case the weapons had to be contrary ideas.

Whatever the reason for the introduction of Gramsci into our interviews, the military and church interviewees clearly understood in 1997 and 1998 that the battle of the epoch was ideological, not military. The churchman who admitted frankly that the battle was against Marxists, not just guerrillas, did not say so, but the implication was that had it been only against revolutionaries carrying arms, there would have been no need for secrecy, concentration camps, intelligence services, book burning, or the torture of intellectuals. His statement was supported by other interviewees, who noted that for every armed revolutionary there was a big support group of ideologues. And one military officer said bluntly that there was no point in just killing the man with the gun; the military also had to kill the one with ideas.

If, as so many inputs suggested, one or more of the Montonero leaders were collaborating with the military forces between 1975 and 1977, then the military had no excuse for carrying on the war. They had decimated the only genuine Marxist army the year before the coup. They had killed a large number of young people and union members in the first few months of the dictatorship, and with the collaborators on side, they could have killed all remaining Montoneros by the end of 1976 (indeed, they may have done so). But it was precisely because it was a war against ideas that the terrorism continued for at least two more years. Convinced that they were engaged in a massive ideological war, the military kept enlarging the potential pool of subversives. *El Proceso* really was a process, in more senses than intended by the label: it was a process by which a military force constantly increased its power over the society by redefining ideological sins.

The holy war explains the motivation of the military and the support of the church and many citizens. It also provides some insight into why the society was unable to control the violence by less extreme means. Other societies in the same period – notably Germany and Italy – coped with revolutionary groups without creating a massive network of concentration camps, torture chambers, and murders. Military men claim that revolutionary groups were smaller in those societies. That may be so, but the revolutionary forces in Argentina were actually a small fraction of the society, and they consisted in large part of teenagers. They were badly armed and poorly trained, and the only revolutionary army that ever actually existed, the ERP, was destroyed in a few months at Tucumán by a regular army.

In any event, if the excuse for a bloodbath was that the military forces were unable otherwise to capture urban revolutionaries and subject them to legal proceedings, then it is, in effect, an admission of their own corruption and incompetence. The same military forces had controlled the state for the previous four decades. In short, they could have controlled the guerrillas by other means had they been intent on controlling guerrillas. The fact was that they were engaged in an ideological battle, and the objective was not simply to control guerrillas but to eradicate ideas. That is absolutely basic to any explanation of why Argentina experienced state terrorism.

Monetarism/Neoliberalism

We have to ask, however, which ideas were central to this mission. Clearly, Marxism was the perceived enemy, but what was the ideology that the military championed? As noted in chapter 12, David Pion-Berlin argues that it was monetarism, and his view is seconded by some of our interviewees. He contends that this economic theory was capable of motivating people to take drastic action in order to implement it. Downsizing the labour force, destroying union power, and decreasing wages would all be consistent with monetarist policies. But monetarism also advocates removal of tariffs and protections for domestic capital and, most particularly, the reduction of the state in economic affairs. Although the economic ministers under both Isabel Perón and the military junta attempted to impose selected monetarist solutions on the economy, neither succeeded, because their masters blocked change where it affected their own interests. The military factories, for an outstanding example, were never privatized. This is problematic for an argument that makes the content of monetarism the core of the military belief system.

One might argue that the military, and the Peronists, indulged in a modified form of state terrorism at an earlier stage when they imposed the opposite economic policy on the nation. Could it be that import substitution has a similar capacity to energize militars and politicians? As well, in the more general case, the century witnessed state terrorism in the name of yet another economic theory – communism. The differences between these three economic theories is so great that one is hard put to discover a common thread that would have the same electrifying impact on military minds. The obvious alternative explanation is that it is not the content of the economic theory that motivates the behaviour; it is the willingness to believe that any single solution to massive problems is capable of saving the nation. Intolerance for nonbelievers in economic theories may well be as strong as intolerance for nonbelievers in religious theories.

If it was not the content of the theory but, rather, the conviction that a particular economic policy is superior to all others, then the extreme actions are more understandable. What we now call neoliberal theories were beginning to be popular at that time. Chile, in particular, had already started to implement them. True, Chile had no success with them until much later, in the closing phase of Pinochet's regime and the early years of democracy. But in 1976 the next decade of Chilean history was not known; all that was apparent was that brutal methods were succeeding in eliminating opposition to economic restructuring. The socialists were being defeated. That might well have been enough for the junta, and when it employed Martínez de Hoz as its minister of economy, this need not have been because of devotion to monetarism (even if he and his cohort were devotees of the theory) so much as opposition to socialism as the junta understood that term.

There is little doubt that the armed forces provided the security for restructuring. They killed the potential opponents and created such a reign of terror that no new opponents emerged, and they maintained "order" even if that required the abrogation of law. In particular, they dramatically undermined the strength of unions and in this respect created a more hospitable climate for foreign investment. The destruction of unions was clearly intended: it began under the Isabel Perón regime and continued through the next several years. The army also ensured that foreign investment could operate in the domestic market on the same conditions as national companies. This destroyed small national companies but provided entrée into the global marketplace for Argentine capital.

These conditions suggest that the restructuring may have been orchestrated by the national financial elite and global-level capital. The problem is that if we entertain the theory that the financial elite was behind state terrorism, we would have to suppose that the military forces were subservient to it. If the military, while in power over the previous four decades, had acted in the interests of such an elite, this might be a credible theory. But the military, as we have learned, was relatively autonomous, and in any case the bourgeoisie was so fragmented that the military would have received conflicting messages had it been intent on heeding this class as its master. Several decades earlier, the military had imposed import-substitution policies contrary to the interests and opposition of the financial-industrial elite. Since the opposition failed to bring down military government, we have to conclude that the military was sufficiently powerful to survive opposition from the economic leaders of the society.

That said, is there evidence of pressure imposed by multinational corporations with which the financial elite was affiliated? There were American, Italian, and French automobile-production units in Córdoba and the province of Buenos Aires during the dictatorship. There were other companies as well, but Argentina was not the recipient then (or now) of massive foreign investment. Its population was similar to that of Canada; it did not constitute a large aggregate market. It was remote – and, in that respect, disadvantaged relative to Canada. Its companies enjoyed no imperial tariff preferences (as did Canada in its formative period). It had no valuable minerals, nothing unique that international capitalism coveted. True, it might have received more investment had it not contained a very powerful union bureaucracy, but there is no proof of that. The foreign automobile companies had at least as great an impact on the union movement as the unions had on their companies. Finally, Argentina had corrupt governments before as well as during the dictatorship. In short, there seems to be very little to go on by way of explaining why Argentina would have been "chosen" by international capital to experiment with monetarism.

In connection with these arguments, one is obliged to look at the actual record. The experiment in monetarism failed. The policies were inconsistent, unpredictable, and frequently self-defeating. The country's financial elite was more inclined to move its money abroad than to invest in Argentina, and foreign companies did not line up for entry. If these capitalists were actively and consciously behind state terrorism, then the most one can say is that they were unwilling to follow through with serious economic restructuring; and if they were not behind it, as seems much more probable, we are left with a military force that wanted to restructure the economy while purifying society. That force simply grabbed a policy it thought would work. This does not preclude influence exerted by Martínez de Hoz and his friends; but the choice might as easily have been influenced by the Chilean example or by Argentine economists who had graduated from the University of Chicago's Department of Economics. Also, it does not preclude acceptance of benefits by foreign or domestic companies from policies that repressed workers and extinguished unions. As described by some of our interviewees who were incarcerated under PEN, their bosses in just such companies had supported repressive policies.

There is one further argument along these lines. It is that international capital, in the form of the World Bank, the IMF, or bilateral and multilateral aid programs, was willing to provide development loans to the military government, but not to Peronist or Marxist governments. That this was so is uncontestable and is borne out in the contrast between the loans made to Chile under Allende and under Pinochet. International financiers are supporters of capitalism and stability. To the degree that these organizations at that time advocated or made loans contingent on monetary policies that downsized unions, wages, and welfare programs, they represented the monetary theories of the time. No one has suggested that the World Bank advocated or was an active party to state terrorism, but a more credible argument was advanced by some of our informants – that the general policies of international financiers and aid programs pushed the society toward such drastic measures.

Strategic Defence Concerns

Our military informants introduced the possibility that external powers used Argentina as a testing ground for the Third World War. In their view, the Argentine military rid the southern cone of communists, yet North Americans and Europeans turned against them after the war. It is certainly true that French and then American military forces encouraged Latin American military officers to take up the "revolutionary" war against communism. Several of our interviewees discussed this, and the objective record supports their contention that external military forces, and presumably the political forces that supported them, put resources into inculcating anticommunism in Latin American military forces. The officers learned methods of fighting revolutionaries, torturing people, and disposing of bodies, as well as the ideological rationale for so acting.

But there is an ironic flaw in the reasoning. It consists of the fact that it was the Soviet Union, not the United States and France, that championed the cause of the military in international forums. As noted in chapter 12, the United States policy toward Argentina was always contradictory and ambiguous. On the one hand, Carter's human rights initiatives became public condemnations of Argentina's military government. On the other hand, economic aid not only continued but increased, and the military was well kept by American money. And this was so even while American businesses were disinvesting in the country. The explanation for these contradictions seems to be that different interest groups within the American government acted independently. The USSR, meanwhile, championed the military, because it needed a source of wheat after the U.S. embargo closed off other sources; and in general, it opposed investigations of human rights cases by the United Nations. If the two superpowers of the Cold War era were fighting it out in Argentina, neither of them was acting consistently with the supposed objectives of the war.

A sidelight to this debate has come to light only recently. American scholars have long assumed that the contras of Nicaragua were created and funded initially by the United States under the Reagan government, with Argentina joining the U.S. counterinsurgency battle later on. But information more recently brought forward argues in favour of a very different version – that it was the Argentine army that established the contras. The United States came in later; and after the United States was fully engaged, the Argentine military forces were relegated to secondary status.[2]

The evidence in favour of this interpretation appears to be strong, and it supports the contention that the Argentine military was absolutely convinced that it was fighting the Third World War against communist subversion and that the war had to be fought throughout the Hispanic world. But the example raises doubts about the primary role of the United States in sustaining that obsession. It seems likely that the United States, in its contradictory fashion, indoctrinated military forces throughout the Latin American countries to adopt the Cold War religion, but was not as active a leader in physically eradicating communists as these converts expected.

Intraclass Power Struggle

The broad middle class of Argentina in the 1970s encompassed the military forces, the priesthood, the academic establishments, the substantial public service bureaucracy, independent professionals, small business, and a layer of union bureaucrats. The institutional nexus of this class was the state itself. Much of the class was organized within or around the state; much of its business was with or on behalf of the state; and a large part of it was employed by the state. A restructuring of the economy would necessarily begin with the state and would challenge many of these people. Restructuring from the right would involve, first, dismemberment of the Peronist centralized union bureaucracy, downsizing of welfare and education systems; and then privatization and the removal of tariffs. ·

To suggest that an underlying reason for this whole tragic episode was an intraclass power struggle is not likely to win friends amongst most of our interviewees. But it does make some sense of the events. The military forces had taken over the reins of the society in the 1930s, instead of permitting an elected government to work with capital and labour as occurred in similar settler countries. By the 1960s, the modernization process headed by the military forces was stuck. One military government after another was locked in battle with unions that were centred in the state. Yet when new American-style unions entered the picture, along with huge automobile industries, both the military and the Peronist unions found them threatening. All the middle-class groups that were organized within the state were afraid of social change. This was the beginning of the violence. The students came later, and they moved into a political vacuum where neither the military nor the unions could control the population, and where neither global nor domestic capital was capable of controlling the military and the unions.

A somewhat different scenario on restructuring involves recognition that this society (like many others that have undergone similar cataclysmic events) was unevenly developed as an industrial society. It had much of what contemporary theorists call "modernity" in its major cities. Science and rational bureaucracies were part of that modernity; modern technologies were embedded in its automobile, chemical, and some other industries. But at the same time, there was growing economic inequality throughout the society; some rural areas were still quasi-feudal, and in most such areas, strongmen *caudillos* still held a good deal of power. Fundamentalist and ultramontanist Catholicism was the religion of the people, and the church was everywhere extremely powerful. Secularism had not made inroads even in the universities.

One of the hallmarks of modernity is that bureaucracies are not headed by charismatic leaders; they are run by career administrators and in accordance with explicit rules in the context of wage labour and capitalism. But Argentina was still in thrall to Juan Perón's charisma and to the icon Evita. Capitalism was embedded but was persistently thwarted by state intervention, wage bargaining through the state, and state-owned or state-controlled economic units. This was not a fully modern society, and its uneven development may well be a crucial element in our explanation.

We have used the term "uneven development" rather than "underdevelopment" because the latter is part of the vocabulary of a major theoretical school in Latin America, mentioned by several of our interviewees and popular in Argentine universities of the early 1970s. As put forward by André Gunder Frank,[3] the argument is that Latin American societies were progressively underdeveloped by the actions of international capital originating in northern rich countries. The rich extracted resources and labour, and in the process impoverished the host societies. In this theory, the word "underdevelop" becomes a verb, and the nouns are the agencies of international capital. The theory has applicability to Argentina during its early history, when British and other European capitalists extracted wealth from the agribusinesses and infrastructure. But that period had passed into history by the time of the 1930 coup, and from that time forward the military forces had substantially more influence over development than external capital did. The military exercised this role, of course, within a capitalist world context, but its geopolitical situation within that context was not the same as Chile's (with its mineral wealth) or Venezuela's (with its oil reserves). Argentina after about 1930 was not a satellite, a dependency, or a branch plant of international capitalism.

This argument, then, is that Argentina was a semimodern, unevenly developed society which, through decades of military rule, had come to an economic standstill. The economy was not only failing to grow; industrial wealth was retreating from its factories. Reconstruction was essential, but there were opposing views on how and in whose inter-ests it might be undertaken. Private capital was not well organized, and much of it was so externally oriented that its owners were unwill-ing, and possibly unable, to attend to the problems of their own society. There ensued a power struggle between the major institution-alized fractions of the middle class, each armed with a powerful and all-encompassing ideology. At that moment in history, the military won with its superior weapon – state terrorism.

EPILOGUE: THE CONTENDERS AND THEIR FATE

Our interviews have built up a picture of the contending forces in the battle for state power. Here we briefly review what we learned in the interviews and ruminate on the changed circumstances in the 1990s.

The Guerrillas

The picture our respondents gave was tragic. These movements were composed of middle-class young people with two compelling beliefs: that they could overturn the military government and transform society; and that they were invincible. The former was their response to exclusion from political involvement in legitimate political parties: the institutions for peaceful transformation did not exist. Having grown up under repressive, authoritarian military dictatorships, they had no personal experience of a secular, liberal, pluralistic society. They could not imagine such a constellation. They had no choice, then, but to engage in violence if they wanted to achieve their version of utopia.

The second belief represented a curious naiveté about consequences and responsibility. As one informant put it, "We said, well what could they do to you if you were caught and you were pregnant?" And as one of the military respondents put it, "They thought they could kidnap and kill people, and there would be no punishment." The reasons for the irresponsibility on the one hand and the heavy-handed punishment on the other lie somewhere deep within the authoritarian Catholic Argentine culture.

The PRT/ERP organizations were virtually destroyed early in the battle. One of our informants told of going to Tucumán in 1975 knowing full well that the end was upon them. Her lover was killed, and she was spirited out of the country – which is why she lived to tell the tale. Many others died. The Montoneros turned out to be a great movement of idealistic teenagers headed by cynical and apparently incompetent leaders. Whether or not Mario Firmenich was in the employ of the armed forces, and whether or not the leadership as a whole was collaborating with the army, these leaders did not show concern for their followers. They went underground when thousands of young people were vulnerable, visible proponents of their ideology. They watched as these children were systematically kidnapped and killed. Then they left the country. How they escaped is not known. They are still living.

The Unions

Our informants and the historical record told us about the turmoil within the union movement. The central problems were structural, not ideological, but they were embedded within an ideological context. The structure involved unions in traditional sectors that were in rapid decline. The economic sectors were losing ground, and technological change was causing a decrease in demand for labour. More modern sectors were growing, and very different unions were being established within them. The Peronist structure was disintegrating. These vast structural changes were encased within the struggles over Peronism and American-style business unionism. We heard of these battles in the interviews, but they were never expressed in terms of the union structure; rather, in terms of ideology and personalities.

In the long run, from the perspective of the military, it mattered not whether the unions were Peronist or modern; both impeded the extraction of surplus value from workers (as a Marxist unionist would have described it). Destruction of the entire union movement was one of the military's objectives after the coup. This, indeed, is a major argument in favour of the hypothesis that neoliberalism was the motivating force for the military. We have argued that reconstruction was part of the objective but that the original motivating force was ideological opposition to Marxism and communism. Neoliberalism and the destruction of unions was an outgrowth of the original ideology.

Unions in the 1990s are much smaller organizations than before the cataclysmic events of the 1970s. There is greater diversity in the union movement. Pictures of Evita and Juan Perón, however, still adorn union offices, and many of the old enmities are still evident in union affairs.

The Church

The Argentine Catholic Church played a pivotal role in the murder of thousands of young believers, union members, and even its own priests. There is substantial evidence that ranking officers of the church informed on them, gathered information about these people, and collaborated with the military in ways that led to their destruction. The question is not whether but why.

Again, we turn to ideology, and again the ideology was a profound antipathy to communism and Marxism, as defined by the church. But why did the church so deeply oppose these ideologies? Three reasons emerged in our interviews: one, that the church was a middle-class institution, and the middle class was threatened by Marxist ideas; second, that the church would have lost its hold on the population if Marxism had become a dominant belief system; and third, that the church had considerable property interests that would have been jeopardized by implementation of socialist ideas of property. A simpler version of all three is to say that the church defended the status quo, because in the existing social and economic structure it, as an institution, and its functionaries, as privileged members of the society, were beneficiaries.

The interviews demonstrated a profound schism between conservative and Third World priests, as well as between both and the middle group who dared to speak on behalf of pluralism and democracy. At the time, priests were almost obliged to choose between extremes; moderation was deemed as sinful as opposition to the conservative church. Thus was the church both a perpetrator of authoritarianism and a victim of it. As an institution it belonged to an earlier era, but its impact on the society continued even while it demonstrated its incapacity to deal with the tragic events occurring in its parishes.

The Military

The defeat in the battle for the Malvinas was the terminal chapter for the military dictatorship. Free elections were called in 1983. Raúl Alfonsín led the Radical Party to victory and instituted the National Commission on Disappeared People (CONADEP) to investigate the disappearances. Various conspiracies and small rebellions in the armed forces sustained tense relations between the government and the military but did not stop the investigations. Alfonsín initially gave the Supreme Military Council the task of conducting trials of military officers; but after lengthy delays the council claimed, in September 1984, that it could not judge the alleged crimes because they had been committed during a war against subversion. By this time the commission's hearings, which were open to the public and televised, had generated a strong public revulsion to the military. This grew with the publication and wide dissemination of *Nunca Más*. Human rights organizations had been energetic and tenacious in gathering evidence for the commission hearings, and they insisted, now with public support, that the military be tried in civilian courts. Trials were at length started in the Buenos Aires federal appeals court during 1985.

The months of testimony were punctuated by bombs in courthouses, threats against prosecution witnesses, and other violence, but eventually the case against military leaders for crimes against humanity resulted in sentences for some of the most notorious. The military defence on the grounds of a "dirty war" was rejected for the 1976–83 period. Ignorance of "excesses" was disproven in specific cases. More generally, the argument that the events had been the direct result of orders given by military leaders was sustained. Prosecution arguments about an interservice and even international conspiracy, however, were rejected.

Five of the junta were given variable sentences: General Jorge Videla and Roberto Viola, Admirals Emilio Massera and Armando Lambruschini, and Air Force Brigadier Orlando Agosti. Ramón Camps, military commander of the Buenos Aires police, was found guilty of six hundred homicides and sentenced to twenty-five years. Other arrests and trials followed throughout 1986. The courts were flooded with claims against military officers in middle as well as high ranks. Tensions in the military were high, threats and violence were endemic, and the government finally introduced two laws to limit the court process. The first was the *Punto Final*. This established a time limit of sixty days for processing future charges, which effectively pre-empted the trials of well over a thousand accused persons. Child stealing was the one crime exempted from this restriction. The second law was the *Obediencia Debida*, which limited the definition of crimes committed by persons acting under orders from higher ranking officers. Human rights organizations protested mightily against both laws, and two judges resigned, but the laws were passed in a context that included threats of military uprisings and also continuing economic decline.[4]

Alfonsín's government lost the 1989 election. The new Peronist government, led by Carlos Menem, granted amnesty to all military detainees and the few guerrilla leaders who also were imprisoned. However, military budgets were gradually cut back. Many generals and other high-ranking officers were obliged to retire. Some of the torturers were weeded out, especially in the army.

In 1998 the Abuelas succeeded in having charges laid against Generals Videla and Bignone and Admiral Massera for the kidnapping of infants, this being the one crime exempted from the laws and amnesty of the late 1980s.

Militars who were active during the dictatorship still claim that they did their duty in defence of the nation and Christianity, and we heard some of this in interviews. But in other interviews we learned of a new generation that has ascended to high posts in the military, and its leaders do not see themselves as saviours of the nation. They say they are content to be servants of the democratic state. Democracy is not yet robust in Argentina, but this transition is a dramatic shift in a culture so long subordinated to military authority.

MÁS QUE MEMORIA

People living near detention centres during the terror could hear the screams in the night, see the police and military cars bringing in prisoners, and were themselves subjected to controls on their movements in the vicinity of the detention buildings. Individuals were picked up by squads of armed but nonuniformed militia in their homes or on the streets, and neighbours were aware of these pickups. It was impossible to avoid knowing about them. Yet it was and remains possible for people to suffer amnesia about such frightening knowledge or simply to be incapable of admitting to themselves or others that they had any inkling of what was going on at that time. Others said they knew what was going on, but they could think of no way to intervene without putting themselves or their families in jeopardy. During one interview a woman said, "We could hear the screams. We tried to protect the children by putting up the volume on the radio. The army claimed that the noise was caused by soldiers dancing and singing. Every day, at any time, before breakfast even?"

In 1996 a group of community-minded citizens organized a series of symposia and other projects under the general title "Más que Memoria" (More than Memory) in memorial of the military period that had started twenty years earlier. They wanted to enable people to speak about their history and to help younger people become informed. One of the projects was to create a video documentary in which they interviewed persons who had lived next to a couple of these concentration camps. One of the organizers of this project described it in an interview:

Our objective was to have the journalists talk with the people who used to live around the different detention centres, and the question would be: "What happened there?" We knew that they used to take people there at any time of day. They also took stolen goods to those centres. We supposed that the neighbours must have heard the screams of those being tortured, or seen something that happened during the dictatorship.

A second organizer continued:

What impressed me most was that fear still continues ... In the video appear only people who agreed to be interviewed, but there were many who refused to speak. We attribute this refusal to the unpleasant aftertaste of fear that has remained from that time. Terror. This democracy is a fragile democracy. I believe that many people are not conscious of the fear that they feel. They do not say that they do not want to speak because they are afraid. Simply they refuse to speak. And many times, erroneously in my opinion, they think that it is better to forget the horror.

In some cases, too, there is a feeling of guilt. There is a feeling, we call it the guilt of the survivors. During that time of state terrorism, some people tried to do whatever they could, collaborating with the persecuted in various ways, helping them to leave the country, hiding them in their houses, taking information abroad. Of course this was all clandestine work. And another sector of society refused to believe what was happening, as a way of survival, denying what was happening, and, of course, there was another sector of society that supported the military dictatorship.

The resulting video, with the same title as the conference, showed an interview with a middle-aged man who claimed that he had never heard or seen anything near the detention centres. Even the most outspoken chose their words with care.

WHO WON?

Often, at the conclusion of a visit, as we were preparing to leave, our interviewees puzzled aloud about who had won the ideological battle. Some of the military bemoaned the success of Marxism. They give it too much credit. Marxism had a very brief run in Argentina, similar to its popularity elsewhere in the late 1960s and early 1970s, but it had then and has now no deep roots in a profoundly Catholic culture. As several of those who had been young at the time emphasized, they regret much of their past. Most would not again use violence to achieve a better world, but most would still prefer a more equitable, more civil, more decent society. Few invoked Marx in our interviews, and even socialism seemed remote for many. They are no longer sure how to define their utopias, and some have lost their taste for the struggle in defence of it. Only the military still call it a war. But whatever it is called, no one came out a winner.

Former guerrilla members were inclined to conclude pessimistically that the democratic government had achieved precisely what the military had tried and failed to achieve with its restructuring process.

Neoliberalism had succeeded, and the market was everywhere dominant over humanistic values. But they too gave too much credit to the ideology they despised. Argentina is much like the rest of the world at the end of the twentieth century – struggling to discover a golden mean between state and market, between particularisms that breed animosities and universalisms that destroy local cultures.

We did not undertake systematic interviews with people now below the age of thirty-five, but in many of the interviews with their parents' generation we heard a bemused recognition that younger people who did not experience these events have very little interest in what happened in that long-ago time; and may even express hostility toward parents who dreamed of a new society. They are interested in the same activities and ideas as young people the world over – dancing, loving, listening to (mostly American) music, dressing in fashion, buying the latest gadgets, attending school and developing career ambitions. The past – even though it is the immediate past of their parents – holds for them no appeal, and they have little sympathy for its victims. Consumerism, not politics, is their passion; and consumption, not citizenship, motivates them.

Two of the many ironies of recent Argentine history are that Peronists supplanted the Alfonsín government and that some of President Carlos Menem's key cabinet ministers are surviving Montoneros. Corruption, attributed by current newspapers to political linkages with the Mafia and drug dealers, is apparently endemic. Occasional gangland-style assassinations shock the country, including the Triple A–style murder of an investigative journalist-photographer, José Cabezas, in 1996. Although there were massive demonstrations and Mercedes Sosa gave a concert in his memory, and although the population pledged that they would not forget Cabezas, there were other deaths in the following year that were just as shocking if less publicized and were also attributable to investigations of criminal behaviour with which prominent politicians, powerful police officers, and wealthy businesspeople were connected. Peronists of the old school insist that Menemism is not true to the Peronist ideal; but then, Perón himself did not live up to that ideal.

Even with all these schisms and the corruption, Argentina is developing some semblance of democracy. Tolerance for opposing ideas is a very difficult capacity to establish in a society, but in the Chamber of Deputies and other institutions one sees its beginnings. When a man such as Alfredo Bravo, incarcerated without cause and tortured for many months because he led a teachers' union, can sit in the same chamber as former torturers and their supporters, there is visible leadership.[5] There was only one human rights group in Argentina before the coup. Now there are many, and they are admirably strong organizations. It was these organizations that pressed for the commission hearings and conducted many of the initial investigations that provided the basis for the prosecution of military leaders. Without their determination, the inquiries and trials would not have gone as far as they did. In the end, justice was meagre, but at least truth was established. Argentines were the first people to undertake an investigation of human rights crimes in their own country. Their report on these crimes, *Nunca Más*, is unique in its honesty and comprehensiveness, and it continues to be easily obtained free in public libraries or for a small sum at street and railway station kiosks throughout the country.

Compared to social movements, permanent, independent institutions are slow to develop. For example, no genuinely new political parties have taken root. There is still not a strong political party of the left, because Peronism still has a hegemonic position as a social movement even more than as a political party. The reader will recall that the Communist Party never had credibility with the left and in fact supported the military regime. There is a socialist party, but it has not attracted voters or strong leaders. At the other end of the income scale, the economic elite of the country has still not invested in the creation of a political party that might represent its interests along with a coalition of other conservative interests. And though the state has privatized many of its holdings and opened up its frontier to investment and trade, the state itself remains a centrist institution.

Universities were so weakened during the entire period from Peronism on through the dictatorship that they have not yet recovered. They charge no fees in most courses and have no serious entrance requirements. The result is that there are insufficient classrooms and teachers for the mass of students who enrol, and instructors are so ill-paid that they depend on other employment as their mainstay. Politics still has a large place in the university schedule. Serious intellectual work and the traditions of disengaged scholarship are not well embedded in public institutions. However, private institutions that emerged during the 1970s have become firmly established. For the most part, these are research institutes that have gradually accepted graduate students. Many of their faculty members obtained degrees in the United States or Europe. They are developing on a trajectory more akin to that of American and European institutes of higher learning.

The mass media have revived somewhat. A number of critical and independent publications have emerged: *Noticias* (for which Cabezas worked), *Página/12* and others. The regular papers that backed the military when it was in power, or otherwise survived by keeping a noncontroversial profile in those years, have gained sufficient courage to report on police brutality and political corruption. They remain subject to legal hassles for their reports. Many politicians have yet to learn how to tolerate an independent press.

The rule of law is even more difficult to establish where the entire justice system has been trashed for the past half century. At this time there is no strong institutional force to ensure the impartiality of judges or the fairness of the system. Law enforcement, moreover, is far from just, and the population has no sense of security. It is generally believed, and the newspapers frequently report, that police officers are routinely bribed or demand protection money, are brutal and still practise torture, are sometimes involved in assassinations (suspected, for example, in the Cabezas case), and cannot be trusted to enforce the law. In addition, the former repressers, paramilitary groups, police, and retired military personnel are at large. Some are employed as private bodyguards and company security officers. Many are unemployed and available on call.

In spite of all these problems, random violence is not characteristic of this society. Indeed, in daily life Argentina's cities in the 1990s are safer for ordinary citizens than many inner cities of the United States. Buenos Aires after dark is a relatively safe environment for pedestrians, and in spite of the police force, its citizens are neither violent nor uncivil to one another. Control of the state remains an unsettled problem, but one thing the state does not do today is perpetrate systematic terrorism. That is an achievement.

APPENDIX

Revolutionary Organizations, 1960s to Early 1970s

This list includes organizations that existed at some point during these turbulent decades.

Camilo Torres Comando. Represented at Havana founding meeting of OLAS (see below), 1967. Named after a martyred Colombian guerrilla priest, led by another priest, Juan García Elorrio. Armed. Eventually joined the Montoneros.

Descamisados (the Shirtless Ones). A term that was used early in the nineteenth century for workers and peasants, and adopted by Evita Perón as a rallying cry to her followers. The group that adopted this name in the late 1960s consisted of Peronists, Catholics, and nationalists. As the Descamisado Political-Military Organization, these members joined the Montoneros in mid-1972.

EGP, People's Guerrilla Army (Ejército Guerrillero del Pueblo). Guevarist operation, led by Comandante "Segundo," Ricardo Massetti, not heard of after 1964 when the Gendarmerie destroyed the group.[1]

ERP, People's Revolutionary Army (Ejército Revolucionario del Pueblo). Formally founded by the Fifth Congress of the Revolutionary Workers' Party (PRT) in 1970 as a political-military organization of professional revolutionaries. It was Guevarist in ideology, though the PRT was the Argentine member of the Fourth International (a legacy of its origins in the Palabra Obrero, see below). Armed. Theoretically subordinate to the PRT, but not all ERP members were members of PRT. ERP broke with international Trotskyism in June 1973. Linked to MLN (Uruguay). The ERP had no ties to Peronism and did not support the Peronists in 1973 elections.

FAP, Peronist Armed Forces (Fuerzas Armadas Peronistas). Established in the 1960s as a Guevarist military organization. Some of its leaders were arrested on 19 September 1968 at San Miguel de Tucumán. Peronist Youth leaders led the organization to merger with the Montoneros in 1974.

FAR, Revolutionary Armed Forces (Fuerzas Armadas Revolucionarias). Established about 1970, directed by Carlos Enrique Olmedo. Guevarist, Trotskyist, and Peronist. Joined the Montoneros in October 1973.

FRIP, Popular Front for Intra-American Revolution (Frente Revolucionario Indoamericano Popular). Established about 1960 by Mario Santucho in the province of Tucumán. After a visit to Cuba in 1962 and conversion to Marxism, Santucho came to an agreement with the Palabra Obrera (PO), and the combined organizations became the PRT in 1965.

JP, Peronist Youth/Young Peronists (Juventud Peronista). Established originally in universities as a movement in opposition to the government of General Onganía. Developed further with various subsidiary groups, including the university chapter (JUP), the regional chapters (JP-R), workers' groups (JP-T), etc. The movement was dominated by Montoneros after 1970.

Montoneros. Probably originated in the Camilo Torres Comando movement, with influences from Guevarism, revolutionary Peronism as interpreted by John William Cooke, and the cult of Evita Perón, but it also had right-wing Catholic nationalist roots. Date of origin unclear: members claimed foundation in 1968, but later research suggests that its beginning coincided with the murder of General Aramburu in 1970.

MNRT, National Revolutionary Movement of the Tacuara (Movimiento Nacionalista Revolucionario Tacuara). Originated in a 1962 split within the Catholic Nationalist Tacuara, a fascist youth organization formed in the 1930s. Ideology of the Spanish Falange but combined with Peronism, with the objective of creating a national syndicalist state. Precursor of the Montoneros.

OAP, Peronist Armed Organizations (Organizaciones Armadas Peronistas). Fusion of FAR and FAP in 1973.

OLAS, Latin American Solidarity Organization (Organización Latinoamericana de Solidaridad). Established in Havana in 1967 by OSPAAL. Che Guevara, honorary president. Decision: Each country to create an Army of National Liberation (ELN).

OSPAAL, Organization of Solidarity of the Peoples of Asia, Africa, and Latin America (also called Tricontinental). Established in Havana, Cuba, in 1966. Successor organization to OAPAA, Organization of Solidarity of Peoples of Asia and Africa, originally established in 1955.

PO, Workers' Word (Palabra Obrera). Established in early 1960s by Angel Bengochea as a Trotskyist party influenced by Guevara's strategy of guerrilla warfare. Bengochea created a Buenos Aires Commando as an urban support group for the People's Guerrilla Army in Salta. Bengochea died when his commando's arsenal blew up a Buenos Aires apartment house, but his organization went on to merge with FRIP in 1965 and eventually became part of the PRT.

PRT, *Revolutionary Workers' Party* (Partido Revolucionario de los Trabajadores). Founded by Mario Roberto Santucho through merger of FRIP and Palabra Obrera in 1965. Became Trotskyist by 1966 and participated in the Fourth International. Formally ended relationship with Trotskyism in June 1973.

PRT-ERP. Merger in 1976, designated itself as the Fourth International. It appears that all leaders and most members of the group had died by 1979.

PST, *Socialist Workers' Party* (Partido Socialista de los Trabajadores), also known as Nahuel Moreno). Militant breakaway group from the non militant Socialist Party of Argentina (PSA), led by Hugo Bressano in 1972.

Ururunco (a Quechua word meaning "tiger"). The first of the pro-Peronist groups. Established in 1960 near San Miguel de Tucumán. Adopting Guevarism as its operating code, it developed into a military operation on a very small scale.

NOTES

CHAPTER ONE

1 The estimate is from Amnesty International, *Political Killings by Governments*, 50–60.
2 Arendt, *The Origins of Totalitarianism*.
3 Says Hannah Arendt: "Terror is not the same as violence; it is, rather, the form of government that comes into being when violence, having destroyed all power, does not abdicate, but on the contrary, remains in full control" ("On Violence," in Lukes, *Power*, 70–71).
4 David Pion-Berlin offers an eloquent theory about the motivational capacity of monetarist theories in Latin America in *The Ideology of State Terror: Economic Doctrine and Political Repression in Argentina and Peru*. This is discussed further in chapter 12.
5 The outstanding theorist regarding economic development up to the early 1970s is Guillermo O'Donnell, *Modernization and Bureaucratic Authoritarianism*, whose work is discussed in the following chapters. See also William C. Smith, *Authoritarianism and the Crisis of the Argentine Political Economy*.
6 The classical definition of bureaucracy is provided by Max Weber: "Precision, speed, unambiguity, knowledge of the files, continuity, discretion, unity, strict subordination, reduction of friction and of material and personal costs – these are raised to the optimum point in the strictly bureaucratic administration ... Bureaucratization offers above all the optimum possibility for carrying through the principle of specializing administrations according to purely objective considerations ... The 'objective' discharge of business primarily means a discharge of business according to calculable rules and without regard for persons" (Gerth and Mills, *From Max Weber: Essays in Sociology*, 215).
7 For discussion of this subject, see Arendt, *Origins of Totalitarianism*, Bauman, *Modernity and the Holocaust*, Friedrich and Brzezinski,

Totalitarian Dictatorship and Autocracy, and O'Kane, *Terror, Force, and States: The Path from Modernity.*
8 Andersen, *Dossier Secreto.*

CHAPTER TWO

1 The phrase "intervened in" is frequently used by way of describing government takeovers of public institutions and unions. During interventions, the government appointed supervisors and sometimes fired existing personnel and replaced them. Professors and teachers were dismissed and replaced by various governments from the 1930s onwards.
2 Secretaría de Informaciones de Estado. This was the secret police organization.
3 The Malvinas/Falkland Islands war against Britain in 1982.
4 José López Rega, a former police corporal who served as valet to the Peróns and rose to be minister of social welfare, was a highly influential adviser of both Juan and Isabel Perón.
5 Universities had special relationships with selected schools throughout the country. These were the schools from which their students were recruited, and the curriculum was designed as a transitional period between school and university. There was stiff competition for entry into these schools.
6 This refers to David Kraiselburd, publisher of *El Día*, in La Plata. See chapter 12 for discussion of the media.
7 A beach resort town south of Buenos Aires.
8 The Cuban guerrilla movement.
9 Ultraleft nationalist members of the Movimiento Todos por la Patria (All for the Fatherland Movement) attacked La Tablada military base, apparently because they anticipated another military coup. More than forty people were killed and about one hundred injured. Some of the captured rebels had been members or supporters of the ERP during the 1970s. (The ERP was defeated in military action in 1975.)
10 Merlo was a mercenary and for a time a member of the ERP. He boasted of killing the former president of Nicaragua, Anastasio Somoza and the president of the sugar cane workers in the province of Tucumán.

CHAPTER THREE

1 Diaz Alejandro, *Essays on the Economic History of the Argentine Republic*, 54–8.
2 Arthur Lewis, *Growth and Fluctuations, 1870–1913*, 197.
3 Waisman, *Reversal of Development in Argentina*, 6, table 1.1.

4 William Smith, *Authoritarianism and the Crisis of the Argentine Political Economy*, 16.

5 Paul Lewis, *The Crisis of Argentine Capitalism*, 50–2.

6 William Smith, *Authoritarianism*, 17, tables 2.1, 2.2.

7 Munck, Falcón, and Galitelli, *Argentina: From Anarchism to Peronism*, 43–4.

8 Hodges, *Argentina's "Dirty War,"* 9.

9 Modern trade unions were established toward the end of the 1870s. For a study of these and early socialist and anarchist movements, see Munck, Falcón, and Galitelli, *Argentina: From Anarchy to Peronism*.

10 Hodges, *Argentina's "Dirty War,"* 24.

11 Bayer, *La Patagonia rebelde*.

12 Deutsch, "The Right under Radicalism, 1916–1930," 40.

13 Ibid., 42–50.

14 Ibid., 47–58.

15 O'Donnell, *Modernization and Bureaucratic Authoritarianism: Studies in South American Politics*.

16 Hodges, *Argentina's "Dirty War,"* 32.

17 This account follows that of Paul Lewis, *The Crisis of Argentine Capitalism*, 93–5.

18 Paul Lewis (ibid., 95) states that over the period 1939–45, local manufacturers increased their share of the domestic market in textiles, paper, chemicals, oil, metal products, and electrical machinery, some of these by as much as 30 per cent.

19 Paul Lewis (ibid., 87) describes published arguments to this effect by Alejandro Bunge, of the wealthy Bunge family, a leading economist of the period.

20 Hodges, *Argentina's "Dirty War,"* 43.

CHAPTER FOUR

1 For an extended description of this period, see Munck, Falcón, and Galitelli, *Argentina: From Anarchism to Peronism*, 127–46.

2 Paul Lewis, *The Crisis of Argentine Capitalism*, 215.

3 Munck, Falcón, and Galitelli, *Argentina: From Anarchy to Peronism*, 182–3.

4 Pion-Berlin, *The Ideology of State Terror*, 65.

5 United Nations Economic Commission for Latin America, *Economic Development and Income Distribution in Argentina*, 170.

6 Pion-Berlin describes the growth in greater detail in *The Ideology of State Terror*, 66–8.

7 According to the Argentine system, the official taking of office following the 1951 election occurred in 1952.

8 Hodges, *Argentina's "Dirty War,"* 69.

9 Paul Lewis, *The Crisis of Argentine Capitalism,* 216.

10 This section draws on Ghio, "Church and Politics: The Argentine Church in Comparative Perspective."

11 Ghio, "Church and Politics," 198.

12 Ibid., 207.

13 Perón proclaimed the "hour of the people," meaning the replacement of liberal democracy by people's democracy, the end of the rule of money, and the overcoming of imperalism through national liberation movements. Also, stated Perón, "We conceive of capitalism as the exploitation of man by capital, and of communism as the exploitation of the individual by the state ... Without capitalism, communism would have no reason to exist ... Without the cause, the effect would also begin to disappear" (Perón, *La tercera posición argentina,* as quoted in Hodges, *Argentina's "Dirty War,"* 49–50).

14 Ibid., 48.

15 In Hodge's view, the two principles of the National Justicialist movement – the union of all Argentines and the principle of social justice – were based on article 26 of the 1934 Program of the Spanish Falange. This version of *falangismo* was populist, in contrast to the fully authoritarian and fascist version expressed by General Franco and, in his later period, by Mussolini.

16 Goldwert, *Democracy, Militarism, and Nationalism in Argentina, 1930–1966,* 113, 117–18, 129.

17 Why Perón chose not to fully arm the workers at this stage and to accede to the military offensive remains a puzzle and is debated amongst Argentine historians. For discussion, see Goldwert, *Democracy, Militarism, and Nationalism,* and Paul Lewis, *The Crisis of Argentine Capitalism.*

18 O'Donnell, *Modernization and Bureaucratic Authoritarianism: Studies in South American Politics.*

19 This term is frequently used in the literature written by Argentines to denote the lower-middle and working classes.

20 See the contributions to di Tella and Dornbusch, *The Political Economy of Argentina, 1946–83,* especially the papers by Jorge Fodor and Pablo Gerchunoff.

21 Mora y Araujo, "Comment," 26.

22 Rouquié, *The Military and the State in Latin America,* 287.

23 Goldwert, *Democracy, Militarism, and Nationalism in Argentina, 1930–1966,* 188–210. The quotation is from James W. Rowe, "Argentina: Reds, Blues and the New Year, ii," *Mimeo,* 1962, in Goldwert (189n2).

24 Springer, 150–2.

25 Goldwert, *Democracy, Militarism, and Nationalism in Argentina, 1930–1966*, 192, from the text of Communiqué no. 150 in Rowe, "Argentina: Reds, Blues and the New Year, 11," 9–10.

26 As expressed by the minister of war, 8 February 1963, cited in Goldwert, ibid., 193.

27 Hodges, *Argentina's "Dirty War,"* 39.

28 Quoted in ibid., 71.

29 Ibid., 79, quoting from "Directivas generales para todos los peronistas," *Perón-Cooke correspondencia*, 2:378–83.

30 Poneman, *Argentina, Democracy on Trial*, 101.

31 Rouquié, *The Military and State in Latin America*, 145–6.

32 General Juan Carlos Sánchez, commander of the 2nd Army Corps headquartered in Rosario, was assassinated by the ERP together with another group, the FAR (Revolutionary Armed Forces/Fuerza Armadas Revolucionarios).

CHAPTER FIVE

1 The phrase "el far west sindical" is from *Confirmado*, 4 Feb. 1970, as reported in James, "Power and Politics in Peronist Trade Unions," 5.

2 Paul Lewis, *The Crisis of Argentine Capitalism*, 408–9.

3 Ibid., 407–8.

4 James, "Power and Politics," 17.

5 Ibid., 21–31.

6 Reported in Paul Lewis, *The Crisis of Argentine Capitalism*, 413, table 16.3, based on CGT statistics.

7 William Smith, *Authoritarianism and the Crisis of the Argentine Political Economy*, 102–3.

8 Ibid., 106.

9 Ibid., 110.

10 Ibid., 114. Regarding the reversal of the slogan, Smith quotes Balve et al., *Lucha de calles, lucha de clases*, 173.

11 William Smith, *Authoritarianism*, 115–25.

12 Ibid., 128–9.

13 Personal interview with Juan Carlos Torre. See also his book, *Los sindicatos en el gobierno, 1973–76*, and *La formacia del sindicalisme peronista*, ed. Torre.

14 This term is used to describe takeovers by the government. See above, chap. 2, note 1.

15 SMATA: Sindacatos de Mecánicos y Afines del Transporte.

16 Perón's third wife, María Estela (Isabel), who became president after her husband's death in 1974 and was deposed by the military coup in 1976.

CHAPTER SIX

1 Mattini, *Hombres y mujeres* PRT-ERP *de Túcuman a la Tablada*, 158.
2 *Latin America*, 1 June 1973, 170.
3 *Latin America*, 8 June 1973, 180.
4 Gillespie, *Soldiers of Perón*, 51. Ironically, the holdup was at the Bank Employees Union Clinic, for the clinic's payroll.
5 As reported in ibid., 90–1.
6 Di Tella, *Argentina under Perón*, 46.
7 Gillespie, *Soldiers of Perón*.
8 Vatican Council II. *Populorum progressio*, 1967.
9 Movimiento de Sacerdotes para el Tercer Mundo.
10 Gillespie, *Soldiers of Perón*, 55, quotes García Elorrio, *Cristianismo y Revolución* 1 (September 1966): 23.
11 Gillespie, *Soldiers of Perón*, 55, reports this as stated in Mario Eduardo Firmenich, "Nuestras diferencias políticas," *El Peronista*, 21 May 1974, 4–8.
12 Fernández Alvariño, *Z argentina, el crimen del siglo*.
13 Other references on this event include Méndez *Aramburo: El crimen imperfecto*.
14 Andersen, *Dossier Secreto*, 65–7, 107, 117–18, 319.
15 *Latin America*, 13 July 1973, 221–2.
16 See Bonasso, *El Presidente que no fue*, for a fictionalized documentary of the Cámpora period.
17 *Clarín*, 12 May 1973.
18 11 September 1973, as cited in di Tella, *Argentina under Perón*, 55.
19 *Latin America*, 1 February 1974, 39.
20 Jelin, *Conflictos laborales en la Argentina, 1973–76*, 29–30; Torre, *Los sindicatos en el gobierno, 1973- 1976*, 87–8; Paul Lewis, *The Crisis of Argentine Capitalism*, 427.

CHAPTER SEVEN

1 Alfredo Bravo, a member of the Chamber of Deputies and a highly respected human rights advocate, objects to the term on the grounds that no war was ever declared. Also, in his view, the terrorism was not yet "state terrorism," because the state did not acknowledge its organization of the paramilitary groups, whereas the military state took responsibility for the second phase. He expressed these views in an interview, 29 December, 1996.
2 The following sources are used in this section: Paul Lewis, *The Crisis of Argentine Capitalism*, 434; Graham-Yooll, *The Press in Argentina, 1973–1978*, 14–16, 35, 42–4, 46, 49, 52–3, 78; Aizcorbe, *Argentina, the Peronist Myth*, 286; Gillespie, *Soldiers of Perón*, 156.

3 Attacks on the press are itemized by Graham-Yooll in *The Press in Argentina, 1971–1978*.

4 Graham-Yooll, *The Press in Argentina, 1971–1978*, entry for 11 March 1974, 45.

5 *Latin America*, 10 May 1974, 142.

6 Di Tella, *Argentina under Perón, 1973–1976*.

7 See, for analysis by the guerrilla groups, Baschetti, ed., *Documentos 1973–1976*, 1: 630–86.

8 González Janzen, *La Triple-A*, 107–16.

9 *Latin America*, 17 January 1975, 18.

10 *Latin America*, 31 January 1975, 33–4.

11 *La Patagonia rebelde* is the Spanish title. It refers to the rebellion that occurred in 1921–22. Bayer is the major historian of the event.

12 Brother of ex-President Arturo Frondizi and former rector of the National University in Buenos Aires.

13 Paul Lewis, *The Crisis of Argentine Capitalism*, 435.

14 Andersen, *Dossier Secreto*, 125–6.

15 Ibid., 130.

16 Ibid., 131–2 and 350n27, citing a pamphlet from *La Gaceta* archive, written by Acdel Vilas and in Andersen's possession.

17 Andersen, *Dossier Secreto*, 134n37.

18 Ibid., 163n27, citing a report in *Clarín*, 31 January 1976.

19 The term "arrogance" is the description of the Montoneros in the title of a book that is widely read in Argentina: Pablo Giussani, *Montoneros: La soberbia armada* (Montoneros: Armed Arrogance).

20 Marriages between teenagers was common in leftist circles of this period. It indicated commitment to the cause more than commitment to romantic love.

21 Graham-Yooll, *The Press in Argentina, 1973–1978*, entry for 6 July 1974, 59.

22 Ibid., entry for 23 August 1974, 60.

23 For a detailed account, see Graham-Yooll, *The Press in Argentina, 1973–1978*.

24 Ibid., entry for 30 September 1974, 62.

25 Frontalini and Caiati, *El mito de la guerra sucia*, 66. The original reads: "El ataque al arsenal 601 y el consiguiente rechazo del intento, demuestra la impotencia absoluta de las organizaciones terroristas respecto a su presunto poder militar, a lo que se agrega su nula captacíon de voluntades populares."

26 Reported in Pion-Berlin, *The Ideology of State Terror*, 5, citing a secret order reprinted in *El diario del juicio 28* (December 1985): 529–32.

27 Gillespie, *Soldiers of Perón*, 38.

28 Economic Minister Emilio Mondelli, speech to the nation, 6 March 1976. Reported in full in *Buenos Aires Herald*, 6 March 1976.

29 He was exiled in July 1975 and accused of absconding with substantial government funds. During the following months he was reported to be dead, ill, and alive in various places; he never returned to Argentina.

CHAPTER NINE

1 "Producir es libertad, " *La Nación*, 22 March 1976 (WM translation).

2 Goldhagen, *Hitler's Willing Executioners.*

3 *Daily Journal* (Caracas, Venezuela), 5 April 1976, 5.

4 John Grundy, "Don't Cry for the Big Banks, Argentina," *Globe and Mail* (Toronto, Canada), 7 March, 1987.

5 See Langguth, *Hidden Terrors*, 124–42; Agee, *Inside the Company: CIA Diary*, 632; Duvall and Stohl, "Governance by Terror," 246.

6 Numbers culled from various sources, including interviews. There does not seem to be an "official" figure.

7 *Clarín*, 18 December 1977, as reported in Frontalini and Caiati, *El mito de la guerra sucia*, 24 This is a collection of speeches by members of the junta that were published in newspapers and periodicals of the period.

8 As quoted by Hodges, *Argentina's "Dirty War*," 192–3.

9 Frontalini and Caiati, *El mito de la guerra sucia*, 75. I have used the translation by Hodges, 181.

10 *La Prensa*, 18 December 1977, as reported in Frontalini and Caiati, *El mito de la guerra sucia*, 22.

11 *La Razón*, 12 June 1976, reported in ibid., 22.

12 As expressed, for example, by Rear Admiral César A. Guzzetti, in *La Opinión*, 3 October 1976, reported in ibid., 21.

13 *Guardian*, 6 May 1977, as quoted in Gillespie, *Soldiers of Perón*, 250.

14 Amnesty International, *Political Killings by Governments,* annual report, 1983.

15 The film *Avellaneda* gives a semi-documentary report on the work of these anthropologists.

16 Adolfo Francisco Scilingo, as told to Horacio Verbitsky, who described it in *El Vuelo.*

17 CONADEP, *Nunca Más* (English translation), 12.

18 Ibid., 16.

19 Ibid., 21–6.

20 Mignone, *Witness to the Truth*, 2.

21 Personal interview, 18 January 1997, MPM notes.

22 Reported in several leading newspapers, as cited by Andersen, *Dossier Secreto*, 185.

23 Testimony of Miriam Lewin de García, reported in CONADEP, *Nunca Más*, file no. 2365.

24 CONADEP, *Nunca Más*, 318–19 (files under the separate names of the six who remain disappeared).

25 These events are described in Seoane and Ruiz Nuñez, *La noche de los lápices*, and in a film available in English as *The Night of the Pencils*, produced by Héctor Olivera in 1986. Seoane and Ruiz Nuñez omit one case that is included in the CONADEP report (Victor Trevino, file no. 4018).

26 In interview with Jorge Asis, *Revista libre*, 13 March 1984, 1–4, as discussed by Hodges in *Argentina's "Dirty War,"* 191.

27 This information is provided in Andersen, *Dossier Secreto*, 258–9. For further information on the Graiver case, see *Wall Street Journal*, 29 July 1977 LI, 15.

28 *Latin America Political Report*, 22 April 1977.

29 Graham-Yooll, *The Press in Argentina, 1973–1978* summary report of April 1977, and itemized reports throughout April, 144–5.

30 Andersen, *Dossier Secreto*, 285.

31 Neilson, "The Education of Jacobo Timerman."

32 Timerman, *Prisoner without a Name, Cell without a Number*, 42.

33 For accounts of these events and the organization of the mothers, see Asociación Madres de la Plaza de Mayo, *Historia de la Madres de la Plaza de Mayo*; Bennett and Simpson, *The Disappeared and the Mothers of the Plaza de Mayo*; Bouvard, *Revolutionizing Motherhood: The Mothers of the Plaza de Mayo*; and Fisher, *Mothers of the Disappeared*.

34 William Smith, *Authoritarianism*, 235.

35 Ibid., 5.

36 Ibid.

37 Ibid., 244–5.

38 Ibid., 246.

CHAPTER TEN

1 The Born brothers, heirs to the Bunge Born fortune, were both kidnapped. Juan was released (circumstances fuzzy). Jorge was ransomed for a reported $60 million.

2 Play on the verb *perder*, meaning to lose.

CHAPTER ELEVEN

1 For discussion of the events in Tucumán from the perspective of the ERP, see Mattini, *Hombres y mujeres del PRT-ERP de Tucumán a la Tablada.*

2 Tucumán, La Provincia, *Informe de la comisión bicameral investigadora de las violaciones de los derechos humanos en la provincia de Tucumán (1974–1983)*. Earlier, local residents compiled a short listing with occupations of the disappeared: *Nomina de 409 personas detenidas-desaparecidas de la provincia de Tucumán (Argentina), denunciadas por sus familiares*, n.d.

3 Atilio Santillón, secretary general of the Federation of Sugar Industry Workers (FOTIA), had been an active Peronist union leader, but he supported the army in Tucumán in 1975. He was killed by ERP gunmen 22 March 1976 in Buenos Aires.

4 The Inter-American Commission on Human Rights (Comisión Interamericana de Derechos Humanos). Organization of American States investigation of 1979.

5 The reference is to Antonio Gramsci, Marxist philosopher in Italy, imprisoned under Mussolini. Gramsci wrote notebooks while in prison which have since become major contributions to the literatuare on culture and politics in modern societies.

CHAPTER TWELVE

1 *Buenos Aires Herald*, editorial, 25 March 1976.

2 *La Nación* editorial, 25 March, 1976 (WM translation).

3 *Buenos Aires Herald*, editorial, 25 April 1976.

4 Translation of instructions from the Secretaría de Estado de Prensa y Difusión, published in Graham-Yooll, *The Press in Argentina*, 118–19.

5 Graham-Yooll, *The Press in Argentina*, 122, 144. The second speech to the Inter-American Press Association was in Cartagena, Colombia, 28 March 1977.

6 Graham-Yooll, *The Press in Argentina*, 153 and appendix A, which provides names of journalists noted by International PEN, Amnesty International, and the National Union of Journalists in London.

7 Ibid., 14.

8 Andrew Graham-Yooll, "All Country's Eyes on Changes," *Buenos Aires Herald*, 15 August 1976.

9 16 Andrew Graham-Yooll, "Bloodbath No Climax," *Buenos Aires Herald*, 22 August, 1976.

10 The *Buenos Aires Herald* under Cox's leadership continued to publish information on missing persons and on robberies by police and military personnel long after other papers had ceased to mention such features of their society.

11 *Buenos Aires Herald* editorial, 22 August 1976.

12 An exclusive private school in Buenos Aires.

13 Graham-Yooll, *A State of Fear.* Graham-Yooll was present when Born was handed over for a $60 million ransom.

14 Andersen, *Dossier Secreto.*

15 Duvall and Stohl, "Governance by Terror," 246; Agee, *Inside the Company: CIA Diary,* 632; Langguth, *Hidden Terrors,* 124–42, 244; Chomsky and Herman, *The Washington Connection and Third World Fascism,* 252–3, 264–71; Poelchau, ed., *White Paper Whitewash: Interviews with Philip Agee on the CIA and El Salvador,* 37–9, 65–9.

16 Duvall and Stohl, "Governance by Terror," 247.

17 Pion-Berlin, *The Ideology of State Terror,* 10.

18 Guest, *Behind the Disappearances,* 76.

19 Ibid., 83 (Guest's translation).

20 Ibid., 85.

21 Previously editor of the left-wing magazine *Nuevo Hombre.*

22 Escuela Superior de Mecánica de la Armada (Navy engineering school). Located near the centre of Buenos Aires on the Avenida Libertador San Martín, the buildings and grounds became a major concentration camp during the regime.

23 Guest, *Behind the Disappearances,* 230.

24 Organization of American States, *Report on the Situation of Human Rights in Argentina,* 186, as reported in Guest, *Behind the Disappearances,* 177 and chapter 13, fns 37, 38.

25 Iain Guest's book provides a detailed, well researched account of the machinations of this individual and the failure of the United Nations Human Rights Commission to keep Argentina on the agenda throughout the mid-1970s.

26 There has never been an explanation for the unexpected and apparently arbitrary release of occasional prisoners, even from ESMA. As well, a few individuals managed to escape. And there were some persons who were tortured briefly but released on condition that they leave the country immediately.

27 Macdonald, "The Politics of Intervention: The United States and Argentina, 1941–46," provides a detailed study of the earlier period.

28 Carlos Escudé, "Argentina: The Costs of Contradiction," 141–2.

29 Ibid., 142–3.

30 Ibid., 148–9.

31 Tulchin, *Argentina and the United States,* 149.

CHAPTER THIRTEEN

1 Emilio F. Mignone, in personal interview and in *Witness to the Truth.*

2 Mignone, *Witness to the Truth,* 3–5.

3 Ibid., 4–6

4 *La Nación*, 6 May and 11 October 1976, as cited by Mignone, *Witness to the Truth*, 6.

5 Speech at Universidad Nacional del Litoral, as reported in the Santa Fe newspaper *El Litoral*, 6 December 1977, cited by Mignone, 6.

6 Mignone, *Witness to the Truth*, 36, citing the Buenos Aires magazine *Radiolandia 2000*, which printed the interview done by its correspondent in Rome.

7 Name used to refer to Saint Thomas Aquinas (1225–74) or to the philosophy and followers of Aquinas. Aquinas is generally credited with reconciling the work of Aristotle, with its emphasis on empirical examination, and of Saint Augustine, with its emphasis on revelation.

8 Capital of the province of Entre Ríos, about 300 km north of Buenos Aires.

9 Antonio Gramsci (1891–1937), Italian philosopher and critic of capitalism, co-founder of the Italian Communist Party in 1921, parliamentarian 1924–26, imprisoned in 1926, authored *Prison Notebooks*.

10 At the church conference in Medellin in 1968, the pope's address was interpreted as authorization to engage in activities to alleviate poverty and suffering. The Conference of the Latin American Bishops held in Puebla, Mexico, in 1979 was more conservative.

11 "Vicenda ingiusta e amara," *Il regno attualità*, July 1997, 385–90.

12 See, for example, *La Iglesia y los derechos humanos*.

13 *L'Iglesia y commune nacional*.

CHAPTER FOURTEEN

1 González Janzen, *La Triple A*, 113.

2 Andersen, *Dossier Secreto*, 110–11, and ftns 27, 28. Andersen notes that there is conflicting evidence, though the killer was named in court cases.

3 This is the only Irish Embassy in Latin America.

4 In response to a question, the padre noted that another group, composed of laypersons, was called Christianity and Revolution. They said they were followers of Camilo Torres. There was interaction between the two groups, but they were separate, and Camilo Torres, though known to the priests' movement, was not their principal figure.

5 Bresci, ed., *Movimiento de sacerdotes para el tercermundo*.

6 NN on a tombstone signified that an unknown body was buried beneath it. This was frequently used by the miltary during the early period, when they buried corpses.

7 "Vicenda ingiusta e amara," *Il regno attualità*, July 1997, 385–90.

8 The phrase was popularized by Che Guevara.

CHAPTER FIFTEEN

1 *Latin America Weekly Report,* 27 January 1998.
2 Interview with General Martín Balza, reported in *Clarín digital,* 16 January 1998.
3 *La otra campana del Nunca Más,* no publisher named, no date given. The book could be purchased at vendors in the railway stations of Buenos Aires, but was unavailable in regular bookstores during September 1997. During that same month a television talk show ("Fleore Clare") had both Etchecolatz and Alfredo Bravo (now a highly regarded deputy in the Chamber of Deputies, who as a schoolteacher in the 1970s had been imprisoned by Etchecolatz) on the same program. There was a widespread outcry against this: Etchecolatz may have been amnestied, but he had been found guilty, and to see him being allowed to challenge Bravo in this way was extremely offensive to many viewers. In our own interview with Alfredo Bravo, he expressed the importance of tolerance and spoke of the difficult necessity for deputies like himself to interact daily, on a reasonable and amicable basis, with former persecutors.
4 Diaz Bessone, *Guerra revolucionaria en la Argentina (1959–1978).*
5 Uturuncos ("tigermen" in the Quechua language) attempted to become established in Tucumán in December 1959. The colonel's reference on this is Diaz Bessone, *Guerra Revolucionaria,* 11–12.
6 Raúl Alfonsín was the first democratically elected president after the military regime. He was elected in 1983.
7 Operativo Independencia, the code name for the war against subversion in Tucumán. Donald Hodges (*Argentina's "Dirty War,"* 102–3) argues that this directive began the "dirty war" in Tucumán, February 1975. The term itself became known through a speech by President Videla on 14 September 1976 in Tucumán province during celebrations of the six-month anniversary of military rule.
8 Karl von Clausewitz (1780–1831), Prussian military theorist. His theories on war (contained as collected essays in *vom Kriege)* were influential in many countries, including Argentina.
9 Diaz Bessone, *Guerra revolucionaria.* The Circulo Militar is the officer's club.
10 Under a political amnesty decree, political prisoners were freed. This included seventy-two ERP members at the Villa Devoto penitentiary and up to two thousand prisoners altogether.
11 The attack by the ERP on a military base at Azul in the province of Buenos Aires occurred January 1974.
12 Ernesto Sábato chaired the National Commission on Disappeared People (CONADEP).

CHAPTER SIXTEEN

1 Ballester, *Memorias de un coronel democrático.*
2 See Arendt, *Origins of Totalitarianism.*
3 Reference is to Pion-Berlin, in *Journal of Interamerican Studies and World Affairs* and in *Liberalization and Redemocratization in Latin America.*
4 Frank, *Capitalism and Underdevelopment in Latin America.*
5 Bonasso, *Recuerdo de la muerte* (Remembrance of Death).
6 Well-known author, journalist, and personality in Buenos Aires of the 1990s.
7 The events at Garín in 1970 were in fact organized by FAR, not the Montoneros. See Gillespie, *Soldiers of Perón,* 107, and Andersen, *Dossier Secreto,* 71–2. The Montoneros took over the town of La Calera in the province of Córdoba in July 1970.

CONCLUSION

1 One collection of Gramsci's work in English is *The Modern Prince and Other Writings,* originally published in 1957.
2 Armony, *Argentina, the United States, and the Anti-Communist Crusade in Central America, 1977–1984.*
3 Frank, *Capitalism and Underdevelopment in Latin America.*
4 The legislation, together with critical commentary, was published by APDH and other human rights organizations at the time. A succinct summary of the circumstances in which the laws were promulgated is given in Brysk, *The Politics of Human Rights in Argentina,* 74–88.
5 Bravo discussed this very experience during an interview.

APPENDIX

1 Massetti learned politics as a journalist on the fascist newspaper *Tribuna* and as a militant in Juan Queralto and Guillermo Patricio Kelly's Alianza Libertadora Nacionalista (ALN), a fascist group organized under Perón in his first term of office.

BIBLIOGRAPHY

Acuña, Carlos H., ed. *La nueva matriz política argentina: La investigación social.* Buenos Aires: Nueva Vision, 1995

Acuña, Carlos, and Catalina Smulovitz. *¿Ni olvido ni perdon? Derochos humanos y tensiones civico-militares en la transición argentina.* Buenos Aires: CEDES, 1991

Acuña, Carlos H., and William C. Smith. "Politica y 'Economía militar' en el cono sur: Democracia, producción de armamentos y carrere armamentista en Argentina, Brasil y Chile." *Desarrollo económico. Revista de ciencias sociales* 34, no. 135 (1994): 343–78

Acuña, C.H., et al. *Jucio castigos y memorias: Derochos humanos y justicia en la política argentina.* Buenos Aires: Nueva Vision, 1995

Acuña, Claudia. "Dios y la patria los demandaron. " *La Semana* 9, no. 8 (1984): 3–33

Agee, Philip. *Inside the Company: CIA Diary.* Harmondsworth, Middlesex: Penguin, 1975

Agencia Informativa Católica Argentina (AICA). "Carta de la comisión permanente de la Conferencia Episcopal Argentina al Presidente Videla, sobre la 'situación de los detenidos, con motivo de la próxima navidad.' (por Raúl Francisco Card. Primatesta, Arzobispo de Córdoba, Presidente de la Conferencia Episcopal Argentina)." Buenos Aires, 3 December 1976

– "Carta de la comisión permanente de la Conferencia Episcopal Argentina a los miembros de la Junta Militar, sobre inquietudes del pueblo cristiano, por detenidos, desaparecidos, etc." (por Card. Primatesta, Arzobispo de Córdoba, presidente de la Conferencia Episcopal Argentina; Juan Carlos Card. Aramburu, vicepresidente 2 de la Conferencia Episcopal Argentina; Vicente Zazpe, Arzobispo de Sante Fe, vicepresidente 1 de la Conferencia Episcopal Argentina). Buenos Aires, 17 March 1977

– "Reflexión cristiana para el pueblo de la patria de la Conferencia Episcopal Argentina." San Miguel, 7 May 1977

- "Caminando hacia el tercer milenio." Doc. 366, Suplemento del Bolet informativo AICA no. 2054, del 1 de mayo, 1996. San Miguel: LXXI Asamblea Plenaria, 27 April 1996

Agosin, Marjorie. *The Mothers of Plaza de Mayo: The Story of Renee Epelbaum, 1976–85.* Trans. Janice Malloy. Stratford, Ont.: Williams-Wallace, 1989

Aguiar, Elina. "Effets psychologiques de l'impunité en relation avec la represión politique: Etude du contexte social." *Revue de psychotherapie psychoanlytique de groupe* 15 (1990)

- "Efectos psicosociales de la impunidad." Mimeo paper produced for Asamblea Permanente por los Derechos Humanos. Published in *Impunidad*, ed. Legie Int. Derechos de los Pueblos. Geneva, February 1993

Aizcorbe, Roberto. *Argentina, the Peronist Myth: An Essay on the Cultural Decay of Argentina after the Second World War.* Hicksville, NY: Exposition Press, 1975

Allende, José Antonio, et al. *Informe sobre el Proceso para la reorganización nacional.* Buenos Aires: Agencia Periodistica CID (prepared 1979), 1981

Americas Watch. *Argentina. Human Rights in Argentina: A Report from CELS in Buenos Aires.* New York: Americas Watch, 1983

- *The State Department Misinforms: A Study of Accounting for the Disappeared in Argentina.* New York: Americas Watch, 1983

- *Truth and Partial Justice in Argentina.* New York: Americas Watch, 1987

Amnesty International. *Report of an Amnesty International Mission to Argentina, 6–15 November 1976.* London: Amnesty International Publications, 1977

- *Testimony on Secret Detention Camps in Argentina.* London: Amnesty International Publications, 1977

- *The Disappeared of Argentina.* London: Amnesty International Publications, 1979

- *The "Disappeared" of Argentina.* London: Amnesty International Publications, 1980

- *Political Killings by Governments.* London: Amnesty International Publications, 1983

- *Torture in the Eighties: An Amnesty International Report.* London: Amnesty International Publications, 1984

- *Argentina: The Military Juntas and Human Rights: Report of the Trial of the Former Junta Members.* London: Amnesty International Publications, 1987

- *Argentina: The Attack of the Third Infantry Regiment Barracks at La Tablada: Investigations into Allegations of Torture, "Disappearances" and Extrajudicial Executions.* London. Amnesty International Publications, 1990

Amnesty International–Argentina. *Actividades sobre Argentina, 1972–1987.* Buenos Aires: Amnesty International, n.d.

Andersen, Martin. *Dossier secreto: El mito de la guerra sucia.* Published simultaneously in English as *Dossier Secreto: Argentina's Desaparecidos and the Myth of the "Dirty War."* Boulder, Colo.: Westview Press, 1993

Anguita, Eduardo, and Martín Caparrós, *La voluntad: Una historia de la militancia revolucionaria en la Argentina, 1966–1973.* Buenos Aires: Grupo Editorial Norma, 1997

Anzorena, Oscar R. *Tiempo de violencia y utopia, 1966–1976.* Buenos Aires: Contrapunto, 1988

– *Historia de la juventud peronista, 1955–1988.* Buenos Aires: Cordon, 1989

Arendt, Hannah. *The Origins of Totalitarianism.* Cleveland, Ohio: Meridian, 1958

– "On Violence." Taken from original (1970) essay in *Power,* ed. S. Lukes, 59–74. Oxford: Blackwell, 1986

Armony, Ariel C. *Argentina, the United States, and the Anti-Communist Crusade in Central America, 1977–1984.* Latin American Series, no. 26. Athens, Ohio: Ohio University Center for International Studies, 1997

Asamblea Permanente por los Derechos Humanos (APDH). *Inconstitucionalidad de la Ley de obediencia debida, actuaciones de la camara federal de apelaciones de Bahía Blanca.* Discussion paper. August 1987

– *Entonces, es licito matar? Pedido de informes al Poder Ejecutivo Nacional por el desprocesamiento de jefes militares.* Para diputados de la Nación: Matilde Fernandez de Quarraccino y Simon Alberto Lázara, 1988

– *Los derechos humanos y el futuro institucional del país en relación a las bases políticas de las fuerzas armadas.* Conferencia del Sr Simon A. Lazara 11. Seguridad Nacional, Sistema Republicano de Gobierno y Derochos Individuals, 1995

Asamblea Permanente por los Derechos Humanos, together with many other human rights organizations in Argentina. *Ley de Obediencia debida.* Discussion paper. Buenos Aires, 1984

– *Ley del punto final.* Discussion paper. Buenos Aires, January 1987

– *Culpables para la sociedad: Impunes por la ley.* (Names persons responsible for the disappearances.) Buenos Aires, 1988

– *Denuncia a la iglesia cómplice: Homenaje a los mártires.* N.d.

Asociación de Periodistas de Buenos Aires. *Con vida los queremos: La voces que necesitaba silenciar la dictadura. Periodistas desaparecidos.* Buenos Aires: Asociación, 1986

Asociación Madres de la Plaza de Mayo. *Historia de las Madres de la Plaza de Mayo. Documentos Página/12.* Buenos Aires: La Página, 1995

Avellaneda, Andrés. *Censura, autoritarismo y cultura: Argentina 1960–1983 / 1.* Buenos Aires: Biblioteca Política Argentina, Centro editor de América Latina, 1986

Azpiazu, Daniel, and Hugo Nochteff. *El desarrollo ausente: Restricciones al desarrollo, neoconservadorismo y elite económica en la argentina. Ensayos de economia politica*. 2nd edn. Buenos Aires: FLACSO, Tesis Gropo Editorial Norma, 1995

Azpiazu, D.E.M. Basualdo, and M. Khavisse. *El nuevo poder económico en la Argentina de los años 80*. Buenos Aires: Legasa, 1986

Ballester, Horacio P. *Memorias de un coronel democrático: Medio siglo de historia política argentina en la óptica de un militar*. Buenos Aires: Ediciones de la Flor SRL, 1996

Balvé, Beba, et al. *Lucha de calles, lucha de clases: Elementos para su análisis (Córdoba 1969–71)*. Buenos Aires: Editorial La Rosa Blindada, 1973

Barcesat, Eduardo S. "Defensa legal de los derochos a la vida y la libertad personal en el regimen militar argentina." In *Represión política y defensa de los derochos humanos*, ed. Hugo Fruhling. Santiago, Chile: Academia de Humanismo, 1986

Baschetti, Roberto, ed. *Documentos (1970–1973). De la guerrilla peronista al gobierno popular*. Buenos Aires: Colección Campana de Palo, 1995

– *Documentos 1973–76. De Cámpora a la ruptura*. vol. 1. Buenos Aires: Colección Campana de Palo, 1996

Bauman, Z. *Modernity and the Holocaust*. Cambridge: Polity Press, 1989

Bayer, Osvaldo. *La Patagonia rebelde*. Mexico: Nueva Imágen, 1980

Beltran, Virgio. "Political Transition in Argentina: 1982 to 1985." *Armed Forces Quarterly* 13, no. 2 (Winter 1987): 215–34

Bennett, Jana, and John Simpson. *The Disappeared and the Mothers of the Plaza de Mayo*. New York: St Martin's Press, 1985

Bienen, Henry, ed. *The Military Intervenes: Case Studies in Development*. New York: Russell Sage Foundation, 1968

Bonafini, Hebe de. *Historias de vida*. Buenos Aires: Fraterna/del Nuevo Extremo, 1985

Bonasso, Miguel. *Recuerdo de la muerte*. Buenos Aires: Edigraf S.A., 1988

– *El Presidente que no fue: Los archivos ocultos del peronismo*. Buenos Aires: Planeta, 1997

Boron, Atilio A. "La militarización de la cultura política: Reflexiones a propósito de la experiencia argentina. " Buenos Aires: Mimeo, EURAL, 1986

– "Los dilemas de la modernización y los sujetos de la democracia." In *Alfonsín: Discursos sobre el discurso*, ed. Luis Aznar et al. Buenos Aires: EUDEBA, 1986

– *State, Capitalism, and Democracy in Latin America*. London, Eng., and Boulder, Colo.: Lynne Rienner, 1995

Bouvard, Marguerite Guzman. *Revolutionizing Motherhood: The Mothers of the Plaza de Mayo*. Wilmington, Del.: Scholarly Resources, 1984

Bra, Gerardo. *El gobierno de Onganía: Crónica*. Buenos Aires: Biblioteca Politica, Centro Editor de América Latina, no. 128, 1985

Brennan, James. *Labour Wars in Córdoba, 1955–1976.* Cambridge, Mass.: Harvard University Press, 1994

Bresci, Domingo, ed. *Movimiento de sacerdotes para el tercer mundo: Documentos.* Buenos Aires: Centro Salesiano de Estudios "San Juan Bosco." Centro Nazaret, Comisión de Estudios de Historia de la Iglesia en Latinoamérica (CEHILA), 1994

Brown, Cynthia. *With Friends Like These: The Americas Watch Report on Human Rights and U.S. Policy in Latin America.* New York: Americas Watch, 1983

Bruno, A., M. Cavarozzi, and V. Palermo, eds. *Los derochos humanos en la democracia.* Buenos Aires: Biblioteca Política Argentina. Centro Editor de América Latina, 1985

Brysk, Alison. *The Politics of Human Rights in Argentina: Protest, Change, and Democratization.* Stanford, Calif.: Stanford University Press, 1994

– "The Politics of Measurement: Counting the Disappeared in Argentina." In *Human Rights in Developing Countries,* ed. David Louis Cingranel. Greenwich, Conn.: JAI Press, 1994

Caraballo, Liliana, Noemi Charlier, and Liliana Garulli. *La dictadura (1976–1983): Testimonios y documentos.* Buenos Aires: Universidad de Buenos Aires, 1996

Castiglione, Marta. *La militarización del estado en la Argentina (1976/1981).* Buenos Aires: Biblioteca Política Argentina, Centro Editor de América Latina, 1992

Cavarozzi, Marcelo. *Autoritarismo y democracia, 1955–1983.* Buenos Aires: Centro Editor de América Latina, 1983

– "Argentina's Political Cycles since 1955." In *Transitions to Democracy,* ed. Philippe Schmitter, Guillermo O'Donnell, and Lawrence Whitehead. Baltimore: Johns Hopkins University Press, 1986

La Central de los Trabajadores (CTA). *Documentos 1er congreso nacional de delegados, noviembre 1996* (and other CTA pamphlets)

Centro de Estudios Legales y Sociales (CELS). *Terrorismo de estado, 692 responsables: Programa de documentación, estudios y publicaciones.* Buenos Aires: CELS, 1986

Argentina y la tortura: Obligación de juzgar a los responsables. By George C. Rogers, in *Cuadernos del CELS* 2 (Nov 1990).

– *Informe anual sobre la situación de los derechos humanos en la Argentina* (CELS annual). Buenos Aires: CELS/Facultad de Filosofia y Letras, Universidad de Buenos Aires, 1994, 1995, 1996.

Chomsky, Noam, and Edward S. Herman. *The Washington Connection and Third World Fascism.* Boston: South End Press, 1979

Clarín. "Cincuenta años de politica nacional." Suplemento aniversario. *Clarín,* 28 August 1995

Coggiola, Osvaldo. *El trotskysmo en la Argentina, 1960–1985.* Vol. 1 (no. 133). Buenos Aires: CEAL, 1986

Comisión nacional sobre la desaparición de personas. *Anexos CONADEP.* Buenos Aires: Editorial de la Universidad de Buenos Aires, 1985

– *Nunca más: Informe de la Comisión nacional sobre la desaparición de personas.* Buenos Aires: Editorial Universitaria de Buenos Aires, 1985

– *Nunca Más (Never Again): A Report by Argentina's National Commission on Disappeared People.* English translation by Writers and Scholars International Ltd, publishers of *Index on Censorship.* London and Boston: Faber and Faber, 1986

Confederación de Trabajadores de la Educación de la Republica Argentina (CTERA). *Con la pluma y la palabra: Cuentos premiados de maestros y profesores.* Edición especial auspiciada por CTERA. Buenos Aires: Colihue, 1992

Conferencia Episcopal Argentina (CEA). *Democracia, responsibilidad y esperanza.* Buenos Aires: CEA, 1984

– *Iglesia y comunidad nacional: XLII Asamblea plenaria, 4–9 de Mayo de 1981.* Buenos Aires: CEA, 1984

– *La Iglesia y los derechos humanos* (Extracts from documents, etc., 1970–82). Buenos Aires: CEA, 1988

– *Boletin oficial de la conferencia episcopal argentina.* Buenos Aires: CEA, 11 August 1996

Confines. Special edition containing memories of terror in Argentina, 1976–96. Año 2, no. 3 (September 1996)

Córdoba, Municipalitad de. *Informe: Comisión nacional sobre la desaparición de personas.* Córdoba, 1984

Corradi, Juan. "The Mode of Destruction: Terror in Argentina." *Telos* 54 (Winter 1982–83): 61–76

Corradi, Juan, Patricia Weiss Fagen, and Manuel Antonio Garretón, eds. *Fear at the Edge: State Terror and Resistance in Latin America.* Berkeley: University of California Press, 1992

Cox, Robert J. *The Sound of One Hand Clapping: A Preliminary Study of the Argentine Press in a Time of Terror.* Washington, DC: Woodrow Wilson International Center, 1980

Crenshaw, Martha, ed. *Terrorism in Context.* University Park, Pa: Pennsylvania State University Press, 1995

Crenzel, Emilio A. *El tucumanazo, 1969–1974.* Buenos Aires: CEAL, 1991

Debray, Regis. *Revolution in the Revolution: A Primer for Marxist Insurrection in Latin America.* New York: Grove Press, 1967

Deutsch, Sandra McGee. "The Right under Radicalism, 1916–1930." In *The Argentine Right,* ed. Deutsch and Ronald H. Dolkart, 35–63. Wilmington, Del.: SR Books, 1993

Deutsch, Sandra McGee, and Ronald H. Dolkart, eds. *The Argentine Right: Its History and Intellectual Origins, 1910 to the Present.* Wilmington, Del.: SR Books, 1993

Diana, Marta. *Mujeres guerrilleras: La militancia de los setenta en el testimonio de sus protagonistas femeninas.* Buenos Aires: Planeta, 1996

Diaz Alejandro, Carlos F. *Essays on the Economic History of the Argentine Republic.* New Haven, Conn.: Yale University Press, 1970

Diaz Bessone, Ramón Genaro. *Guerra revolucionaria en la Argentina (1959–1978).* Buenos Aires: Circulo Miitar, 1988

Diaz Colodrero, José, and Monica Abella. *Punto final: Amnistia o voluntad popular.* Buenos Aires: Puntosur, 1987

Di Tella, Guido. *Argentina under Perón, 1973–1976.* London: Macmillan, 1983

Di Tella, Guido, and Rudiger Dornbusch, eds. *The Political Economy of Argentina, 1946–83.* Oxford: Macmillan, 1989

Dolkart, Ronald H. "The Right in the Decada Infame, 1930–1943," In *The Argentine Right*, ed. Sandra McGee Deutsch and Ronald H. Dolkart, 64–98. Wilmington, Del.: SR Books, 1993

Dorfman, Adolfo. *Cincuenta años de industrialización en la Argentina.* Buenos Aires: Ediciones Solar, 1983

Dornbusch, Rudiger. "Argentina after Martínez de Hoz." In *The Political Economy of Argentina, 1946–83*, ed. Guido di Tella and Rudiger Dornbusch, 286–315. Pittsburgh: University of Pittsburgh Press, 1989

Ducatenzeiler, Graciela, and Philip Oxhorn. "Democracia, autoritarismo y el problema de la gobernabilidad en América Latina." *Desarrollo económico: Revista de ciencias sociales* 34, no. 133 (April–June 1994): 31–52

Duhalde, Eduardo. *El estado terrorista argentino.* Buenos Aires: El Caballiot, 1983

Duvall, Raymond D., and Michael Stohl. "Governance by Terror." In *The Politics of Terrorism*, 3rd edn, ed. Stohl, 231–71. New York: Marcel Dekker, 1988

Escudé, Carlos. "Argentina: The Costs of Contradiction." In *Exporting Democracy: The United States and Latin America*, ed. Abraham F. Lowenthal, 125–160. Baltimore: Johns Hopkins University Press, 1991

Escurra, Ana Maria. *Iglesia y transición democrática: Ofensiva del neoconservadurismo católico en América Latina.* Buenos Aires: Puntosur Editores, 1988

Etchecolatz, Miguel O. *La otra campana del Nunca más: Por la reconciliación de los argentinos.* Buenos Aires, 1983

Feijoo, María del Carmen. "The Challenge of Constructing Civilian Peace: Women and Democracy in Argentina." In *The Women's Movement in Latin America: Feminism and the Transition to Democracy*, ed. Jane Jacquette, 72–94. Boston: Unwin Hyman, 1989

Fernández Alvariño, Próspero Germán. *Z Argentina, el crimen del siglo.* Buenos Aires: private printing, 1973

Fernández Meijide, Graciela. "Historia de los organismos de derechos humanos en Argentina y su rol en la democracia." In *Represión politica y defensa de los derechos humanos,* ed. Hugo Fruhling, 70–5. Santiago, Chile: Academia de Humanismo, 1986

Fisher, Jo. *Mothers of the Disappeared.* Boston: South End Press, 1989

Fodor, Jorge. "Argentina's Nationalism: Myth or Reality?" In *The Political Economy of Argentina, 1946–83,* ed. Guido di Tella and Rudiger Dornbusch, 16–24. Pittsburgh: University of Pittsburgh Press, 1989

Fontana, Andres. *Fuerzas armadas, partidos politicos y transición a la democracia en la Argentina.* Buenos Aires: Centro de Estudios del Estado y Sociedad, 1984

Foro de Estudios sobre la Administración de Justicia. *Definitivamente nunca más: La otra cara del informe de la* CONADEP. Buenos Aires: Foro de Estudios sobre la Administración de Justicia, 1985

Frank, André Gunder. *Capitalism and Underdevelopment in Latin America.* New York: Monthly Review Press, 1969

Friedrich, C.J. and Z.K. Brzezinski. *Totalitarian Dictatorship and Autocracy.* Cambridge, Mass.: Harvard University Press, 1965

Frontalini, Daniel, and Maria Cristina Caiati. *El mito de la guerra sucia.* Buenos Aires: CELS, 1984

Funes, Carlos. *Perón y la guerra sucia: Documentos criticos.* Buenos Aires: Catalogos, 1996

Galtieri, Leopoldo. "Celebración el dia del ejercito." *Revista del circulo militar* 702 (1979–80): 4–11

Garcia, Prudencio. *El drama de la autonomía militar.* Madrid: Alianza Editorial, 1995

Gendarmería Nacional 2 (1996)

Gerchunoff, Pablo. "Peronist Economic Policies, 1946–55." In *The Political Economy of Argentina, 1946–83,* ed. Guido di Tella and Rudiger Dornbusch, 16–24. Pittsburgh: University of Pittsburgh Press, 1989

Gerth, H.H., and C. Wright Mills, eds. and trans. *From Max Weber: Essays in Sociology.* London: Routledge and Kegan Paul, 1958

Ghio, José María. "Church and Politics: The Argentine Church in Comparative Perspective." PhD thesis, University of Chicago, 1990

– "The Argentine Church: From Integralist to Populist Nationalism." Working paper no. 34, Universidad Torcuato di Tella, September 1996

Gillespie, Richard. *Soldiers of Perón: Argentina's Montoneros.* Oxford: Clarendon Press, 1982

Giussani, Pablo. *Montoneros: La soberbia armada.* 1984. New edn. Buenos Aires: Tiempo, 1992

Goldhagen, Daniel Jonah. *Hitler's Willing Executioners and the Holocaust.* New York: Alfred A. Knopf, 1996

Goldwert, Marvin. *Democracy, Militarism, and Nationalism in Argentina, 1930–1966: An Interpretation.* Austin: University of Texas Press, 1972

Gomez, José María. "Derochos humanos, politica y autoritarismo en el Cono Sur." In *La etica de la democracia,* ed. Waldo Ansaldi. Buenos Aires: Consejo Latinoamericano de Ciencias Sociales, 1986

Gonzalez Bombal, María Ines, and María Sonderreguer. *Derechos humanos y democracia.* Working paper. Buenos Aires: Centro de Estudios del Estado y Sociedad, 1986

Gonzalez Janzen, Ignacio. *La Triple A.* Buenos Aires: Contrapunto, 1986

Graham-Yooll, Andrew. *The Press in Argentina, 1973–1978.* London: Writers and Scholars Educational Trust, 1984

– *A State of Fear.* London: Eland; New York: Hippocrene Books, 1986

Gramsci, Antonio. *The Modern Prince and Other Writings.* New York: International Publishers, 1957

– *Selections from Prison Notebooks.* New York: International Publishers, 1971.

Graziano, Frank. *Divine Violence: Spectacle, Psychosexuality, and Radical Christianity in the Argentine "Dirty War."* Boulder: Westview Press, 1992

Groisman, Enrique. *A corte supreme de justicia durante la dictadura, 1976–1983.* Buenos Aires: CISEA, 1983

Grupo de Iniciativa por una Convención Internacional Sobre la Desaparación Forzada de Personas. *Jornadas sobre el tratamiento juridico de la desaparición forzada de personas.* Facultad de Derocho y Ciencias Sociales de la Universidad Nacional de Buenos Aires. Buenos Aires: Asamblea Permanente por los Derechos Humanos, October 1987

– *La desaparición forzada como crimen de lesa humanidad: El "Nunca más" y la comunidad internacional.* Coloquio de Buenos Aires, Octubre. Buenos Aires: Paz, 1989

Guest, Iain. *Behind the Disappearances: Argentina's Dirty War against Human Rights and the United Nations.* Philadelphia: University of Pennsylvania Press, 1990

Gurr, Ted Robert. "The Political Origins of State Violence and Terror: A Theoretical Analysis." In *Government Violence and Terror: An Agenda for Research,* ed. M. Stohl and G. Lopez, 45–71. New York: Greenwood Press, 1985

Hodges, Donald C. *Argentina 1943–1976: The National Revolution and Resistance.* Albuquerque: University of New Mexico Press, 1976

– *Argentina's "Dirty War": An Intellectual Biography.* Austin: University of Texas Press, 1991

Howard, Rhoda, and Jack Donnelly. "Human Dignity, Human Rights and Political Regimes." *American Political Science Review* 80, no. 3 (Sept. 1986): 801–17

Huntington, Samuel P. *Political Order in Changing Societies.* New Haven, Conn.: Yale University Press, 1968

Independent Commission on International Humanitarian Issues. *Disappeared! Technique of Terror.* London: Zed, 1986

Isla, Alejandro. "Terror, Memory and Responsibility in Argentina." Paper presented to Workshop on Memory, Responsibility and Terror, International Centre for Contemporary Cultural Research, Department of Social Anthropology, University of Manchester, 29 November 1996

Izaguirre, Ines. *Los desaparecidos: Recuperación de una identidad expropiada.* Buenos Aires: Cuadernos del Instituto no. 9, 1992

James, Daniel. "Power and Politics in Peronist Trade Unions." *Journal of Interamerican Studies and World Affairs* 20, no. 1 (February 1978): 3–36

– "The Peronist Left, 1, 1955–1975." *Latin American Studies* 8, no. 2 (1981): 172–296

– "Rationalization and Working Class Response: The Context and Limits of Factory Floor Activity in Argentina." *Journal of Latin American Studies* 13, no. 2 (1981): 375–402

– *Resistance and Integration: Peronism and the Argentine Working Class, 1946–76.* Cambridge: Cambridge University Press, 1988

Jelin, Elizabeth. *Conflictos laborales en la Argentina, 1973–76.* Buenos Aires: Biblioteca Política Argentina, Centro de Estudios de Estrada y Sociedad, 1977

– *Los nuevos movimientos sociales / 2. Derechos humanos. Obreros. Barrios.* Buenos Aires: Biblioteca Politica Argentina, Centro Editor de América Latina, no. 125, 1985

– *Movimientos sociales y democracia emergente / 2.* Buenos Aires: Biblioteca Política Argentina, Centro Editor de América Latina, 1987

Joxami, Eduardo, Pedro Paz, and Juan Villarreal. *Crisis de la dictadura argentina: Política económica y cambio social (1976–1983).* Buenos Aires: Siglo veintiuno editores, 1985

Kennedy, John J. *Catholicism, Nationalism, and Democracy in Argentina.* Notre Dame, Ind.: University of Notre Dame Press, 1958

Kirkpatrick, Jeane. *Leader and Vanguard in Mass Society: A Study of Peronist Argentina.* Cambridge, Mass.: MIT Press, 1971

Kordon, Diana R., et al. *Efectos psicologicos de la represión política.* Trans. Dominique Kliagine as *Psychological Effects of Political Repression.* Buenos Aires: Sudamericana/Planeta, 1988

Langguth, Arthur J. *Hidden Terrors.* New York: Pantheon, 1978

Leon, Carlos A. "El desarrollo agrario de Tucumán en el periodo de transición de la economia de capitalismo incipiente a la expansion azucarera." *Desarrollo económico: Revista de ciencias sociales* 33, no. 130 (1993): 217–36

Lewis, Arthur. *Growth and Fluctuations, 1870–1913.* London: George Allen & Unwin, 1978

Lewis, Colin M., and Nissa Torrents, eds. *Argentina in the Crisis Years (1983–1990)*. London: Institute of Latin American Studies, University of London, 1993

Lewis, Paul H. *The Crisis of Argentine Capitalism*. Chapel Hill: University of North Carolina Press, 1990

– "The Right and Military Rule, 1955–1983." In *The Argentine Right*, ed. S.M. Deutsch and R.H. Dolkart, 147–80. Wilmington, Del.: SR Books, 1993

Linea. "Paro y Después" (round table discussion with union leaders). *Linea* 144 (August 1997): 24–31

Lobaiza, Humberto J.R. *La Argentina indefensa? Crisis, oportunidades y propuesta*. Buenos Aires: Circulo Militar, 1997

López, Ernesto, and David Pion-Berlin. *Democracia y cuestion militar*. Quilmes: Universidad Nacional de Quilmes, 1996

Lopez, George. "National Security Ideology as an Impetus to State Violence and State Terror." In *Government Violence and Repression: Agenda for Research*, ed. Michael Stohl and George Lopez. New York: Greenwood Press, 1988

– "Terrorism in Latin America." In *The Politics of Terrorism*, 3rd edn, ed. M. Stohl, 497–524. New York: Marcel Dekker, 1988

Lopez, George A., and Michael Stohl. *Liberalization and Redemocratization in Latin America*. New York: Greenwood Press, 1987

López Laval, Hilda. *Autoritarismo y cultura. Argentina 1976–1983*. Madrid: Espiral Hispano Américana, 1995

Lozada, Salvador María, et al. *Inseguridad y desnacionalization: La "doctrina" de la seguridad nacional*. Buenos Aires: Ediciones Derechos del Hombre, 1985

McClintock, Michael. *Instruments of Statecraft: U.S. Guerrilla Warfare, Counter-Insurgency, and Counter-Terrorism, 1940–1990*. New York: Pantheon, 1992

Macdonald, C.A. "The Politics of Intervention: The United States and Argentina, 1941–46." *Latin American Studies*. 12, 2, 365–96.

Mallimachi, Fortunato. "Catolicismo y militarismo en Argentina (1930–1983): De la Argentina liberal a la Argentina católica." *Revista de ciencias sociales* (Universidad Nacional de Quilmes), 4 (August 1996)

Marín, Juan Carlos. *Conversaciones sobre el Poder (Una experiencia colectiva)*. Buenos Aires: Instituto de Investigaciones "Gino Germani," Universidad de Buenos Aires, 1995

– *Los hechos armados: Argentina 1973–1976: La acumulación primitiva del genocidio*. Buenos Aires: PICASO/La Rosa Blindada, 1996

Mattini, Luis. *Hombres y mujeres del PRT–ERP de Tucumán a la Tablada*. 2nd edn. De la Campana, 1995

Méndez, Eugenio. *Aramburu: El crimen imperfecto*. Buenos Aires: Sudamericana-Planeta, 1987

Mignone, Emilio F. *Iglesia y dictadura: El papel de la iglesia a la luz de sus relaciones con el regima militar*. Ediciones de Pensamiento Nacional, 1986

– *Witness to the Truth: The Complicity of Church and Dictatorship in Argentina, 1976–1983*. Trans. Phillip Berryman. Maryknoll, NY: Orbis Books, 1988

– *Derechos humanos y sociedad: El caso argentino*. Buenos Aires: Ediciones del Pensamiento Nacional, 1991

Molas, Ricardo Rodriguez. *Historia de la tortura y el orden represivo en la Argentina*. Buenos Aires: Editorial Universitaria de Buenos Aires, 1984

– ed. *Historia de la tortura y el orden represivo en la Argentina: Textos documentales*. Buenos Aires: Editorial Universitaria de Buenos Aires, 1985

Mora y Araujo, Manuel. "Comment." in *The Political Economy of Argentina, 1946–83*, ed. G. di Tella and R. Dornbusch, 25–30. Oxford: Macmillan, 1989

Moreno Ocampo, Luis. *Cuando el poder perdió el juicio: Como explicar el "Proceso" a nuestros hijos*. Buenos Aires: Planeta Espejo de la Argentina, 1996

– "Corruption and Normative Systems." Working paper. Mimeo. N.d.

Morero, Sergio. *La noche de los bastones largos: Treinta años después*. Buenos Aires: Documentos Página/12, Gustavo la Cava Ediciones, 1996

Most, Benjamin A. *Changing Authoritarian Rule and Public Policy in Argentina, 1930–1970*. Denver, Colo.: University of Denver, 1991

Moyano, María José. *Argentina's Lost Patrol: Armed Struggle 1969–1979*. New Haven: Yale University Press, 1995

Munck, Ronaldo, with Ricardo Falcon and Bernardo Galitelli. *Argentina: From Anarchism to Peronism. Workers, Unions and Politics, 1855–1985*. London: Zed, 1987

Neilsen, James. "The Education of Jacobo Timerman." *Books and Writers*. London, 1981

Nino, Carlos Santiago. *Radical Evil on Trial*. New Haven: Yale University Press, 1996

Norden, Deborah. "Democratic Consolidation and Military Professionalism: Argentina in the 1980s." *Journal of Interamerican Studies and World Affairs* 32, no. 3 (Fall 1990): 151–76

Nun, José. "La democracia y la modernización, treinta años después." *Desarrollo Económico* 31, no. 123 (Oct.–Dec. 1991): 375–93

Nun, José, and Juan Carlos Portantiero. *Ensayos sobre la transicíon democrática en la Argentina*. Buenos Aires: Puntosur, 1987.

O'Brien, Philip, and Paul Cammack. *Generals in Retreat: The Crisis of Military Rule in Latin America*. Manchester: Manchester University Press, 1985

O'Donnell, Guillermo. *Modernization and Bureaucratic Authoritarianism*. Berkeley: Institute of International Studies, 1973

- "Reflections on Patterns of Change in Bureaucratic Authoritarianism."
  Latin American Research Review 13, no. 1 (1978): 3–38
- "State and Alliances in Argentina: 1955–76." *Journal of Development Studies* 15, no. 1 (1978): 3–33
O'Kane, Rosemary H.T. *Terror, Force, and States: The Path from Modernity.* Cheltenham, UK: Edward Elgar, 1996
Ollier, Maria Matilde. *Orden, poder y violencia / 1 and 2 (1968–1973),* nos. 273 and 274. Buenos Aires: Biblioteca Política Argentina, Centro Editor de América Latina, 1989
Organización de los Estados Americanos Comisión Interamericana de Derochos Humanos. *El informe prohibido. Informe sobre la situación de los derechos humanos en Argentina.* Buenos Aires: Talleres Impresores "La Constitución" (from original 1980 English text)
Organization of American States. Interamerican Commission on Human Rights. *Report on the Situation of Human Rights in Argentina.* Washington, DC, 1980
Página/12. *Documentos: Semanario CGT,* nos. 1 and 2. Buenos Aires: La Página, 1997
- *Los tiempos de Rosas: Una historia argentina,* no. 7. Buenos Aires: La Página, 1997
- *La Argentina se organiza: Una historia argentina,* no. 8. Buenos Aires: La Página, 1997
- *Los tiempos de Perón,* ps 1 and 2. *Una historia argentina,* nos. 11 and 12. Buenos Aires: La Página, 1997
Paoletti, Alipio. *Como los Nazis, como en Vietnam: Los campos de concentración en Argentina.* 2nd edn. Buenos Aires: Ediciones Asociación Madres de Plaza de Mayo, 1996
Paz y seguridad en las Américas. Various editions, 1996
Peralta-Ramos, Mónica. *Acumulación del capital y crisis política en Argentina (1930–1974).* Mexico City: Siglo XXI, 1978
- "The Structural Basis of Coercion." In *From Military Rule to Liberal Democracy in Argentina,* ed. Peralta-Ramos and Carl H. Waisman, 36–68. Boulder, Colo.: Westview Press, 1987.
Peralta-Ramos, Mónica, and Carlos H. Waisman, eds. *From Military Rule to Liberal Democracy in Latin America.* Boulder, Colo.: Westview Press, 1987
Perdue, William D. *Terrorism and the State: A Critique of Domination through Fear.* New York: Praeger, 1989
Perrone, Alberto M. "Habla el cura que interrogaba desaparecidos." Reportaje exclusivo al padre Cristian von Wernich. *Siete Dias,* 25–31 July 1984, 3–9
Pion-Berlin, David. "Political Repression and Economic Doctrines: The Case of Argentina." *Comparative Political Studies* 16, no. 1 (April 1983): 37–66
- "The Fall of Military Rule in Argentina, 1976–83." *Journal of Interamerican Studies and World Affairs* 17, no. 2 (Summer 1985): 55–76.

– *The Ideology of State Terror: Economic Doctrine and Political Repression in Argentina and Peru*. Boulder: Lynne Rienner, 1989

Pion-Berlin, David, and George Lopez. "Of Victims and Executioners: Argentine State Terror, 1975–1979." *International Studies Quarterly* 35, no. 1 (March 1991): 63–87

Poelchau, Warren, ed. *White Paper Whitewash: Interviews with Philip Agee on the CIA and El Salvador*. New York: Deepcover Books, 1981

Poneman, Daniel. *Argentina: Democracy on Trial*. New York: Paragon House, 1987

Portantiero, Juan Carlos. "Political and Economic Crises in Argentina." In *The Political Economy of Argentina, 1946–83*, ed. Guido di Tella and Rudiger Dornbusch, 16–24. Pittsburgh: University of Pittsburgh Press, 1989

Pozzi, Pablo. *Oposición obrera a la dictadura (1976–1982)*. Buenos Aires: Contrapunto, 1988

Reich, Walter, ed. *Origins of Terrorism: Psychologies, Ideologies, Theologies, States of Mind*. Cambridge: Woodrow Wilson International Center for Scholars, and Cambridge University Press, 1990

República Argentina. *Observaciones y comentarios criticos del govierno argentino al informe: CIDH sobre la situación de los derechos humanos en la Argentina*. Buenos Aires: Registro Oficial, 1980

– *Documento final de la junta militar sobre la guerra contra la subversión terrorismo*. Buenos Aires: Registro Oficial, 1983

– *Ley de obediencia debida*. Dibujo de tapa tomado de Ediciones el EIP, Suiza, 1984

– *Ley del punto final* (Law no. 23, 492, 14 December 1986). Discussion paper distributed by nineteen human rights groups, 1986

Reyna, Roberto. *La Perla*. Córdoba: El Cid Editor, 1984

Rock, David. *Authoritarian Argentina: The Nationalist Movement, Its History and Its Impact*. Berkeley: University of California Press, 1993

– "Antecedents of the Argentine Right." In *The Argentine Right, Its History and Intellectual Origins: 1910 to the Present*, ed. Sandra McGee Deutsch and Ronald H. Dolkart, 1–34. Wilmington, Del.: SR Books, 1993

Rogers, George C. *Argentina y la tortura: Obligación de juzgar a los responsables*. Buenos Aires: Cuadernos del CELS, November 1990

Rosenzvaig, Eduardo E., and Luis M. Bonano. *De la manufactura a la revolución industrial: El azucar en el norte argentino*. Tucumán: Universidad Nacional de Tucumán, 1992

Rouquié, Alain. *The Military and the State in Latin America*. Berkeley: University of California Press, 1987

Sabato, J.F. *La pampa pródiga: Claves de una frustración*. Buenos Aires: CISEA, 1981

– *La clase dominante en la Argentina moderna: Formación y caracteristicas*. Buenos Aires: CISEA/GEL, 1988

Salvioli, Fabian, ed. *La constitución de la Nación Argentina y los derechos humanos: Un análisis a la luz de la reforma de 1994.* Texto completo de la constitución de la Nación Argentina (aprobada por la Convención Nacional Constituyente, Paraná, Santa Fe, 1994). Declaraciones y pactos incorporados con jerarquía constitucional. Buenos Aires: Movimiento Ecumenico por los Derechos Humanos (MEDH), 1995

Schenone, Maria Teresa, and Horacio Ricardo Ravenna. "The Right to an Identity." In *Derechos del niño: Declaración de la Plata, Republica Argentina, su debate y aprobación. 1er encuentro extraordinario de legisladores sobre derechos del niño, 16–18 Octubre 1989,* 69–78. Buenos Aires: UNICEF, Ministerio Relaciones Exteriores, para Hon. Camara de Diputados de la Provincia de Buenos Aires, Comisión de Derechos Humanos y Garantias, 1989

Schoultz, Lars. *Human Rights and U.S. Policy Towards Latin America.* Princeton: Princeton University Press, 1981

Seoane, María. *Todo o nada: La historia secreta y la historia publica del jefe guerrillero Mario Roberto Santucho.* Buenos Aires: Planeta, 1991

Seoane, María, y Héctor Ruiz Núñez. *La Noche de los lápices.* 1986. Buenos Aires: Planeta, 1992

SER *(Seguridad Estratégica Regional) en el 2000.* "Seguridad Publica Seguridad Privada." SER 10 (July 1997)

Sikkink, Kathryn, and Lisa L. Martin. "U.S. Policy and Human Rights in Argentina and Guatemala, 1973–1980." In *Double-Edged Diplomacy: International Bargaining and Domestic Politics,* ed. Peter Evans, Harold K. Jacobson, and Robert D. Putnam, 330–62. Berkeley and Los Angeles: University of California Press, 1993

Smith, Brian. "Churches and Human Rights in Latin America." In *Church and Politics in Latin America,* ed. Daniel Levine, 155–94. Beverley Hills, Calif.: Sage, 1979

Smith, Peter H. *Argentina and the Failure of Democracy: Conflict among Political Elites 1904–1955.* Madison, Wis.: University of Wisconsin Press, 1974

Smith, William C. "Reflections on the Political Economy of Authoritarian Rule and Capitalist Reorganization in Contemporary Argentina." In *Generals in Retreat: The Crisis of Military Rule in Latin America,* ed. Philiip O'Brien and Paul Cammack, 37–88. Manchester: Manchester University Press, 1985

– *Authoritarianism and the Crisis of the Argentine Political Economy.* Stanford: Stanford University Press, 1991

Smulovitz, Catalina. "Constitución y poder judicial en la nueva democracia argentina: La experiencia de las instituciones." In *La nueva matriz política argentina: La investigación social,* ed. C. Acuña, 71–114. Buenos Aires: Nueva Vision, 1995

– "Ciudadanos, derechos y política." Seminario, Acciones en Defensa del Interés Público, Universidad Di Tella, Buenos Aires, 19 April 1996

Springer, Philip. "Disunity and Disorder: Factional Politics in the Argentine Military." In *The Military Intervenes: Case Studies in Development*, ed. Henry Bienen. New York: Russell Sage Foundation, 1968

Staub, Ervin. *The Roots of Evil: The Origins of Genocide and Other Group Violence.* New York: Cambridge University Press, 1989

Stepan, Alfred. "State Power and the Strength of Civil Society in the Southern Cone of Latin America." In *Bringing the State Back In*, ed. Peter Evans, Dietrich Rueschemeyer, and Theda Skocpol, 317–46. Cambridge: Cambridge University Press, 1985

Stohl, Michael. "Outside of a Small Circle of Friends: States, Genocide, Mass Killing and the Role of Bystanders." *Journal of Peace Research* 24, no. 2 (June 1987): 151–66

– ed. *The Politics of Terrorism.* 3rd edn. New York: Marcel Dekker, 1988

Stohl, Michael, and George A. Lopez, eds. *Government Violence and Repression: An Agenda for Research.* New York: Greenwood Press, 1985

Tiano, Susan. "Authoritarianism and Political Culture in Argentina and Chile in the mid-1960s." *Latin American Research Review* 21, no. 1 (1986): 73–98

Timerman, Jacobo. *Prisoner without a Name, Cell without a Number.* London: Weidenfeld and Nicolson, 1981

Torrado, Susana. *Estructura social de la Argentina: 1945–1983.* Buenos Aires: De la Flor, 1992

Torre, Juan Carlos. *Los sindicatos en el gobierno, 1973–1976.* Buenos Aires: CEAL, 1983

– ed. *La formacia del syndicalisme peronista.* Legasa, 1988

Torres Molina, Ramon. *Inconstitucionalidad de la ley de punto final.* Buenos Aires: Abuelas de Plaza de Mayo, n.d.

Troncoso, Oscar. *El Proceso de reorganización nacional.* Vols. 1–5. Buenos Aires: Biblioteca Política Argentina, Centro Editor de América Latina, 1992

Tucumán, la Provincia de. *Informe de la comisión bicameral investigadora de las violaciones de los derechos humanos en la provincia de Tucumán (1974–1983).* Salamanca, Spain: Instituto del Estudios Políticos para América Latina y Africa [1986?]

Tucumán, la Provincia de. *Nomina de 409 personas detenidas-desaparecidas de la provincia de Tucumán, denunciadas por sus familiares.* N.d.

Tulchin, Joseph. *Argentina and the United States: A Conflicted Relationship.* Boston: Twayne, 1990

Turner, Frederick C., and José Enrique Miguens, eds. *Juan Perón and the Reshaping of Argentina.* Pittsburgh: University of Pittsburgh Press, 1983

United Nations Economic Commission for Latin America. *Economic Development and Income Distribution, Argentina.* New York: United Nations, 1969

Universidad Nacional de Tucumán. *Informe de la comisión bicameral investigadora de los derechos humanos en la provincia de Tucumán.* Imprenta de la Universidad, San Miguel de Tucumán, 1991

Verbitsky, Horacio. *Ezeiza.* Buenos Aires: Contrapunto, 1985

– *Robo para la corona: Los frutos prohibidos del árbol de la corrupción.* Buenos Aires: Planeta Bolsillo, 1991
– *El vuelo.* Buenos Aires: Planeta, 1995
Villalba Welsh, Alfredo. *Tiempos de ira tiempos de esperanza: 50 años de vida política a traves de la Liga Argentina por los Derechos del Hombre.* Buenos Aires: Rafael Cedeno, 1984
Villarreal, Juan. *El capitalismo dependiente: Estudio sobre la estructura de clases en Argentina.* Mexico City: Siglo veintiuno, 1978
– "Changes in Argentine Society: The Heritage of the Dictatorship." In *From Military Rule to Liberal Democracy in Argentina,* ed. Mónica Peralto-Ramos and Carlos H. Waisman. Boulder, Colo.: Westview Press, 1987
Waisbord, Silvio. "Politics and Identity in the Argentine Army: Cleavages and the Generational Factor." *Latin American Research Review* 26, no. 2 (1991): 157–70
Waisman, Carlos. "The Legitimation of Liberal Democracy under Adverse Conditions: The Case of Argentina." In *From Military Rule to Liberal Democracy in Argentina,* ed. Mónica Peralta-Ramos and Carlos H. Waisman, 97–110. Boulder, Colo.: Westview Press, 1987
– *Reversal of Development in Argentina: Postwar Counterrevolutionary Policies and Their Structural Consequences.* Princeton, NJ: Princeton University Press, 1987
Waldmann, Peter. "Guerrilla Movements in Argentina, Guatemala, Nicaragua, and Uruguay." Trans. Michael R. Deverell and Richard Fleischauer. In *Political Violence and Terror: Motifs and Motivations,* ed. Peter H. Merkl, 257–82. Berkeley: University of California Press, 1986
Walsh, Mary. "The Tucumán Case." *Wall Street Journal,* 1988
Walter, Richard J. "The Right and the Peronists, 1943–1955." In *The Argentine Right,* ed. S.M. Deutsch and R.H. Dolkart, 99–118. Wilmington, Del.: SR Books, 1993
Yannuzzi, Maria de los Angeles. *La modernización conservadora: El peronismo de los 90.* Buenos Aires: Editorial Fundación Ross, 1995
– *Politica y dictadura.* Buenos Aires: Editorial Fundación Ross, 1996
Zanatta, Loris. *Del estado liberal, a la nación católico: Iglesia y ejercito en los origines de peronismo, 1930–43.* Quilmes: University of Quilmes, 1996
Zapata, Edgar Antonio. *Guerrilla y Montoneros: Ensayo sobre el origen y evolución.* Buenos Aires: Editorial Fundación Ross, 1996

PERIODICALS AND NEWSPAPERS

Buenos Aires Herald
Clarín
La Nación
La Prensa
La Semana

La Voz
Latin America
Latin America Economic Report/Andean Times
Latin America Political Report
Noticias
Página/12
Siete Dias

FILMS

Avellaneda. Documentary on forensic anthropology's contribution to identifying bodies found in mass graves. Buenos Aires, 1996

Cazadores de Utopia. Documentary on Montoneros. By David Blaustein, Instituto Nacional de Cinematografia y Artes Audiovisuales y Zafra Cine Difusion S.A. [probably 1995]

Falcon buen estado. A film about the disappearances. The title refers to the green Ford Falcon cars used by the kidnappers. Video issued by Madres de la Plaza de Mayo, 1995

La historia oficial. Fictionalized documentary on kidnapped babies during *el Proceso.* Libro Cinematográfico de Aida Bortnik y Luis Puenzo. Issued in English as *The Official Story.* N.d.

Las madres: The Mothers of Plaza de Mayo. Film by Susana Muñoz and Lourdes Portillo, 1986

Malajunta 76. Documentary about the dictatorship. Producción: Cecilia Landaburu y María Angélica Pacheco, 1996

La memoria ahora. Amateur video by various individuals in Buenos Aires, about how residents remember others being taken off the streets. 1996

La noche de las lápices. Docudrama about the abduction of schoolchildren. Issued in English as *The Night of the Pencils.* 1986

La republica perdida. Documentary about Argentine history. 1 and 2. Noran Producciones y Enrique Vanoli, n.d.

Teatro abierto. Film produced by Arturo Balassa about the independent theatre movement in Argentina during the final years of the dictatorship. N.d.

INDEX

Abal Medina, Fernando, 312, 313; death of, 97, 100; and guerrilla tactics, 96; as Montoneros founding member, 96

Abal Medina, Juan Manuel: Perón's appointment of, 102

Abuelas de la Plaza de Mayo, 11, 155, 163, 164–5, 274; and charges against Videla, Bignone, and Massera, 334

Actis, Gen. Omar: death of, 308

Agosti, Brig. Gen. Orlando: and junta, 148–9; sentencing of, 334

Alemann, Roberto: as economic superminister, 168

Alfonsín, Raúl, 38, 243; election of, 357n6; election loss of, 334; government of, 268–9, 297, 337; national commission under, 36; as Radical Party leader, 333; and trials of junta leaders, 223, 312

Algeria, 226, 240, 279, 281, 294, 302, 304

Allende, Salvador, 113, 226, 248, 327

Alonso, José, 78, 79; murder of, 76, 90

Alvear, Marcelo T. de, 50; presidency of, 49

amnesty: granted by Campora government, 103; granted by Menem government, 334

Amnesty International, 123, 144, 155; investigation by, 227–8; and release of Graham-Yooll, 222; report of, 228

Andersen, Martin, 14; and events in Tucumán, 120; on Firmenich as double agent, 100, 220–2

Angelelli, Bishop Enrique, 197; murder of, 160–1, 243, 251, 258, 262

Anna (voice), 205–6, 207–8, 208–9

anti-Semitism: in Argentina, 12–13, 48, 49, 96, 146; among Peronist Youth, 96; and Timerman case, 161, 162

APDH (Asamblea Permanente por los Derechos Humanos), 143, 165, 197; and laws to limit court process, 358n4 (ch. 17)

Aramburu, Cardinal Juan Carlos, 235, 236; statement of on the disappeared ("living in Europe"), 246, 259

Aramburu, Gen. Pedro E.: kidnapping and murder of, 33, 96, 97, 99–100, 101, 116, 178, 179, 182 187, 188–9, 219, 243, 262, 268, 271–2, 292, 299, 312–13, 314, 342; presidency of, 66, 67; and the press, 216; responsibility of for 1955 coup, 69

Arancibia, Isauro: murder of, 201

Arendt, Hannah, 293; analysis by of Nazi regime, 6; on terror vs violence, 345n3

Argentina: daily life in contemporary, 336; principal allies of, 230. See also Catholic Church; economy; governments; historical and political background; human rights; media, mass; military (general); pluralism; unions and labour

Argentine Anticommunist Alliance. See Triple A

Argentine bishops' document, 254–5

Argentine Communist Party, 303